Conversation Analysis for Social Work

What do the stories youth in state care tell us about life in their family of origin? What stories do they tell us about coming into care, living in care, and relationships with foster-parents and social workers? This book presents the stories of youth in care, though not in splendid isolation, but as interactively produced, turn by turn in interviews, and in conversations with other youth.

By using tools from conversation analysis (CA), the author examines interviews with youth in care and social workers, to unfold the essential and incorrigible reflexivity of story production. CA allows us to grasp the ways that a youth's story emerges turn by turn, and is an artefact of a social relation between a youth and an interviewer. A turn to CA moves us past mere words, language, and meaning to consider just how people use talk to interact and to produce every-day occasions as such.

This text provides social work readers with a sense of art, artistry, and ambiguity at the heart of social interaction. It will be required reading for all social work students and academics looking for a deeper, more philosophical understanding of the profession.

Gerald A. J. de Montigny grew up in a proud working class family, with parents, Monty and Betty, who supported his socialist activism. When still 19 he met Andrea, who remains his partner and love, and together they have three adult children, Brendan, Julia, and Sarah. With a MSW completed in 1978, he worked in child protection, mental health, and forensic psychiatry, and began teaching social work in 1985. Gerald uses a Marxist materialist analysis which begins with people's living practices and social interactions, as bringing about their experienced worlds. He was fortunate to have studied with Dorothy Smith and Mary O'Brien, both second wave feminists.

Routledge Advances in Social Work

Conversation Analysis for Social Work

Talking with Youth in Care

Gerald A. J. de Montigny

Routledge
Taylor & Francis Group

LONDON AND NEW YORK

First published 2019
by Routledge
2 Park Square, Milton Park, Abingdon, Oxon OX14 4RN

and by Routledge
711 Third Avenue, New York, NY 10017

Routledge is an imprint of the Taylor & Francis Group, an informa business

British Library Cataloguing in Publication Data
A catalogue record for this book is available from the British Library

Library of Congress Cataloging in Publication Data
[CIP data]

ISBN: 978-0-8153-9180-7 (hbk)
ISBN: 978-1-351-20075-2 (ebk)

Typeset in Times New Roman
by Taylor & Francis Books

For Monty and Betty.

Contents

Acknowledgements

On reflection I recognize that the children I first worked with as a social worker in Prince Rupert, BC, are between 35 to 52 years old today. It is likely that many have had their own families, and it is equally likely that some will have become involved as parents with child protection systems. The dilemma and the necessity of child protection work is that we are caught between the injustice, social and economic oppression of people, and the compelling necessity to act to protect children.

In the research process I was aided by a team of dedicated research assistants, and by the support of social workers. We interviewed many youths whose voices and stories could not be addressed in this book. Even for those whose voices are represented in this text, we glimpse only a thin slice of their remarkably thick life stories. As social workers we are privileged to be in a position to listen to people, and if we can still the voices of professional obsessions long enough, we can learn from those who give us the gift of their time and their voice. I want to thank those youths who came forward and allowed themselves to be interviewed, and by doing so gave us a small glimpse into the fabric of their lives in their families of origin and in care.

This research could not have been possible without the support of the Social Sciences and Humanities Research Council funding.

My brother Brian de Montigny, a man with thousands of songs inside his head, aided me with editing and proofing. "Thanks bro!"

Finally, I could not have dedicated the work necessary to produce this book without the continual support of my spouse, Andrea Trudel.

1   Conversation analysis: Categories, contexts, and reality

Talk and social work

Talk is ubiquitous. We use talk day-to-day in a largely taken-for-granted practice for conducting our lives. As social workers, we use talk to communicate with and to understand clients, and to navigate face-to-face conversations with colleagues, staff meetings, case conferences, telephone calls, and so on. Though talk is everywhere around us, and though generations of scholars have examined language and communication it is only relatively recently, following the ready availability of audio-recording devices, that we have been able to focus in a detailed manner on the unfolding practice of talk-in-interaction. Although, it is self-evident that understanding talk demands understanding the use of words and language, the work we accomplish through talk is not entirely understandable through attention to language or to communication as such. A focus on talk-in-interaction brings to light the embodied production of talk in relationship and the reflexive accomplishment of iterative and identifiable forms of relationship through the art of differential forms of talk.

Today, what we know as conversation analysis has its origins primarily in the work of Harvey Sacks in the 1960s. Sacks' attention to every-day ordinary conversation was informed by Harold Garfinkel's own ethnomethodological attention to the mundane, ordinary, and every-day. Sacks and Garfinkel, although having met as early as 1959, did not begin working together until 1963, at which time Sacks joined Garfinkel at the Center for the Scientific Study of Suicide (Silverman, 1998:28). As Silverman points out, "the Suicide Prevention Center data were central to Sack's first set of UCLA lectures in 1964–65" (1998:28), addressing such issues as "Rules of conversational sequence", "On suicide threats getting laughed off", "The correction-invitation device", "Suicide as a device for discovering if anybody cares", and importantly, "The MIR (Membership Inference-rich Representative) membership categorization device" (Sacks, 1995:v).

Sacks' conversation analysis (CA) directs us to examine the relationships between forms of talk and the interactive and reflexive accomplishment of recognisable social contexts and socially relevant purposes. CA paid close attention to such simple things as greetings or conversational openings

(Schegloff, 1968), turn taking or the sequential nature of talk (ten Have, 2007; Schegloff, 2007; 1990; 1968; Sacks et al., 1974), question/answer response structures (Heritage, 2002; Button, 1992), and other distinctive features, such as the use of acknowledgement tokens, 'so ...' formulations (Hutchby, 2005), and so on. Simply expressed, how do two people do, or perform an interaction as a conversation between friends, rather than as an interview between a social worker and a client? Though both are occasions in which talk-in-interaction feature as a primary form of exchange or interaction between participants, are there structured differences in the forms of talk? Can a close analysis of the embodied production of talk, that is, its form or shape, mechanics, tone, sequencing, and structure indicate the different accomplishments of relationships? What are the resources and practices members draw on to perform such different occasions? How are these resources and practices both similar and different?

While talk might conventionally be thought of as providing a window into self and others, it is also in and through the activities of talking, formulating the right words, and reaching past the ineffability of embodiment that a self emerges, as one's narrated existence, as recognised, as sensible, and as oriented and located inside of social relations. In our day-to-day worlds it is through talk, of course combined with other activities, whether pureeing vegetables, wiping food from an infant's face, changing diapers, dressing a child for school, and so on, that parents produce relationships with children, demonstrate attention, concern, and caring, and do the work necessary to constitute this constellation of relations as a family. It is through talk, as combined with gestures and bodies intertwined that people become lovers. It is through talk, combined with showing a client a chair in our office, positioning our own chair opposite his or hers that social workers produce helping relationships.

Although much of the stuff of relationships is accomplished through talk, and while this book is concerned with analysing talk, it must be stated that while talk is often necessary for relationships it is rarely sufficient in itself. Talk as performed unfolds and is accomplished within successive moments and inside the orders of a social landscape. Talk, is a vital moment or element in the embodied performance for accomplishing both work and play, whether as talk at supper, a chat with a friend over coffee, a funeral, a court room, an interview, a team meeting, a case conference, and so on. Talk is always and everywhere produced by living people, embodied people, as located in shared lived-time and space, that is as Schutz observed, borrowing from Bergson (2001), in a social durée in which "we grow old together" (Schutz, 1962:174). Talk-in-interaction is somebody's lived speaking with someone else. It comes to be produced here and now as incarnate activity. On the other hand, when analysts take up talk as the subject of interest, talk as the object of analysis, can all too easily become fetishised. Talk as an 'it' becomes the object of attention, and as such becomes abstracted, separated, and removed from the actual embodied activities of speakers. Additionally, when talk is taken up as an analytic subject, it can easily be transformed yet again into an agentic subject. Conversation analysis disrupts such analytic transformations of talk to redirect our enquiry to the embodied enactments of people in interaction, who use talk in situ, that is their talk, to produce the sense, coherence, and order of occasions. Talk should not be treated as separate from the people whose talk it is, despite our ability to record, transcribe, create taxonomies, orders, and analyses. Precisely as a result of the instantiation of talk-in-interaction as a manifestation of embodied, situated, and in vivo social interaction, it is vitally important that we also recognise the fundamental transformation effected by representing talk-in-action through transcription or conversation analysis as such.

It is hardly surprising that a feature of human life as pervasive as talk, albeit transformed into a study of grammar and language, logic and argument, and rhetoric and communication,[1] has been an object of intensive study across diverse fields, whether philosophy, communications, literature, or linguistics. What is perhaps surprising is how little attention was given historically to analysis of people's actual talk as interaction, or to their talk as productive. It must be noted that the ephemeral nature of talk, that is its character as sound waves, as uttered, heard or misheard, and as situated in lived space and time, made the complex elements of talk elusive. Our ability to dissect and to discern the enormous complexity of talk-in-interaction is largely dependent on the development and evolution of readily available audio recording technologies. These technologies were not available in a convenient form until at least mid-20th century, first with the development of reel-to-reel tape recorders, then cassette recorders, and today with the advent of hand-held digital recorders. The technology of recording and endless replay subject to a disciplined attention to turn-by-turn processes of talk-in-action allowed for the development of conversation analysis. Through attention to the details revealed by recordings of talk those doing conversation analysis were able to probe and unfold the art of talk-in-action.

Historically the focus has been on language as systematised, idealised, abstracted, and written about. Wittgenstein, although understanding that "language games" developed within a "form of life" (2009:11), arrived at his analysis of language through consideration of abstracted forms and usage, albeit using examples that in their apparent simplicity seem readily sensible to speakers and listeners. Similarly, Searle, who employed the extremely rich notions of "speech acts", develops his analysis through consideration of a philosophy of language, and an abstract "class of utterances", e.g. performatives (Schegloff, 1995; Searle, 1979; 1969). Even the work of the Palo Alto group, which included Gregory Bateson, Paul Watzlawick, Jay Haley, and Don Jackson, and which had significant influence on social work, did not look at talk-in-interaction as such. Despite the promise of *The pragmatics of human communication* source data relied primarily on extracts of dialogue from fiction, plays, and other literary products.[2] They derived their analysis of paradox and other problems in communication primarily from consideration of literary and linguistic analysis of formal properties of language and communication (Watzlawick, Beavin, & Jackson, 1967). It was on the basis of literary, general, and abstracted forms that the Palo Alto group developed schematisations and systematic rules to account for language use. In contradistinction to such theorising, Harvey Sacks directed his attention front-and-centre to audio recorded instances of people's local and mundane talk-in-interaction.

Silverman observes that Sacks, though praising linguistics as "the most advanced social science" noted that, "Linguists tended not to look at conversations; indeed many did not go beyond the analysis of a sentence" (Silverman, 1998:50–51). Sacks wanted to redirect attention to the ways that speakers were able to produce, as a socially organised matter, understanding and sense in and through their conversations achieved across sequences. For Sacks analysis of talk revealed actual people's living and embodied practical accomplishment of specific forms of social relations. Those who do conversation analysis focus on "talk-in-interaction" (Hutchby & Wooffitt, 1998:13) as that by which people in their every-day, mundane, ordinary, taken-for-granted lives go about producing coherence, understanding, and society itself. Through CA we develop a close analysis of the details of talk-in-interaction to unfold the ways that participants produce, concretely, and palpably the coherence of socially organised forms of life as that which is experientially at hand, lived, and present.

Through the use of CA, talk becomes the focus of attention as it is produced day-in and day-out in conversations between friends, in interviews, in exchanges over a telephone, in short, wherever talk is employed interactively between people. Talk which is audio-recorded and then transcribed provides a detailed series of empirical specimens (ten Have, 2007), as at-hand, material evidence of how people in mundane and ordinary situations performed various forms of social interaction. People, when engaged in the acts of talking use their lungs, diaphragm, thorax, larynx and vocal chords, and mouth to produce sounds of varying tone, pitch, intonation, rhythm, volume, and so on. That which we call talk is a quite complex species-specific activity, which warrants study in and of itself. Beyond the physiology of talk are the effects or accomplishments achieved through talk, especially talk-in-interaction.

We use talk to instruct and coordinate activities with others, to share observations and understandings, and to signal or communicate feelings, emotions, and relationships of self with others. Talk as spoken is a physical practice which shapes relationships, whether as care, attention, animosity, work, and play, etc. The taken-for-granted coherence and order of every-day and local settings is actively and repeatedly produced by people in interaction, and as such is their lived coherence and order. Talk along with other disciplined physical movements, whether walking, driving a car, standing at a pedestrian crossing, or lecturing in a classroom emerges as embodied and interactive. Order in local scenes is as people accomplish it and bring it into being. Lived and experienced every-day orders emerge as essentially reflexive[3] (Watson, 1987). Psathas (1995) has outlined that: "1. Order is produced orderliness. 2. Order is produced by the parties in situ; that is, it is situated and occasioned" (Psathas, 1995:2). For CA, as in ethnomethodology (EM) order is not imposed by the analyst, nor is it to be derived from the analyst's generic, essentialist, idealist, or even empiricist imposition of concepts, categories, and theories. Instead, any and all social orders are recognised as produced in the living energy, practice, and socially oriented performances of members in situ as their quite practical accomplishment. Garfinkel differentiated EM from formal analysis (FA), and argued that "The premier policy of the worldwide social science movement, 'There is no order in the plenum,' is contradicted by the unique coherence of the things of immortal ordinary society" (2002:97). In contradistinction, Garfinkel advanced a program of studies which posed "the discipline-specific workplace question":

> How, in starting with everyday activities, being unavoidably and without remedy or alternatives in the midst of ordinary activities, not knowing nothing and certainly not knowing how to proceed knowing nothing. But to the contrary being answerable to the contingent facticities of produced everyday things, just how and just in any actual case, is the coherence of those ordinary things made? How in the unavoidable midst of immortal, ordinary society, and therein just in any actual case is the congregationally witnessable coherence of the most ordinary things in the world made in the details in and as of their empirical generality? In the details of their generality how is their coherence made accountable? How are they made demonstrable? How are they made examinable and researchable?
>
> (2002:138–139)

Although Garfinkel's language is not ordinary, he directs us to take up ordinary and every-day activities in their plenty, as they surround us, as we are surrounded by them, and as we participate in them. For social workers this means beginning with the quite mundane, ordinary, and every-day sites of our practice as reflexively accomplishing the orders of our offices and our professional work.

Order is iterative and recurrent. Analysis that aims to discover the production of orderliness turns to what people do in situ. This way of working provides for an analysis of "structures of social action" (Psathas, 1995:2–3) as lived, taken-for-granted, relied on, and as practically effected. Malone succinctly notes, "Conversational talk exhibits orderliness because it is produced in such a way that it will make sense for those for whom it is intended" (1997:36).

Given that so much social work comes to be achieved in and through talk, whether as interviews, assessments, case conferences, and so on, it seems natural that the concerns of CA should resonate with those of social work (Hall, Juhila, Matarese, & Nijnatten, 2014; Hall, Juhila, Parton, & Pösö, 2003). As noted above, until recently social workers have generally turned not to CA but to communication theory with the unfortunate effect that the analytic focus has been on talk not as practically realised but as idealised, theorised, taxonomised, and categorised. This has been most unfortunate, as social workers in their day-to-day practice work face-to-face with people and as a result need simple practical tools to understand how talk is actually effected. ten Have points out the traditional focus in thinking and writing about talk has been to address "how one should speak, rather than how people actually speak" (2007:3). Similarly, in social work much attention has been paid to directing students to emulate preferred forms of talking, e.g. reflection of feelings (Kadushin & Kadushin, 2013), reaching into silences (Shulman, 2016), paraphrasing responses, using open ended questions, seeking concreteness (Hepworth, et al., 2010). Of course, it is not surprising that social workers' writings that address interviewing aim to help workers to improve their practice. Yet the attention to specifying optimal or preferred forms of communication has meant that little attention is given to the specific structures of talk by which these preferred forms actually come to be accomplished. Though social workers have given considerable attention to identifying those forms of talk which advance professional purposes, e.g. trust, open communication, dialogue, client self-disclosure, problem solving, and so forth, only by examining in vivo instances of talk-in-interaction can we move to understand how such dynamics are achieved and accomplished as accountable and warranted features of professional work.

Despite the historical hegemony of communication some social work theorists have recognised the importance of talk itself. For example, Turner questions the familiar adage that social workers should "start where the client is and let the client lead the way" by noting:

> We need to remind ourselves that such things as the way we speak, the gestures we use, our opening comments, what we look like, where we are, who we are, and how we respond all influence "where the client is" and thus what clients say and do. If we truly believe that an interview is a dynamic process between two or more people, then to say that the client is the one who directs the interview contradicts this.
>
> (2002:54)

Fortunately, CA provides tools for examining the sorts of quite practical puzzles Turner has identified. Indeed, as any practitioner knows, the success or failure of an interview or a moment of work with a client depends not only on choice of words and content, but on the form of a response. For example, performing an empathic response is conditioned by tone of voice, pitch, matched pace of talk, control of interruptions, shape of vocal ejaculations and sounds – e.g. acknowledgement tokens such as mmm, yah, mmhuh, umm, etc. The sorts of close attention to the details of talk in CA can provide social workers with a technology and a focus for rendering talk-in-interaction available for review and attention.

Conversation analysis

Mundane, ordinary, every-day, and taken-for-granted talk-in-interaction can provide a very useful pathway for analysis of rather complex social scenes, whether these are courtrooms, police stations, or social work interviews. CA, along with EM, redirects our enquiry to an examination of the mundane ways that people go about producing the largely unremarkable orderliness of their every-day worlds.[4] Through CA our attention shifts to the specific ways that order is produced through talk-in-interaction (Hutchby & Wooffitt, 1998). Harvey Sacks, working in the 1960s, discovered that ordinary talk in its detail revealed members' orientation to, and ongoing accomplishment of complex social settings and relationships. He set out a program for study of talk-in-interaction as allowing for analysis of "human sociality" (Silverman, 1998:27). Schegloff, in his introduction to the two-volume set of Sacks' lectures, notes:

> There is the distinctive and utterly critical recognition here that the talk can be examined as an object in its own right[5], and not merely as a screen on which are projected other processes … The talk itself was the action, and previously unsuspected details were critical resources in what was getting done in and by the talk; and all this in naturally occurring events, in no way manipulated to allow the study of them.
>
> (1995:xviii)

Introductory texts into CA, such as ten Have's, recommend analysis of transcripts oriented to "turn-taking organization; sequence organization; repair organization; and the organization of turn-construction/design" (2007:125). CA creates an opening for analysis of the concrete, local, and at-hand practices by which members co-produce both the warrantable forms for specific occasions and, through the systematic and replicable aggregations of such occasions, agencies, organisations, and institutions (Boden, 1994).

Through detailed study of such seemingly mundane matters, those doing CA have identified the ways that people through talk not only reproduce the orderliness of every-day settings, whether family dinners, putting children to bed, queuing for coffee at a local shop, riding a bus, etc. Additionally, others have turned to examine just how practitioners talk institutional orders into being (Boden, 1994).[6] Indeed, through such seemingly simple matters as turns, sequences, and repairs participants to talk-in-interaction ensure that they are oriented to a listener, and that listeners are oriented to their talk, and furthermore that both are oriented to the relevancies of the setting in and through their talk. As participants talk they enact and revive as at-hand and presently experienced settings so that such matters as agency policy, protocols, and mandates are accountably and warrantably relevant in and through talk as work. The implications of this recognition are profound for analysis, as study of every-day talk-in-interaction, provides a rich resource for examining the in vivo, at-hand, and mundane accomplishment of agency, organisational, and institutional settings.

The concern in CA with such mechanics as turns and sequences discloses "the inferential order of talk" that is "the interpretive resources participants rely on in order to understand one another in appropriate ways" (Hutchby & Wooffitt, 1998:39). Mutual understanding demands, as Silverman points out, that members "produce activities as observable and reportable" (Silverman, 1998:74) and that they manage to do so turn by turn, in the minutia of listening, shaping responses, effecting repairs, and interacting together in sequence.

The emergence of conversation analysis arises from the ready access to a technology for audio-recording and transcribing of ordinary conversations and interviews. Unlike post-facto reconstructions of conversations effected through reliance on memory, the medium of audio-recordings can be subject to veridical and repeated detailed review. Further, the audio recording captures not only those discrete vocalisations we identify as words, but those vocalisations that are not words as such. Audio-recordings capture the spacing between utterances, the depth of overlapping talk, specific starts, stumbles, and interruptions, and the prosodic rhythm and tonality of living talk.

The body

Talk, that most basic of human skills, must be understood as rooted in the physical exercise of the body through the movement of bodily organs and appendages. When we talk, we bring our bodies actively and palpably into a particular type of performance, concerting the activities of complex and diverse organs that include lungs, trachea, larynx, mouth, tongue, and which express in turn the biochemical activities of our brain. Talk as activity is irremediably physical. Talk demands the exercise of our bodies. Talk is not simply the rational and orderly stuff of the mind or the head, but articulates fully the embodiment and physical presence of speakers and their intentionalities. As embodied and as practically accomplished talk is replete with spasms, twitches, and neurological reflexes. Hence talk is replete with what we call errors, stumbles, stutters, mis-starts, unintended pronunciations, misspeaking, lisps, and various physical, rather than ideal, manifestations of vocalisations. To recognise the troubles with talk underscores the fact that as we talk to each other, that which we do together is not merely mind or intention, but speaks to a full physical presence and embodied engagement with another. Through such attentions talk becomes visible as socially organised activities and as practice.

In the following segment an eleven-year-old boy, when describing how he had tried to kill himself, relied on a series of sound effects to convey his experience of choking, as a string constricted about his neck, until it broke.

H: why did ju wanna try te kill yerself
D: no:o don know

H: no

D: jist came te mind te kill myself

H: did ju do anything

D: yah

H: what didja do

D: ah one time, I tried it with a butcher knife, the next time I tried it with
ah belt, hangin myself, an another time I tried it was a::h butter knife,
or fo:rk, string, a special kindsa string, that didn't break easily . . but it
broke the same, thank heaven ya::h. heh. that's a when cchh ((choking
sound)) so hard it broke cha ((breaking sound))=

H: when di, when was the first time that you tried [te ki//]

D: [an another] time I tried it like this with my ring

It is not just children who routinely use vocalisations to capture sounds and
emotions. With the technology of audio-recordings, analysts were not only
able to review talk in its minutia, but through such review, were able to
examine the prosodic and emotive dimensions of talk. Talk in CA is rescued
from the narrow focus on language as words spoken, to be appreciated as
embodied, socially coordinated interaction. As already noted above, audio
recordings allow for almost unlimited replay, starting, stopping, marking of
time measurement, review and recovery of muffled, garbled, and indistinct
sounds, and, of course, transcription. Through these technologies those in CA
were able to identify patterns and consistencies in matters as seemingly mundane as turn taking, overlapping talk, response tokens, pauses and gaps in
talk, and interruptions.

Although audio-recordings provide an invaluable technological resource for
listening to talk as performed they are but a thin trace of the actual physically
executed activity we call talking. Audio-recordings cannot communicate the
physicality of the occasion in which the talk was performed. Thus audio-
recordings, while able to represent modulations of words spoken, cannot
capture the richness of the face-to-face embodied occasion. So it is that the
visual tapestry of the talk-in-interaction escapes detection, as do the smells
and tastes that encircle the participants to the moments of talk. Indeed, as
social workers who wish to understand talk, we must also locate talk as a
performance in actual space and time enacted through our bodies.

Our ability to produce talk which is understood by others, in its audibility,
depends not only on our controlled use of a voice box, but on the reception of
that talk by the ears of another. Talk is an activity of the body that speaks
and hears. Consider the following two transcriptions of the same passage
from an interview:

G: Oh she is eh..{door closing: boom boom}. So she doesn't werk outside the
home {background voice on audio-recording: no I'll try te tell you}...
Okay, so L (_) held a knife, a knife te yer mom's fthrot, she goes inta th'
-is that the first time ya went inta care

B: na ths w' ths wen I wuz livin wi' my mom..I wuz small, like smal sma, i's like tha big

G: yah how come ya went inta care then

B: i wen n'ta care w' livin wi my granma

G: yah

B: she alweys ah.every time when we didn' do nuthin she would ah hitus

G: who did

B: my granmof'r

G: yer grandma would beat on yu.yah.an how cum ya went te live wi yer grandma

B: b'cus my mom had surgry.[til]

G: [ok]ay

B: time wen we hadta go, wm wmy muther

G: okay so yer mom had surgery and you went to live with yer grandma . she would hit chu.How di//

B: an anah we wente go the pleese were there

In this transcription, which was very painstaking in the making, I have attempted to preserve the sound of the utterances and to capture a finer sense of the timing between utterances, hesitations and pauses. Even a cursory attempt to transcribe recorded talk, even that recorded on the highest quality equipment, will quickly reveal the variation between spoken and written language. It should be clear that people do not speak with the precision of printed words, and indeed, that the attempt to capture sounds using the conventions of properly spelled words is quite inadequate.

Now consider a second transcription produced from the same interview. This segment has been cut and pasted from a complete transcription of the interview.

G: Oh she is eh, so she doesn't work outside the home. Okay, so L (_) held a knife, a knife to yer mom's throat, she goes into the hos,..is that first time you went inta care

B: no that was when, when I was still with my mom, I was small, like small small, like that big

G: yah how come you went inta care then?

B: I went inta care when I was living with my grandma, she always ah, every time that we didn't do anything, she would ah, hit us

G: who did

B: my grandmother

G: yer grandma would beat on yah, yah. Now how come you went to live with yer grandma

B: because my mom had surgery

G: okay,

B: tell me we hadta go live with my grandma

G: okay, so yer mom had surgery, you went to live with yer grandma, and she
would hit you, how di//
B: e.a.an when we were at school, the police were there

It should be clear that the second transcription relies more on a taken-for-granted or ordinary written representation of words. The production of such a transcript relies on the ordinary focus on words, sentences, and meaning, irrespective of the mode or format of delivery.

The variation between the two transcribed versions is not insignificant. In the detail of the first transcription we can glimpse the synthetic artfulness and subtlety of talk-in-interaction as an articulation of a speaker's thought (ideal) and delivery in a matrix of physical interaction with another. We can begin to recognise the ways that co-participants interact in a given space, in a given time, and use the available physical resources of their particular bodies to recover and produce sense from the utterances of their co-participant. It is important to remember that talk-in-interaction long preceded the written word, and as such talk-in-interaction is richly tonal, varying in pitch, speed – laconic or compressed – pacing, combining gestures of face and hands and body, which as a totality articulate matters of specific relationship and lived context.

Of course, on reflection there is little surprising in this. It is part of everyday and common-sense that talking with another is not simply about the use of words. Rather recovering sense and meaning from another's talk demands attending to and making sense of the morphology of talk, that is tone, pace, volume, and so on. Such common-sense knowledge is a resource for both parents and infants, who coo, gurgle, babble, and make noises mimicking each other, both vocally and through facial and bodily gestures. In courtship rituals, we readily recognise just how feeble words are as a foundation for communication. Lovers communicate with glances, hand gestures, visual focus, smiles, and even tender touching of hands or face. An appreciation of the embodied nature of talk-in-interaction is of long-standing in conversation analysis. Olsher notes the "mutual elaboration of talk and embodied practices" and sequential practices has been central in, which has included studies of:

> (1) the relative timing of gestures and the utterances which they accompany (Schegloff 1984); (2) the use of facial manipulations (such as an eyebrow flash) and gestures in conjunction with assessments, including concurrent assessments (Goodwin and Goodwin 1987); and (3) assessment gestures which mirror and amplify the gestures associated with the assessments to which they respond.
>
> (2004:222)

We reach past words as embodied in the cultivation of relationships with those whom we meet and to whom we speak. To pretend that meaning can be recovered through words alone is a futile exercise. Fortunately, as noted, CA points past words to the very forms and structures of talk-in-interaction, that is talk as physically realised as two or more people interact, to try to represent some sense of the complexity of that which is accomplished by actual people interacting, and talking to each other.

Listening, response tokens, and repairs

In the preceding I have rather simplistically asserted that talk is heard. I want to turn now to address the active work involved in hearing. As noted, talkers may misspeak, have slips of the tongue, and not realise that they have misspoken, and hearers let talkers know that this has occurred through utterances or non-verbal signals, that act to repair the problem. In CA such repairs are referred to as "other initiated self-repair" or "other initiated other repair" (Hutchby & Wooffitt, 1998:61). In addition to repairs, listeners may signal that they are hearing and understanding the other's talk through the use of a wide variety of response tokens, e.g. mmhuh, yah, okay, nnn, etc. (Gardner, 2001).

The embodied and interactive nature of talk is revealed through analysis of response tokens.[7] Though response tokens are a feature of every-day talk in interviews, in social work, they are particularly worthy of attention as essential tools for eliciting talk, and then signalling to the speaker that their talk does or does not make sense. Certainly, just as competence in every-day conversation relies on the ability to not only talk but to listen, so too is it true in social work interviews. Indeed, response tokens are an essential form for signalling that a listener is listening.

A person spoken to may suffer from any number of problems which might also interfere with the ability to recover sense and meaning from the talk as performed by another. The proper hearing of talk is interactive. Talk, although relying on speaking and hearing, is not just a function of sound. As someone who is hearing impaired – I have relied on hearing aids for more than 25 years – I appreciate that people often talk to me, assuming that I am hearing them, when in fact, I am not able to discern with any reliability what they are saying. Instead, I struggle to synthesise sense from out of fragments to arrive at conjectures of their words and their meaning. Indeed, in most conversations I miss important bits and pieces. As people speak to me I often mishear. I struggle to recover meaning by synthesising expected sounds and tones into words, which are not those which the speaker actually means to communicate or did communicate. As I listen to others I struggle to shift sounds, rhythmic pulses, tones, ascending and descending volumes into understandable words and phrases.

From out of my own hearing loss, I have come to have a deep appreciation for the enormous variations between spoken talk, and the absolute dependence of talk-in-interaction on the embodied interactive coproduction of sense. The possibility of synthesis of understanding from the diverse physical processes, of speaking and hearing, suggests that talk is much more than mere words, or even sentences strung together. Rather, the recovery of sense from talk-in-interaction demands attention to the plenitude of talking and listening as embodied activities. Just as speakers attend to listeners so too do listeners attend to speakers, and both do so, at least those who are not visually impaired, through attention to the plenitude of facial gestures, movements of eyes, raising of brows, pursing of lips, wrinkling of foreheads, and so on. Speakers and listeners signal attention through smiles, frowns, yawns, eye contact, movements of fingers, posture, and so forth. Such a simple matter as interacting with a person who does not speak our language demonstrates the embodied nature of talk, for in the struggle to communicate we may exaggerate facial gestures, pitch and tone of voice, volume, speed of talk, and use various means to communicate using our arms, legs, torso, and head to convey meaning.

CA has identified turn-taking systems and adjacency pairs as structures of talk, as forms of order that participants produce when talking, and it follows that troubles can emerge, and in fact routinely do emerge, as participants speak, anticipate the response of others, struggle to understand the utterances of the other, and move to craft their response in their turn. Silverman argues that turn taking and repairs are embedded in each other (1998:122). Schegloff observes, "Any of the systems and contingencies implicated in the production and reception of talk – articulatory, memory, sequential, syntactic, auditory, ambient noise, etc. – can fail" (1979:269). As a result, problems routinely arise between speakers and listeners, as speakers may stumble, misspeak, struggle to recall a word or a name, and listeners, in and through their reactions may alert a speaker to effect a repair, or a listener may even initiate a repair in their next turn (Schegloff, 1979). Repairs point to more than just specific techniques speakers and listeners use to correct or fix troubles in talk. Repairs point to the very sociability of talk-in-interaction and the co-production of workable interactions and interpretations.

Repairs point to the social organisation of our individual bodies, and physical interactions in coordination with others as integral to the production of discrete social scenes. A recovery or construction of sense and sensibility from others' naturally occurring speaking emerges through a memetic, concerting, and matching of bodily movements, whether as expressions of joy, sorrow, contemplation, and so forth. It is in and through the interstices of interaction that people coordinate accountable and warranted performance of recognisable social occasions. When talking, people actively deploy the plenitude of embodied being in interaction. Embodiment, while providing for the phenomenal possibility of talk, simultaneously suggests a liminality and a horizon or limit through which talk-in-interaction cannot reach. Simply, the plenitude of talk-in-interaction as embodied interaction means that simple attention to matters of sequences, turns at talk, topics, and substance of talk, provides only a narrow window into the plenitude of interaction between people.[8]

Talk as living activity

Consideration and analysis of conversation must recognise and be attentive to the recurrent and mundane use of our bodies in situ, and embodied interaction as instrumental for the production of social relationships. While a relationship may be partially accomplished through talk, the productivity of a face-to-face encounter also expresses exchanges of gestures, hand movements, and body proxemics. Further, talk in situ is not merely words spoken, nor is it a simple use of an established language, but as Volosinov points out, "word is a two-sided act" that is "determined equally by whose word it is and for whom it is meant" (1973:83). Talk in its form as actually expressed is embedded in discrete moments of interactional work. Smith connects this two-sided understanding of Volosinov (1973) to Bakhtin's (1993; 1986) analysis of speech genres, as articulating individual utterances to socially organised "spheres of activity" (Smith, 1999:143). The "two-sided" nature of speech is that it is always both external and internal, individual and social, general and particular, then and now, there and here (1999:142).

For Bakhtin "language grew up in the service of participative thinking and performed acts, and it begins to serve abstract thinking only in the present day of its history" (1993:31). Beyond the word, speakers and their talk always and everywhere express motivation, intention, and purpose. Similarly, Volosinov observes:

> Verbal intercourse is inextricably interwoven with communication of other types, all stemming from the common ground of production communication. It goes without saying that word cannot be divorced from this eternally generative, unified process of communication. In its concrete connection with a situation, verbal communication is always accompanied by social acts of a nonverbal character (the performance of labor, the symbolic acts of a ritual, a ceremony, etc.), and is often only an accessory to these acts, merely carrying out an auxiliary role. Language acquires life and historically evolves precisely here, in concrete verbal communication.
>
> (1973:95)

Talk does not simply exist as a dead letter placed on a shelf. Rather, talk is generated in living, breathing, acting people who use their talk, this particular talk, this once-occurring talk (Bakhtin, 1993) as one resource among many to perform social relations. Talk is the stuff of sitting at a table and talking to one's spouse, sharing comments on the progress of the day, planning activities for the weekend, coordinating drives for the children, identifying grocery lists, and so on. Talk is used by people as one tool among many to perform and to accomplish the experienced every-day and taken-for-granted orders of their lives.

The embodied roots and expressions of talk draws our attention to this person or that person who is talking in this moment of social interaction.

Attention to talk as enacted in and through bodies brings us face-to-face and into interaction with others. We present before them, and they before us, and as we subject them to our judgements so too do they. From a hermeneutics for reading bodies and for reading and interpreting talk we arrive at series of judgements, assessing age, race, gender, ability, intelligence, class, relative beauty, and so on. Talk so considered ceases to be a lofty philosophical or academic domain, and becomes simply a mundane action that contributes to the practical, at-hand, and every-day production of ourselves, others, and a world in which we live. The mundane nature of talk is both its curse and blessing. The curse of talk is that it is ubiquitous, ever present, recurrent, and seemingly unremarkable. The blessing of talk is that if we can see that it is not unremarkable, then talk itself becomes a rich resource. Talk becomes a means for studying the practical and every-day production and reproduction of that which formal analysis calls "social structures". The study of talk moves language out of texts, away from rules of grammar, to look at actual speakers, and actual listeners in interaction and "what people are doing in their talk" (Silverman, 1997:viii). Talk, because it originates in the body is properly profane. A sacred attention to the word and to language is enacted through linguistic priestly rituals, dividing holy words from defiled bodies that talk, to discover in the conceptually abstract and pure, the indwelling of an undefiled spirit. Linguistic transubstantiation transforms words as spoken, and words as realised by speakers whose words they are, into analytically structured language and discourse.

Practice

Precisely because talk is a thing produced by living people, inside their living bodies, talk needs to be approached and understood as a form of practice. Social workers rely on the common-sense concept of practice when they refer to direct practice, clinical practice, therapeutic practice, and so forth. But what is it that they are pointing to as that which is practice? As noted talk is performed using the resource of language, that is words, with forms of meaning which are in turn rooted in a culture or a form of life. Any single moment of talk, thus any conversation, for instance between myself and my son or daughters, is itself embedded in extended and ongoing social relations. When I sit across the kitchen table talking to my daughter about troubles she is having finding work in Canada, our talk, though here-and-now and embedded and performed in a discrete moment and place, is also rooted in our ongoing life course. Our talk while articulating the troubles of finding work simultaneously reproduces the fabric of our relationship, both actually and as idealised both in this moment and in the transcendent intentionality of ideal space and time. Thus, as we talk I accomplish here and now, to a greater of lesser degree various idealisations of what I take it to being a loving, supportive, caring, and attentive father. Reciprocally, my daughter responds to me from out of the fabric of her life, and following from her differential location, as seeking her father's guidance, support, and comfort.

Similarly, talk performed in an interview between social workers and youth in care bridges both the practical and mundane orientations of the participants as well as anticipating and articulating their practice to the idealisations, expectations, forms, and orders of formal, organisations and institutionalised social relations (Smith, 1987:160). The seemingly local practices of social workers and youth in care are always and everywhere rooted in forms of organisation that extend beyond the particular moment of the interview, the physical location of the interview space, and the face-to-face encounter between social worker and client. While attention to individual practices are essential as a point of departure, it is equally essential that these practices be grounded (Bologh, 1979) as moments of extended social relationships. Certainly, what people do is critical for producing a social reality, however, they do not produce this social reality individually, but collectively.

Whether that which is being produced is a thing in hand, a commodity for sale, or an interview for a research project, the processes by which it comes to be produced draw on prior moments of work. Any present moment of work articulates extensive social relations which neither begin nor end in the experienced reality of the participants. Yet, perhaps most importantly it follows that if all knowledge producers, whether social workers, sociologists, or researchers, are located or grounded in actual life processes, then what they count as knowledge will itself be embedded in those life processes. What counts as knowledge expresses the social organisation of knowledge producers' locations, and as such all knowledge is fundamentally political, situated, and interested.

In EM this connection has been addressed as "the problem of 'institutional context'" (Zimmerman & Pollner, 1970), which as Hak points out provides an "occasioned corpus of setting features" (1995:134). Hak explains that, "the features of a setting are not 'given' but rather are achieved by participants who 'assemble the corpus'" (1995:111). The "occasioned corpus of setting features" directs an ethnomethodologist to spurn the temptation of conventional or positivist sociology which would have us read categories back into settings as explanations of the settings determinate features. Both EM and CA favour an approach that discovers sociological categories only to the degree that they are demonstrably present as features oriented to by actors on particular occasions. For example, Zimmerman outlines,

> Thus conduct situated in formal settings or occasions and oriented to institutional aims can be understood as "institutional" (as opposed to "mundane") interaction only in terms of the deployment of general conversational resources activated and configured not only to produce but to provide the relevance and recognizability of specific types of activity.
>
> (1992:36–37)

Schegloff has expressed similar methodological strictures through the dual notions of "relevance" and "procedural consequentiality" (1997; 1992) which be examined in more detail in Chapter 3.

However, for now it is important to affirm that there is a lively interest in conversation analysis not only for mundane and every-day talk but for the ways that people through talk come to bring institutional orders, authority, and reality into being. Indeed, that which we identify as the distinctive elements or characteristics of institutional work, especially social work, emerge as realised in and through the quite ordinary, mundane, and everyday practical activities of people as they go about performing an office, an interview, a team meeting, a community consultation, and so on. Conversation analysis allows us to probe and unfold the essential reflexivity of institutional orders as practically accomplished day after day, from which as Garfinkel noted, there is no time out (2002).

Notes

1　Since the middle ages, grammar, logic, and rhetoric have been identified as the trivium or the lower division of the seven liberal arts. Their identification articulates a process of formulating sound argument. Grammar identifies assembling words into cogent sentences with meaningful propositions, logic identifies rules and orders for sensible propositions one might make with sentences, and rhetoric is about using grammar and logic when talking to others and making arguments that they will find cogent and convincing. The trivium articulates a work process and a process for thinking which aims to identify rules and laws for communication. Conversation analysis aims to shift the approach to talk and talking from its orders, to attention to people's situated practices and activities of talking.

2　The authors turn to transcripts in their analysis of pathological communication, and again, albeit briefly, in their analysis of paradoxical communication. They come close to recognising the importance of the dimensions identified by CA as they conclude their analysis of pathological communication by making two points, "First, content fades in importance as communicational patterns emerge" and second, "No given statement in isolation can be symmetrical, complementary one-up, or whatever. It is the response of the partner that is of course necessary for the 'classification' of a given message" (Watzlawick, et al., 1967:117).

3　Watson observed, "that reflexivity is not merely something which one 'does,' like engaging in self-reflection or seeking validity, but is, rather, an essential and inevitable property of all discourse (including, of course, this)" (1987:29–30). The problem of EM and CA is working out just how these actual people, in this place, at this time actually went about, interactively producing the lived and experienced coherence, not as abstract but as lived and shared as a moment in their lives.

4　The relationship between EM and CA although close, has given rise to some tensions, as Lynch notes that "the professional discipline of conversation analysis has moved progressively away from explications of its ethnomethodological foundations in favor of procedural accounts of conversational method" (2000:518). Despite these concerns he effects a recovery of CA as still ethnomethodological, as it "retains its ethnomethodological foundations in its technical vocabulary" (518).

5　Although Schegloff's entreaty that talk be treated as "an object in its own right", talk is not properly speaking an object, but rather talk as performed is an activity. Talk is always someone's talk, as their living activity, and as the expression of their embodied existence, being, and performance. To treat talk as an object risks replicating the formal analytic turn which threatens to separate that which is achieved in and through talk from the plenum of member's lives, accounts, and orders.

6 It must be noted that Hester and Francis identify a tension or conflict between CA proper and what they call "the institutional talk program" (2000). They argue that the focus on institutional rather than ordinary conversation aims to "elucidate the relationship between the social organization of interaction and the social order of institutions" (393). This they argue promises rapprochement between CA and mainstream sociological interests in structure, and redirects attention from "members' phenomena" to "analysis' phenomena" (406). Indeed they remind us again of the importance of discovery of institutional categories in and through members' practically coordinated work.

7 Gardner has pointed out some response tokens, such as "falling Ah: (unlike the uttering of a word Beautiful or How sad for example) resemble continuers in that they have no readily identifiable semantic content, but their impact appears to hang on ... their intonation contour and prosodic form being fitted appropriately to the talk to which they respond" (2001:5). What is most remarkable about this recognition is that it suggests that people routinely use forms of talk that do not rely on words. Rather people use forms of talk that rely on sounds to convey mood, emotion, and connection with the other. In this sense sounds function as caresses, touches, and physical communication between talkers.

8 For a fascinating example of the complementarity between talk-in-interaction and body motion see Schegloff's (1997) analysis of a video segment of two couples at dinner. Schegloff, writing about a participant, observed, "Shane's body behavior has preceded his talk" (181) and that this was central to opening a new sequence. Also noteworthy is Schegloff's earlier paper on gestures and talk (1984).

References

Bakhtin, Mikhail M. (1986). *Speech genres and other late essays* (Trans. Vern W. McGee). Austin, TX: University of Texas Press.

Bakhtin, Mikhail M. (1993). *Toward a philosophy of the act* (Trans. Vadim Liapunov, Eds. Vadim Liapunov & Michael Holquist). Austin, TX: University of Texas Press.

Bergson, Henri. (2001). *Time and free will: An essay on the immediate data of consciousness* (Trans. F. L. Pogson). Meneola, NY: Dover.

Boden, Deirdre. (1994). *The business of talk: Organizations in action.* Cambridge, England: Polity.

Bologh, Roslyn Wallach. (1979). *Dialectical phenomenology: Marx's method.* London, England: Routledge & Kegan Paul.

Button, Graham. (1992). Answers as interactional products: Two sequential practices used in job interviews. In Paul Drew & John Heritage (Eds.), *Talk at work: Interaction in institutional settings* (pp. 21–231). Cambridge, England: Cambridge University Press.

Gardner, Rod. (2001). *When listeners talk: Response tokens and listener stance.* Philadelphia, PA: John Benjamins.

Garfinkel, Harold. (2002). *Ethnomethodology's program: Working out Durkheim's aphorism.* Lanham, MD: Rowman & Littlefield.

Goodwin, Charles & Goodwin, Marjorie Harness. (1987). Concurrent operations on talk: Notes on the interactive organization of assessments. *IPrA Papers in Pragmatics,* 1(1): 1–55.

Hak, Tony. (1995). Ethnomethodology and the institutional context. *Human Studies,* 18, 109–137.

Hall, Christopher, Juhila, Kirsi, Maqtarese, Maureen, & Carolus van Nijnatten (Eds.). (2014). *Analysing social work communication: Discourse in practice.* Oxford, England: Routledge.

Hall, Christopher, Juhila, Kirsi, Parton, Nigel, & Pösö, Tarja (Eds.). (2003). *Constructing clienthood in social work and human services: Interaction, identities and practices.* London, England: Jessica Kingsley.

Hepworth, Dean H., Rooney, Ronald H., Dewberry Rooney, Glenda, Strom-Gottfried, Kimberly, & Larsen, Jo Ann. (2010). *Direct social work practice: Theory and skills* (8th ed.). Belmont, CA: Brooks/Cole.

Heritage, John. (2002). The limits of questioning: Negative interrogatives and hostile question content. *Journal of Pragmatics,* 34: 1427–1446.

Hester, Stephen, & Francis, David. (2000). Ethnomethodology, conversation analysis, and "institutional talk". *Text,* 20(3): 391–413.

Hutchby, Ian. (2005). "Active listening": Formulations and the elicitation of feelings-talk in child counselling. *Research on Language and Social Interaction,* 38 (3): 303–329.

Hutchby, Ian, & Wooffitt, Robin. (1998). *Conversation analysis.* Cambridge, England: Polity.

Kadushin, Alfred, & Kadushin, Goldie. (2013). *The social work interview: The guide for human service professionals* (5th ed.). New York, NY: Columbia University Press.

Lynch, Michael. (2000). The ethnomethodological foundations of conversation analysis. *Text,* 20(4): 517–532.

Malone, M. J. (1997) *Worlds of Talk: The Presentation of Self in Everyday Conversation.* Cambridge, England: Polity.

Olsher, David. (2004). Talk and gesture: The embodied completion of sequential actions in spoken interaction. In Rod Gardner & Johannes Wagner (Eds.), *Second language conversations* (pp. 221–245). London, England: Continuum.

Psathas, George. (1995). *Conversation analysis: The study of talk in interaction.* Thousand Oaks, CA: Sage.

Sacks, Harvey. (1995). *Lectures on conversation (Volumes 1 & 2)* (Ed. Gail Jefferson). Oxford, England: Blackwell.

Sacks, Harvey, Schegloff, Emanuel, & Jefferson, Gail. (1974). A simplest systematics for the organization of turn-taking for conversation. *Language,* 50(4): 696–735.

Schegloff, Emanuel A. (1968). Sequencing in conversational Openings. *American Anthropologist,* 70: 1075–1095.

Schegloff, Emanuel A. (1979). The relevance of repair to syntax-for-conversation. *Syntax and Semantics,* 12: 261–286.

Schegloff, Emanuel A. (1984). On some gestures' relation to talk. In J. Maxwell Atkinson & John Heritage (Eds.), *Structures in social action: Studies in conversation analysis* (pp. 266–296). Cambridge, England: Cambridge University Press.

Schegloff, Emanuel A. (1990). On the organization of sequences as a source of "coherence" in talk-in-interaction. In Bruce Dorval (Ed.), *Conversational organization and its development* (pp. 51–77). Norwood, NJ: Ablex.

Schegloff, Emanuel A. (1992). On talk and its institutional occasions. In Paul Drew & John Heritage (Eds.), *Talk at work: Interaction in institutional settings* (pp. 101–134). Cambridge, England: Cambridge University Press.

Schegloff, Emanuel A. (1995). Introduction. In Harvey Sacks, *Lectures on conversation* (Volumes 1 & 2) (Ed. Gail Jefferson) (pp.ix–lxii). Oxford, England: Blackwell.

Schegloff, Emanuel A. (1997). Whose text? Whose context? *Discourse and Society*, 8 (2): 165–187.

Schegloff, Emanuel A. (2007). *Sequence organization in interaction: A primer in conversation analysis I.* Cambridge, England: Cambridge University Press.

Schutz, Alfred. (1962). *Collected papers I: The problem of social reality* (Ed. M. Natanson). Dordrecht, Netherlands: Kluwer.

Searle, John. (1969). *Speech acts: An essay in the philosophy of language.* London, England: Cambridge University Press.

Searle, John. (1979). *Expression and meaning: Studies in the theory of speech acts.* Cambridge, England: Cambridge University Press.

Shulman, Lawrence. (2016). *The skills of helping individuals, families, groups, and communities* (8th ed.). Toronto, ON: Thompson Brooks Cole.

Silverman, David. (1998). *Harvey Sacks: Social science & conversation analysis.* Cambridge, England: Polity.

Silverman, David. (1997). *Discourses of counselling: HIV counselling and social interaction.* London, England: Sage.

Smith, Dorothy E. (1987). *The everyday world as problematic: A feminist sociology.* Toronto, ON: University of Toronto Press.

Smith, Dorothy E. (1999). *Writing the social: Critique theory and investigations.* Toronto, ON: University of Toronto Press.

ten Have, Paul. (2007). *Doing conversation analysis: A practical guide* (2nd ed.). London, England: Sage.

Turner, Francis J. (2002). *Diagnosis in social work: New imperatives.* New York, NY: Haworth Social Work Practices Press.

Volosinov, Valentin N. (1973). *Marxism and the philosophy of language* (Trans. Ladislav Matejka & I. R. Titunik). New York, NY: Seminar Press.

Watson, Graham. (1987). Make me reflexive—But not yet: Strategies for managing essential reflexivity in ethnographic discourse. *Journal of Anthropological Research*, 43(1): 29–41.

Watzlawick, Paul, Beavin, Janet Helmick, & Jackson, Don D. (1967). *The pragmatics of human communication: A study of interactional patterns, pathologies, and paradoxes.* New York, NY: W. W. Norton.

Wittgenstein, Ludwig. (2009). *Philosophical investigations* (4th ed.) (Trans. G. E. M. Anscombe, P. M. S. Hacker, & J. Schulte). Sussex, England: Wiley-Blackwell.

Zimmerman, Don H. (1992). Achieving context: Openings in emergency calls. In Graham Watson & Robert M. Seiler (Eds.), *Text in context: Contributions to ethnomethodology* (pp. 35–51). Newbury Park, CA: Sage.

Zimmerman, Don H., & Pollner, Melvin. (1970). The everyday world as a phenomenon. In Jack Douglas (Ed.), *Understanding everyday life: Toward the reconstruction of sociological knowledge* (pp. 80–103). Chicago, IL: Aldine.

2   Structures of talk-in-interaction

It may seem self-evident, if not banal, but the recognition that a social work interview is a talk-centred activity provides a rich resource for study and analysis. Unlike other social activities, e.g. eating a meal, playing cards, playing hockey, or jogging with friends, doing an interview, as with having a conversation, centres on activities of talking, taking turns, responding to another, and creating a sensible occasion as such. Furthermore, unlike a conversation between friends in which asymmetry in turn taking is likely random or accidental, in an interview asymmetry is an intentionally designed and achieved feature of the interaction (Buttny, 1996; Button, 1992). Indeed, asymmetry in turn-taking between interviewers and interviewees is one of the distinctive markers of interviews, and is brought about through their intentional co-construction of differential contributions (Kadushin & Kadushin, 2013; Mazeland & ten Have, 1996; Drew & Heritage, 1992). Drew and Heritage have identified the following as relevant dimensions for examining the distinctive features of institutional talk: "(a) lexical choice; (b) turn design; (c) sequence organization; (d) overall structural organization; and (e) social epistemology and social relations" (1992:28–29).[1]

This chapter focuses on an examination of the structural features of talk performed as interviews. Through detailed study of the interactions for doing an interview we can begin to glimpse the ways that matters such as organisational context are practically produced in and through the concrete and determinate forms of participants' conduct in interaction. As Drew and Heritage point out, it is in the ways that people organise their conduct that institutional realities are realised "recurrently and pervasively" (1992:26). By studying the ways that participants produce certain structured features of talk-in-interaction as interviews we can explicate or unfold how it is that the interviews as such are performed, that is for practical and at hand purposes.

Indeed, it is through the detailed analysis of the talk-in-interaction that we can glimpse the practical techniques whereby participants produce not just interviews, but specific types of interviews, i.e., unstructured research interviews to address the experiences of youth of coming into care and living in care. In such so-called unstructured[2] (Pawson, 1996) or open-ended interviews (Mazeland & ten Have, 1996), the interviewer's objective was to elicit, entice,

and seek out information from the interviewee. For the youth being interviewed there was also a recognition, more or less articulated, that the success
of the interview depended on his or her ability to meet the objectives of the
interviewer, that is to provide the interviewer with answers to questions.

This chapter, although addressing structural features of talk-in-interaction
does not seek to discover or establish that particular structures of talk-in-
interaction – sequences, repairs, response tokens, etc. – work in this or that
fashion, or work according to this or that rule. My objective is not to advance
conversation analysis (CA) as a discipline.[3] My primary interest is not in
developing the disciplinary corpus and understanding of talk as sequential
action. Rather, it is simply to make a case that social workers can benefit by
taking up CA's tools, methods, and analytic frameworks and by deploying
these in analysis of social work practices and interactions with clients. By
analysing some of the common structural features of talk-in-interaction as
producing warranted forms of social work, e.g. an interview, I hope that
social workers can better recognise, appreciate, and understand the complex
details that comprise the art of their practice.

An economy of turns at talk

In one of the first articles which advanced CA, Sacks, Schegloff, and Jefferson
noted that "the presence of 'turns' suggests an economy, with turns for
something being valued–and means for allocating them, which affect their
relative distribution" (1974:696). Hutchby and Wooffitt took up this insight to
note that the turn-taking model recognises "turns in conversations are
resources which, like goods in an economy, are distributed in systematic ways
among speakers" (1998:47). The idea that there is an economy of turns is a
rich and surprisingly useful metaphor as it allows us to unfold the foundations of talk-in-interaction. As with any economy, something of value must be
exchanged, whether it is a commodity or a turn of talk. What is it that gives a
turn value? What are the values of a turn of talk? How does membership in
different speech communities shape the value of specific turns of talk, e.g.
patient and counsellor, youth and interviewer, social workers and client?

It is important, to add, as Hymes (1996) so astutely points out, that not all
participants to talk, and thus not all turns come to be treated as having equal
value. Hymes provides a critical examination of the ways that linguists have
glossed over and erased the problems of inequality of speakers, based on
gender, accent, race, class, age, ability, and so forth. Additionally, Hymes in
contradistinction to Habermas' "ideal of unrestricted communication"
(Hymes, 1996:54), draws attention to the problems of restriction or constraint
placed on some participants to talk and to remain silent, and the expectations
and license that others will talk, when in interaction. We can easily identify
settings where such differences exist, such as a courtroom when a defendant
on the stand talks only when asked a question, and is expected to talk only in
a way that is deemed by a judge to answer the question, while a judge, when

delivering a judgement, is expected to talk without interruption. Hymes' insight applies as well to interviews between social workers and youth in care. What are the differential obligations, at different moments, for the social worker or the youth to talk? Who is expected to talk? Who is expected to be silent? Who expects? What are the resources that participants to talk-in-interaction bring to the talk that inform such expectations?

The question about the value of turns, coincidentally is illuminated by a turn to Marx. If we think about a turn-at-talk as a 'thing', that expresses people's actual interaction over the time needed for this spate of talk, and as such expresses the energy, time, and attention of their actions, we can begin to glimpse some similarity with the problem of the values of commodities. Indeed, to understand the value of commodities as things that are exchanged, Marx developed a "labour theory of value" (Marx, 2010c). He argued that it was 'labour power', not just labour as an abstract concept, but rather the power, energy, and time of work that was the origin of the exchange value of the things people produced and consumed. His enquiry began with a relatively simple question, what is it that gives a commodity, or produced thing, its value as exchanged (Marx, 2010a; 2010b; 2010c; 1973). He noted that there is a difference between "use value" and the fact that some very useful things are neither bought nor sold, e.g. air, oceans, and (until recently) water, and "exchange value", that seemingly elusive quality of things that give them value as bought and sold. The puzzle Marx faced was figuring out just what it was, in a commodity, that made this thing have, or gave it exchange value. Marx observed that "exchange-value is the only form in which value of commodities can manifest itself or be expressed" (2010a:48). So, when people exchange one commodity for another, whether in primitive barter, a sheep for a small cart, or $550.00 for a cell-phone, some sort of calculation of equivalencies is being performed. But what is it that is being considered as equivalent?

Marx's unique contribution was to identify and to unfold that the source of exchange value arose from labour power. But, what is labour power? We can only understand labour power by beginning with an attention to people at work. We recognise that when people work they work in the time of their life, e.g. Monday to Friday from 8:30 a.m. to 4:30 p.m. every day. They also work with energy, using the capacities, movements, and strength of their bodies. Though lamentably, the implication of a focus on people in action, and people's actions, has all too often been missed, it follows that if the source of all exchange value is derived from people at work, then the source of all value is human life itself. The placement of human activities as the foundation for all exchange value needs to be recognised as profoundly humanist. The structures of the world around us, the streets, buildings, electric power grids, and the things of day-to-day lives, whether computers, pens, paper, washrooms, dinner tables, and so on, are the sedimentations, memories, and voices of generations of working people who have bequeathed to us through their labour the taken-for-granted contours of our lived world. Commodities, and exchange value are nothing more nor anything less than human life itself. They are the expression of our lives, expended over time, and as emerging from the directed energy of our minds and bodies. Simply, people, in the time and energy of their lives are the source of all values. People through the work of their bodies in the world come to produce a social world. All exchangeable values that make up an economy are founded in living human activity. It follows, perhaps not surprisingly, as articulated by a social worker, that the only source or 'thing' of value, is that which is never a thing, and this is human lives and human beings.

So, to return to talk-in-interaction, we ask: What is produced in a conversation? The words, sentences, and forms of exchange are produced in lived time, using the energy of our bodies, expressed through our lungs and our voices, and augmented by our gestures, and registered in the recognition of each other's actions. What is being exchanged in conversational turns is nothing more nor less than the time and energy of our lives. If a turn has value this articulates the intentionalities of position and projection of the participants to talk-in-interaction, the value of holding the floor, or being listened to by another, of commanding, ordering, directing, or of exploring, sharing, etc. As in a political economy where there are socially organised rules, laws, or regulations shaping the exchange of commodities, so too are there rules that shape an economy of turns between participants. So, if there is an economy of turns, it follows that a turn has value, though turns produced by different people also have different value. This is more than simple metaphor. We have come increasingly to recognise the inequalities of not only of 'voice', but who has voice. Who and what powers, authority, status, social positions, regulations, and norms are brought into play to manage the distribution of turns? Furthermore, even when one person, a client talks, what value does that spate of talk have relative to the spate of talk of the social worker, counsellor, or interviewer? Talk and turns at talk come to be produced for exchange with another. A turn's value is realised in an economy of talk, that is the intensity of engagement in the activity of talking with another, and the duration of talk-in-interaction, that presupposes engagement between people as talkers and listeners. What counts as 'value', whether abstract labour power, or talk itself, will articulate a form of life in which socially organised distribution of 'value' is organised.

The brilliance of Marx's analysis was that he was able to see through the mystifications and fetishisations obscuring the source of what gave commodities an exchange value. He was able to see that underneath the commodity form, that the exchange value of things was realised in and through the everyday and largely taken-for-granted work of people. Work was realised as people came together, in determinate, i.e. socially patterned and organised ways, to spend the time of their lives (duration) together, and bringing into the interaction the energy of their bodies (intensity). Yet such essential elements of oneself, that is the capacity to expend energy as work over the time of one's own life, can become a commodity, even in talk, as we recognise through the employment of social workers, and the costs and charges clients and patients must pay for counselling and therapy. Wendling notes, "Humans become a calculable resource like any other within the economy. Within this economy, resources are all subject to exchange-value, and must therefore be made calculable in terms of one another" (2009:4).

Once entered into the calculations of commodity exchange, one's work, energy, and life-time become subjected to an 'alien' control by others. Industrialisation and today globalisation, subordinate one's local work to the orders, management, administration and regulations of a cadre of professional managers, who are in turn accountable to owners of capital, who due to their wealth, and as a result of the complex legal webs of corporate ownership, live predictably far removed from sites of production. Such external controls over a labour processes effected through divisions of labour, divisions of authority, and divisions of classes results in processes of alienation (Marx, 2010c; Ollman, 1976; Rubin, 1972; Rubin, 1970).

Alienation is a manifold phenomenon, as Wendling observes, covering multiple dimensions, "theological, political, psychological, economic, and technological" (2009:37). Indeed, that which we point to and reference as alienation includes the human capacity to project, displace, and convert our every-day frustrations and rage, into fetishised images of a just god and a just ethics. Of course, the structures of alienation of capitalist production are in turn legitimised by the structures of a state apparatus, through which relations of property, ownership, and inequality are legitimised. Particularly important for social workers, alienation articulates our otherness to self. Alienation emerges from the every-day experience of self as fragmented, divided, and separated from the humanity of others. Just as I become a 'thing' in the form of a commodity for myself, so too are others, for me, 'things' and commodities. Yet, in the agony of relationships formulated on a terrain of calculation, manipulation, and consumption we desire something otherwise.

The systematic technological innovations of production, expressed through divisions of labour and the factory, damage not only people themselves, but the natural worlds where they live (Dickens, 1996). Indeed, the alienation generated through divisions of labour, result in not only loss of self and a loss of one's own authenticity and humanity, but a concatenating rupture between self and others (Dickens, 1996). Alienation in a capitalist society is fundamentally expressed in the separation of a worker from himself, as ruptures in the fundamental forms of life, as recognition of self as a commodity, and as people become living things to be bought and sold in a labour market. When at work, the experiential structures of alienation are reproduced daily. Alienation emerges as a worker's life energy is directed toward production and its products, in work removed from the worker's own control, and through legal structures which assure that a worker's productions are appropriated by an employer. So, as workers lose control over a work process (Braverman, 1998), they lose control over time and embodied direction of energy. In this loss, reproduced day-after-day, working people lose control over their own lives, as well as control over the commodities and the values that are produced.

Alienation, understood as emerging from out of and expressing forms of social relation, comes to be expressed for social workers, and other 'professionals'[4] through ritualised subordination and absorption of self into the structured and ideological orders of professional regulation and institutionalised forms of work. Alienation is effected day after day as a person makes herself over into a professional social worker, realising the mandates, mission, and objectives of the organisation as her own, and as expressed in her work.

Simply, the hidden source of exchange value was the mundane and everyday activities of actual people expressed in socially organised forms of work. In this profoundly reflexive and humanist move Marx opened up the possibility that work could be a congruent and authentic expression of human desire and creativity. As useful as Marx's insight is, two addenda or modifications are necessary. First, as Mary O'Brien observed in *The Politics of Reproduction* (1981), Marx and Engels both, perhaps as men, failed to recognise the organic 'reproduction' of people through labour and birth. O'Brien insisted that human reproduction needed to be recognised and examined dialectically, that is a fully human process. Second, as Baudrillard so insightfully pointed out in *The Mirror of Production*, human attention, energy, and time is also directed to discharge, waste, profligacy, sexuality, and play (Baudrillard, 1975). Clearly much of what is performed as talk-in-interaction, particularly when shaped as conversations between lovers, sexual intimates, as well as family and friends, overflows a simple conception of labour as work, to touch on elements of human reproduction, sexuality, and play.

It follows that to understand what is being exchanged, and the forms by which that which is being exchanged comes to be recognised as having value, demands explicating the social organisation of actual exchange systems in differential forms of talk-in-interaction. As noted, a conversation is different from an interview, and the reflexive accomplishment of the differential forms and locations of such activities demands close attention to the forms of practice and interaction. The structures of exchange and value are different, by virtue of differential intentionality of the actors who produce the social organisation of such occasions.

The economy of exchange for distributing turns in talk-in-interaction is every bit as complex as that for distributing goods and services in our society, and just as dependent on the forms of life and social relations in which people live. Indeed, the allocation and distribution of turns can readily be seen as being dependent on such social relations. We can imagine turn-exchange systems in which people speak only when spoken to, for instance between upper class employers and servants, between a judge in court and a witness, or between strict parents and their children. We can also imagine turn exchange systems where complex rules of age, gender, vocabulary, energy, body size, emotional energy, and so on are resources for negotiating turns among a group of ten-year-old children in a school yard. We can also imagine turn exchange systems in which though there is unequal power to determine turn distribution, that the one with least power is encouraged to do most of the talking, such as in interrogations and interviews.

Even when talk-in-interaction is produced as a form of work, as with all work, the moment of working is alive to the synthetic possibility of conjoining use-value with exchange value, as an immediate moment of pleasure. Further, work with people, as talk, always involves engaging with another, who like oneself is alive. Work performed as talk is always living, always dynamic, and always unpredictable. Just as workers even in the most oppressive organisations find opportunities to play at work (Roy, 1959–60), so too can people whose talk is work find opportunities to play at talk. Even talk which is performed as work, such as that as an interview, when performed 'well', as we can see below between M and G, expresses a sense of engagement, commitment, joy, and creativity. In short, talk becomes a source of pleasure. At times we are pleased by our talk with others. The work of coordinating talk with another can itself be a source of laughter, amusement, and joy.

G: = So::h And you've bin in care for a long time eh?
M: Quite a long time, yeah
G: So::h, d'you wanna:a..jist
M: ((laughter and inaudible)) Do you want me to jist . . Do ya want to just spit it out hehehe((laughing))
G: hehehe ((laughing))Yeah! Spit it out!
M: I have no idea where ta begin. I don't know wha=
G: =OK. Whe-where did you begin in care, I mean yo-you were pretty young, right?
M: M-hmm. I was very young, very. I was(-) uh:h three days old I think.
G: Oh, I see.
M: Yes.

What is it that causes the youth M to initiate laughter, and G to follow by laughing herself? If we assume that laughter expresses some form of pleasure, and that pleasure is of value, what is it that M and G find of value? The laughter seems prompted by G's questions, "So:oh, d'you wanna:a.. jist", which unlike the question in the first line, "And you've bin in care for a long time eh?", is quite elliptical, indirect, and vague. The joke as it works arrives in M's repair to G's turn (more on repairs below), hence the perceived necessity that M take over leadership of the interview from the interviewer. Essentially M in her turn is saying: someone has to take control of this interview, and if you won't do it then I will. It seems to me that the source of pleasure and value in this turn is that together M and G recognise that they have work to do, and that to get it done they will need to work cooperatively. Thus, what is of value in these turns of talk is the very humanity of each other in interaction.

If we return to the question of the value of the exchange of turns in talk-in-interaction we see that the source of that which is valued in a turn ultimately expresses the organisation of social relations of power. Watts notes, "Whenever people interact verbally, power is exercised. One person acts, another reacts, and either interpersonal balance is achieved or imbalance is created" (1997:87). The allocation and distribution of turns is ultimately tied to the social organisation of the settings in which talk is performed. Though it may be the case that what is of value in a commodity is "congealed labour" (Marx, 2010c), what comes to be seen as of value in a turn of talk articulates the social organisation of the life and labour of speakers. Curiously, just as Marx dedicated Volume II of *Capital* (2010b) to tracing the "circulation of capital", conversation analysts, notably Sacks, Schegloff, and Jefferson (1974) and Schegloff (2000; 1990) can be seen to examine a circulation of turns and sequences in talk-in-interaction.

Indeed, in the interviews conducted with youth in care the interviewers did largely manage the distribution of turns and sequences throughout the interview. They effected control over the direction of the interview by asking relevant questions about coming into care and living in care, and by providing appropriate response tokens, and follow-ups requesting elaboration of detail. Interviewers generally attended very carefully to youth's talk and indicated that they were concerned with the issues that the youth raised. In general, interviewers exercised an executive direction over length and topical shaping of turns. For their part, the youth did most of the talking in interviews. They generally held the floor for the longest periods. Of course, that which was talked about, hence the topic of the talk, was centred on the youth's life experiences in their families and in care, not those of the interviewers.

When interviewing youth, or for that matter any client, social workers struggle to produce interviews, or forms of social interaction, in which the interviewee is demonstrably engaged and interested in the occasion. Interest is signalled through the emotional tone of the talk, through a willingness to reveal personal details, through the length and details of responses, and so on. Experienced social workers, when conducting interviews with clients, are wary of talking too much. A social worker's talk, as invested with professional authority, education, and organisational office, can function to impose the worker's beliefs, evaluations, views, and interpretations on clients. Indeed, it has long been recognised that a social worker's talk in an interview can be produced to advance their power over a client's. A social worker's talk in an interview can be manipulative and controlling.

From the standpoint of the client or interviewee, a good interview is one where the social worker's questions make sense, and can be applied as cogent, relevant, and meaningful points of entry to talk about his or her own life. In a good interview a client can frame their talk to address the questions posed by the social worker, while at the same time speaking through these frameworks to the relevant structures of his or her own life. In this sense, a good interview arises from the ability of the social worker to frame questions such that they resonate with this client. Simultaneously, the client is able to interpret the social worker's questions in such a manner that they are able to find resonances with familiar forms for narrating their life story, forms that they have used in the past to account for their lives. A good interview is one where the client speaks candidly, using their own language. By turning to close evaluation of the structures of talk-in-interaction in interviews we can better understand not only how coherence is produced in interviews, but in social work generally.

Turn taking

Central to any talk-in-interaction is the structure participants use to signal turn transitions between participants. My concern in this section is not to set out rules governing the use of this or that device, but rather to demonstrate the utility for social workers of close analysis to such matters as turns, overlapping talk, and interruptions. The following somewhat lengthy segment displays a series of turns at talk between N, the interviewer, and S, the youth, that taken together build up interactive "clumps of talk" (Schegloff, 1990:53) or sequences that work to fulfil the purposes of the interview.

N: So you came inta foster care when you were seven=
S: =yah=
N: =For the first time. What was goin on with you at the time? Do you recall much of that?
S: I'w's jist, I was jis gettin in a lotta trouble.
N: Yah↑?
S: Yah.
N: What kinda trouble.
S: Life, like I said, all like stealin, gettin kicked outta school and stuff, when I was in school, when I was five, I was, like in grade, I was getting kicked outta school. I was jist a total bad ass and stuff. But jis, I don' know why, it's jis how I was.
N: Do you remember how you felt at the time?
S: I like had no friends. I's pretty lonely except fer my cousin O(_)=
N: yah=
S: he's only seventeen now, he cou- I jist hung out with him and stuff=
N: =yah=
S: but I like was jis, I was, I was jist too hyper.
N: Okay.
S: like nobody liked me and stuff.
N: Have you had any, are you ah A D D, or anything like that.
S: Well I wa:s, well I'm (proud of showing but fuck) it doesn't come out.
N: Yah=
S: =I've been able te ah control it.
N: Yah.
S: But, that's my own perspective of it=
N: =yah=

S: =I don't know what their, right perspective of [it is], but=
N: [yah]
S: =but up till grade eight. I was always hyper=
N: =yah=
S: no-body liked me, and then up then, first half of grade nine, had no friends,
   and nobody te hang out and stuff like then, but then I got kicked outta X
   (town), and went te ah Y (town), an made some friends there, started
   acting maturish and stuff, stopped actin like an idiot. Got some friends,
   stopped that, and people started following me, and now I'm starten to go
   to Y (town). My cousins, pretty popular, and everybody likes him. He's
   not, like he's ah, he's able te hang out with the preppy group=
N: =yah yah=
S: =and the teenage group, and the people that'll, always bad, and always
   doin stuff bad. He's like a neutral guy=
N: =yah

This segment begins as N, draws on an earlier statement by S's, "so its pretty
weird, bin in care since I was seven years old", to shape a statement posed as
a question "So you came inta foster care when you were seven". Although S
signals that N's understanding is correct, the latched "yah" is heard by N to
be a continuer, allowing him to move past questions of age and chronology to
questions about experiences in care, "What was goin on with you at the
time?" S's response then opens up a series of turns that focus on "I'w's jist, I
was jis gettin in a lotta trouble."[5] N recognises that S considers that his turn is
complete, but wants more information, so responds with an affirmative,
"Yah↑?", shaped with ascending tone to act as a question to elicit further
information. S attempts to avoid the invitation, by responding "Yah", which
most likely was designed to signal his sense that the topic of 'trouble' had
been adequately addressed. N refuses to accept S's indication that the
sequence of talk about troubles is complete. N moves to continue to expand
the sequence on 'troubles' by replying, "What kinda trouble", to push S to
provide specific details and descriptions of things that might be trouble. N's
strategy works, as S moves to provide an extended turn that provides several
examples of what he meant by trouble.

Once S has provided what counts for N as an adequate account of troubles,
N returns to the theme of experiences and feelings by asking, "Do you
remember how you felt at the time?" N's probe for information resonates with
S, as he responds, "I like had no friends. I's pretty lonely except fer my cousin
O (_)". S then shifts to a description of his cousin, N provides a response token
'yah', and S returns to talking about his own troubles, and explains, "I was jist
too hyper". N provides a response token, "okay", which unlike "yah" that acts
as a continuer, indicates interest, and signals a readiness to take a next turn.

As a result of the signal, when S finishes his turn, which centred on
explaining the troubles with friends, "like nobody liked me and stuff", N,
rather than pursuing this topic, as noted, picked up on S's claim that he was

"too hyper" to explore whether or not S is "ADD". The next five turns, beginning with S's agreement, "Well I wa:s", except when N provides an overlapping response token, reveal a grammatical structure in which S uses full sentences, while N replies with response tokens that act as continuers, encouragers, and supporters. N's use of response tokens has the overall effect of indicating to S, that that which he is talking about is worth saying, interesting, and relevant for this interview. S responds by producing an extended and very personal sequence that is a confession of events that are extremely stigmatising, shameful, and hurtful. Of course, S is able to provide this narrative because it is characterised as being about events and ways of being that are in his past.

Clearly, central to the art of interviewing is the interviewer's skilful recognition of those interactive devices that will keep the interviewee talking. One sign that an interview is going well is that there is an eagerness to participate by the person being interviewed. This eagerness is often expressed through tone and through close latching of utterances, such that one person's turn is followed up quickly by the other, thereby indicating excitement and engagement. The following segment demonstrates a social worker's close latching of acknowledgment tokens and of thought completions.

M: = and had had problems so I didn't know if anybody had said [anything
SW: [Mm.hmm]
M: [to] her about it. Uh:mm... As for M, sh:e... was very bad when it comes to that.=
SW: =Mm..hmm=
M: =I constantly...there was a little book I got from (Organisation), u:h=
SW: On your rights?=
M: stating my rights=
SW: =right=
M: and everything else and it says "right to privacy" and it shows a door with a kid in front of saying "Do not enter, I have my right to privacy"=
SW: =Mm . . . hmm

When M indicates that she received "a little book" but hesitates, "u:h=" the social worker fills in, by proffering a sentence completion, offered as a question, "On your rights?", to which M responds, agreeing, "stating my rights". The social worker's next turn "right" both signals a satisfaction that her completion was correct, and a readiness for M to proceed, having established the identity of the "little book". M then develops a story about her reading of the text.

Interruption and overlap

Although interruptions are often the source of trouble, as they threaten to irritate the person who is interrupted, in interviews interruptions also function to maintain the preferred focus of the interviewer.

S: i/bi/ it was harder for me to adapt because it was safe, I mean, you know what I mean? I was used to the house being kinda loud, and you know, being really quiet, there I could express myself. I got really angry a lot and ah, and always just/ I could tell it was different, I wa/ it was really confusing. Oh, I mean I can tell// [you]

W: [Were] you frightened, anxious//

S: I was frightened, I was frightened because ah it was a new, it was a different environment for me.

W: Yah

In this segment S talks about his experiences moving from home where, "I was used to the house being kinda loud", and about his troubles adjusting to life in a group home. S indicates that "I got really angry a lot", "I could tell it was different", and "it was really confusing", to then expand the narrative, by providing an example, "Oh, I mean I can tell//" when W the social worker interrupts him, to provide a further interpretation to the difficulties S faces, "[were] you frightened, anxious//". The tactic works as S then takes up the first of the two offers, "I was frightened, I was frightened", signals that as he speaks he is working to apply the concept to describe his experience in care. In this sense S makes the social worker's insight work for him, by playing with it, and applying it to explore its relevance as a descriptor of his experience.

Another fascinating feature of talk-in-interaction is the issue of overlapping speech. In the following example, B is passionately engaged in narrating troubles in the group home.

B: turn on the lights, an turn on my music an stuff, an then she'll li', she'll come in an start bitchin at me, "Turn off yer lights, go te bed right now, or I'll turn off yer power↑" (increased volume and higher tone) I'd jist ma:ad at her, I's like, "Who the hell do you think you are, walkin in my room like that."

G: yah=

B: =an she's like, "Well yer drunk." I's like, "Well can I get my fuckin pajamees on." She's like, "Well." So they'd jist kinda barge in.

G: so they're not [respectin yer privacy]

B: [an they lock you] out like, if you AWOL for a really long time, er drink lots=

G: =yah yah=

B: =they'll, they lock you out fer like seven days

G: now, what're you supposed to do?

As B enumerates grievances against the group home parent, G, the interviewer, follows up what he takes to be B's turn completion, "So they'd jist kinda barge in" by attempting to offer an interpretation, "so they're not [respectin yer privacy]". However, before G can complete his utterance, B begins, with an overlapping turn, "[an they lock you]", thereby taking back the floor and providing yet another example of complaint. G does not try to regain his turn, but rather offers encouragers, "yah yah=", which allow B to continue, "they'll, they lock you out fer like seven days".

The next segment provides a further example of overlapping talk, however here it is the interviewee, A, who produces the overlap in her willingness to help the social worker, F, establish dates.

A: cause my mom got us back.
F: oh, I see, I see. After five years, [yer mom got chu]
A: [nineteen ninety-five] yep
F: yah. An it looked like she had straightened out.

The social workers, "oh, I see, I see" functions both to indicate that a confusion has been addressed, and that clarification has come from A, the youth. In this sense F signals that A has helped him to understand, and in so doing elevates A's status within the interview. Indeed, it would seem that F's positioning of A as expert seems to have worked, because A expresses her confidence and leadership by initiating her turn overlapping F's talk.

Similarly in the next segment Y, the social worker, is overlapped twice by S, who provides information about his experiences moving in care.

S: I think, ha, hum, I'm not sure at that age. I think I went right to my uncles=
Y: =okay, [an
S: rel]atives.
Y: okay [s]
S: and then
Y: so then] at your uncles was that close to you in your neighborhood, or was that abou//
S: We lived in the country, near ah, just out, W (town),=
Y: =mmhuh

S's responsibility, ownership, and priority to produce the narrative is signalled both through the overlaps and through the interruption. In this sense, the interviewer has clearly managed to engage S in the process of producing his story, as evident by his commitment to get it out and to shape the relevant details.

Repairs and interviews

As we talk to each other we stumble, stutter, start using one word then interrupt ourselves mid word, and begin again with another word. Sometimes we might use one word in our turn, hesitate, and then the listener completes a word, or provides the right word. At other times, after our turn, and as we listen to the listener's response, we realise that what we had said has been misinterpreted, and we may interrupt the other, or wait to provide a correction, "n. no that's not what I mean". Ten Have notes that "any utterance can be turned into a repairable" (2007:133). Schegloff defines repair as referring to "practices for dealing with problems or troubles in speaking, hearing, and understanding the talk in conversation" (2000:207).

As we talk to each other we continually effect repairs to our talk. Hutchby and Wooffitt outline that, beginning from the turn in which trouble originated, there are four types of repair: 1) Self-initiated self-repair; 2) Other initiated self-repair; 3) Self-initiated other repair; and, 4) Other initiated other-repair (1998:61). I will not provide examples of each of these but will instead address only the first two types below.

In the next sequence we see, an instance of self-initiated self-repair in the first position:

Y: okay . . Uhm, so yu/your reaction you just said was that yu/you were expressing anger a lot?
S: Well, yah, like, I used to ha/ when I was that young I used to have really a lot of anger problems. Like emotionally jist, I jist, I was jist out of, really hard to get into, like hard to reach me.
Y: mmmhuh

This example is fairly typical, as S in his turn is struggling to articulate Y's question in his own words and as connected to his life experiences. S begins by expressing agreement with Y's question about anger, "Well, yah, like, I used to ha/", but then self-initiates a repair to his sentence, self-interrupting, to begin another sentence that provides contextual information, "when I was that young I used to have really a lot of anger problems". This sentence is followed by another, marked by a series of self-initiated self-repairs, "Like emotionally jist, I jist, I was jist out of, really hard to get into, like hard to reach me." Y's attempts to begin the sentence with "Like emotionally jist" effects a next repair by clarifying that the utterance is about himself, "I jist", and then effects a third repair, " I was jist" to provide temporal context. This then allows him to address the matter of being "really hard to get into", which he recognises may not be very clear, by providing a final repair, "like hard to reach me".

The matter of self-initiated self-repair brings to the fore the ways that speakers as they tell their stories are oriented continually to the listener, and the ways that through this orientation, they internalise criteria to continually monitor and evaluate the shape and form of their utterances, effecting repairs to ensure coherence and clarity. In the self-initiated self-repairs Y effected we can see that he was concerned to provide a temporal context for "expressing anger" as a matter in the past.

The next segment demonstrates self-initiated self-repair first occurring in what Schlegoff has described as a third position repair (1992) followed by a fourth position self-repair. This is a repair effected following the response of the listener to a speaker's utterance, that indicates that a misunderstanding has occurred requiring that the original speaker effect a repair.

S: and it'll be eliminated. A:ah, after the research is over all the recordings will be erased, and ah, but the key thing really is to protect your confidentiality. I'll bring in the consent=
J: =okay=
S: =next week=
J: =yah, had the//
S: it may not be tomorrow=
J: =mmhuh=
S: =because all us at work have a meeting, so we are going out for a lunch, and it depends how//
J: so you may not be here next Wednesday, you said?
S: No to[morrow]
J: [or tomo]rrow, oh tomorrow=
S: =yah
J: oh that's right, this is tomorrow//
S: =yah so we're going out to a restaurant, and it depends ah=
J: =yah, okay

Trouble develops because S, the interviewer, promises to bring in the consent for J to sign next week indicating that "it may not be tomorrow", which relies on S's understanding that J might expect to see S at a regularly scheduled weekly meeting they both attend next week. S says, "we are going out for a lunch", to which J replies, "so you may not be here next Wednesday, you said?" S recognises that she has been misunderstood, and effects a repair in line 12, "no to[tomorrow]"[6] which overlaps with J's expression of understanding in what Schegloff calls a "fourth position repair", and self-correction, "[or tomo] rrow, oh tomorrow". Schegloff explains that,

> fourth position repairs allow retrieval of the next turn position by the recipient of the trouble-source turn by having the recipient reintroduce the trouble source as revised and understood differently, which, when confirmed, provides a new next turn position after it, in which a new – and different – next turn can be done.
>
> (1992:1325)

S effects a further repair, outlining, "yah so we're going out to a restaurant ..." to ensure that J understands that he will not be available to meet tomorrow.

The next example is a simple but clear instance of other-initiated self-repair. Y's opening question is responded to by S with "pardon?" Y begins to repeat the question, but meanwhile S was able to process it's sense and interrupts Y with his response, "[yah, a sister]".

Y: D-do you have brothers and sisters?
S: pardon?
Y: Do you ha:[ave brothers an]
S: [yah, a sister]
Y: Hm, yah, okay. Where's she?
S: With my mom.

"Pardon", signals an indication of trouble that leads Y to effect a correction in his turn. Whether the trouble resulted because S did not hear Y, or because S was not paying attention, before Y was able to effect a complete repair, S has responded in overlapping talk. Y, on hearing S's response, signalled S has understood his opening question, "Hm, yah, okay. Where's she?"

The next example also provides a nice look into the use of other-initiated self-repair as tool for elucidating not only more information, but for shaping the direction of topics and flow of information. In this exchange G is commenting on the fact that J "had a week's notice" before moving from a group home.

J: so I had to pack up all my stuff, an::d, it took me about a week,
G: so you had a week's notice
J: no we had te wait until somebody finally took us
G: yah, when you say us, who's us
J: D, my sister
G: oh, you and D, maybe we should go back, uhm, you were with your aunt
J: mmhuh, with D and with her

Though J's response, "no we had te wait until somebody finally took us" is a repair, it is worth recognising that his repair of G's "so you had a week's notice" creates a further source of ambiguity. G is uncertain who the "us" refers to, and asks "who's us", to which J responds "D, my sister". This then underscores for G, that he has failed to understand the composition of J's family, so that he proposes, "maybe we should go back".

I want to look at one last segment, which elegantly displays the manifold nature of repairs, self-initiated, and other initiated.

J: Do you think it's harder when long term homes are gettin, when long term homes break down.
M: I don't think it is, I mean I went through two of them. Oh long term homes, or the long t-hermhe ((laugh)) foster homes//
J: Yah well foster homes, that's what I'm talking about, long term foster homes. You don't think that that's hard, you think that you should//
M: Well I mean the last one, it kinda, it bothered me but I, I thought it was the right thing then, because I mean wasn't a crown ward, I'm like, I can't in a family, eh, unless I'm surely not going home, but right then it wasn't a, a not bad thing.

J: So, so do you think in your case it would have been better if we had made you a crown ward sooner?

M: No.

We see that the interviewer, J, begins by asking M, "Do you think it's harder when long term homes are gettin'", but then self-initiates a self-repair, offering, "when long term homes break down." Obviously there is a difference of attention provided by the initial formulation and the second. Just as obviously the direction of M's response, that which he talks about, and how he talks about it, is itself shaped by J's question. M begins by responding "I don't think it is, I mean I went through two of them." Then catches himself, as possibly having misunderstood the question, and offers, in a louder voice, "Oh long term homes, or long t-herm foster homes//", to thereby identify an ambiguity between homes that he might have lived in for a 'long term', and homes that are organisationally classified as 'long term homes'. His correction leads J to self-correct, "Yah well foster homes, that's what I'm talking about, long term foster homes". Clearly, attention to repair in this sequence underscores the ways in which both M and J struggle to produce a shared sense of talk that works for the purposes at hand.

We might ask why do repairs matter? They matter because they demonstrate the ways in which participants to talk-in-interaction progressively shape their utterances to accord with the reactions of listeners. Repairs point to the foundational sociability of talk, hence to our willingness to craft our talking performances to take into account the reactions and understandings of others. Repairs underscore that talk, and accordingly stories are always and everywhere interactional events.

Schegloff observes, "when a source of misunderstanding escapes the multiple repair space, a whole institutional superstructure that is sustained through talk-in-interaction can be compromised" (1992:1337). Indeed, social workers can ill afford sustained misunderstandings as the core of helping interviews is demonstrably reaching out to the other, to develop an understanding of the person being interviewed. Without continual reliance on repairs talk would not only be narcissistic and a-social but incomprehensible. The stories that are produced in interviews demonstrate in the very structures of their production the orientation of storytellers and listeners to each other, and to the production of this story-telling occasion as a particular sort of interaction.

Response tokens

Everyday talk is marked by single word turns and sound smatterings uttered by participants who listen, e.g. mm, mmhum, hm, uh huh, yah, yeah, nn, ahh, and so on. In CA these have been called response tokens. The production of response tokens is not accidental, but rather are deployed to do particular types of work. Participants to talk use response tokens for a wide range of purposes. Gardner, in a detailed text that looks exclusively at response tokens, summarises they are used: to function as continuers; to signify either agreement or understanding; to provide news-markers that express surprise – e.g., really, oh; to act as "idea connectors"; to signify "change-of activity" before moving to new topics – e.g., okay, alright; to give assessments of agreement or disagreement; to question – huh-; to collaboratively complete an utterance; and, to provide "non-verbal vocalizations and kinesic actions (e.g. sighs, laughter, nods and head shakes)" (Gardner, 2001:2–3). He points out that the primary function of response tokens is "not to make reference to the world, but to provide some information on the course the talk is taking" (2001:14).

The following short segments provide some simple examples of response tokens and the ways that they are used in interviews. In the first segment T begins an extended narrative about troubles in the group home:

T: [some of the staff] didn't care, (-) like that night that C[7] (_)broke that(-) gave me I lost it, I picked up the dresser and threw it through the wall I just flipped right out and, and instead of like, he never even apologised me for it you know what I mean, like I remember that too, he never even said I'm sorry, he just, I got into major major crap for flipping out but I mean (-)but I mean he was the one freaking in the first place over thing, over someun . . . . . really stupid, and he broke my, it was a glass bowl at the time=

SW: =um huh

T: like one of those snow ball things=

SW: =um huh

T: Snowball, snowball things whatever, that broke=

SW: =um huh

T: and it was like not even three days after my grandma died=

SW: =um huh

T: but then there was other stuff like S[8](_), he was really nice like he was real, he was a great guy=

SW: =um huh

The social worker repeatedly responds to T's extended narrative with a series of latched "um huh". Close examination of SW's "um huh" indicates that it designed to do two types of work. First, the use of a latched "um huh", is situated and understood as functioning inside the context of T's extended turn. T's turn is extremely complex as it touches on multiple matters – staff that didn't care, objects were being broken, C, another youth in care who flipped out, C's failure to apologise, C freaking out, and C breaking her glass. Although the function of "um huh" is ambiguous, it signifies a weak agreement, most likely that SW follows and understands what T is saying. In addition to signalling that SW understands, it functions to signal that T can continue to talk, and to invite her to provide more detail to her story. Indeed the repeated use of "um hum" seem less ambiguous as they operate as encouragers, prompting T to continue producing her story.

In the next example D, another a youth in care, talks about troubles with her mother. This segment begins about three-quarters through her extended turn.

D: ... And then I jist lef..I was going upstairs, and she was coming up behind me and uhm, like a friend of mine was sitting on the bed. And she had me cornered against the wall, and she had her face right here::hheh ye you know, this personal space.
SW: yah=
D: =I didn't have it, hehehheheheh..
SW: no personal space

Though the transcript does not indicate it, D's claim, "and she had her face right here:hheh" most likely relies for its effect on some bodily movement to signify violation of personal space – e.g. rapidly raising her hand to within an inch of her nose – leading to a laugh. SW's response token "yah" provides a strong agreement, most likely acknowledging the impact of a violation of personal space. D uses SW's agreement, to quip, "I didn't have it" and then breaks into laughter at her own joke. SW then assumes the role of the straight man, to observe, "no personal space".

The use of response tokens such as "um huh" and "mmhuh" bring to light in practical terms the dimension of interaction Garfinkel addressed as "ad hocing", or "letting it pass" (1967). Through the use of such tokens social workers signify that the story as it is unfolding in time, in this moment holds together, and makes sense. Unlike this moment, when we can work from a transcript, talk as it unfolds, and because it is unfolding, does not communicate a transparency, other than as searched for through the form of talk that precedes it. Working off talk-in-interaction is not the same as working off a transcript. Schegloff points out,

> some first sentence (or set of sentences) can have a diversity of potential relevancies, and a hearer (in real time) does not have what follows as a way of selecting among them; he or she must produce what will turn out to have followed, based on an analysis of the initial item(s) without the "later text".

(1990:54)

Response tokens must be recognised as essential elements between speakers and listeners which signal that that being produced is being received, that it makes sense, at least provisionally, and that the speaker should continue.

Silence and turn transitions

While it is readily recognised that each of us have personal styles of talking, marked by pace, tempo, prosody, and lexical choice, to express our emotions, we also rely on silence or gaps in talk to communicate emotional content.

Social workers have long recognised gaps between turns, or silences, as an essential element in work with clients (Shulman, 2016). Shulman was one of the first social workers (1979) to look beyond the troubles posed by silence, to recognise the tremendous power of reflecting on silence, bringing silences to attention, and in so doing "reaching inside of silence" (1979:35) to give clients the opportunity to speak about lived hurts and emotional pain.

The pace at which we speak changes from slow and deliberate to rapid and spontaneous. The spacing or gaps between turns – our use of silence – can be measured in micro-seconds or spans of fifteen or twenty seconds. A speaker can signal that it is the next speaker's turn in a clear and direct manner, "Jim, what do you think?", or obliquely and indirectly, "aa:ah". Similarly, the next speaker can begin their turn with a clear enunciation of a thought, "Yes I like the play", or it may be initiated hesitatingly through extended sounds that convey uncertainty – "u:uh", "ya:aah↑", "au:ah", "mm" – about both the nature of the response and the speakers' willingness to take the turn. Turns may occur in close proximity, as participants add onto and complete the sentences of the other; or, they may even be marked by each other's eager interruptions. Although the issues of space, pace, and silence may have differential effects on participants to a conversation, as Tannen points out, silence "is always a joint production" (1985:100). She observes, "when there are two or more participants in a conversation … anything that happens or doesn't happen, is said or unsaid is the result of interaction among the two" (100).

Silence does not simply exist or emerge separate from talk. Rather as, Sobkowiak argues, communicative silence "is deliberately produced for communicative purposes" (1997:44). Sobkowiak argues that silence is "volitional, teleological, substitutive and contextual"[9] (44), which leads to exploration of the particular types of work participants do through their use of silence. It is generally recognised that silence has at two major functions. First, through silence people produce an emotional tempo, rhythm, and mood. As in music, silence in talk is used to communicate mood, feeling, and emotional content. Silence, much like a rest in music, is a tool that allows speakers to modulate the acoustic and prosodic structures of their talk (Sobkowiak, 1997; -Troike, 1985). Second, silence, is conjoined to the non-verbal architectonics of the body, that is gesture, proximity, and facial expression, to achieve quite pragmatic interactive objectives (Sobkowiak, 1997) such as to elicit and produce statements or propositions (Saville-Troike, 1985). For example, an interviewer might not take up his or her turn following an interviewee's use of a normal "transition relevance place" (Sacks, Schegloff, & Jefferson, 1974:708), that is a place in talk where the current speaker signals that they have completed their turn and that it is the other's turn, e.g., what? ; huh?; ya:h; u:uh. Such transition relevance places are usually effected through the creation of an awkward silence or palpable gap in talk that presses the interviewee to talk. Similarly, an interviewer may choose to withhold a repair to the other's talk (Button, 1992) by relying on a gap in talk, in order to allow the speaker to work through an issue, or to reveal content that otherwise might have been concealed if a repair was effected.

For social workers the use of gaps in talk, as silence, is an essential tool for the conduct of interviews. Silence can be used to elicit information, to allow a speaker to continue to speak in an unimpeded way, to give the social worker time to assess what a client has said, and to signal to the client that the social worker is thinking about what was said, and so on. By recognising the importance of gaps in talk, and silence social workers join with clients.

In the following J, the youth in care, talks about witnessing drunken fights between her mother her mother's boyfriend. G, the interviewer, follows up, offering support and a question for more information:

J: sometimes in the apartments, uhm, a guy she was with at that time, V and
    her, uhm, they use' get inta fights after they drink=
G: =yah °yah°, and the fights would become physical
J: not that bad, they're jist like push each other, and yell at each other
G: yah, that's not a very good, that's not very pleasant for you as a child to be
    around that eh . yah, yah, no I I can see that. Were you ever hurt . . .
    nobody ever hit chew er...
J: no I don't think anyone hit me, probably forced me to go in the bedroom or
    something
G: yah

This segment begins with J's claim that "they use' get inta fights after they drink". G then follows up by offering a potential clarification/proposition, "and the fights would become physical". Though it is not clear what G might count as "physical", to J it seems that G is suggesting more aggressive, harmful, and violent forms of action than those she meant to identify. J offers her version, by signalling disagreement with G, "not that bad, they're jist like push each other, and yell at each other". Though pushing each other clearly denotes some form of physical contact, J demonstrates that her understanding of "physical" indicated something different than, and perhaps more severe than pushing each other, e.g. slapping, kicking, punching, resulting in bruising, lacerations, or broken bones.

Although J may attempt to downgrade the seriousness of the fighting between her mom and V, G resolutely adheres to standard social work understandings about the trauma of witnessing violence, to counter, "yah, that's not a very good, that's not very pleasant for you as a child to be around that eh.", whereby he indicates an acceptance of J's correction, of what counts as "fighting", but continues to hold to the claim that harm was done. Further, by ending the re-frame as a question, with "eh", G invites J to enter into talk about the fighting which addresses the harm or pain it caused her.

In the one second silence, following G's re-frame, we can assume that there was some non-verbal cue, most likely a look of sadness, or an affirmative nod of a head, that allowed G to continue, "yah, yah, no I I can see that. Were you ever hurt . . . nobody ever hit chew er...". G picks up on J's non-verbal cue, to signal that he has recognised her agreement "yah, yah", captures the awkwardness of the moment, expressed through the stumble "I I", and moves to explore the effects of fighting on J. Again, we see that "were you ever hurt" is followed by a full three second silence in which, again, J must have sig-nalled some non-verbal response, indicating that she had not been physically hurt, for G tentatively continues, " nobody ever hit chew...". Though J seems to have indicated that she was not hurt when fighting occurred, G sticks with the issue, using a more concrete approach by transforming a claim that "nobody ever hit" J, into a question, and then allowing a full 2.5 seconds for a response.

From the preceding we see that silence is used in multiple ways. It provides a client with time to process provocative statements, to allow this processing to create an emotional response, to allow clients time to compose a response when emotionally overwhelmed, and even to create a degree of awkwardness which induces anxiety resulting in a repair of silence through a client's response. Though silences may be a source of trouble in interviews, they can also be a powerful tool for eliciting client stories, as they play off against a sense of social obligation as well as the deep emotional impact of raising difficult topics. Saville-Troike notes that "silence 'means' what it conveys" and that "the time-spaces occupied by silence constitute and active presence (not absence) in communication" (1985:10).

Lexical choice: Struggles over words

The next example provides an exquisite look into the ways that talk-in-inter-action provides an at hand forum for negotiating and struggling over the appropriate ways to describe events. In talk-in-interaction participants dis-agree, modify, and alter each other's accounts in a way that belies the putative objectivity of standardised survey responses. Although a survey may allow the person filling it in to determine which categories should or should not apply, in talk-in-interaction participants, to the extent that they are engaged, are able to make these choices for themselves.

J: D (_) and S (_), what was happening with them that you weren't getting along.
C: W::ell just basically we got inta a lotta fights
J: yah
C: that's basically it . .
J: Do you remember how you felt living with them.
C: aaaoouuuuuhhhh (yawn) Ihh didn't like feel happy sad mad, I actually felt all of them at the same time, but...I's happy there, but not that happy there...a::nd
J: So. Cus my dad[10] would just give me a few belts, not like, h'd like when I deserved it, not like when I didn't deserve it, like when I like uhm . smk (lip smack) I ran h'- away from home a lotta times back then

J: °uhhuh°

C: and when we went to (the village) there's a lotta houses that were abandoned and they still had a lotta supplies, and it was, they were, they were
open fer people hehh te stay, and that didn't have a house or anything, so
I ran away to there and one of the one's that didn't have people in it,
hmm, basically that's it, and then I'd go back home °heh

J: So, so S(_) had trouble controlling his anger when when you did thin[gs
that he didn't]

C: [No, H' He] didn't, he didn't have, he didn't have any trouble con=

J: °okay=

C: trolling his anger. He . he was just very worried about me eh, so..

J: °okay. And, . d' were you hooked up with B (the social worker) at this time.

C: No I was with . . . . actually I don't think I had a social worker in X
(town)

This sequence begins with the interviewer J trying to get C, a twelve year old
girl to outline the circumstances that led to the breakdown of her foster-home
placement. From previous sequences the interviewer knows that something
resulted in the foster-home breakdown. At this point the interviewer is trying to
elicit a coherent account from C of the events that led to this state of affairs.

C begins by claiming that, "Cus my dad would just give me a few
belts". She then provides an explanation that these belts were "deserved",
and moves in the same turn to give an example of why the belt would be
deserved, moving into a story about running away and staying in abandoned houses. C appreciates that her activities of running away warrants
punishment, even to the extent of being subjected to being hit with a belt.
J clearly understands the direction that C's narrative is taking, and
understands that C believes that being hit by a belt is "deserved". Yet, J
does not commit herself to accepting this account, as evidenced by the
weak, and barely audible acknowledgment token "°uhhuh°". Indeed, at
the next turn, J proceeds to subject the narrative to a 'proper' professional
reframing, "So, so S had trouble controlling his anger when when you did
thin[gs that he didn't]". It is worth recognising that C, a twelve year old
child, not only recognises the reframe, but repudiates it with the force of
an assertive and deep interruption, stopping J, and insisting on her version
of S's actions.

J: So, so S(_) had trouble controlling his anger when when you did thin[gs
that he didn't]"

C: [No, H' He] didn't, he didn't have, he didn't have any trouble con=

J: °okay=

C: trolling his anger. He . he was just very worried about me eh, so..

The interviewer, faced with such an obvious sign of trouble, moves even
before C has completed her turn to signal her acceptance of C's version. J

demurs to C's version through the latched and softly spoken "°okay". This a capitulation which is issued even before C has had an opportunity to provide reasons or justification for her understanding "He . he was just very worried about me".

The interviewer's assessment must be seen as originating in the stock-in-trade of professional understandings in child welfare about acceptable and unacceptable methods for child discipline. Simply, J, as a social worker does not accept that this child, or indeed any child, would ever deserve to be hit by belt by an adult. The interviewer relies on such background frameworks to arrive at an understanding of the reported interaction, in which the child is blameless. Further, quite contrary to the child's belief, the blame needs to be attributed to the adult who used the belt, that is to S. It follows then that the adult's behaviour is understood to be problematic, and the only remaining task is to provide some explanation for why an adult would engage in such abusive behaviour. In this instance J postulates that S had "trouble controlling his anger" (a formulation that resonates with the socially pervasive phrase, anger management problems). C hears J's interpretive framework, and immediately disagrees. She insists that S was motivated by "worry". Hence S's actions were impelled by positive and caring emotions, expressing commitment to C.

Fortunately, J happened to be a very experienced social worker, youth worker, and interviewer, and when faced with C's redemptive interpretation of S's actions, she demurs. She chooses to not voice disagreement, challenge, or continue to win the case for her analysis. Why? Clearly, the shape of the interaction is not about J saving face, or winning arguments, but about conducting an interview which nurtures C. Though it is not explicit, it is quite transparent that the child has a commitment to her foster father S. Further C needs to believe that S cares and is committed to her, and that S hitting her with the belt was motivated by S's care. The interviewer allows C to preserve and hold onto the positive view of her foster father, as this may be one of the few emotional bonds and commitments in C's life. While the issue of a "few belts" would certainly be an indicator of abuse requiring intervention, J recognises that the matter cannot be resolved at this time with C, and accordingly moves on to another topic.

This sequence provides a nice demonstration of disjunctions and lack of fit between professional and client understandings of events. Further we can see that when trouble arises from an interviewers' use of professional categories and schemata, that one strategy is to get off troubling topics. An interviewer can insist on the relevance of a particular category, though by doing so, they risk an escalation of a client's emotions and possible conflict, or we saw in this segment they can let the disagreement pass, and move onto less troublesome issues. Of course, in letting the disagreement pass, they will most likely register the client's understanding as a source of potential trouble, or as an area warranting future work, i.e. helping the client to see things differently (Buttny, 1996).

Conclusion

Attention to the structural matters of talk-in-interaction has been quite peripheral to the study of interviews in social work. It is worth noting that the latest edition of Kadushin and Kadushin' classic social work text, *The Social Work Interview*, recognises the contribution of ethnomethodologists who "have studied the minute details of commonplace events such as face-to-face conversation" (2013:6). Unfortunately, despite this insight the text remains silent on the potential contribution of conversation analysis to social work practice. Further, despite the acknowledgement of EM, Kadusin and Kadushin's analysis of interview skills proceeds as though the structures of talk-in-interaction do not matter. Talk-in-interaction as an in vivo process is displaced by generalist attention to the phases of interviewing, the use of questions in interviews, non-verbal communication, and recording. Sadly, their inattention to CA is symptomatic of social workers failure to examine the potential contribution of CA not only for analysis and understanding, but education in the art of social work interviewing.

While the foci of standard social work texts are essential elements in educating students to carry out good interviews, my objective in this chapter has been to open up for consideration the importance of such seemingly trivial matters as turn allocation, response tokens, gaps in turns, and lexical choice for the accomplishment of interviews. Social workers can only benefit by audio-recording interviews with clients, transcribing segments from these interviews, and examining the mundane structures of their talk for performing an interview. As a social work educator, I have encountered tremendous resistance by social work students when I have required that they submit audio-recordings of their interviews with clients. Unfortunately, many supervisors collude with student resistance by raising concerns about confidentiality, the imagined intrusiveness of the audio-recording, client discomfort with being audio-recorded, and so on. Against these imagined fears it has been my experience that youth were delighted to have their stories recorded. Further, those social workers who participated by recording interviews with youth felt that the exercise was very useful.

It is my resolute belief that social workers must listen to the interviews that they conduct with clients in order to improve their practice. The very process of transcribing what was said, in the detail provided for by conversation analysis, and then examining these transcripts has the effect of revealing some of the tremendously complex interactive dynamics whereby information exchanged between clients with social workers is shaped by virtue of social workers' professional powers. The process of transcribing and analyzing the structures of talk-in-interaction reveals whether or not a social worker is making good use of such important tools as response tokens, silences, open-ended questions, and so on. To the degree that social workers are better able to understand the art of their performances in and as an interview they can develop greater insight and awareness of interviewing practices that provide for mastery of the art of interaction with clients.

By tracking such mundane matters as response tokens or silence social workers can better understand the importance of emotional bonding with clients beyond words. Indeed, it is precisely through the use of such non-semantic physical utterances, which express tone, cadence, and emotionality that we create an interactional mood, and a solidarity with clients. To produce depth and emotional bonding in relationships we reach for forms of communication beyond words. Analysis of interviews must look beyond mere words to capture the brilliant humanity enacted in the plenitude of forms of interaction. This is a humanity expressed in the sounds, tones, prosodic structures, rhythms and even silences that speakers and listeners use together in sequential interaction to craft and shape an occasion as an interview.

Notes

1 Lexical choice directs attention to the language participants use and don't use in institutional interviews. Although lexical choice is notably evident as professional jargon in institutions, it is also important for organising speakers' talking and performing organisational relevance, e.g., taking up the language of an interview guide. Lexical choice also shapes preferred ways of speaking, such as refraining from swearing or the use of vulgar or derogatory terms. Turn design directs us to examine what participants respond to in their turn, e.g. selection of organisational relevances such a 'child abuse', 'violence', 'anger management', as well as the shaping of responses, e.g. length of turn, amount of detail provided, emotional tone of talk, etc. Sequence raises matters of turn by turn organisation of talk, e.g. reliance on question and answer structures. The overall structured organisation of an interview demands attention to the talks shape and stages, e.g. the orientation to a set time period, preset orders of topics, identification of beginning, middle, and ends. Finally, the concept of social epistemology requires examination of the disposition of the participants to such matters as professionalism and future accountability.

2 Collins observes that the dichotomy between unstructured and structured interviews is "misleading and ultimately unhelpful" as "even the apparently most 'unstructured' interviews are structured in a number of sometimes subtle ways" (1998:2). His position matches that developed in this book. The mechanics of producing an interview signal a series of structures into which both the social worker and the client enter. The interviews referenced throughout this book were produced as part of a research project, and as such are closest to what Kadushin and Kadushin (2013) identify as information gathering or social study interviews. These interviews are not like therapeutic interviews, in which the focus is on converting "clients' problem tellings and accounts into the therapist's version" (Buttny, 1996:126).

3 Excellent examples of detailed attention to the structures of talk-in-interaction have been produced by Schegloff (2007; 2000; 1992; 1990).

4 The perennial question of whether or not social workers are professional was addressed by Abraham Flexner, who in 1915, after setting out the criteria for defining a profession, announced, "Now that we have run through the marks of the professions and have found that on the whole at this stage, social work is hardly eligible" (2001:163). In the years that followed social workers fretted, worried, and responded by trying to articulate the professional and scientific foundations of their craft (Bartlett, 1969). The debate continues today as Lymbery insists that, at best, "… social work is not able to claim the same status as the established professions" (Lymbery, 2000:125).

5 This turn demonstrates a structure of repair very similar to that addressed in the section, Repairs and Interviews, below.

6 The form of this "third position repair" conforms to that identified by Schegloff, "most commonly it takes the form of 'no,' singly or in multiples ('no, no'; 'no, no, no'), or in combination with 'oh' ('oh no'), which also occasionally stands alone ('oh')" (1992:1305).

7 Another youth in care living in the group home.

8 A group home staff member.

9 It should be noted that silence may also be 'involuntary' in the sense that the speaker is too emotionally overwhelmed to be able to express him or herself in words. Silence may also be an effect of psychiatric disturbance. Recognition of 'involuntary' silence does not however negate the importance of examining the contextually based work performed through silence.

10 C's 'dad' is her foster father, later referenced as S.

References

Bartlett, Harriet. (1969). *The common base of social work practice*. Washington, DC: NASW.

Baudrillard, Jean. (1975). *The mirror of production* (Trans. Mark Poster). St. Louis, MO: Telos.

Braverman, Harry. (1975, 1998). *Labour and monopoly capital: The degradation of work in the twentieth century* (25th anniversary ed.). New York, NY: Monthly Review.

Buttny, Richard. (1996). Clients' and therapist's joint construction of the clients' problems. *Research on Language and Social Interaction*, 29(2): 125–153.

Button, Graham. (1992). Answers as interactional products: Two sequential practices used in job interviews. In Paul Drew & John Heritage (Eds.), *Talk at work: Interaction in institutional settings* (pp. 21–231). Cambridge, England: Cambridge University Press.

Collins, Peter. (1998). Negotiating selves: Reflections on "unstructured" interviewing. *Sociological Research Online*, 3(3): 1–20.

Dickens, Peter. (1996). *Reconstructing nature: Alienation, emancipation and the division of labour*. London, England: Routledge.

Drew, Paul, & Heritage, John. (1992). Analyzing talk at work: An introduction. In Paul Drew & John Heritage (Eds.), *Talk at work: Interaction in institutional settings* (pp. 3–65). Cambridge, England: Cambridge University Press.

Flexner, Abraham. (2001). Is social work a profession. *Research on Social Work Practice*, 11(2): 152–165.

Gardner, Rod. (2001). *When listeners talk: Response tokens and listener stance*. Philadelphia, PA: John Benjamins.

Garfinkel, Harold. (1967). *Studies in ethnomethodology*. Englewood Cliffs, NJ: Prentice-Hall.

Hutchby, Ian, & Wooffitt, Robin. (1998). *Conversation analysis*. Cambridge, England: Polity.

Hymes, Dell. (1996). *Ethnography, linguistics, narrative inequality: Toward an understanding of voice*. London, England: Taylor & Francis.

Kadushin, Alfred, & Kadushin, Goldie. (2013). *The social work interview: The guide for human service professionals* (5th ed.). New York, NY: Columbia University Press.

Lymbery, Mark. (2000). The retreat from professionalism: From social worker to care manager. In Nigel Malin (Ed.), *Professionalism, boundaries and the workplace* (pp. 123–138). London, England: Routledge.

Marx, Karl. (1973). *Grundrisse: Foundations of the critique of political economy* (Trans. Martin Nicolaus). New York, NY: Vintage.

Marx, Karl. (2010a). Capital Volume III. In *Karl Marx & Frederick Engels, Collected Works* (Volume 36). Electric Book. London, England: Lawrence & Wishart.

Marx, Karl. (2010b). Capital Volume II. In *Karl Marx & Frederick Engels, Collected Works* (Volume 36). Electric Book. London, England: Lawrence & Wishart.

Marx, Karl. (2010c). Capital Volume 1. In *Karl Marx & Frederick Engels, Collected Works* (Volume 35). Electric Book. London, England: Lawrence & Wishart.

Mazeland, Harrie, & ten Have, Paul. (1996). Essential tension in (semi-) open research interviews. In Ilja Maso & Fred Wester (Eds.), *The deliberate dialogue: Qualitative perspectives on the interview* (pp. 87–113). Brussels, Belgium: VUB University Press.

Mészáros, István. (1970). *Marx's theory of alienation*. London, England: Merlin.

O'Brien, Mary. (1981). *The politics of reproduction*. London, England: Routledge & Kegan Paul.

Ollman, Bertell. (1976). *Alienation: Marx's conception of man in capitalist society*. New York, NY: Cambridge University Press.

Pawson, Ray. (1996). Theorizing the interview. *British Journal of Sociology*, 47(2): 295–314.

Roy, Donald F. (1959–60). "Banana Time": Job satisfaction and informal interaction. *Human Organization*, 18: 158–168.

Rubin, Isaak Ilich. (1972). *Essays on Marx's theory of value* (Trans. Miloš Samardija & Fredy Perlman). Detroit, MI: Black and Red.

Sacks, Harvey, Schegloff, Emanuel, & Jefferson, Gail. (1974). A simplest systematics for the organization of turn-taking for conversation. *Language*, 50(4): 696–735.

Saville-Troike, Muriel. (1985). The place of silence in an integrated theory of communication. In Deborah Tannen & Muriel Saville-Troike (Eds.), *Perspectives on silence* (pp. 3–18). Norwood, NJ: Ablex.

Schegloff, Emanuel A. (1990). On the organization of sequences as a source of "coherence" in talk-in-interaction. In Bruce Dorval (Ed.), *Conversational organization and its development* (pp. 51–77). Norwood, NJ: Ablex.

Schegloff, Emanuel A. (1992). Repair after next turn: The last structurally provided defense of intersubjectivity in conversation. *American Journal of Sociology*, 97(5): 1295–1345.

Schegloff, Emanuel A. (2000). Overlapping talk and the organization of turn-taking for conversation. *Language in Society*, 29: 1–63.

Schegloff, Emanuel A. (2007). *Sequence organization in interaction: A primer in conversation analysis I*. New York, NY: Cambridge University Press.

Shulman, Lawrence. (1979). *The skills of helping: Individuals and groups*. Itasca, IL: F. E. Peacock.

Shulman, Lawrence. (2016). *The skills of helping individuals, families, groups, and communities* (8th ed.). Toronto, ON: Thompson Brooks Cole.

Sobkowiak, Wlodzimierz. (1997). Silence and markedness theory. In Adam Jaworski (Ed.). *Silence: interdisciplinary perspectives* (pp. 39–61). Berlin, Germany: Mouton de Gruyter.

Tannen, Deborah. (1985). Silence: Anything but. In Deborah Tannen & Muriel Saville-Troike (Eds.), *Perspectives on silence* (pp. 93–111). Norwood, NJ: Ablex.

ten Have, Paul. (2007). *Doing conversation analysis: A practical guide.* London, England: Sage.

Watts, Richard J. (1997). Silence and the acquisition of status in verbal interaction. In Adam Jaworski (Ed.), *Silence: Interdisciplinary perspectives* (pp. 87–115). New York, NY: Mouton de Gruyter.

Wendling, Amy E. (2009). *Karl Marx on technology and alienation.* Houndmills, England: Palgrave Macmillan.

3   Accounting for conversations

Relevance and procedural consequentiality

We begin by asking, both for participants and for those engaged in conversation analysis (CA), what resources are needed to produce and to account for occasions of talk-in-interaction? When people talk with each other just how do they assemble coherence and order? How do they both understand and produce the context of their interaction as such, as well as relevant sets of participant categories, e.g. male/female, mother/daughter, adult/child, manager/employee, etc.? How does the physical context or in situ location of the talk get taken into account in the performance of the talk, e.g. a queue at a grocery store, an interview in a child protection office, a conversation on a telephone? How do participants orient to context and to social categories to shape the forms and meaning of their activities? How do the participants to the talk orient themselves and interactively perform context and social categories as relevant organisers for their interactions?

Similarly, when we listen to audio-recordings of talk, and 'automatically' identify participants' identities as male and female, adult and child, social worker and client, what sense making resources do we draw on to assemble such identifications? When we identify an audio-recording as being an interview or a chat, again we ask, what are the resources we draw on to make such distinctions?

Of course, audio-recordings usually do not just 'arrive' unannounced. Instead, they are produced and assembled as part of a work process. Thus, I know that this interview was 'conducted' by a social worker, or a research assistant, or myself, with a youth. So, as I listen to the audio-recording, just how does knowledge and understanding of people's identities and the context of interaction shape and form my understanding of just what it is that is occurring as recorded? Is the interaction rendered as sensible through reference to context and social categories, or do we examine just how participants to the talk-in-interaction actually went about performing context and social categories as accountably consequential or relevant on that occasion? As conversation analysts, are we able to suspend or put out of play our own understandings of contexts and taken-for-granted identities, to shift our focus to consider how the context is 'talked into being' (Zimmerman & Boden, 1991:9)? Fortunately, CA does allow us to hear, process, and assemble audio cues, tone, pitch, speed of talk, question and answer sequences, and so on. Through CA we can begin to unfold the complex activities participants engage in to make taken-for-granted social categories relevant. So what are our requisite social resources for finding and recovering sense and meaning? Are our resources any different than those that participants to interaction draw on? When doing CA to what extent are the resources relied on by participants necessarily our own?

Conversation analysis, as with ethnomethodology (EM), requires a 'respecification'. Such respecification is fundamentally rooted in a phenomenological turn, that is in an *epoché* of the natural attitude (Husserl, 1990), or what EM recognises as a bracketing of the 'taken-for-granted'. For CA, as for EM, the social facts of an occasion – e.g. that this is an interview between a social worker and a youth – are bracketed or suspended, such that we turn to examine the ways that the participants actively constitute the occasion as such, for self and for each other. Both CA and EM require a reflexive turn toward examination of members' practices for constituting such characteristics as a sensible and present feature of their interaction. Garfinkel wrote:

> For ethnomethodology the objective reality of social facts, in that and just how it is every society's locally, endogenously produced, naturally organised, reflexively accountable, ongoing, practical achievement, being everywhere, always, only, exactly and entirely members' work, with no time out, and with no possibility of evasion, hiding out, passing, postponement, or buy-outs, is thereby sociology's fundamental phenomenon.
> (1988:103)

Unlike conventional social science where social identities are conceptualised as roles or are taxonomically ordered category sets with explanatory power, e.g. male/female, mother/child, student/teacher, client/therapist, etc., in conversation analysis and ethnomethodology we examine "how identity is done, managed, achieved, and negotiated in situ" (Housley & Fitzgerald, 2015:2). Through CA we approach recordings as artefacts of social action, wherein participants reflexively produce, turn-by-turn their own identities in situ and in an unfolding of a relationship, in whatever identifiable forms it might take, as practically accomplished.

When doing conversation analysis we are challenged to identify and work through the foundational knowledge or resources relied on by participants as well as those we share with those participants. Our work of recovering meaning from talk in interaction, as with the work of doing talk-in-interaction, relies on taken-for-granted resources for reflexively accomplishing and for accounting for occasions as such. How does our knowledge that this is an interview conducted at a Children's Aid Society, at the CAS office, with a child in care, shape our understanding and sense of this recorded talk? Can we suspend or put out of play such knowledge, to allow to be heard just how participants to an occasion actually went about producing the occasion as such, and thereby to recognise social occasions as artefacts grounded in people's embodied interactive work together? How do we hear and recognise a context of talk as an effect of talk?

To answer such questions we turn to Schegloff's identification of the two related issues of relevance and procedural consequentiality (1997; 1992). First, he identifies the relevance of categories, that is "how 'members' characterise, identify, describe, refer to, indeed 'conceive of' persons in talking to others" (1992:107). Schegloff proposed that, when doing conversation analysis, before relying on the good sense of social categories we instead demonstrate just how whatever categories we think might be deployed are actually rendered sensible and are derived from the talk-in-interaction of the participants to that talk. Thus, categories must be shown to be "demonstrably relevant to the participants, and at the moment – at the moment that whatever we are trying to provide an account of occurs" (1992:109). What can we hear in the forms of interaction, in the materials, that reveal that participants orient themselves to this or that social category? How do taken-for-granted social categories come to be 'relevant' for "conduct in the interaction" (1992:109)?

When we do conversation analysis, the ethnomethodological strictures that problematise 'formal analysis' and the taxonomic imposition of categorical orders (Garfinkel, 2002) continue to apply. Hence, caution is needed before relying on the taken-for-granted and common stock-in-trade of social categories, e.g. "man/woman, protestant/catholic/jew, doctor/patient, white/black/chicano, first baseman/second baseman/shortstop and the like" (Schegloff, 1992:107). Schegloff begins with Sack's discussion of Pn-adequate devices[1] and the idea that people rely on using 'collections' to "categorize any member of a population whether or not it has been specified" (Schegloff, 1992:107). While there are any number of collections that can reasonably be applied to describe actors, not all are applied or might be deemed by participants to be relevant, and accordingly we need some means for determining just which sets of categories members to talk-in-interaction relied on when engaging each other.

As we return to social work we see that we routinely account for clients through recourse to standard category sets. For example, when doing child protection we work with mothers and children, fathers and mothers, grandparents and grandchildren, family and friends, men and women, and so on. Our recourse to such category-sets to describe peoples' actions and interactions is common-sense and as such largely taken-for-granted. Yet the questions remain, just how do we determine, when do we determine, and for what purposes do we determine which sets of categories are relevant to this moment of interaction, and which are not? Schegloff addresses social categories by observing:

> We may share a lively sense that indeed they do matter (social categories), and that they mattered on that occasion, and mattered for just that aspect

of some interaction on which we are focussing. There is still the problem of showing from the details of the talk or other conduct in the materials that we are analyzing that those aspects of the scene are what the parties are oriented to. For that is to show how the parties are embodying for one another the relevancies of the interaction and are thereby producing the social structure.

(1992:110)

Of course, social categories do matter, not only for sociologists, social workers, and those who do conversation analysis, but for all of us, all of the time. Yet, what is novel in conversation analysis and ethnomethodology, is an invitation to approach talk-in-interaction reflexively, that is as interactive practice through which people quite practically, and turn by turn, go about bringing into being the situated and local orders of an every-day world. What Schegloff develops is a way of approaching talk as an activity whereby people come together to produce as the reflexive effect of their work social structures themselves. In this way social structure ceases to be treated as alien or distant, but as that which is brought into existence as the effect of people in interaction as their living accomplishment. This occurs moment by moment, and as Garfinkel observed, "there is no time out" (Garfinkel, 2002:118).

Building on his discussion of relevance Schegloff moves to examine 'the context' of talk-in-interaction. As we saw with the problem of relevance and categories, so too with context, whether an office, an interview, a social service agency, a hospital, or a court, rather than presume its effects, we need to pay assiduous attention to the reflexivity of talk-in-interaction as a means by which participant's themselves produce context. Schegloff directs us to try to recover from the talk just how participants make the context procedurally consequential. Conversation analysis demands demonstrating just how participants to an occasion actually go about making for each other, as a relied-on matter, a socially recognisable context as consequential for their talk.

Just as the problem of relevance addresses the problem of determining the relevant categories participants are oriented to and performing in this or that moment of interaction, the problem of procedural consequentiality directs attention to determining the ways that participants perform and enact 'context' in interaction (Schegloff, 1992:111). Schegloff insists that:

Even if we can show by analysis of the details of the interaction that some characterization of the context or the setting in which the talk is going on (such as "in the hospital") is relevant for the parties, that they are oriented to the setting so characterized, there remains another problem, and that is to show how the context or the setting (the local social structure), in that aspect, is procedurally consequential to the talk. How does the fact that the talk is being conducted in some setting (e.g. "Hospital") issue in any consequence for the shape, form trajectory, content, or character of the interaction that the parties conduct? And what is the mechanism by which the context-so-understood has determinate consequences for the talk.

(1992:111)

Schegloff does not want to abandon the connection to context, but as with his treatment of relevance, he insists on analysis which in close attention to talk-in-interaction explicates or unfolds the relationship between the forms of talk, its ordering and accomplishment, as achieving and producing as a relevant matter for participants a 'context', e.g. a doctor's office, a court of law, a drop-in clinic, etc. He uses research by Atkinson and Drew (1979) to explore speech exchange systems in a court of law. He notes that only those in front of the 'bar' speak, and that they do so in quite distinct ways, and that an audience behind the bar does not speak. The distribution of turns of talk among participants – judge, lawyers, witnesses, accused, and audience – in its distinctive character can be seen as participants organise their talk to achieve or perform a court room.

Schegloff argues that it necessary to discover the ways that the categories that sociologists, and I would add social workers, believe are relevant, are actually accomplished as relevant through the talk-in-interaction of participants. Second, he demands that we discover the ways that the seemingly inescapable effects of context are actually made to matter, or are brought into being as a resource that is "demonstrably consequential for some specifiable aspect of that interaction" (1992:128). For example, it is not sufficient simply to assume that the power of a social worker was that which organised a segment of talk. Instead, the claim that a social worker exercised her power would need to be demonstrated as a necessary feature of the structure, sequencing of turns, or the content, as at-hand and demonstrable matters. Similarly, any claim that an interview is a different type of talk-in-interaction from a street corner chat or a conversation between friends, must be demonstrated through close analysis to the structures of talk-in-interaction itself (1992).

While I have considerable sympathy with the imperative to discover both the relevant categories of identification of actors, and the accomplishment of context from the form of the talk itself, it is clear that what counts as admissible materials constitutive of any occasioned corpus extend before and beyond a particular moment of practice. For instance, when examining talk in a court Schegloff does not address the ways that "courtroom-ness" (1992:112), observed in participants' practices, is also organised by a series of prior practices and institutionalised injunctions, textually mediated rules, and methods of enforcement. Certainly, for those inside this courtroom at this time such constraining forms of practice are not fully visible, although they can be inferred through observation of the spatial organisation of the courtroom – i.e. rails dividing an audience from court participants, a raised dais for the judge, a stand for witnesses, etc. – symbolic decorations – i.e. coat of arms, flags on staffs, photograph of the Queen, etc. –, the activities of participants, the presence of people in uniform, and so on. For instance, consider the work of the court stenographer, who records the talk inside the court, which will in turn become a matter of record, to be housed in a court registry, as a production of the court.

Warrantable practices and interactions for accomplishing "courtroom-ness" are revealed precisely on those occasions when proper performance is breached or brought into jeopardy, e.g. if a participant shouts obscenity towards the judge, talks out of turn, is deemed to have arrived in court inappropriately dressed, or acts in a manner which is deemed to violate the decorum of the court. However, it should also be noted that such in situ breaches also reveal that seemingly local and here and now productions of "courtroom-ness" are achieved not solely on the basis of this particular group of people's actions, on this occasion. Rather, participants interact to accomplish as a warranted matter, reference to regulations, codes, legal frameworks, and so on. Any particular occasion as a court articulates member's ability to bring into being the relevances of an extended institutional and ruling apparatus (Smith, 1990a). Indeed, the actions of a judge, in a Canadian court, facing an offender charged under the Criminal Code, derives authority from a reading and knowledge of powers granted to judges and to the court under various documents, e.g. the Criminal Code (R.S. 1985) that gives him or her, "authority to preserve order in a court" (Sect. 485). The judge's work to preserve order in the court in turn relies on the work of sheriffs and police officers who are expected to assist the judge and as needed to physically restrain and remove anyone who is deemed to be disrupting the decorum of the court. Against the sorts of constriction of the admissible "occasioned corpus" recommended by Schegloff, a turn to Smith's notion of an institutional ethnography (2005) broadens our sense of an occasion. Thus, whatever any specific occasion is deemed to be is recognised as accomplished as such by members who by virtue of practice – that is the iterative replication of forms of action and interaction – go about engaging in the congregational production of an occasion as such. Peoples' in vivo and interactive self-organisation realise this moment as articulating institutional courses of action, expectations, knowledge, skills, and ethical orientations and obligations. They simultaneously accomplish this specific occasion such that it is warrantably and accountably a proper performance of a general form, whether the court, an interview, a child protection assessment, a team meeting, and so on.

Questioning relevance and procedural consequentiality

As set out above, while Schegloff's directions are important for conversation analysis, as social workers we have a lively and acute sense that what participants to talk intend and mean is not always what they say, nor that which they reveal in words and in talk. Thus, it is vital that we identify the limitations of an empirical, or empiricist, focus on "details of the talk or other conduct in the materials" (Schegloff, 1992:110). Beyond what any audio-recording might indicate as the "details of the talk", social workers need to have an acute sensitivity to that which is not said, elided, implicit, hinted-at, or even avoided and not talked about. Further from Gestalt therapy, we learn the importance of attending to another not just as talking, nor to ourselves as simply talking, but to the embodied and gestural dimensions of interaction, in which processes of mutual transformation occur in and through the interaction. Clemmons notes,

> The Gestalt therapist, by focusing on the immediate embodiment in the client and his/her own, allows a deeper dialogic resonance to become possible. Nowhere is this more salient than in the pas de deux of psychotherapy where minute movements, gestures, tone, and glances communicate and co-create meanings, the sense of wholeness and relatedness for the client.
>
> (2012:40)

Indeed, just how it is that any of us, when engaged in talking with another, orient ourselves to another person is incorrigibly embodied. As embodied we bring ourselves in the plenitude of physical being to interaction, performing ourselves for another through facial gestures, movement of arms, legs, back position, and so on. Even when sitting, the physical dance of engagement and response mark interactions with a signature that transcends mere words. This is not a novel insight, as it has resonance with Goffman's, albeit dramaturgical, attention to presentation of self and 'impression management' (1959). Goffman's attention to interactive performance and actors 'parts' in a performance presented to an audience directs us to consider not just talk-in-interaction in this moment, but the ways that participants to that talk orient themselves to background expectations, understandings, and rituals.

There are substantial slips between what might be recorded, and what two participants engaged in talk-in-interaction are doing. The potential for slippage becomes more pronounced when we consider what any single participant to an occasion might imagine him/herself doing, is likely different from the intentions and imaginings of another. We know that just how we act with others emerges out of complex tensions between desire, habit, emotion, role, responsibility, situation, context, and so forth. Prosaically we recognise the importance of masks, deception, lying, pretending, dissembling, avoiding, mimicking, and so on, as perhaps unwelcome but necessary elements of interaction with others. Finally, we also recognise that along with that which is said comes that which is best not said, that which is thought but not said, and that which is on the tip of the tongue, yet never gets said. Given such considerations, it must be conceded that whatever it is that is captured on an audio-recording represents a residue of talk-in-interaction and interaction itself. It is at best a thin glimpse into the actual moment of embodied and engaged talk-in-interaction in situ between two participants.

First, it cannot and likely should not be presumed that both parties to an interaction are oriented to either shared social categories or even shared context. We all recognise those situations where one person intends one form of interaction, while the other intends something quite different. Our recognition that some encounters are deceptive, phony, fake, manipulative, and so on points to the possibilities of slippage between the projects and intentions of participants. Although the disjunction between the participants might not be identified during the interaction as such, through memory and reflection certain words, tones, looks, gestures, grimaces, and so forth routinely come to be interpreted post-facto. Indeed, the very practices of naming, or demonstrating that we are oriented to particular categories is routinely avoided, particularly as naming the interaction often articulates a complex dance or play, e.g. making friends, courtships, supervisory relations, management, and so on.

Consider the following instance. I have just attended a keynote lecture at my university, and afterwards there is a reception. After getting my plate of hors d'oeuvres I migrate to one of the stand-up tables in the reception area. There I join another person. 'He' is someone I have seen on campus, and though we haven't spoken before, I assume that he is a professor in another department. Imagine I begin with a standard opener, "What did you think of the lecture?" As I pose the question, and he responds, our interactions are shaped according to complex background understandings about how to interact with colleagues. Now, if in addition to gender I read[2] my colleague as a 'black'[3] man, how might this shape our interaction?

Before proceeding let us step back. How did I recognise gender, race, class, and age? What resources or understandings did I draw on to read this man's body, colour, and dress to assemble this assumption that he is likely a university colleague? How did the context of our interaction, a reception following a lecture, inform the reasonableness of my identifications? Reciprocally I assume that he will look at me, and at the colour of my skin, and likely identify me as a 'white man'. As we begin to talk, I will monitor his reactions to me, as I anticipate that he will monitor my reactions to him. I will read him, as I expect that he will read me, though it is likely that we will not give voice or explicitly address the layering of our reading. It is likely that 'race' will be a seen but unsaid element shaping our talk. Whether or not racial categories get addressed or are made remarkable, given the sociological contours of our lives in the contemporary world they will quite likely shape, albeit in implicit fashion, that which we say or do not say. Furthermore, while the forms of presence or conduct in the materials might be shaped by our mutual orientation to the performance of a context, the forms of absence are virtually infinite, bounded not only by concealed intentions and imagination, but by the complexities of the unconscious[4] (Parsons & Shils, 1962).

If our talk were being recorded, whether or not his race or my race would become explicitly addressed in our talk would depend very much on the context and the history and nature of our relationships with each other, as well as our disposition towards members of racialised categories. If this is our first conversation together we will draw on a complex background knowledge and

repertoires to manage and shape our responses in order to create civil, collegial, and hopefully respectful interaction. The categories informing our interaction in this moment are not bound to this interaction nor just as certainly
to any audio or video recording of our interaction. We have come together
inside of a social order, in which we have learned, albeit as differently positioned, to see our skin colour and our physical features as 'race'. When talking to another each of us deploys a repertoire of intentional strategies to
manage potential troubles of 'race' (and racism), e.g., stereotypes, invidious
and negative assumptions, hostile and negative words toward each other, and
so on.

It is also important to recognise the double binds at the heart of talk. First,
as we interact I see him, and he sees me. I see him seeing or watching me, and
reciprocally I know that he sees me seeing or watching him. I anticipate that
he will likely imagine that I am seeing him as a 'black' man, just as I imagine
that he will see me as a 'white' man watching a black man. However, what it
means for him as a black man to be seen and watched by a white man, is
likely quite different than what it means for me as a white man to be seen and
watched by a black man. Yet, as I watch him watching me, anticipating my
seeing him as 'black', I will likely experience anxiety, as I fear that I might say
or do something that will lead him to see me as 'racist'. I wonder just how he
imagines that I see his black skin and black body? What does my seeing
myself in interaction with him 'mean' for me? What does his seeing himself in
interaction with me 'mean' for him. Furthermore, how he imagines I might
see his 'blackness', will likely shape how he shapes himself in interaction with
me, and how he answers what he imagines my seeing and sense making of
him 'being black'. Now if I name my whiteness, I fear being seen by him as
adhering to an essentialist belief that there is a 'white race'. Yet, if I do not
name my whiteness I fear that he might see my as failing to recognise my
'privilege' as a 'white man'.

As we talk, quite apart from overtly speaking to the lecture, I will be trying
to assess his understandings of race categories, i.e. are they essentialist or
social constructivist? If I identify being 'white' as an essential marker of my
being, and if he takes a constructivist approach to race, ala Ta Nehisi Coates
(2015), [5] then my identification as such, will be perceived to be unenlightened,
and likely an expression of racism. On the other hand, if I fail to identify
myself as 'white', and he takes the view that this is a valid marker or identifier
of my form of being, then he will likely see me as 'other'. Further, it is more
than likely that I will not reveal this operative framework, though I might
probe, and we might dance around it, until such time as I have a better sense
of his orientation to these questions, just as I suspect that he will dance
around his own presumptions about just who I am.

In the preceding, I have aimed to unfold some of the present but unsaid
issues that can come to shape interaction which although relevant, will most
likely not be revealed through the conduct of the materials. The question
emerges as to whether or not we, or even an analyst who records our talk, can

recover from this talk or this conduct a cogent demonstration of the apparently paradoxical situation that he and I 'do' race by avoiding making race remarkable. Such situations are indeed "Knots" in precisely the sense described by Laing, "They are playing a game. They are playing at not playing a game", and as Laing further pointed out, they pose an intractable problem for the observer/analyst for, "If I show them I see they are, I shall break all the rules and they will punish me. I must play their game of not seeing I see the game" (1970:1).

Of course, the problem with knots, as anyone who has ever encountered one along a length of rope, is that their unravelling demands finding either the beginning or the end of the rope. Similarly, unravelling a social knot demands a way of working which moves the focus away from the bundled knot, to look down the social line so to speak, to find an appropriate beginning. Just as a knot in a rope cannot be untied without passing the start of a rope back through the knot, a social knot cannot be untied without injecting knowledge derived from a life course in a series of multiple social relations. Unravelling a social knot demands drawing on resources, in which the analysis rather than foreclosing access to categories and contexts, uses these in an eclectic movement to produce a cogent and sustainable account.

If my objective is to interact as though the other's race does not matter, and if his objective is to perform similarly, that is as if neither his or my race matter, and if together we manage to achieve this effect through a conversation about the lecture or even by getting off topic and talking about cross country skiing in the Gatineau Hills in winter, is it the case that 'race' does not matter on this occasion? Must the consequentiality of race be omnipresent? Must it be presumed to be a texture of relevance? Alternatively, might its relevance be inferred should certain events occur, e.g. what did the trail attendant say to my colleague? Is it that race was not remarkable because neither he nor I dared make it remarkable, or is it that race can be glossed over strategically at this moment in this occasion?

Can an analyst who might have access to our audio-recorded conversation conclude, that because race did not seem to be relevant in the talk or in the conduct, that it had no relevance for the interaction? Or could it be that the polite tone of our voices, the measured reciprocity, the expressions of mutual interest in each other's skiing exploits were designed to produce a particular form of interaction, e.g. collegial talk between male colleagues in which race and racism did not matter. As we will see below, the analytic problem is that observation of either the details of the talk or the conduct of the participants cannot account for the constellation of motivations, hidden agendas, and different purposes (Hak, 1995) that each participant brings to the interaction.

Institutional talk

Psathas, in very helpful paper (1999) distinguishes between what he calls the "Schegloff/Jefferson tradition" (140) with its focus on ordinary conversation and attention to "sequential analysis" (141), and the study of talk-in-interaction within institutional and organisational settings. Here he notes the focus is on how "talk is 'modified, shaped, influenced, or constrained' by contextual factors" and how talk is organised differently from ordinary talk (141). Psathas then argues for the utility of using Sacks' idea of a "membership categorization device, MCD" (143) to unfold the ways that participants to talk-in-interaction in institutional settings can be shown to be oriented to, and to perform interactively. It follows that an explication of what is going on in so called institutional instances of talk may not be adequately recoverable by a simple focus on the structures of talk-in-interaction, that is its sequences, turns, repairs positions, and so forth.

The problem with a narrow focus on conversational features is addressed by Hester and Francis (2000) who divide ethnomethodology (and perhaps a properly executed conversation analysis) from the problematic offspring they call the "institutional talk program" (ITP). They outline that EM is to be distanced from the institutional talk program as the latter is purportedly concerned to effect a rapprochement between the interests of CA "in the organization of interaction" and those of "mainstream sociologists in the forms and processes of 'social structure'" (393). Hester and Francis critically analyse three strategies employed by those advancing the institutional talk program: 1) A focus on "structure in action", by which structure becomes a "members' notion" (396); 2) A focus on the "institutionality of interaction" (394), by which utterances are treated as informed by institutional dynamics –doctor/patient relations– and; 3) An analysis of the sequential structures of institutional talk (394), by which the distinctive nature of sequences are ascribed to institutional relevances. Hester and Francis complain:

> The institutional talk program's concern is not simply with analyzing the 'participant produced and managed' characteristics of talk between professional or bureaucrats and those with whom they deal, but also with interpreting such data with reference to generic features of such relations presupposed in mainstream theoretical accounts, features such as conflict, power, and control. In consequence, institutional talk program studies are notable for their failure to meet Schegloff's 'relevance' requirement.
>
> (2000:401)

They observe, "We question the viability, from an ethnomethodological point of view, of the analysis of the formal properties of institutional talk alone as a method for understanding the recognizable accomplishment of institutional activities" (394). Hester and Francis indicate that a necessary feature of analysis of institutional talk is the recognition that "the intelligibility and recognizability of any interactional activity is a situated accomplishment" that relies for performance on "members' orientations and competencies" (405).

Today, with a growing focus on so called anti-oppressive practice (Shulman, 2016; Mullaly & West, 2017) social workers are reminded of the need for vigilance when using categories that negatively label or pathologise clients. Similarly, social workers must guard against relying on stereotypes and generalisations when working with diverse clients, notably those who are racialised or from minority ethnic backgrounds. Indeed, competent practice demands struggling against subsuming complexity – particularly as presented by each client – within the comforting spaces of standardised categories and concepts. Front-line social workers are well advised to hold off or forestall recourse to the professional stock-in-trade of organisational categories and labels for treating clients. Yet we can hear in the concern of CA to demonstrate relevance and procedural consequentiality the imperative of explicating the practical accomplishment of every-day social work descriptors of action as abuse, violence, oppression, sexism, racism, etc. Against the leap into the conceptual social workers are enjoined through CA to pursue a process of discovery, explication, and analysis of the mundane forms of interaction between participants.

While professional authority may be partially recoverable from the differential allocation of sequences in a counselling interview, from the question and answer structure of responses, in the prosodic and lexical construction of talk-in-turns, and so on, an adequate explication of authority demands examining processes and relations that neither begin nor end in the interview as such. In this sense the coherence of an occasion depends on extended courses of action, and extended movements before and after, and which though not consequentially visible on this occasion, can become extremely consequential later. Hak (1995) has argued that in some ethnomethodological studies the "occasioned corpus of setting features" that are considered for study "is arbitrarily confined to elements that display considerations that are relevant for the immediate tasks at hand" and that they "dismiss as elements of the corpus orientations to concerns ... that though not visible in their data, are no less immediately relevant in the course of the work studied" (1995:122). He explains:

> Ethnomethodological and conversation analytic studies in work in institutional settings tend to depict encounters in these settings as harmonious events that are characterised by mutual understanding and cooperation. This way of depicting these encounters is justified in one respect, namely, in that these encounters rarely break down. Parties usually display a mutual orientation to cooperation within a 'context' that is made observable to each other in their actions. This, however, does not imply that parties do not orient to other 'contexts' at the same time, without this being observable for the other party. Phenomena of this kind (such as, for instance, 'hidden agendas', 'different purposes') are usually neglected in ethnomethodological and conversation analytic studies.
>
> (1995:134)

As Hak outlines, the problem with such interactions as may occur between a social worker and a client is that one of the participants, that is the social worker, performs as a practitioner, which necessarily demands an orientation to considerations outside the purview of the talk-in-interaction. As Hak notes, "the practitioners' point of view will only rarely be made part of a mutual understanding between the participants" (1995:134). In professional relationships participants are not only not equally situated, they are oriented to quite different systems of relevance in and as they engage in talk-in-interaction. There are tremendous imbalances of power, knowledge of organisational categories, motivations, agendas and so forth (Hak, 1995) between the professional and the client. Though it may be readily discernible that participants are demonstrably engaged in producing themselves as social workers and youth, as opposed to some other set of identifications such as friends in the mall, mentor and student, and so forth, such practical and strategic positioning must be explicated as grounded in extended courses of actions and consequentiality.

Surely it is not a violation of the "occasioned corpus" to recognise that the participants to institutional action recognise that an interview emerges by virtue of other socially organised antecedent and anticipated contexts. Watts, who uses close analysis of conversation segments to address silence and acquisition of status, argues that the extracts he uses must be seen "within a far wider social framework", and adds, "It is important to know what occurred prior to the interaction, to assess the possible states of mind of the participants when the interaction begins, to consider events of great importance to the participants themselves" (Watts, 1997:111).

For social workers these include the processes of formal education in schools of social work, applications for employment, employment in Children's Aid Societies, performance of job descriptions defined in documents, enactment of Child and Family Services legislation and so forth. Whether the materials in hand are tape-recordings from the optical discovery of a pulsar (Garfinkel, Lynch, & Livingston, 1981), or distress calls to a 911 number (Whalen & Zimmerman, 1998), audio-recordings of children at play (Hamo, Blum-Kulka, & Hacohen, 2004), or even audio-recordings of interviews between social workers and youth in care, all materials subjected to analysis need to be treated as artefacts. As artefacts they come to be, express, and articulate multi-layered and extended corporate capitalist (recorders as commodities), technological (development from tape-recording, to disk, to electronic recording devices), and institutional forms of life (organisations, agencies, ethics review boards, legislative authorities, and so on) that provide for their possible emergence.

Expanding the corpus

Perhaps because conversation analysis is an offspring of ethnomethodology there is a general discomfort or worry concerning expanding the 'corpus' of investigation past talk. Thus while 'context' is as practically accomplished on specific occasions, it must also be recognised that the iterative, replicable, and familiar nature of certain contexts, one's own home, one's place of work, the office, and so on, speak to 'institutional' (Smith, 1999; 1990a) webs of practice and relationships that knit this moment to that, thereby allowing for the discrete identification of this or that context. Although both conversation analysis and ethnomethodology appear, to my mind, to be quite correct in the insistence that analysis begins with interactive practices and materials visibly at hand, it is also the case that the corpus of attention must be expanded beyond the immediate forms of practical accomplishment. Of course some ethnomethodologists recognise this imperative.

A plea for a modification of the corpus has roots even among those who might be understood as ethnomethodologists properly speaking. For example, McHoul observed, "Why 'in situ' and 'in text' should be treated any differently, then, in the first place – whether as topic or resource – is dubious" (1982:6). McHoul called for a modification of "ethnomethodology's rejection of (theoretical) textual resources for its investigation and its preference for conversational topics (and the like) over textual ones" (1982:7) Similarly, Searle argues that "all meaning and understanding goes on against a background which is not itself meant or understood" (1992:29). Smith reminds us that "we should grasp entities as moments in social relations; we should grasp how the property of being an entity itself is a specific form of socially organized practice" (1990a:201), and indeed such a grasp of 'entities' must extend to conversation itself. Hak too has joined his voice to demand that an essential element that must be "admitted to the corpus" includes texts (1995:135).

Searle provides an important insight into the limits of procedural consequentiality and relevance as he argues, "you can't explain the general structure of conversation in terms of relevance, because what counts as relevance is not determined by the fact that it is a conversation" (1992: 14). Searle outlines that information in "lexical meanings" (1992:27) may be extremely sparse, the information communicated between speakers may be extremely thick. Searle asserts, "all meaning and understanding goes on against a background which is not itself meant or understood, but which forms the boundary conditions on meaning and understanding, whether in conversations or in isolated utterances" (1992:29).

The approach I adopt explicitly recognises that any given audio-recording is but a moment, and certainly as such its analysis requires looking beyond the narrow temporal window of its production. Explication demands connecting this moment to other moments both local and extra-local; past, present, and future. Schegloff wants to refuse to account for relevance of content in conversations as to do so is to refer to pre-existing or external social structures or sociological concepts, e.g. roles, gender, class, power, status, organisation, etc. (1992:106). Though this may seem to be a compelling move to resist the imposition of categories so characteristic of formal analysis, the problem is Schegloff presumes that the analyst's attention and selection of talk-in-interaction is not, as Smith observes, already, always, thoroughly organised by the social context and the work of a sociological analyst herself

(Smith, 1990b). The arbitrary circumspection of that which is admissible to a corpus of investigation itself arises from the analyst's own context and functional purposes. The analyst's desire to derive an account strictly from consideration of the sequences of talk-in-interaction, articulates the analyst's own intentionalities, projects, and designs.

An analysis of talk-in-interaction which demands that whatever reference to social dimensions might be made must be derived from the talk-in-interaction itself, as explicitly referenced, cannot be sustained, simply because all occasions of talk-in-interaction are performed in the embodied here and now. Any immediate instance of talk-in-interaction is bound to a concrete and at-hand, present and palpable social landscape – whether street corners, hallways, offices, or parks. The contours of the talk-in-interaction is in turn structured by this landscape, its temporal press – stop lights, setting of the sun, scheduled bookings for rooms, the sandwiching between meetings – and it is such unremarked features of talk, such implicit orderings that act as resources organising interactants' turns at talk. That which emerges as talk on this or that occasion is incorrigibly linked to such extended social processes. Thus, the social is not fully contained either in the explicit or discoverable forms of the talk.

Talk and "What actually happened"

Although CA may be an extremely useful tool for social workers, particularly as it makes available a series of techniques for close analysis of audio-recorded interviews, it must be acknowledged that social workers cannot be indifferent to the actual content or substance of interview materials. Social workers must continue to focus on the representational adequacy or cogency of the client accounts produced in and through talk-in-interaction. Social workers need to see beyond that which is produced to that which is being claimed to have happened or happens. Social workers must look for the connections between utterances and actual events.

As a social worker I am obliged to be oriented to the content and substance of the interviews, not just to the process, and certainly not just to the issue of "talk-in-interaction" as producing the occasion of the interview as such. Social workers are compelled to grapple with client's talk as putatively 'representational' of actual occurrences or actual life events, that is as awaiting confirmation, corroboration, assessment for consistency, coherence, rationality, logical order, and so forth. Simply, social workers grapple with slippage between our client's talk as 'representational' and actual occurrences or actual life events. For example, if in the course of an interview a child 'discloses' information that could be construed as indicating 'sexual abuse', 'physical abuse', or even 'emotional abuse', as a social work researcher I am morally, professionally, and legally obliged to act on that 'disclosure' of information. My actions, which would consist of reporting the 'incident' to the Children's Aid Society, would in turn initiate an assessment and investigation process that could itself result in dramatic interventions in the every-day routines, relationships, and life of the child.

Of necessity, we must include consideration of the organisation of these moments of talk inside the structures of a Children's Aid Society, the work processes of social workers, the professional and discursive codes for sense making, and so on. Indeed, consideration of such background is essential for uncovering the sense of the talk itself.

Despite the imperative to treat stories told by youth as representative of what actually happened (Smith, 1990a) the youth's talk not only intends and struggles with recovering sense from the social organisation of a personally experienced history, but it performs an occasioned social relation, between the child and the social worker. Drew and Heritage observe:

> First, utterances and actions are context shaped. Their contributions to an ongoing sequence of actions cannot be adequately understood except by reference to the context in which they participate ... This contextual aspect of utterances is significant both because speakers routinely draw upon it as a resource in designing their utterances and also because, correspondingly, hearers must also draw upon the local contexts of utterances in order to make adequate sense of what is said ... Second, utterances and actions are context renewing. Since every current utterance will itself form the immediate context for some next action in a sequence, it will inevitably contribute to the contextual framework in terms of which the next action will be understood ... Moreover each current action will ... function to renew (i.e. maintain, adjust, or alter) any broader or more generally prevailing sense of context which is the object of the participants' orientations and actions.
>
> (1992:18)

What is told as a story is grounded in the contexts of the production of the account. The context of these stories has been what we might commonly see as institutional, that is interviews conducted between social workers and children in care; interviews between the primary researcher and children in care; and weekly Children's Aid Society Teen meetings. Despite this attention to the relationship between utterance and socially organised background – reality – hence to what might be construed as a representational epistemology – social workers also have an acute sense that the relationship between the client's utterances and an actual state of affairs, and an actual order of events, may not be treated as in perfect correspondence. Social workers are not 'cultural dopes' (Garfinkel, 1967). On the contrary, they understand all too well that clients' accounts are interested, motivated, and strategic. They recognise that clients' claims need to be checked out. Social workers operate as practical phenomenologists in that they appreciate that client accounts are unreliable indicators of what actually happened, and accordingly they bracket such accounts by treating them as claims which are unfolding, putative, tentative, and awaiting assessment.

The bracketing of client accounts assumes several forms. First, accounts may be treated only as claims that await further exploration before being substantiated. Second, accounts may be treated as multi-layered, such that a series of separations and distinctions may be imposed on the talk, for example content may be conceptualised as both explicit and implicit, or content may be separated from form. Third, social workers appreciate, much as do conversation analysts, that as talk is performance, the client may be engaged in a moment of "impression management" in which they aim to please, "to present the appropriate image, to give required recognition to administrative authority, to 'bow properly to immense institutional power, understand and flatter the bureaucratic personality'" (Ferguson, 1985:95). Fourth, social workers approach any presently unfolding account and interaction against a background of prior contact, understandings, and case history. Accordingly, the account is read against what the social worker already knows about the child or the background case or documentary details. Finally, the sensibility of the account produced in the interview is understood as emerging and unfolding. Just what any particular utterance might mean is to be discovered through a process of focused interviewing which gives the social worker permission to return to a claim, topic, or subject, to thereby explore the issue in greater detail.

Zimmerman documented precisely such procedures in his analysis of the practice of social workers in a welfare office (1976). He noted that competent social workers employ an "investigative stance" marked by "being skeptical", which treats client's utterances as putatively factual to thereby establish the actual "facts of the matter" (1976:331). Through experience social workers learn to elicit client accounts to check for sensibility, coherence, order, plausibility, and ultimately veridicality. Competent practice demands routinely 'bracketing' a client's utterances, such that what the client says is transformed into a series of unverified but potentially verifiable claims. A social worker who believes a client's account, takes up a client's claims at face value, joins with the client in outrage or defence, may be seen as being inexperienced, naive, and colluding with the client. On the other hand, a social worker who tests out client accounts as they unfold demonstrates experience and competence.

Reflections on CA and social work

Despite the strategic necessity of treating what clients might say as a series of claims, social workers are nevertheless obliged by virtue of their organisational locations – particularly those in mandated child protection services – to pursue courses of action that 'treat' or 'respond' to client stories, narratives, or utterances, as located in concrete, knowable, and actionable worlds of daily life. It is through a client's stories of disclosure of sexual abuse, physical abuse, and neglect that a child is brought into care and placed in an approved resource. Child protection social workers do not have the liberty of treating client's accounts as mere narratives or stories. Indeed a client's claims are necessarily interpreted by social workers using "stocks of interactional knowledge" (Peräkylä & Vehviläinen, 2003) rooted in textually mediated theories and approaches. In addition to an orientation to issues of interaction – or as expressed in social worker's jargon 'process' – social workers in specific fields such as child protection must be alert continually to content as indicating potential 'risk', e.g. indications of physical, sexual or emotional abuse of a child, or parental behaviour such as alcohol and drug abuse. The perpetual struggle facing social workers, such as those doing child protection, is to establish adequate, defensible, and warranted accounts of 'what actually happened' based on evidentiary matters such as talk-in-interaction, body signs, behaviours, affect, presentation, and so forth.

As a social worker my attention is to the abiding concerns of social work practice. I am compelled to take the utterances of youth in care about being in care as pointing to, intending, and articulating the forms of their lives as 'wards' of the state. I am disturbed by the youth's articulation of anger, loss, and confusion as they talk about being moved from placement to placement, relationships with parents or social workers, or dealing with the effects of government cut-backs. I remained dissatisfied with my ability to address the concerns that the youth raised in the 'interviews'.

As we will see in the next chapter the stories told by youth in interviews must be approached as reflexive accomplishments. Yet, attention to reflexivity as a problem inherent in the constitution of accounts is unsettling as it disturbs the confident, authoritative, and controlling orientations made possible through the claims of positivistic research. Pollner observes:

> There is nothing intrinsically problematic about incessant reflexivity or the regresses and abysses by which it is supposedly accompanied. They are constituted as unacceptable, intolerable, or unintelligible within forms of life that place a premium on positivist discourse as the basis for subsequent action and inference. These demands are more intense for inquirers who are responsible to objectivist ontology as the grounds for deciding the significance and intelligibility of a claim.

(1993:78)

Attention to reflexivity directs us to consider how the talk in interaction in itself produced the occasion as an interview, how the participants constituted the 'topicality' of the talk, and how the participants oriented themselves each to other, and jointly to the project of producing the distinctiveness of the "social scene" (Varenne, 1990:240) as an interview that examines the experiences of coming into and being in care.

The reflexive turn creates a tension between attention to the constitutive practices which produce narratives and the 'content' of these narratives, hence to matters of representation between what children in care have to say and actual events. As a social worker I am obliged to make determinations concerning the "significance and intelligibility of a claim" (Pollner, 1993:78). Social workers must be oriented to the content and substance of the interviews, not just to the process, and certainly not merely to the issue of "talk in interaction".

To conclude those doing EM and CA would do well to attend to Marx's dialectical conceptualisation of work. That is, people in the instances of doing talk-in-interaction are engaged in multiple levels and various forms of work. As participants in a present-and-at-hand moment of talking and listening they draw on prior experiences and extended courses of action to produce this moment, as sustained and sustainable. When this moment, through the wonders of modern technology, comes to be audio-recorded, the recording can be transported to the intellectual factories of conversation analysis, where it can be subjected to various forms of post-facto revision and review.[6] These moments of consumption and reproduction remake that which was performed in situ into the reasoned fragments of conversation analysis and ethnomethodology. Whatever moment of talk-in-interaction is taken up articulates not only a bridge with the work of EM and CA, but the contingent, particular, local, and embodied performance to transcendent, extra-local, disembodied, textually mediated, and universalised forms of action.

Notes

1 Sacks addressing the problem of identifying and categorising people, developed the idea that there were some devices that could be used to categorise any member of the population (P) where members were not specified (n). Hence there were category sets with broad application, thus Pn adequate devices, e.g., mommy and baby, mother and child, father and son, wife and husband, and so on (Sacks, 1995).

2 When addressing race we need to appreciate our reliance on a hermeneutics for reading, assembling meaning, and interpreting the bodies and actions of others. Skin colour, physiognomy, comportment, dress, adornments, hair, style, accent, and so on are assembled as markers and signifiers of race, gender, and class. Such readings are not 'innocent' (Rossiter, 2001), particularly in a society marked by systematic racism and the mundane accomplishment of differential identities and sites as more or less privileged, powerful, and dominant. As I recognise race I am simultaneously buffeted by a reflexive troubling of innocence, as my gaze is disturbed by acknowledgement of the assembling of my own privilege and complicity in racist social relations. Though I simultaneously struggle to build solidarity, alliances, and allyship (Bishop, 2015), I recognise that this cannot be taken-for-granted interactively.

3 The issue of capitalisation of race is contentious and fraught, as white supremacists tend to capitalise white though they refuse to capitalise black. African American activists, working from an acknowledgement of a history of slavery, segregation, and racism in the United States, argue that African Americans are an identifiable group, and therefore Black warrants capitalisation, in the same manner as nationality as identity warrants it. I do not disagree. However, in this text and in this section, the focus is on interpersonal interaction, and a hermeneutics of reading, assembling, and identifying race as a feature of another in interaction. Certainly, while the interpersonal is decidedly political I have decided against capitalisation, in order to identify a reciprocity in the problematics of reading race.

4 Parson's and Shils identified five dichotomous pattern variables shaping interaction, i.e., 1) Affectivity–Affective neutrality; 2) Self-orientation–Collectivity-orientation; 3) Universalism–Particularism; 4) Ascription–Achievement; and, 5) Specificity–Diffuseness (1962:77). Largely due to Parsons' profound understanding of psycho-analysis their effect was not just a manifestation of habit but of the structures of the unconscious, the libidinal, and the imperative for constraint and control.

5 Coates in *Between the World and Me* relies on a non-essentialist view of race, in which he recognises that "these new people are, like us, a modern invention" and observes, "The new people were something else before they were white—Catholic, Corsican, Welsh, Mennonite, Jewish ..." (2015:7). Coates' approach to race is resonant with that of Theodore Allan, who in his comprehensive examination of *The Invention of the White Race*, characterised race and racism as a "social control formation" (2012:204).

6 Hamo et al. note, "Every transcription system involves a reduction of the social reality it seeks to capture" (Bucholtz, 2000; Ochs, 1979; Psathas & Anderson, 1990), often turning the continuous stream of the interaction into discrete units (Schegloff, 1984) and transforming people from social actors with goals, identities, and moti-vations into 'A's and 'B's (Bucholtz, 2000; Moerman, 1988)." (2004:76)

References

Allen, Theodore W. (2012). *The invention of the white race: Volume one: Racial oppression and social control.* New York, NY: Verso.

Atkinson, J. Maxwell, & Drew, Paul. (1979). *Order in court: The organisation of verbal interaction in judicial settings.* London, England: Macmillan.

Bishop, Anne. (2015). *Becoming an Allie: Breaking the cycle of oppression in people* (3rd ed.). Halifax, NS: Fernwood.

Bucholtz, Mary. (2000). The politics of transcription. *Journal of Pragmatics, 32,* 1439–1465.

Clemmens, Michael Craig. (2012). The interactive field: Gestalt therapy as an embodied relational dialogue. In Talia Bar-Yoseph Levine (Ed.), *Gestalt therapy: Advances in theory and practice* (pp. 39–48). East Sussex, England: Routledge.

Criminal Code (1985). Revised Statutes of Canada (R. S. C.) c. C-46, s. (484).

Coates, Ta-Nehisi. (2015). *Between the world and me.* New York, NY: Spiegel and Grau.

Drew, Paul, & Heritage, John. (1992). Analyzing talk at work: An introduction. In Paul Drew & John Heritage (Eds.), *Talk at work: Interaction in institutional settings* (pp. 3–65). Cambridge, England: Cambridge University Press.

Ferguson, Kathy E. (1985). *The feminist case against bureaucracy.* Philadelphia, PA: Temple University Press.

Garfinkel, Harold. (1967). *Studies in ethnomethodology.* Englewood Cliffs, NJ: Pre-ntice-Hall.

Garfinkel, Harold. (1988). Evidence for locally produced, naturally accountable phe-nomena of order, logic, reason, meaning, method, etc. in and as of the essential quiddity of immortal ordinary society (I of IV): An announcement of studies. *Sociological Theory, 6:* 103–109.

Garfinkel, Harold. (2002). *Ethnomethodology's program: Working out Durkheim's aphorism.* Lantham, MD: Rowman & Littlefield.

Garfinkel, Harold, Lynch, Michael, & Livingston, Eric. (1981). The work of a dis-covering science construed with materials from the optically discovered pulsar. *Philosophy of the Social Sciences, 11:* 131–158.

Goffman, Erving. (1959*).* *The presentation of self in everyday life.* Garden City, NY: Doubleday.

Hak, Tony. (1995). Ethnomethodology and the institutional context. *Human Studies,* 18, 109–137.

Hamo, Michal, Blum-Kulka, Shoshana & Hacohen, Gonen. (2004). From observation to transcription and back: Theory, practice, and interpretation in the analysis of children's naturally occurring discourse. *Research on Language and Social Interaction* 37(1): 71–92.

Hester, Stephen, & Francis, David. (2000). Ethnomethodology, conversation analysis, and "institutional talk". *Text – Interdisciplinary Journal for the Study of Discourse,* 20(3): 391–413.

Housley, William, & Fitzgerald, Richard. (2015). Introduction to membership categorization analysis. In Richard Fitzgerald and William Housley (Eds.), *Advances in membership categorization analysis* (pp. 1–21). London, England: Sage.

Husserl, Edmund. (1990). *The idea of phenomenology* (Trans. William P. Alston & George Nakhnikian). Dordrecht, Netherlands: Kluwer.

Laing, Ronald David. (1970). *Knots.* London, England: Routledge.

McHoul, Alec W. (1982). *Telling how texts talk: Essays on reading and ethnomethodology.* London, England: Routledge & Kegan Paul.

Moerman, Michael. (1988). *Talking culture: Ethnography and conversation analysis.* Philadelphia, PA: University of Pennsylvania Press.

Mullaly, Bob, & West, Juliana. (2017). *Challenging oppression and confronting privilege: A critical approach to anti-oppressive and anti-privilege theory and practice* (3rd ed.). Toronto, ON: Oxford University Press.

Ochs, Elinor. (1979). Transcription as theory. In Elinor Ochs & Bambi B. Schileffelin (Eds.), *Developmental pragmatics* (pp. 43–72). New York, NY: Academic Press.

Parsons, Talcott, & Shils, Edward A. (1962). Categories of the Orientation and Organization of Action. In Talcott Parson & Edward A. Shils (Eds.), *Toward a general theory of action* (53–109). Cambridge, MA: Harvard University Press.

Peräkylä, Anssi, & Vehviläinen, Sanna. (2003). Conversation analysis and the professional stocks of interactional knowledge. *Discourse & Society,* 14(6): 727–750

Pollner, Melvin. (1993). The reflexivity of constructionism and constructionism of reflexivity. In Gale Miller & James A. Holstein (Eds.), *Constructivist controversies: Issues in social problems theory* (pp. 69–82). New York, NY: Aldine de Gruyter.

Psathas, George. (1999). Studying the organization in action: Membership categorization and interaction analysis. *Human Studies,* 22: 139–162.

Psathas, George, & Anderson, Timothy. (1990). The "practices" of transcription in conversation analysis. *Semiotica,* 78, 75–99.

Rossiter, Amy. (2001). Innocence lost and suspicion found: Do we educate for or against social work? *Critical Social Work,* 2(1): (no page numbers on-line).

Schegloff, Emmanuel A. (1984). On some gestures' relation to talk. In J. Maxwell Atkinson & John Heritage (Eds.), *Structures of social interaction: Studies in conversation analysis* (pp. 266–296). Cambridge, England: Cambridge University Press.

Schegloff, Emanuel A. (1992). On talk and its institutional occasions. In Paul Drew and John Heritage (Eds.), *Talk at work: Interaction in institutional settings* (pp. 101–134). Cambridge, England: Cambridge University Press.

Schegloff, Emanuel A. (1997). Whose text? Whose context? *Discourse and Society,* 8(2): 165–187.

Searle, John. (1992). Conversation. In Herman Parret and Jef Verschueren (Eds.), *(On) Searle on conversation* (pp. 7–29). Amsterdam, Netherlands: John Benjamins.

Shulman, Lawrence. (2016). *The skills of helping individuals, families, groups, and communities* (8th ed.). Toronto, ON: Thompson Brooks Cole.

Smith, Dorothy E. (1990a). *The conceptual practices of power: A feminist sociology of knowledge.* Toronto, ON: University of Toronto Press.

Smith, Dorothy E. (1990b). *Texts, facts, and femininity: Exploring the relations of ruling.* London, England: Routledge.

Smith, Dorothy E. (1999). *Writing the social: Critique, theory, and investigation.* Toronto, ON: University of Toronto Press.

Smith, Dorothy E. (2005). *Institutional ethnography: A sociology for people.* Lanham, MD: AltaMira.

Varenne, Hervé. (1990). Parents and their children at talk. In Bruce Dorval (Ed.), *Conversational organization and its development* (pp. 239–275). Norwood, NJ: Ablex.

Watts, Richard J. (1997). Silence and the acquisition of status in verbal interaction. In Adam Jaworski (Ed.), *Silence: Interdisciplinary perspectives* (pp. 87–115). New York, NY: Mouton de Gruyter.

Whalen, Jack, & Zimmerman, Don H. (1998). Observation on the display and management of emotion in naturally occurring activities: The case of "hysteria" in calls to 9–1–1. *Social Psychology Quarterly*, 61(2): 141–159.

Zimmerman, Don H. (1976). Record-keeping and the intake process in a public welfare agency. In Stanton Wheeler (Ed.), *On record: Files and dossiers in American life.* New Brunswick, NJ: Transaction Books.

Zimmerman, Don H., & Boden, Deirdre. (1991). Structure-in-action: An introduction. In Deirdre Boden & Don Zimmerman (Eds.), *Talk and social structure: Studies in ethnomethodology and conversation analysis.* Cambridge, England: Polity.

4 Topic as a resource for coherence

This chapter examines the issue of topic as a source of coherence in conversations and in interviews. Although as school children we are taught that topic is what defines a story, in what follows topic is examined as a resource for sense making. Topic, that is the identification that this talk is about this or that, along with sequence and turn-exchange are resources or tools members rely on to accomplish coherence and order in and as talk-in-interaction. The coherence and orderliness of talk in an interview relies on participants warrantably orienting themselves in their turns to producing a content, subject, or topic of talk that can be treated by the other as relevant either to the immediate stream of the conversation – e.g. we were talking about your summer vacation – or the overall purpose of the interview – e.g. an interview with youth about coming into care and living in care.

Schegloff has outlined some problems with using topic as an exclusive resource for coherence in talk-in-interaction (1990), suggesting that "the structure of sequences in talk-in-interaction is a source of coherence in its own right" (1990:72). While such matters as sequence and the turn-by-turn structure of talk-in-interaction provide essential structures, any adequate understanding of coherence must also attend to the ways that people draw on topic, albeit as fluidly recognised as a resource for ordering talk. Participants and analysts' identification of coherence requires attention to both topic as a resource and to sequence, and reciprocally analysis of topic demands attention to sequence, and vice versa. While sequence points to the form and structure of the activity of doing talk, topic (as implicit, emerging, changing, and as explicit) points to what is being done in and as talk-in-interaction turn by turn.

Schegloff argues that it is difficult determining "what the topic is" even for a single sentence; that in conversations topics shift turn to turn – topic shading –; that it is not feasible to characterise the topic "as an organizing unit for talk in interaction"; that while an analyst might identify the topic in a stretch of talk, that this identification does different work than that being done by the participants to talk; and that attention to topic addresses what talk is about rather than what participants to talk are doing with each other (1990:51–52). Against relying on topic as a source for coherence, he outlines:

First, that the "sequence structure" of a spate of talk and its topical aspect or structure are analytically distinct and can be empirically at least partially independent; and second, that the sequence structure itself can provide for the organizational coherence of the talk ... third ... even when misunderstanding and trouble arise, these can be coherently shaped by sequence structure in conversation.

(1990:53)

While Schegloff's argument quite rightly corrects the move to locate coherence solely in topic, without regard to turns and sequence, it would seem that he overstates the case in an equally untenable and opposite direction. Against Schegloff, I argue that, while it is possible to make "analytic distinctions" between sequence structure and topic, the making of such distinctions is itself an artefact of moments of analysis rather than the practices of talking. Just as Schegloff objected to "the status of unconstrained formulation of topics by professional analysts" (1990: 52), so too should we object to the bifurcation of sequence from topic.

Indeed, it is important to recognise that talk-in-interaction, as with all other forms of practice is accomplished in and as particular forms or structures – habits, expectations, rituals – of embodied expression – talking, hammering, walking, smiling – and as organised by a motivational or intentional complex. The coherence of talk-in-interaction, as Schegloff so ably demonstrates, does depend on sequence structure, but it also relies on the ability of participants to produce and to find coherence in that which is talked about. While sequences of talk-in-interaction provide a form and structure for order they do not in themselves provide for the substance of that order. Order is also accomplished in the simple fact that people talk to each other, or to do something with another. Talk is produced in situ, and is accomplished as realising relevance or irrelevance of content. In talk participants progressively realise as an accountable matter the coherence of utterances that demonstrably indicate in their unfolding an orientation to a topic. Thus, as a speaker moves sound by sound, word by word, clause by clause, past stutters, stumbles, false starts, and repairs, coherence emerges for a speaker and listener such that they come to see that this talk is about or at least seems to be about this or that. As an interview unfolds members' orientation to some topics provide resources for accomplishing this occasion as such. They co-construct coherence and accountability turn-by-turn such that, as their time together unfolds, that which is talked about demonstrates an orientation to topically organised work of interviewing.

To explicate the problem of coherence and order, our analysis must look beyond the topic as a descriptor of the talk, to topic – or specification of content or substance – as a device for ordering talk. As we will see below, the clearest form through which such specifications occur in interviews is in the question and answer sequence structure.

Question/answer sequences and topic control

Asking questions is an integral skill in the repertoire of social workers, professional helpers, and social science interviewers (Bergmann, 1995; Sacks, 1995; Button, 1992). Button (1992) has noted that "the interview overwhelmingly consists of talk that is organised into a series of questions and answers" (214). Through adherence to turn design as questions and answers, participants jointly produce talk-in-interaction that allow the person asking questions to set out preferred topics for the next speaker's turn. Of course, the next speaker need not address themselves to the questions that are asked, however not doing so becomes a remarkable response.[1] The effect of the question/answer structure, as Sacks observes, is that, "as long as one is doing the questions, then in part one has control of the conversation" (1995:55). This is a control of conversation that allows the questioning to shape what gets talked about, both through the questions as formulated, and through follow-up re-directions and questions. Sacks argues that once a response is given, questioners can continue "to hold the floor",[2] hence initial questions can be followed by other questions that dig and probe for more details, clarifications, resolution of ambiguities, and so on. Yet equally relevant to holding the floor is the aspect of questioning that Sacks calls "this rule that persons asking questions have a right to make the first operation on the answers" (1995:55), that is to evaluate the response to the question, to add up answers to questions, to reach a conclusion about responses, and to follow up with additional questions (54).

The following two short segments demonstrate the ways that the social worker, W the interviewer, uses statements and questions to shape initial and follow up responses. W's questions cumulatively function to elicit details from S, which will combine to create a coherent story about coming into care and living in care. What counts as coherence speaks to W's reliance on topics or themes, as well as skilled deployment of certain structures of talk – e.g. repairs, silences, sequences – which demand that certain types of information be elicited.

In the first segment W uses questions to encourage S to provide information about: the number of siblings; the relative ages of siblings; the number of siblings "at home"; the entry of S and her siblings into CAS care; the ages of S and her siblings at that time.

W: Ok. So when you were two, you had three siblings↑?
S: When I was two I had two siblings=
W: =Two siblings=
S: =Yeah
W: So there were three children at home?
S: Yeah
W: Were you all taken into the CAS care?
S: Yep

w: And how old were your siblings?

s: One was four when I was two and the other one I don't know cause I don't remember but I know I have another one.

w: So was she younger than you or older=

s: =yep she was younger=

This segment begins as W shapes her turn as a proposition with intonation rising at the end, to thereby indicate this can be treated as a question. W's propositional question invites S to effect a repair if necessary, "Ok. So when you were two, you had three siblings↑?" By using this form W both invites S to help W understand her story, while acknowledging that W might not have the facts right. It is implicit in the use of this form that W acknowledges dependence on S for the production of a coherent and sensible story about coming into care, and living in care.

Coherence arises for S as she works to answer W's questions, and as she produces answers that she anticipates or hopes W will hear to be sensible, coherent, proper, and adequate answers to W's questions. For W topical coherence articulates manifold relevances: First, W struggles to elicit from S a story that can count as being about S's experiences of coming into care and living in care. In this sense coherence is as organisationally defined in relation to research purposes. Second, W must develop questions that S can hear as relevant to the interview. W must anticipate that S will most likely not be able to recover or understand the theoretical connectives between questions, and accordingly she must pose follow-up questions that can be seen as relevant to previous answers, or as transparently connected to research purposes. Third, given the real possibility that W might pose questions which S might treat, or might regard as irrelevant, W must build in the talk-in-interaction positive relationship dynamics. Simply, W needs to anticipate that she may have to rely on resources other than questions to elicit answers, i.e. she must elicit S's trust, she must encourage S's desire to please, she must create an interactional pattern in which S responds to questions, even those she does not immediately see as relevant, in a positive and friendly way, trusting that W's questions are relevant. Fourth, W works to recover coherence and understanding turn-by-turn as she listens to and processes S's responses to questions, drawing on not just the last response, but using as a resource earlier responses to earlier questions. In this manner coherence practically unfolds in a turn by turn accretion of responses so that by the end of the interview both W and S can count the talk that has unfolded as having produced a coherent story about S's experiences of coming into care and living in care. The progressive unfolding through W's questions matched by S's responses provides for the progressive and at-hand interactive production of an ordered and orderly story.

Of course, if W's propositional question was correct it would not require a repair. If correct S would most likely have provided a simple 'response token', i.e. "yah", "right". However, because W acknowledges through the question that the proposition might not be correct, she gives permission or invites S to initiate a correction or repair. W's turn may be described as a "self-initiated-other-invited-other repair".

The effects of such a device are profound. In counselling, the invitation of such "self-initiated-other-invited-other-repair" has the effect of underscoring that the interviewer is in a subordinate position concerning the facts. This move by the interviewer acknowledges the possibility that the interviewer may get it wrong or may be mistaken with respect to those facts over which the youth has knowledge. This has a number of positive strategic interactive effects. First it allows the person being interviewed to act as the expert of their own story. Indeed, that interviews were arranged, and that interviewers met with youth in care demonstrated a genuine interest in youth's life experiences and stories. The fact that these interviews occurred underscored that youth's experiences and stories are important; and that others are interested in what they have to say. Simply, the youth count, their stories matter, and others care. Second, the implicit acknowledgment by the interviewer that he or she might not understand has the effect of taking the interviewer off a professional pedestal. The interviewer's demonstration of their own vulnerability undercuts the youth's potential presumption of the worker's power, confidence, and certainty. It signals to the youth that the interviewer is human and can make mistakes, and thereby decentres presumptive professional authority. Third, precisely because the interviewer does not understand the youth's experiences, youth come to understand that if the interview is to succeed then they must help the interviewer. Youth understand that they must take on the role of instructor, teacher, and expert of their life story. This has the effect of communicating that the youth has power, a measure of control over the narrative, and as such is a necessary and valued participant in the interaction. Of course, such moves by the worker help to ensure engagement by the youth in the work of producing a story.

The paradoxical effect of such devices is that although the interviewer continues to be responsible for shaping the topical direction of the interview, the youth's focus on telling their story, and helping the interviewer to understand creates the appearance that it is the youth who is in control. The interviewer's power to pose questions is counterbalanced by the youth's power to answer questions that only the youth can answer, thereby positioning the youth as the guide through her own life story. The semblance of the youth's expertise, albeit limited to his or her own story, appears to create an equalising effect that mitigates the problems of interviewer power and authority. Indeed, to encourage youth to produce coherent and relevant stories the interviewer must use practical techniques to secure the youth's cooperation and eager involvement in the interview work.

The practical effect is that the youth is empowered as an expert, and as the only one who has the resources to provide the facts of a proper narrative of her life. S takes up the invitation for repair, by providing a repair to the "trouble source" (Schegloff, Jefferson, & Sacks, 1977). She provides a next turn repair initiation (Schegloff, 2000; 1992) not as an explicit correction, but as a simple statement of fact. She refrains from drawing attention to the error or trouble, i.e. she does not say "no, that is not correct", or "no you are mistaken". Instead S shapes a response that uses the common repair device of replicating the grammatical form of W's statement/question (Schegloff, Jefferson, & Sacks, 1977), though substituting first person singular, "When I was two I had two siblings". The effect of this sequence is that W has been able to establish not only a correction concerning the overall number of S's siblings, but some preliminary sense of birth order, as well as the number of children in the family at the time.

W indicates, following S's turn, that she now understands that when S was two she had "Two siblings". In the turns to follow W relies on "an if-this-then-that" question structure. She builds up a picture to construct a working account of S's family members' relations to the child protection organisation. Whatever coherence emerges in this sequence is as worked at and achieved through W's orientation to determine the number of children in the home, their birth order, and the relationship of the children to child protection interventions. Coherence emerges in this spate of talk as W and S coopera-tively orient their responses to in turn explore and explain matters of birth order, sibling numbers, age, and relations to child protection.

The next segment builds on the information set out above, to explore the effect coming into care had on S's relationships with her siblings.

W: So e where did your siblings go?
S: One lived with me for a while, the other one I have no idea. The one lived with me for a while by the age of seven I was separated from him he went to, into a different home and I went to a different home.
W: He was the four year old?
S: Yeah.
W: What was his name?
S: F (_)=
W: =F. So F and you lived together for maybe how long?
S: Bout three years
W: At P's (_) house ?
S: ya

W's questions centre on eliciting a story that allows W to understand the chronology of S's movement through care and the effects this had on contact with siblings. That which drives the sequences is W's need to understand events in quite specific ways. W's next turn, "He was the four year old?", picks up on the ambiguity of S's "for a while", and the specification that "by the age of seven I was separated from him" addresses chronology by estab-lishing F's (a sibling's) age. W's question, "He was the four year old?", indi-cates a reliance on S's understanding of actual chronologies and ages of siblings, and processes of coming into care. As we saw above, W asks S if this or that understanding is correct, not explicitly, but by proffering a proposition as a question, to thereby allow S to correct or repair the statement. W tries to arrive at a provisional age-based identity of S's siblings, and accordingly ties specific age identities with generalised theoretical understandings to arrive at some sense of the impact going into a "different home" might have had for each child. The question "What was his name?" aims to establish the particular identity based on name, to then allow a return to matters of chronology in the next line. The overall effect is to create a story that the social worker can follow without becoming confused with respect to the identity of actors, that is addressing siblings, and addressing foster care providers, probable differential effects of CAS action on children of different ages, and an overall chronology of events.

This capacity to add up the answers to questions and to reach a conclusion is integral for the operation of what social workers call assessment. The question/answer structure allows the questioner to determine the topics or agenda for the talk. Shebib (2003), in a text on counselling skills, notes, "Questions focus the work of the interview on particular topics and themes" (126). As such questions are always informed by the interviewer's understandings, theories, desires, and intentions. Of course, that these need not be disclosed to the interviewee creates an imbalance of power and authority. Hak has argued "in most institutional encounters only one party can be considered a practitioner and that the practitioners' point of view will only rarely be made part of a mutual understanding between the participants" (Hak, 1995:134). Hak employs this distinction to lever an opening for the consideration of institutional context for ethnomethodology, though it also brings into focus the institutional and professional work performed by social workers to assemble particulars into an account about a client, and making sense of client utterances through such assembling practices. These in turn provide background details for organising talk using professionally relevant topics.

The observation that a question/answer sequence is the normal foundational structure for interviews is at first glance hardly newsworthy. Social workers, and others, whose work centres on counselling recognise that asking questions is one essential part of the routines for developing an understanding of clients and their life situations. Yet even the question/answer structure is conditioned by a series of aphoristically expressed understandings about techniques for performing a good interview congruent with social work values. This is most clearly revealed in the potential tension created by the notion of 'starting from where the client is at'. Of course, the dilemma is how a social worker can start from where the client is at and still end up achieving their professional and organisational objectives for the interview. Indeed, 'starting from where the client is at', is an aphorism that points to the need to craft an appearance or a strategic beginning so that a client comes to believe that the social worker cares about them, listens to them, is concerned, and is prepared to take action on their behalf. From the standpoint of the social worker, 'starting from where the client is at' is itself part of a strategy for keeping the client on side, not losing the client, and avoiding making the client angry, hostile, or resistant to joining the social worker as a participant in organisational work.

Experienced social workers have an acute sense of the various problems that can arise from their questions, as gauged by the responses of the client. For example, Shebib outlines some of the blocks that emerge for clients when answering a social worker's questions. These include, occasions when a client does not understand what was meant due to vocabulary or idiomatic usage; those times when clients do not understand the purpose of a question; those times when a client might not know the answer to a question; or those times when clients feel that the question invades a private or personal matter (Shebib, 2002:131–132). A client can signal a failure to understand either intentionally, by saying, "what do you mean", or unintentionally by formulating a response, which a social worker hears as not addressing that which the social worker had imagined or intended was to be addressed by the question. The social worker's understandings of how the client hears questions itself becomes part of the assessment process. A client's consistent failure to understand simple questions as an interviewer intends will likely be taken-up by the social worker to indicate intellectual disability, mental health problems, or even psychiatric symptoms.

Although use of questions is often essential for conducting interviews, skilled social workers recognise that a question can be pursued that is not formulated as a question. For example, the following short segment demonstrates the use of a combination of grammatical questions and propositions that function as questions to gather information.

G: yah, wha what's yer dad's name
J: John X
G: John X
J: yah
G: an yer mom is
J: Joan B
G: okay so you you've kept yer mom's name
J: yah
G: yah now yer first nations
J: yah
G: are you registered
J: yah

Similarly, a question can be pursued through statements of confusion, by offering up re-frames for client consideration, or similarly by advancing formulations that are exploratory, and which lead a client to work it through. All such techniques are deployed to shape the interaction that develops as an interview.

I hold that a social worker's professional power becomes visible in the differential exercise of topic control, and further that there is an organisation of topic and form of control that is essential for the warrantable production of the occasion as a proper interview. Furthermore, as noted above, if we recognise that posing questions is a powerful tool for holding the floor, that is for eliciting and directing the nature of the response from the co-participant, and that the production of an interview is marked by the interviewer's differential responsibility, then it becomes clear that posing questions is integrally related to maintaining control over the topical direction of the interview.

Open and closed questions

If the preferred structure for an interview is marked by the interviewer proffering simple and clear questions, followed by an interviewee's response, that can be treated as relevant and sufficiently detailed by the interviewer, the dispreferred structure is one in which the social worker either does most of the talking, or issues a steady stream of questions, followed by short responses from the interviewee. Social workers have a variety of techniques at their disposal to both elicit and to avoid yes/no answers. Hepworth, Rooney, and Larson observe that "closed-ended questions restrict the client and elicit limited information" whereas "open-ended questions and statements invite expanded expression and leave the client free to express what seems most relevant and important" (2002:142).

The following segment demonstrates both the stylistic and prosodic problems that can result from the use of close-ended questions.

J: Tell me where you were born.
T: Two Trees
J: how many years ago
T: twelve
J: when was the first time you had anything to do with social services.
T: Since I was born.
J: Do you know, what what involvement your mom had with them?
T: No
J: Was your mom with a partner, was it your mom and dad or just your mom?
T: My mom and her boyfriend.
J: Was it your dad.
T: Yep.
J: Is he in Two Trees too?
T: Nope
J: where is he?
T: Don't know
J: okay, but you've met him at times?
T: yep

Although all the questions developed by the interviewer in this segment can be responded to as "close-ended", it is likely that the interviewer intended the question "Do you know, what what involvement your mom had with them?", to open up a discussion in which T could have provided a narrative. The cumulative effect of this barrage of close-ended questions is that there is a sense of 'topic stacking' as the interviewer tries to have the youth address where they were born, the youth's age, age of contact with social services, parental involvement with social services, mother's relationship with the youth's dad, the dad's location, and whether or not the youth knows her dad.

Although T provides the social worker with essential demographic information there is no voluntary elaboration beyond the limited, literal scope of the questions asked. The obvious issue for the social worker over the course of the interview is figuring out how to engage and interest the youth in the process so that the youth will provide her story. While the topics stack one on top of the other the effect is that there is little obvious topical coherence. The monosyllabic and single word replies to questions creates a potential crisis for the interviewer, who struggles to discover some subject that will interest the youth and elicit more detailed replies.

Co-operative shaping of topic

Just as we have explored the troubles that can result from a youth who volunteers too little, the following extended segment examines some of the issues that arise when a youth volunteers 'too much information'. This segment begins as B, the youth, talks about her conflicts with J, the group home parent.

B: an,...J (group home parent) she was tellin, I don' know, I think it was, she was tellin uhm, cause a' at court then, she was tellin the judge//

G: you had court

B: yah

G: for

B: under age

G: oh

B: f', n' yah, under age, an fraud, an uhm, she was tellin the judge that I was takin unprescribed drugs, an all this other stuff=

G: yah=

B: an comin home high every day=

G: yah

B: an drunk, an li' she made it as a paper thing, it didn't say anything about it, but one of us got an infection,

G: mmhuh

B: in this ths' s' like down there,

G: yah yah

B: like one of us got an infection, but she didn't put any name on it, an one of us came home drunk, an she pissed her pants, an another one of us uhm, ended up in the hospital, an that was me, an another one of us, I d', she wrote down a bunch of things on paper, she gave it t' each of us, she made us sound so bad, she's like, "Oh, yah, youth came home drunk an peed her pants."

G: who's this again

B: J (group home parent)

G: who's she.

B: She's the owner of group home

G: well it sounds like she's also partially responsible for you, isn't she

B: yah

G: an for all these behaviours, maybe she's not reachin out to you in a way that, in a way that works

B: I don' know, she's like wrote down that a youth pissed her pants, a youth ended up in hospital, a youth has a sexually transmitted di[sease]=

G: [disease]=

B: a youth does unprescribed drugs, a y'/ this youth comes home drunk every night, an. She gived it t', she didn't put no names on it, but we all knew who it was, an it made us mad, cause it wasn't an STD=

G: =yah=

B: it was jist an infection=

G: =yah, so is she presenting that to the court

B: I I don' know, I don't even know why she made them.

G: Well how didja hear [about this list]

B: [she jis made em] she told us, she gave it to us

G: oh, I see, my lord...an I guess at that point you were feelin pretty desperate

B: I didn' care=

G: =yah=

B: =I jist ripped it up in her face an called her down=

G: =yah=

B: =an another time I came home drunk there, well I wasn't drunk, I had a', a drink a two-six an I wasn't even drunk, but//

G: two-six=

B: =uhm, baccardi, like a bottle, an me an M, and B were walkin home, uhm, me an M were goin back to receiving home an then, I wasn't drunk, but I smelled like alcohol, an cops stopped an they picked up me an B, an I got another ticken, an that made me mad because I wasn't drunk, an then they took me home, an I I jis freaked out, an I threw all my stuff everywhere, an I hit staff in the head with a fire extinguisher

G: ouch

B: I think it was the head or the knee

G: yah

B: an then I took off again, an that cops like, "you stay outta trouble now." I did' really care.

G: what's that like, not caring, you've said that a number of times.
B: doin whatever you want not w//
G: what's that about

In the process of listing complaints against J the group home parent, B indicates, "... cause a' at court then, she was tellin the judge//", which opens up what G recognises to be an important topic, requiring some further explanation, prompting his interruption of B's turn, "you had court". G's response aims to open up a new topic focused on court. Although B attempts to handle G's questions with an affirmative response token "yah", G refuses to accept this as an adequate response, prompting B to provide further information, "for". Fortunately for G, B does not prove reticent to talk about her experiences with the court and the law, as she launches into a detailed description of her troubles only to return to complain about J, the group home parent, "an li' she made it as a paper thing", to indicate that the J compiled and kept written reports on her and the other young women's transgressions.

B's turns at talk from "she made it as a paper thing" through to "I jist ripped it up in her face and called her down=" are oriented to describing troubles with J. B details J's activities of taking certain events involving the young women in care, and putting them on a list. An interesting feature of this sequence of talk, organised around the topic of the list, is the content, "one of us got an infection ... down there", which G, a male interviewer "lets pass" with acknowledgment tokens, rather than requesting further details, e.g. What kind of infection? Was it a venereal or sexually transmitted infection?

An additional feature of this segment is that G attempts to re-frame B's animus towards J the group home parent. G, notes, "well it sounds like she's also partially responsible for you, isn't she". G's intervention follows after B's listing of troubles in the home "like one of us got an infection", "and one of us came home drunk, an she pissed her pants", "an one of us uhm, ended up in the hospital, an that was me". In his position as a social worker and interviewer G plays on B's admission of troubles to indicate that the group home parent, as the responsible adult really doesn't have a choice but to take responsibility, and to try to eliminate the problematic and potentially dangerous behaviours of the young women in the home. B responds to G's reframe through a simple acknowledgment token – somewhat reluctantly – which leads G to try a tactic of spreading the blame, acknowledging B's anger towards J, and suggesting, "maybe she's not reachin out to you in a way that, in a way that works".

G's re-frame for troubles is implicit, and likely informed by his position as a social worker, and understanding the imperative to do counselling and professional social work. At the centre of this work is helping B to move away from simply blaming J to seeing her responsibility for J's actions. The problems in the relationship between B and the group home parent are explained not in terms of the malevolence or evil intention of the parent, but as issues of the parent's ability to reach out "in a way that works". G's proposal is designed not only to elicit information, but as Buttny observes in an analysis of talk between therapists and clients, "the therapist tells the clients things about themselves, not solely to elicit information, but also to suggest, propose, or open up the clients to different ways of seeing their circumstances" (1996:128). B recognises the re-frame, but indicates her uncertainty that it is correct. She signals her right to hold to her version, to resist – albeit weakly – and to respond, "I don' know". She next provides additional information to support her version of the problematic behaviour by the group home parent, "she's like wrote down ..."

This segment demonstrates the ways that the interviewer shapes the topic according to the background imperatives of professional work, namely to help clients to understand situations that move them past blame towards accepting responsibility for their own actions. The interviewer is not necessarily wedded to the explanation, as it is proffered in a manner that suggests or opens up for consideration potentially novel understandings. The re-frame is offered to expand a repertoire of possible explanations for conflict in such a way that B does not feel bound to accept it. Though B signals disagreement, G does not challenge this, but rather allows the proposition to 'sit there' and to percolate in the hope that B may at some time, either within the interview or later, examine its potential relevance. Importantly, this signals the tactical nature of interviews, in which an offer of a novel or different understanding is made, allowing that it might very well be rejected initially, but with the worker expecting that its novelty or challenge will in turn result in the client returning to the issue and the worker's interpretation. When B declines the explanation, G does not counter, but allows B to continue to enumerate grievances against the staff. Further interventions from G act as continuers for B's talk. By avoiding conflict over versions, G works to ensure that B will expand her talk about her experiences, while also recognising that he might have planted doubts, and seeds for new ways of sense making.

Topic drift and shading

Any given sequence of talk as it unfolds suggests numerous topics and direction. When analysing talk-in-interaction, it is essential that we recognise that, while a complete audio-recording of an interview might be in hand, reviewed using a transcriber, and transcribed into text, the ability to scan the transcribed text to search for topic is a post-facto artefact of the research work process. The complete interview was not available to the participants as they produced it as a moment in their lives. Rather, as Schegloff so ably recognises, "in real talk-in-interaction, coherence and topic must in the first instance be constructed into the talk and progressively realized, not found" (1990:54). In talk-in-interaction – in contrast to talk as transcribed and read – that which any individual's utterance is about needs to be realised through a turn by turn interaction system. The following segment displays the multiple ways that an utterance opens up both explicit and implicit shadings and drifts of topic.

J: Do you talk to your worker, A about how you are feeling?

K: I guess not, some things, yes.

J: Can you tell her how angry you are feeling?

K: I could tell her yah.

J: Would you bring up the subject?

K: I don't know, usually when I am there I don't think of it because A is kinda nice.

J: It sounds like you have some blanks you need filled in?

K: Yah.

J: Can A fill them in.

K: Yes, but I don't think it matters, because even if I did know it wouldn't change anything. I learned a lotta things by asking a lotta questions.

J: What does that mean?

K: They said that when we're under permanent care, I asked why and how, and everything, and it all came out then. But some things didn't. I don't think if I had asked a lotta questions it wouldn't have made any difference, but I asked a lot anyways.

J: So a couple years ago was the first time you knew about what transpired, about why you originally got otta the home?

K: yes.

J: Was that when you pieced it all together?

K: Yes.

The interview asks the question, "Do you talk to your worker, A about how you are feeling?", which can clearly be taken in two directions, that is to respond to the issue of talking to your worker, or to respond to the issue of feelings that get talked about. The duality of the question does in fact seem to produce some confusion, for K responds in a contradictory fashion, beginning, "I guess not, some things, yes."

In the next turn J, the interviewer, again seems to invoke both issues, "Can you tell her how angry you are feeling?" It is unclear whether K should be addressing the issue of telling the social worker, or her ability to speak about her anger. In her next turn K chooses to focus on the issue of talking to A, her social worker, by responding, "I could tell her yah", and this seems to be a resonant move for J, as it results in further enquiry into K's relationship with A. J asks, "Would you bring up the subject?" This question is obviously designed to tap into K's level of comfort talking to A. K responds, "I don't know, usually when I am there I don't think of it because A is kinda nice." Although K's characterisation of A as "kinda nice" does address the issue of K's relationship with A, in that it indicates that K sees A positively, somewhat paradoxically, it attributes K's uncertainty about talking to A, because she is "kinda nice". Indeed, one possible next response could have been to explore why being "kinda nice" made it difficult for K to discuss her problems. Is it because K thinks that if she complains to A that she will take it as personal criticism? Is it because K does not want to upset A? Is it because K does not want A to see how angry, and hence 'bad', she really is? However, J does not focus in on such issues, which as noted deserve greater exploration, and instead focuses on K's ability to talk to A, though she links the ability to talk to A to background issues about lack of information, "It sounds like you have some blanks you need filled in?"

In K's next turn she responds, "Yes, but I don't think it matters because even if I did know it wouldn't change anything. I learned a lotta things by asking a lotta questions", to which J asks, "What does that mean?" K then turns to the issue of how she came to be in permanent care. K's turn provides a remarkable transition point, as the focus on K's relationship with her social worker is displaced, as K announces "I don't think if I had asked a lotta questions it wouldn't have made any difference". In this single segment we see that the question of topic is exceedingly complex. Topic in talk skims over multiple dimensions of performance. For participants that which is said explicitly plays off against an implicit background of that which is not being said, e.g. why is the fact that the social worker is described as "kinda nice" relevant to whether or not K can talk to her? What work does K do in this characterisation of the social worker? How does K position herself as a person for J through such characterisations? When K indicates that she asks a "lotta questions" what is the intended portrait of self she produces for J?

Getting off troubling topics

Although social workers and interviewers may use the resource of asking questions to shape the unfolding and direction of the interview, precisely because interviewees are not passive, interviews will quite predictably move in directions not preferred by the interviewer. Rather routinely within interviews, responses open up potential topics and trajectories either implicit or explicit, which can cause considerable trouble for the interviewer. For example, Gail Jefferson notes that Sacks outlined that some topics are so embarrassing or controversial that the participants have "to do getting off of them" (Jefferson, 1984:191). In the following segment, the youth continually returns to the issue of her love for her boyfriend while the social worker appears to want to move onto the warranted topics covered in the Interview Guide (see Chapter 5):

SW: Do you remember how you felt when you first came in?
S: scared=
SW: =mmhuh=
S: =very scared. Uhmm my fiancé, Nat (X), he ah, he wanted te come with me to the foster home and that. I.I tried to get him to come, I wanted him to come so bad, they said "no", that he had ta like separate from me at the school=
SW: =mmhuh=
S: =and uh, I cried real hard=
SW: =mmhuh

S: I had a very hard time because he ((clears throat)) was more like my life-
   line↑, like he was helping me=

SW: =mmhuh=

S: through this. He was the only one that was there fer me, and they were
   taking me away from that and it..it hurt=

SW: =mmhuh

S: It hurt a lot but . . . initially I know, that it was fer my own good, to jist get
   away from everybody at the time so:↓o.

SW: How long didja end up stayin at Hilda's?

S: Uhm:mm, abou↑t three months=

SW: mmhuh

S's response to the social worker's enquiry about her feelings when coming
into care is to talk about the pain she felt at being separated from her boyfriend, Nat X. S claims that this experience caused her considerable emotional turmoil and pain, "I wanted him to come so bad", "and uh, I cried real
hard", "it hurt ... It hurt a lot". Throughout repeated confessions of deep
pain, the social worker's only audible response is the repetition of the
acknowledgment token "mmhuh".

Of course, it is fairly easy to imagine other interventions that the social
worker might have made. She could have asked for more details about the
relationship with the boyfriend, that is its duration, its intensity, whether it
was sexual, the sorts of activities they engaged in together, and so on. Similarly, she could have explored the issue of the young woman's pain, and could
have asked where she cried, when, and whether or not anyone was available to
help her during this period. Further, she could have explored the kinds of
thoughts which elicited crying, the sorts of thoughts she entertained to ease
her pain, and so on. Yet, such detailed exploration is passed over, with the
effect that S's story is allowed to stand as an adequate representation of
"feelings" on coming into care.

Finally, the social worker effects a move off the topic of the boyfriend by
selecting a topic suggested in S's narrative, that is the foster home. The social
worker asks, "SW: How long didja end up stayin at Hilda's?", to which S
responds, "Uhm:mm, abou↑t three months=". By raising a question about
Hilda's the social worker shifts the focus from the "heart of the matter" to an
"ancillary" concern (Jefferson, 1984:202), that is S's experience of living in the
foster home. The link to an ancillary concern enables the social worker to
move towards discussion of other matters, while at the same time
demonstrating attention and respect for S's local concern about life in the
foster home.

Working through difficult/taboo issues

Social workers often need to help clients to address extremely traumatic and
difficult issues in their lives (Saxe, Ellis, & Brown, 2016; Prock, 2015). Social

workers appreciate that sexual matters, notably abuse, sexuality, and sexual practices and preferences potentially comprise a field of trauma and often unresolved emotional troubles. In the following segment, a teenage girl describes the events preceding coming into care:

W: And what happened when they {{L's family}} called?
L: Well the police had told them ok keep her there, make sure she don't go
   nowhere ah the social worker came, we talked and I told her wha everything
   what happened happened, that this man had had ra:a↑ped me an, an things
   like that. We went to court, an:d my mom beat me, a:nd I described what
   the- she used, she hit me with a board, umm she smacked me=
W: mmhuh
L: all over different places, a::nd . . . . [hhhheh]
W: [you're doing fine] no that's what we want to hear is is=
L: =uhm=
W: =is how it was for yo:[u]
L: [hhh] (exhale)
W: . . . so when you were eleven di you go into care at that time.
L: yep

In this sequence the issues of emotional trouble is signified at different levels, that is most obviously through content, but also through tone, hesitation, repetitions, and laughter.[3] As the talk about rape and beating unfolds the social worker attempts to reinforce the ongoing production of the narrative, through the use of an 'acknowledgment token' in the form of a continuer, i.e. mmhuh. The interviewer recognises that the material following her continuer has created difficulty for the teen, and responds to this difficulty by offering, "[you're doing fine] no that's what we want to hear is is … is how it was for you". Closer attention to this single utterance provides a fascinating view into the dynamics of eliciting talk about trauma and trouble.

First, social workers understand that rape and beatings are fundamentally traumatic events occasioned with physical and emotional pain, both at the time of the event itself, and in subsequent moments of recollection and telling. The eliciting of memory of the abuse and violation of oneself re-occasions and elicits, albeit as therapeutically supported and mediated, elements of the emotional trauma and hurt. The difficulty facing an interviewer is being able to balance the evocation of hurt, and the need to respond supportively, against a variety of competing demands. These include, ensuring that the interview proceeds according to a professionally appropriate purpose. Thus, the interview is not simply about a worker's curiosity, or about developing a friendship with the teen, or allying with the teen to attack her family. Rather, a professional mandate and orientation in child protection requires that the social worker engage the teen with an objective of ensuring that the teen emerges at the end of the interview without 'damage', and indeed as stronger for having participated. It is easy enough to imagine that evocation of such past pain and trauma could leave a client feeling unable to continue, being overwhelmed by memory, sobbing uncontrollably, and refusing to go on. In such an event the social worker could be deemed to have been remiss for failing to help the client work through, recognise, and move through her pain.

Talk about sexual issues, notably sexual assault or rape, is recognised as highly sensitive material. As Shulman (2016) observes, sex is a taboo area, and we know that sexual assault and sexual abuse of children are especially so. For generations talk about sexual abuse of children was deeply transgressive. Today while we can speak about sexual abuse of children such discussions are understood to be emotionally volatile and likely traumatic for victims. Implicit in the worker's response is the recognition that the taboo, stigma, and shame surrounding sexual abuse are relevant for this client. When the worker says, "[you're doing fine] no that's what we want to hear is is ... is how it was for you", she signals that, even if the client might have been told by family and friends, or might herself think that it is not okay to talk about being 'raped', that it is okay to talk about it. Indeed, the social worker's 'no' signals a contradiction of an implicit, and unstated understanding of reticence, that was likely read from the shape of the client's utterances, and of course the young woman's body gestures (body language) which are unseen and inaccessible from an audio-recording.

A detailed examination of this seemingly simple intervention/segment by the social worker reveals a surprising nesting of multiple dimensions and multiple sensitivities and understandings. This segment provides a clear window for viewing the complex reflexivity of talk-in-interaction necessary for producing an interview as such, between a social worker and a client. In this segment trouble is not just produced by the client, but is co-produced by the worker, who signals that trouble is expected given the nature of the content. Even though the client did not say, "I don't know if you want me to talk about these matters.", or "I don't think it's okay to talk about being raped and beaten", the worker's 'no' not only acknowledge such potential and likely background thoughts. Against closure, the worker sets into place permission, encourages, invites, and creates a space and an opening for the youth to provide tellings about highly personal and sensitive events in her life. The social worker enjoins the client in the special moment of an interview, to work with her to give voice against conventional prohibitions. Further, the 'no' signals that although such taboos or prohibitions against such talk may normally be in place, they are to be disregarded here, in this interview as, "no that's what we want to hear is is ... is how it was for you". Through these moves the social worker both signals and creates the functional nature of the interview as different from, and governed by different expectations, conventions, and rules than those that apply in an ordinary conversation with a family or friend.

The youth, L, signals to the worker that this is a difficult narrative to produce through a number of different cues. First, she stumbles and repeats the word, "happened happened", thereby demonstrating some level of hesitation and discomfort. Then she signals, through the specification of content, "this man had raped me and things like that"; "we went to court"; "my mom beat me"; and "she hit me with a board", that she is prepared to trust the worker enough to share such potentially stigmatising, taboo, and emotionally painful memories. Finally, she signals her discomfort both through pausing, considering next offerings, and through laughter.

Controlling the order of the story

A challenge facing an interviewer is to acquire a coherent sense of a youth's story during the interview. The problem we all face when producing stories of our lives is delivering them in such a way that others can follow. As we meet with friends to talk about events in our lives we orient ourselves to relevant, and often context dependent themes. If we are talking to a friend while in a queue, surrounded by others waiting to get in to see a play, our talk will most likely be different from that produced sitting in a private living room on a couch, reminiscing about 'old times'. When we engage in talk-in-interaction with another we are unavoidably oriented to preferred ways of presenting self, the unfolding reading of the dynamics of this interactive relationship, and to our own preferences and perseverations for certain themes, level of detail, length of turns at talk, and so on.

Similarly, as youth enter into interviews they weigh out the forms for delivery of their story. Is their story to be ordered by topical themes such as violence, hatred of life in care, family disruption, and so on, or by chronological sequence. How can they make the interviewer understand the key themes, that which matters, and that which they think is important in their lives? Should they even bother to invest the energy needed to share their story with the interviewer? Who and what are the relevances for the story? Is there a focus on family actors, mothers, fathers, brothers, sisters, and so on, or on social workers and friends? How much detail about events should be provided? How can the story be developed to sustain the story teller's interest as well as the interest of the listener?

In the following segment the interviewer attempts to elicit from a teenage girl what might count as a coherent story about coming into care. The worker attempts to order the flow of the narrative by setting limits on the delivery of the story, that is by deferring what is recognised as an extended narrative on "really bad experiences".

SW: okay, uhm, so you grew up on..the island.
S: Yah, I actually, I never lived past (XX) er whatever, like I never was on YY and that, but then when I moved te foster care I was kinda scared, cause they sent me up there with, and I was crying te go home cause I was so far way from home, and then I got inta bad experiences when I lived up there. Really bad experiences=
SW: =okay=
S: =when I was living on YY Island and stuff.

SW: I definitely want te get to those, I jist wanna figure out how you ended
    up, sorta, what was happening, you were ten when you, nine or ten.
S: Yep, sorta.
SW: What was happening in your life that sorta ended up=
S: =Uh[mm]
SW: [end]ed up in care=
S: =my mom was goin around with an idiot that really I really hate, Joe Z. He
    was really mean man, he was like hittin my mom an stuff, at the time,
    and he was in jail, and he never told me he was in jai.er, got outta jail,
    stuff, so. They sent me up there and I was like scared, I though I'd never
    see my mom again. I wasn't seeing my//mom
SW: So did they send ya up because of him, or [because of yer mom?]
S: [I don' know] my mom said that, but I don't believe her at all either=
SW: =was he hurting you.

In this sequence the social worker seeks to explore general background
information, that is where S "grew up", with the intention of exploring how S
"[end]ed up in care". In opening up this topic of growing up in a certain place
the social worker relies on a complex background series of understandings for
assessing transiency, disruption, to determine whether or not she grew up on
"the island". This query then elicits a detailed response about moving to
strange and unfamiliar places which made S feel "kinda scared" and "I was
crying te go home cause I was so far way from home." This leads S to recol-
lect, "and then I got inta bad experiences when I lived up there. Really bad
experiences." Though a narration about these "really bad experiences" is
relevant for S, and for the social worker, who indicates "I definitely want te
get to those", the social worker seeks to defer these narratives until she has
accomplished the task of determining how S came into care.

At the heart of the preceding segment is a puzzle. How can an interviewer
communicate respect for the client/interviewee who wishes to address the
concerns and preoccupations that matter to them, while working to ensure
that the interview produces a coherent story that is relevant to the purpose
and focus of the research? Interviewers encounter clients who are more or
less coherent in producing stories about their lives, more or less temporally
linear, more or less focused, more or less preoccupied by certain concerns
and issues, and more or less talkative etc. The youth in the preceding segment, S, tended to provide lengthy, detailed, if somewhat rambling responses
to questions. For her the interview was a welcome opportunity to tell her
story. The challenge facing the interviewer was to help S shape a narrating
of her experience such that it could be a coherent account of life in care.
Additionally, the interviewer needed to acknowledge that S was being heard,
while also redirecting her talk to coming into care, that is, "how you ended
up, sorta, what was happening".

The social worker's move to postpone the delivery of the story about 'really bad
experiences', by responding "I definitely want te get to those, I jist wanna figure

out ..." is rife with danger. S might refuse to return, later in the interview, to that which was detoured away from. She might think that the social worker is not interested in her experiences or her story. Or she might have felt 'shut down', taken offence and become more guarded. On the other hand, for S, the reference to 'really-bad experiences' signifies that something happened that was 'really-bad' hence patently remarkable, and worth telling. However, what is less clear is whether or not S, other than acknowledging that something really bad occurred, will be prepared to provide the details of a story about those experiences. For a social worker, the offering is both seductive, as it may elicit curiosity about those experiences, while also indicating a source of potential danger. The disclosure might require forms of action beyond a research interview, requiring relaying information to the youth's social worker or even to the police (Cohen, et al., 2006). Further, if S provides information which might lead the interviewer to believe that there continue to be significant issues of risk in S's life and that S might continue to be in danger, either to the possibility of re-victimisation or due to the effects of post-traumatic reactions, then the interviewer is required, by child protection law, to breach the confidentiality of the interview. Secondly, as S begins to recount painful and traumatic information, the concern emerges that recollection of painful memories, if previously not processed, may result in an uncontrollable emotional escalation, avoidance, or emotional shutting down, and/or withdrawal, which will of necessity require that the interviewer shift her role and direction, from conducting the interview, to providing emergency therapeutic intervention.

Conclusion

By exploring the use of topic as a resource for construction of interviews, this chapter has highlighted the interactive and power dynamics inherent in the construction of a youth's stories about being in care. Every account, whether in the natural sciences or the social sciences, relies on a repertoire of powers or abilities to employ theory, knowledge, and skills to craft the account. In their interactions with clients, whether in the form of the interviews for this research project, or in the form of their day-to-day work, social workers are required to adhere to choreographed forms of interaction. The choreography for their dance with clients is informed by the responsibilities of their office as child protection workers; the background demands of legislation; the organisation of their workday and routines; professional theories for ordering phenomena; and the imagery for doing an interview, or what we might call professional skills. Such restrictions on action are hardly accident, for they are referents to an actually existing socially organised world, whose contours while perhaps may be expressed in specific moments through language, are neither wholly expressed nor wholly defined in and through language. As Smith observes,

> Referring is not achieved wholly within language; beyond any given utterance, it relies on a differentiation in the world that is humanly discoverable and discriminable somehow or other. Referring is a social act in

which the category used by the speaker provides something like a set of instructions for the hearer to look for and recognise an object that can be treated as fitted to the category. The hearer may not be successful; she may get it wrong; or the instructions may be inaccurate and misdirect her. But a good map will tell the truth if we know how to read from it to the features it indexes (they become features in the reader's local practices of indexing) - the complex of differences between pavement and sidewalk, the lined-up houses, the street lights, the signs at the intersections -and how to carry on the dialogue it potentiates.

(1999:126)

Simply stated, the organisation of youth's stories about being in care emerge from out of a material world, with determinate contours, and which as such can be known and talked about, so that when a social worker provides a category such as "abuse", or "sexual abuse" the child can locate events in their life which match the category. Indeed, such acts of recognition and identification work to transform experiences into places of awareness and even resistance.

There is a determinate facticity to the accounts of youth's experiences of being in care. Their narratives, albeit interactively constructed, also point back to, and arise from out of a life course that is more than merely a narrative. Youth, along with their social workers attempt to make sense out of the dramatic and even traumatic events of their lives. They try to find the words to account for real pain, and real experiences of abuse, abandonment, and betrayal in their families of origin. At the same time social workers in their struggle to help youth develop stories about their lives that work for the youth, are constrained by the horizons of their own location inside, and unfortunately often absorbed by, the organisational action and discourse. Yet, it must be appreciated that while there are determinate choices to be made by social workers, in the work of helping a child to craft their story, different theoretical organisations for determining what matters in stories will produce different effects. Social workers and youth in care although at times working at cross purposes, inside relations of power, control, and authority, occasionally do manage to muddle through to produce an account of an experience which in naming sources of pain and hurt, provides a route for improved living.

Notes

1 There are contexts where those being asked a question are not expected to answer the question. Robert McNamara in the film Fog of War reflected on his experience as Secretary of Defense during the Kennedy and Johnson presidencies, and the troubles he faced when called to question by the press. His adage was, "Never answer the question that is asked of you. Answer the question that you wish had been asked of you."
2 "Holding the floor" need not mean talking, but rather can refer to the ability of the questioner to control the topic, and that which the other can talk about.

3 This interview was conducted by a research assistant who also did the transcribing. In the original transcription she described the laughter as anxious, i.e. (anxious laughter).

References

Bergmann, Jörg. (1995). Veiled morality: Notes on discretion in psychiatry. In Paul Drew & John Heritage (Eds.), *Talk at work: Interaction in institutional settings* (pp. 137–162). Cambridge, England: Cambridge University Press.

Buttny, Richard. (1996). Clients' and therapist's joint construction of the clients' problems. *Research on Language and Social Interaction*, 29(2): 125–153.

Button, Graham. (1992). Answers as interactional products: Two sequential practices used in job interviews. In Paul Drew & John Heritage (Eds.), *Talk at work: Interaction in institutional settings* (pp. 21–231). Cambridge, England: Cambridge University Press.

Cohen, Judith A., Mannarino, Anthony, & Deblinger, Esther. (2006). *Treating trauma and traumatic grief in children and adolescents*. New York, NY: Guilford.

Hak, Tony. (1995). Ethnomethodology and the institutional context. *Human Studies*, 18, 109–137.

Hepworth, Dean H., Rooney, Ronald H., & Larsen, Jo Ann. (2002). *Direct social work practice: Theory and skills* (6th ed.). Pacific Grove, CA: Brooks Cole.

Jefferson, Gail. (1984). On stepwise transition from talk about a trouble to inappropriately next-positioned matters. In J. Maxwell Atkinson and John Heritage (Eds.), *Structures of social action: Studies in conversational analysis* (pp. 191–222). Cambridge, England: Cambridge University Press.

Levinson, Stephen C. (1995). Activity types and language. In Paul Drew & John Heritage (Eds.), *Talk at work: Interaction in institutional settings* (pp. 66–100). Cambridge, England: Cambridge University Press.

Prock, Lisa Albers. (2015). *Holistic perspectives on trauma: Implications for social workers and health care professionals*. Oakville, ON: Apple Academic Press.

Sacks, Harvey. (1995). *Lectures on conversation (Volumes 1 & 2)* (Ed. Gail Jefferson). Oxford, England: Blackwell.

Saxe, Glenn N., Ellis, B. Heidi, & Brown, Adam D. (2016). *Trauma systems therapy for children and teens* (2nd ed.). New York, NY: Guilford.

Schegloff, Emanuel A. (1990). On the organization of sequences as a source of "coherence" in talk-in-interaction. In Bruce Dorval (Ed.), *Conversational organization and its development*, (pp. 51–77). Norwood, NJ: Ablex.

Schegloff, Emanuel A. (2000). Overlapping talk and the organization of turn-taking for conversation. *Language in Society*, 29: 1–63.

Schegloff, Emanuel A. (1992). Repair after next turn: The last structurally provided defense of intersubjectivity in conversation. *American Journal of Sociology*, 97, #5: 1295–1345.

Schegloff, Emanuel, Jefferson, Gail, & Sacks, Harvey. (1977). The preference for self-correction in the organization of repair in conversation. *Language*, 53(2): 361–382.

Shebib, Bob. (2002). *Choices: Interviewing and counselling skills for Canadians* (2nd ed.). Toronto, ON: Prentice Hall.

Shulman, Lawrence. (2016). *The skills of helping individuals, families, groups, and communities* (8th ed.). Toronto, ON: Thompson Brooks Cole.

Smith, Dorothy E. (1999). *Writing the social: Critique theory and investigations*. Toronto, ON: University of Toronto Press.

5   It says here...

Techniques of textual absorption and resistance

This chapter explores the relationship between texts[1] and day-to-day social work practice. Initially, the focus is on social workers' largely instrumental approach to texts, as produced and guided by professional practice. Next, we shift focus to textual production as a form of practice for bridging local and extra-local, particular and universal, hence as expressing a dialectic. Then, we turn to examine the ways that social workers, who agreed to interview youths on their caseloads for the research project that informed this book, actually took up and applied an Interview Guide. By examining the artful ways that social workers reference the guide during interviews we can begin to detect the strategies, moves, and devices workers deploy, to present and to manage textual realities and documents in 'here-and-now' interactive encounters with clients. By focusing on social workers deployment of the Interview Guide we can glimpse the ways that social workers 'work' or realise textually mediated realities (Smith, 1990a) as present in their day-to-day practice with clients.

As already noted, this book grew out of a research project that aimed to explore the experiences of youth when coming into and being in care. In addition to the interviews conducted by the research team, we also recruited a small number of social workers to interview youths on their caseloads. When listening to and transcribing the interviews conducted by social workers, it became evident that they deployed skilful and strategic practices for referencing and working with the Interview Guide, which I as a former front-line social worker recognised as similar to the moves I had made to bridge and manage documents in face-to-face work with clients. By analysing transcripts produced from the audio recordings of the interviews conducted by social workers, I will identify and explore the artful practices in their repertoire for reading, interpreting, and applying texts in their work with clients.

The instrumental text

Social workers are required to be both producers and users of various texts, whether legislation, policy manuals, standardised records, and so on. They have long understood the importance of generating case records and ensuring that those records, when read and reviewed by supervisors and managers, warrantably demonstrate the worker's adherence to recognisable regulations and policies. In the main social work theorists, when addressing documents and texts, have focused primarily on the instrumental dimensions of record keeping, that is the 'how to', selection and tone of writing, the institutional organisation of records, and issues of confidential storage (Kagle, 2008; Prince, 1996; Little, 1995; Timms, 1972). The focus has been on development of the skills and protocols needed to ensure the production of good or adequate recordings, professional assessments of client problems, confidentiality of recordings, safe and secure storage, the ethics of information storage, and so on. For example, Ames, after having outlined the centrality of records for social work practice argues that recording needs to be integrated into social work curriculum, to address, "improving basic writing skills" (1999: 232), "learning information-gathering techniques" (233), "helping students understand the importance of recording in social work practice" (233), "familiarizing students with forms and formats" (233), "applying recording skills" (233). Similarly, social workers have examined records and issues of bias and reliability (Holbrook, 1983), ethics risk (Cumming et al., 2007; Reamer, 2001, Wilson, 1978; Prochaska, 1977), and client access (Abel & Johnson, 1978). Indeed, social workers have been rightly concerned about the ethics of record keeping, especially unanticipated future and prejudicial use of records, potential negative effects for clients, and the potential for violation of confidentiality and privacy. For example, a fascinating paper from Australia examined the reactions to their personal records by adults who had left care.

> Some of the participants experienced great distress about the language that had been used about them, their parents or other family members. Years – sometimes decades – later these insulting remarks continued to anger and upset them. Others found information that was incorrect, and again this could cause great distress. Sometimes the detail of the inaccuracies themselves were less concerning than what they symbolised – a complete disregard for them as individuals and a lack of care.
>
> (Murray & Humphreys, 2014:220)

Such studies underscore the ways that recording is not just a bureaucratic function distinct from face-to-face work with clients. Additionally records are recognised as expressing the social worker's own "values, attitudes and needs" and that records provide a tool for reflecting on their professional practice (Blake, 2010:1).

It should also be noted that record keeping and textually based activities come to absorb increasing proportions of social workers' working days (Fook & Gardner, 2007; Jones, 2001). The function of records for mitigating risk and liability, as well as for documenting the scope and nature of agency service and hence for securing agency funding and justifying budgets, has resulted in an increase rather than diminution of record keeping. Edwards and Reid (1989), writing in the previous era of 'paperwork' and records, examined the introduction of the Uniform Case Record (UCR) in New York child welfare agencies and found that "Workers reported spending almost 60 percent of their 40-hour workweek on paperwork" (50). Similarly, an Ontario Provincial Service Employee Union paper, 'Peoplework not Paperwork', found that 70% of front-line social workers' time was consumed doing "administrative" work (2001:3). Beyond the issues of time and the restructuring of a workday, the active work and process of articulating and producing practice records has profound epistemological effects on the accomplishment and accountability of front-line social work practice.

Textual practice

What remains largely unexamined are the epistemic foundations of practice as achieved and effected through textual representations and structuring. Even purportedly progressive texts ignore the interplay between texts, documents, and records and sense-making in front-line practice. The realities of institutional contexts, the demands for routine production of accounts and for accountability made manifest through documentary practices are systematically erased, ignored, and silenced, even surprisingly by radical, progressive, and anti-oppressive social work theorists. For example, though Mullaly in *Challenging Oppression and Confronting Privilege* (2018) addresses oppression at personal, cultural, and structural levels, he leaves unexamined the foundational relationship between a documentary articulation of state and organisational policies, the demand that social workers produce records of their services, and 'oppression'. This foundational relationship between social work records, sense making, and accounts and the organisation of state services is glossed and ignored. Mullaly's failure to examine records is replicated similarly by Fook in *Social Work: Critical Theory and Practice* (2001). Although Fook addresses 'contexts of practice' and 'contextual practice' she nevertheless manages to assiduously avoid addressing the routine demands faced by front-line practitioners to produce and to maintain documents and records. Similarly, in her earlier text *Radical Casework: A Theory of Practice* (1993) despite identifying the problem of "casework and social control" no attention was given to texts at all. Similarly, Leonard's *Postmodern Welfare: Reconstructing an Emancipatory Project* (1997), although addressing the effects of organisational location on practice, did so through a typically abstract Foucauldian analysis of discourse,[2] rather than through a detailed analysis of the production of 'texts' or practices for mediating 'textual realities' (Smith, 1990a). Unfortunately, although social workers may worry about negative effects on clients of bureaucratic demands, notably the trade-off between time spent with clients and time spent filling out forms, maintaining agency records, and filing reports, they have paid far less attention to the pervasive structuring effects of such texts on their practice.

While social workers in every-day talk may matter-of-factly describe their activities as guided, directed, shaped, controlled, and determined by various texts, just how they make texts do this work itself needs to be the object of enquiry. Working with and through texts becomes part of the taken-for-granted fabric of front-line practice. Therefore exploring how such work is practically accomplished is an essential moment for understanding the relationship between texts and professional practice (de Montigny, 1995; Smith, 1990b). It is clear that social workers readily adopt language that attributes agency to texts, hence, "the legislation defines child abuse as", "policy demands that we file a report within 24 hours", "child protection protocols guide our practice", and so on. What such nominalised transformations (Kress & Hodge, 1979) gloss, or conceal, are the practical activities that social workers engage in to perform a text, as a working tool, in hand, as read, mentally processed, understood, effected, and represented in turns at talk.

An examination of work-place texts reveals the dynamic relationship between writers – whether policy makers or researchers – and professional readers, such a social workers. Paré urges that we "think of writers, readers, and texts not as objects or discrete entities but as sets or structures of relations" (Paré, 1991:50). It follows then that the interviews are not simply an object as recorded and in hand, but express far more complex sets of relationships between researcher and social workers, social workers and employer, social workers and profession, and so forth. The interviews produced for the research project by virtue of being audio-recorded are in fact 'authored'. While they may not have been produced in an immediate 'textual' form, they were produced as destined for transcription and for textual representation. Understanding the interviews as 'authored' allows us to apply Olson's analysis that:

> When creating a piece of discourse, an author—especially a successful author—considers the discourse community or audience for the discourse; tries to tailor the discourse to the needs, values, assumptions, conventions, and expectations of the community; and is judged as successful partly in relation to the extent to which the discourse community has been satisfied.

> (1993:188)

What emerges is an acute sense of the interviews as a performance directed to an anticipated audience and thereby intended to demonstrate competency, and warrantability as a piece of professional social work.

A central question guiding the analysis which follow is dialectical, i.e. how do social workers read, translate, and apply texts – written as universal guides to practice – to specific and contingent situations at hand? I will argue that the techniques social workers used in the interviews conducted for this research project draw from the general repertoire of techniques they use to perform their day-to-day work. Pare's observations about professional social work writing hold equally for 'interviewing', as "discourse regulations do influence and the composition and interpretation of texts, and therefore the thinking of community members" (Paré, 1993:122–123).

By turning to the transcripts of audio-recorded interviews I will draw out the repertoire of practices social workers employ to realise the text in, through, and as an interview. Paradoxically, to perform an interview social workers not only accomplish the extra-local and universalised authority of the text in a local space, they simultaneously perform both their location in and conformity to such universalised discourses, as well as accomplishing the artfulness and sympathy of their individual practice to the contingencies of the situation at hand. As Smith observes, "The realities to which action and decision are oriented are virtual realities vested in texts and accomplished in distinctive practices of reading and writing. We create these virtual realities through objectifying discourse; they are our own doing" (Smith, 1990b:62).

On the one hand the practices social workers used to make the Interview Guide visibly present in interviews with youth in care are also employed to produce an institutionally present, governable, and governed reality, yet on the other hand, these practices, when artfully and skilfully executed, produce a social worker's individuality as a competent professional. Through such mundane practices social workers accomplish organisational power as concrete, incarnate, and locally realised, while simultaneously realising their own autonomy, integrity, and professional self-identification. Whether social workers made the Interview Guide present in hand, crinkled, flipped through the air, searched for, talked about, read out loud, or indirectly referenced through memory, they re-produced the authority of the text, both as visible and invisible presence. Thus, the warrantability of the occasioned interaction between social worker and child or youth as an interview relied on the constitution of a verisimilitude with the text. By examining such discrete practices for reproducing a text both as in hand and in memory, this chapter unpacks the contours of struggle situated at the interstices of universalised organisational conformity and situated and locally realised autonomy.

It is worth noting that a detailed examination of social worker's use of texts in actual practice provides a corrective to the rather one-sided and negative portrayals of professional practices as necessarily oppressive or controlling. For example, in his examination of what he calls "bureaucratic subsidizing", Burman argues that, "The concrete individual—with his or her motivations, formative contexts, narrative history, standpoint—is not really present at the Welfare interview" (1996:93). Now, while I am sympathetic with Burman's poetic identification of an erasure of clients by universalised enactments of regulations, it must be recognised that the job of a skilful worker is to translate the unique client situations, motivations, contexts, and history into universalised categories and structures of a welfare application. While there is a poetic evocation of the claim that subjectivity is erased in the encounter with a bureaucratic monolith, there remains nevertheless a trace of the subject. Agency documents are a palimpsest written over the lives of clients. Indeed, as I shall argue, skilled social workers effect alliances with clients to simultaneously absorb and signal resistance of the erasures of categorical and universalist policies. A close look at social workers' work with and through texts reveals a much more complex and nuanced play inside, across, and outside the spaces of power.

The textually mediated interview

To prepare the social workers who agreed to participate in the research project, I met with them to discuss the research objectives, methodology, and analytic framework. I presented the social workers with a copy of the five page project description I had submitted to the Social Science and Humanities Research Council (SSHRC) for funding, a two page set of instructions for interviewers, and an Interview Guide (reprinted here in Appendix A) outlining issues and questions to address when meeting with youth in care.

The Interview Guide addressed what for social workers are generally considered to be the major issues surrounding the processes of coming into and being in care. During orientation meetings I outlined that "there are no surprises in the Interview Guide" as it addressed familiar issues for social workers doing child protection. I also suggested that there was no need to bring the Interview Guide into the room when they interviewed a youth, as it was more important to allow the youth to focus on issues that they felt were important. I indicated that I would prefer that they use their relationship with, and knowledge of the youth to identify and explore what they and the youth felt to be the significant issues. I explained that I trusted that the social workers would be able to develop a dialogue with the youth around the identified topics, to thereby explore pertinent dimensions, e.g. feelings when coming into care, perceptions of the process of coming into care, perceptions of the people involved with their 'case', and so forth.

The Interview Guide originated in my own background knowledge as a front-line child protection worker. It was passed on to social workers in briefing meetings about the research project where I provided it in the form of a photocopy. This document, along with a set of instructions to social workers (see Appendix A) was developed to provide only the most general form of direction to social workers when meeting with youth in care. The development of the Interview Guide was informed by two quite distinct trajectories. First, in order for my research project to receive Research Ethics Board approval, I was required to set out the substance and order of interviews with youth by presenting the Board with a copy of an Interview Guide. Second, quite separately, I had hoped that by developing the Interview Guide, it would help social workers to address some core issues youth face when coming into and living in care. My sense was that the guide would serve as a heuristic and mnemonic device. Indeed, I was extremely reluctant to create a fixed interview structure, preferring instead to elicit the frameworks and categories youth and social workers doing child protection work believed to be paramount.

Despite my instructions, most social workers not only routinely brought the guide into the interview rooms, but actively used it to direct their interviews with youth. At first this puzzled me. However, when reflecting on this apparent transgression, I realised that I had inadvertently structured a task that replicated day-to-day work. Simply, I had asked social workers to engage youth as directed and guided by a document or text. Once the social workers agreed to participate in the research project and to conduct the interviews, they understood that the Interview Guide would be a useful tool for doing the work. Rather than rely on memory, or engage in an ad hoc and unstructured encounter, the guide provided some measure of order, direction, and even safety.

Furthermore, as a tool the Interview Guide provided social workers with a reference point. It provided organisation, direction, and a sense of control or foreknowledge over what would unfold. The Interview Guide as a document in hand provided a point of reference such that what might unfold could more easily be warranted and sustained as an interview. Lipsky (1980) writing about street level bureaucrats, including social workers, observed, "The most important aspects of interactions with clients are those affecting the structure of the interactions: when they will take place, with what frequency, under what circumstances, with what resources commanded by the parties" (1980:61). By using documents or texts to structure interaction social workers can control that which occurs interactively. Now it must be noted that 'control' need not be treated as abusive or authoritarian, but rather as an expression of an imperative to perform interactively as warrantably and accountably professional.

Indeed, to conduct an 'interview' is to engage in a controlled interactional process such that what unfolds can be upheld both presently and retrospectively as properly such. This mundane imperative became emphasised and accentuated by the simple fact that social workers, when engaging with youth in care, audio-recorded their interactions and submitted these to the researcher, who had informed them that the interviews would be transcribed and used for research purposes. Understood in this light possession and application of the Interview Guide provided social workers with a tool that could be invoked as needed to ensure a verisimilitude between an idealisation of an 'interview' expressed in the text, and the actual unfolding of interaction between the social worker and the youth. Whether the Interview Guide was enlisted as a text in hand or as a guide resting in memory, it provided social workers with a point of reference through which they could fulfil their promise to participate in the research by conducting interviews with youth in care.

Furthermore, the provision of an Interview Guide replicated the task structure of day-to-day work in which social workers meet clients inside the terrain of getting some piece of documentary production completed.[3] Social workers routinely employ such documents as guides to follow when performing any number of activities, including assessments of various situations – foster homes, adoption homes, children's homes, parenting skills, presenting problems, risk factors – as well as applying for services – child care workers, referral to treatment facilities, allowances, etc. The dilemma facing social workers is similar to that of other workers in situations of alienated labour, that is, how can the tools and productive forms developed by managers or authoritative others be implemented through workers' actual practices, while preserving their own identity and integrity? How can workers' transcend the alienation inherent in carrying out the orders, directives, and dictates of others?

The challenge social workers face is to apply texts to the situation at hand in a manner that subverts the authority of the text, such that the social worker is able to recover a sense of her own integrity and presence as an actor/subject in the interchange. By delivering the Interview Guide to social workers I recreated the dynamic of external direction of situated practice. This is a dynamic which demands strategies for effecting compliance to direction through intentional shaping of one's own activities to make them warrantably concord with anticipated and expected forms. A social worker's activities must be shaped as oriented to and expressive of the forms prescribed by documents. Yet, this must be effected to avoid appearing mechanical, robotic, scripted, and not genuine. The imperative to appear genuine, and authentic (Kadushin & Kadushin, 2013) demands that social workers struggle to work in ways that communicate to clients that they are not just working, following orders, being bureaucrats, or automatons in institutional systems.

Yet, the requirement that practice be oriented to documents poses a threat to the imperative to appear genuine. The universal quality of a document, as posing questions before and outside the context of interaction, to be ordered into standardised textual formats, to present lists of questions, to identify different categories of people, and so on, can easily vitiate the imperative that the worker be present, genuinely engaged, and attentive to this individual client. Even when orienting their work to a text and even when following the orders of questions in an Interview Guide, the challenge for social workers is to establish a distance between themselves and the text. It is in the spaces of this distance that a social worker displays her genuine humanity, her caring, her attention to this particular client, and accordingly an alliance with the client in and against the text.

Social workers employ a variety of seemingly contradictory devices to differentiate between themselves and textually organised projects. For example, a social worker might review a text before an interview with the aim of memorising its major points – or they may have memorised the main dimensions or topics through repeated use – so that when they enter the interview they can ask questions without seeming to be relying on a text. In the latter case the text is hidden, and if the social worker is skilful it may even seem to a client that the questions the social worker asks are simply a logical response to the flow of the interview. In this sense, questions appear as seamlessly woven into the topics of the conversation. Another strategy, which at first sight seems to be contradictory with respect to the relationship to the text, is for the social worker to make his or her use of the text visible for the client. Social workers do this by putting the text on the table in clear view, picking up the text, and reading from the text. Yet, both strategies, if performed skilfully, can serve to effect a differentiation between the social worker and the text while simultaneously establishing a sense that it is the worker and not the text which is directing the interview.

In the sections that follow, I will examine in detail some extracts from interviews that demonstrate such different strategies for managing the text. These range from the very obvious use of the text as a tool in hand, which can be read either silently or out loud, to the more covert invocations of an absent text through memory. The analysis which follows will begin with the most transparent manifestations, moving progressively to more tangential and veiled reference to the text where only a thin trace[4] is evident in the unfolding of the interview.

Reading from the text

When I transcribed the sequence below, it was clear to me as a reader that the social worker was performing as a transparent matter a reading from the text.

SW: uhm, okay. Describe each placement to the best of your ability. Focus on what you like or disliked about the placement. What made this placement enjoyable or difficult?
O: I've already explained that=
SW: =You've already explained that?
O: The ups and downs and all that?
SW: How have you changed since being in care?

The transparency of reading was evident as a result of the word by word correspondence to the Interview Guide. It read:

> Describe each placement to the best of your ability. Focus on what you liked or disliked about the placement. What made this placement enjoyable or difficult (e.g., other children, the condition of the house, the food, entertainment, the neighborhood, etc.)? ...
> How have you changed since coming into or being in care?
> (Appendix A).

Yet beyond the simple correspondence of words, it was evident through the audio-recording that the social worker was reading the text. Indeed, the social worker signalled her shift from having a conversation to reading from the text through a series of performance moves. By using the break marked by the "uhm, okay" followed by a marked shift in tone and voice modulation she engaged in speaking practices that I, and others as competent speakers and readers, readily recognise as reading. It is also necessary to recognise that in that moment of reading, the social worker must have picked up the document – the audio records a crackle of paper – and in view of the youth, fixed her gaze to it and read out loud the words of the text. When considering this, it makes sense to speak of the social worker's practice as a reading performance. By picking up the document, and by reading it, she obviously and intentionally signals to the youth that she is changing the register of the interaction. Though they are talking here-and-now, this present becomes a performance scripted and bridged to the relevances, orders, and intentions of a document, which originated elsewhere outside this moment. The turn to reading, and its performance, signals entry into activity that is not immediately focused and located in the interview. Reading bridges this moment with the structures of institutional order, time, and locations.

By performing a transparent reading, or by transparently reading, the social worker simultaneously establishes a separation from the text. Thus, she is here, visible, and present, and there is the text, which her reading displays, as implicitly demanding that she reads it, to do the work in this moment. By reading, the social worker shares a structured design expressed in the order of words in the text, which simultaneously, and paradoxically, signal a dissonance and distance. This enables her to display both work and play in the unfolding of the interview. Reading allows the social worker to treat the text as an artefact. Its physical presence reveals, that it is from another time. It was produced elsewhere. The questions which were read, in turn speaks to the demand of the text, and behind that, the demand of its author, for a reading, hearing, and orientation. Yet, even in invoking these demands of text and author, embedded in and through the text, the social worker acknowledges that there is still this here and now with this youth, this relationship, and the primacy of this moment. Thus while the text is to be followed, there is also this place and time together outside the text. By performing a reading of the question, the social worker establishes a complicity, and an invitation to the youth, to join with her in the exercise of answering the text. The social worker implicitly signifies her willingness to join with the youth in a mutual task of not only managing the text, but by playing with its authority, topical constructions, and mechanistic definition of issues, transcending the text and valorising the face-to-face encounter at hand.

By reading from the text, reviewing an area that had already been "explained" the social worker produces the otherness of the text, as a mechanical tool insensitive to their talk. Indeed, it follows that both the social worker and the youth need to ally against the incoherence that adherence to the text would produce. Yet, in the disturbance of referencing the text, the social worker constructs a paradoxical situation in which the occasion at hand appears both as a piece of work and as promising something other than work. Successful execution of an interview effects that semblance of an erasure of the text and its externality, and an affirmation of the importance of the immediate moment, the subject positions of the participants, and their reciprocal involvement in a moment of caring. Yet, the affirmation of a relationship beyond the text is but a semblance for the text whether in the form of an Interview Guide, child and family service legislation, or agency protocols, remains as a (viral) presence, which for the social worker must shape the form of the practice that unfolds if it is to be sustained as properly social work, professional, and skilful. The paradox the social worker faces arises from the circularity of what Garfinkel has called the documentary method of interpretation (1967), or what Smith has called an ideological circle. Smith observed:

> An interpretive schema is used to assemble and provide coherence for an array of particulars as an account of what actually happened; the particulars, thus selected and assembled, will intend, and will be interpretable by, the schema used to assemble them. The effect is peculiarly circular.
>
> (1990a:104)

The invocation of the text not only marks off what is transpiring as not a routine conversation, but sets into place a series of practices for discovering particulars through the application of discursive schema. Thus, what emerges as the child's story is itself discursively organised by the schema, or topics made available through the discourse and the text.

Through the obvious reading of the text at this moment the social worker establishes that what she is doing is reviewing their work together, at this point in the interview, essentially in light of the text, to which O replies, "I've already explained that", eliciting in turn the social worker's confirmation, "You've already explained that". Through this move the social worker transforms the present moment as answerable to the structure of the text and simultaneously elicits and elides the dissonance between her own and the child's desires and the intensions expressed in the text.

The problem of accomplishing an interview that appears motivated by the warmth of human engagement and concern rather than the cold rationality of textual determination and indifference is a continual puzzle facing front-line practitioners. Skilled social workers become rather adept at constructing a location outside and in opposition to texts. The social worker we encountered above employed a familiar and effective stratagem for creating distance from the text. Consider the following:

SW: That..I think, that's the interview. I think what he really wants though..he didn't want us to go through and read through that list of questions, and have you say, yes no to questions. It was more ah: (throat clearing). Now that you sorta know, what the..the questions are, is there anything that you want them to know about being a kid in care.

O: Uhm, its really, really hard for youth in care. Its really, really, really hard, cause if you look..I was good kid before I went into care, and when I was in care, I was a bad kid the whole time. The whole time I was in care I was a bad kid e::yshh

The social worker surely recognises that I will, when listening to the audio-recording of the interview, encounter this passage referencing the nature of my directions. Although as noted above the social worker did repeatedly read from the list of questions, however, she did so in such a fashion that O did not merely produce "yes no to questions". Indeed, the social worker's suggestion at the start of the interview, "So O's going to tell you her story", had obviously been fulfilled by the point the above quote occurred fully half an hour later.

In reviewing this passage, the question is whether the social worker was aware of the tension between her sense that, "He didn't want us to go through and read through that list of questions", and the fact that she did read the questions, albeit, not as a list, nor as eliciting a simple series of "yes no answers". This passage appears to do two things. First, the social worker 'excuses' her reading of questions, indirectly asserting that she did not simply read from the list. Further, even when she did read, such reading was blended with an extended and skilfully effected series of probing and follow up question. Thus reading was but a moment in a more extensive performance of excellent interviewing skills. Second, this passage signals that while the text may have provided for a list of questions, what really mattered was letting O tell her story. Indeed, I had insisted in my meetings with the social workers that a primary purpose of the research was to help the youth to tell their stories about coming into and living in care.

The social worker represents her action of reading the questions as but a strategy for letting the youth know "what the questions are". Thus, visibly and accountably reading provides a move for creating the sense that the social worker and the youth are working together with reciprocal knowledge in the enterprise of getting the story out. Reading from the text allows the youth to move beyond the questions to address "anything that you want them to know about being a kid in care". Curiously, this move also creates an opening for elaboration as it casts what has gone on before (13 pages of transcribed text) as preliminary.

There is also the possibility that the social worker by explicitly addressing the fact that "He didn't want us to go through and read through that list of questions" may be signalling a resistance to and defiance of my directives, to thereby simultaneously enlist the youth as a co-conspirator against the rules. This is a familiar social work tactic, as it positions the worker as an ally with a client, as resisting rules prescribed by invisible but nonetheless authoritative and powerful others. It creates a space for alliance, as both worker and client join to resist authority. This is both deliciously wicked and transgressive, as a social worker and a youth become co-conspirators against the dictates of anonymous others, who don't understand what we are doing together.[5] They signify their mutual resistance to the control of their interaction and their moment together by an external force. They signify that what transpires between them cannot be controlled, reduced, or perhaps even understood by a third party. Indeed, it is through such moves that skilled social workers enlist their clients in the social worker's projects, so that together, social worker and client address themselves to documents at hand, while simultaneously resisting the reduction of their work to outside authority. However, despite the positions of resistance, they nevertheless collude to work through the texts together. They are on the same side in the struggle to reclaim their own working space and to assert their living presence against the a-temporal, decontextualised spaces of the text.[6]

The social worker's conversion of the pronoun "he", in the first line, to "them" in the last line also warrants attention. While "he" obviously refers to my directions in our face-to-face meetings, the invocation of the plural "them" appears to reference a corporate other. If it holds that for social workers, as for all of us, that face-to-face disagreements and trouble are far more distasteful than disagreements with formal, corporate, and nameless others, then the social worker's move to invoke a corporate "them", against which the present interaction unfolds, provides a buffer for resistance. It transforms a face-to-face violation into the more familiar violations of corporate policies. The social worker's transformation of a specific "he" into a generalised "them" generates an ambiguity with respect to a controlling and authoritative other. A concrete "he" becomes an abstracted "them" and as such can be taken up into the standardised discourse of resistance to bureaucratic and organisational intrusion into ideally autonomous professional practice.

Transformations and improvisations

The Interview Guide given to the social workers asked that they explore the constellation of issues surrounding the effects of coming into care on family. For example the guide asked:

> d   What initial changes occurred between you and your family?
>   i.   How do you think coming into care affected your relationships with your parent(s), sibling(s), or other significant relatives?
>   v.   Did your parent(s) have access? Did your parent(s) visit?
>   vi. If he/she didn't visit what do you think prevented him/her from visiting?

When I developed the Interview Guide I attempted to anticipate a range of different situations, through the use of brackets to enclose the plural (s), to thereby accommodate situations where the child might not have two parents, more than one sibling, and so forth. Although the guide is written in the form of direct questions to the child, as noted it was anticipated that the actual wording social workers would employ to explore the areas of relations with parents would vary.

Before proceeding into an examination of the conversational extracts below it is necessary to point out that the Interview Guide by identifying "relationships with your parent(s) ..." simultaneously establishes a schema through which particulars can be elicited as sustaining the cogency of notions of family, normal families, dysfunctional families, and accordingly legitimisations of

Children's Aid Society interventions. In this way the Interview Guide is similar to agency documents, as it relies on "plain fact", that is the assumption of "accomplished-events-in-society" which can be referenced or produced on specific occasions to tie "the activity to a record-keeping enterprise" (Zimmerman, 1976). While I will touch on the circularity of such discursive constructions below, this will not be the centre of analysis, for I am more interested in how social workers actually manage the text in their day to day work, rather than the ideological effect of the texts on the topics of the talk.

The four extracts below, each conducted by a different social worker, reveal a preliminary range of artful applications and transformation of the text to the situation at hand. In these interviews there are no audible indications that the text was in hand, nor are there any transparent moments when the social worker can be heard to be reading the text. These interviews are marked by the appearance that the social workers were *speaking in their own voices*. Cicourel's analysis of physicians' interviews with patients applies equally well to interviews between social workers and youth in care, as "indirect, direct, leading or probe-like questions" are used to transform "the patient's responses into mental and/ or written general or specific categories or facts that might lend support to general or specific hypotheses ..." (1985:174). Although it may seem tautological, it follows that which is discovered in the interview is that which is discoverable given a professionally organised discursive horizon. That which is beyond the horizon is only available as a trace, discomfort, and disturbance.

In the following I will begin by presenting an extended transcribed extract concerning the question about contact with a parent. This extract was preceded by the social worker asking M "What would you have changed? If you had more control of the situation, what would you change?", which then prompted a discussion of the lack of privacy M experienced in a particular foster home, the problem with the foster parent searching her room for drugs as M had "done drugs in the past", a review of rights while in care, to a discussion of tensions with the foster parent when she stayed overnight with her boyfriend after staying up late playing cards:

M: uhmm..I was gone for a night to a friend's place. I had gone to play cards actually? Me and my boyfriend and there was a couple of people there and I called her and said, "listen, I'm goin to be home tomorrow morning"=

SW: =mm..hmm=

M: =in time to meet my Children's Aid worker. I'm just...I'll just stay the night here because it's already late a:nd she made me walk home at 12:30 at night=

SW: =mm..hmm=

M: =and I knew that I was supposed to meet with my worker and she did meet. She didn't seem to understand that=

SW: =mm...hmm. When you were in care, when you were at the receiving home or even at any foster homes, did you visit with your mum?

M: uh:mm at the foster home I..I would go to my mum's every once in a while=

SW: =mm..hmm=

M: = didn't do that until I was at Michele's for probably three or four months=

S: W =mm..hmm=

M: =uh..mm=

SW: =then you started to visit your mum?

M: =yes. Uh..mm...the first initial contact with my mother was, uh, actually, June xx, 199x. Uh, me and my boyfriend got into a motorbike accident=

S: W =mm..hmm=

M: =as soon as I got in, uh to make sure I was OK and that was the first point of contact a::nd, uh:hh, it wasn't very . . u:hhm . . y'know (laughs)=

SW: =mm.hmm. Positive?=

M: =it's hard..it's hard to explain. Yes, yah, it wasn't very positive and we=

The shift to a focus about mid-way through the preceding to M's relationship with her mother, "did you visit with your mom?", is remarkable, simply because it seems to introduce a stark rupture or shift off topic. The social worker, while employing the latched "mm.hmm", uses the space to shift topic from M's concerns about privacy, rights, and tensions with foster parent to a direct question apparently derived from the Interview Guide.

Asking what might have prompted the social worker to use this moment to explore M's relationship with the mother reveals the bridging between text and immediate reality. Was the question prompted by boredom with M's extended narrative about troubles with her foster mother, or was there something in M's narrative that resonated with a concern about relationship with mother? Did the social worker hear in M's talk an attention to relationships that would bring into focus the primary relation with mother? Further the question arises as to whether there are palpable indicators in talk that might have triggered the social worker's apparent topic shift?

Although what follows may appear speculative if the context of the interaction is brought into focus then the shift in topic begins to make sense. First, we must recognise that this is an account of problematic relations with foster parents that occur inside the organisational space of protecting the child from problematic relations with natural parents. As such, the topic shift back to contact with mom plays off against an ironic sense that perhaps intervention by the Children's Aid Society has proven to be no more useful at resolving the issues of drug abuse that brought M into care than if she had remained at her mother's. Simply, intervention may have been futile. In this context, questions about the relationship with her mother are directly relevant, for if foster homes and receiving homes have not prevented M from engaging in the problem behaviours that brought her into care, perhaps she would be as well off returning to live with mother. In short, the apparent topic shift can be understood only by reference to a complex interplay of elements that are hardly transparent in the talk. These include the possible influence of the text, the social worker's sifting of M's talk through the frameworks of organisational mandate and background, the invocation of professional discursive frameworks that provide for the linking of 'teenage acting out' with family forms, and the background information/history shared between the social worker and this child.

While there are no obvious indicators on the audio recording that the Interview Guide was "in hand", this segment indicates that it was most likely proximate. We can hear the social worker engage in a series of transformations and corrections, that indicate a beginning inside the general category, "being in care", but which then move to locally relevant issues for the youth, i.e. When you were in care, when you were at the receiving home or even at any foster homes, did you visit with your mum?"

In this segment we can see the social worker works at effectively transforming the generalised direction of the questions outlined in the Interview Guide, into situationally relevant questions resonant with the topic at hand. Through the shifts from the general to the specific the social worker progressively moves, clause by clause closer to establishing relevance and congruence with the topic at hand. Through such processes of taking up a client's words and categories the social worker transforms the client's reality into the discursively organised relevancies of a textually mediated space. The social worker produces a simulacrum of attention, following, and caring, through which the particulars from a client's life can be ideologically absorbed in organisational and professional discursive frameworks. Specific problems that this child might have faced in day-to-day living with others, becomes organisationally relevant as "problems in foster care", and the textual topic of "relationships with your parents".

In the next interaction the question of the relationship with the mother is approached via an extended discussion about relations with a brother, and in the sequences just prior to the question about the mother, by a discussion of the ongoing relationship with foster parents. In this way the social worker locates interaction with parents inside the broader theme of interaction with adults in parental capacity, including foster parents, as well as relations with other family members, i.e. a brother.

T: I was living on my own then, then I moved back in, with M and N
SW: But you felt that you could go over any time and visit them
T: oh yah=
SW: =yah=
T: oh yah
SW: okay
T: Definitely, like i..it was a welcome (walk in), an
SW: Now when you were at M and N's or when you were at your ah, previous foster homes, did you have visits with your parents?

T: °mmmhuh°

SW: Now with your mom, was it supervised? Would've been a supervised visit?

T: yep

Through this sequence we can see that a general directive to explore relationships while in care with family become thoroughly particularised, such that the text that guides the interview process is rendered invisible. In this strategy the text is present only as a residue, as that outside the immediate moment of the talk, but which when the talk is transcribed, reviewed, and analysed can be invoked as guiding that which unfolded.

Here the text is available as a mnemonic device, through which the social worker sifts through utterances as they unfold, shaping responses, and guiding the direction and topics addressed in the talk. It is significant that in such applications of the text to the interview there is a profound disjuncture between the social worker and the youth. In a sense the social worker plays the youth as an instrument for producing a story that can be warranted as meeting the expectancies laid out in the Interview Guide. The paradox is that while this social work strategy seems to escape the text, the absence of the text is only a disguise, and as such the integrity of conversation is both reality and a similitude.

Taking up the standpoint of the client, we can readily understand that the simulation of conversation raises a point of danger and tension. Work is going on that the client may only dimly understand, and as such the dynamics guiding the interview are always hidden and secret, no matter how thoroughly the social worker attempts to disclose the background organisation of the moment. Hak observed:

> Utterances can legitimately be described as oriented to a 'context' that is not observable to the receivers of those utterances ... practitioners' orientations to an institutional context of reporting enables the analyst to describe not only how practitioners such as psychiatrists 'discover' and 'finish off' reportable 'objects', but also how they can accomplish this in conversations with patients who are not aware of their own contribution to the practitioners' work".

(1995:130)

The issue here is that the parties to a conversation are not equally oriented to the conversation. In social work interviews the viewpoint of the practitioner is not, nor can it be made fully available to the client. The social worker and child are located in differential positions marked by a fundamental inequality. The talk that unfolds is oriented to background considerations which from the client's standpoint is both invisible and largely irrelevant, but which for the social worker are absolutely crucial for sustaining her 'professional' persona. Thus the interview demonstrates the social worker's ability to identify relevant topics, to help the client express her life story through these topics, to

redirect tangential movements back to these topics, to cover the topics outlined in the Interview Guide, to assist the client to address difficult issues, to
demonstrate proper care and empathy for the client, and to conduct the
interview with appropriate attention to professional distance, self-disclosure,
and so forth.

In the next sequence the opener to a discussion of the relationship with
mother is accomplished via the issue of becoming a crown ward. The social
worker in this sequence recognises that crown wardship, while permanently
severing the parent's right to guardianship over the child, may not necessarily
terminate access. Thus, a legal and juridical category becomes part of the
terrain for addressing the client's relationship with her mother.

SW: So then you were made a crown ward after that?
D: Yah, at ten yah, they finally called it quits, more or less saying, "She's not
   going back, its not gettin better." Uhm, so they always tried to send me
   back to my home I guess. Its basically what they've told me.
SW: Yah, do you have contact with your mother?
D: yah
SW: how does that work?

In this segment the social worker relies on background organisational and
legal knowledge about the possible meaning of crown wardship. Thus, crown
wardship, usually means for infants that all ties with parents are severed and
that they are placed for adoption, whereas as the child gets older crown
wardship, while severing guardianship, may not necessarily result in a permanent severing of access. Therefore, it is necessary to determine what form
crown wardship takes for this youth, and whether the question of access to
her mother is even relevant.

The seemingly simple reference to crown wardship relies on a complex and
dense weave of background understandings which are not available through
this moment of conversational interaction. This background articulates a
history of work inside this agency, and possibly other agencies. This background may include legislation, policy manuals, experience in the court-room,
and knowledge of other cases involving crown wards. Given that the notion of
crown wardship references a thick array of possible sources, history, and
forms of information, a retrieval of its sense and associative meanings cannot
possibly be recovered from this, or any other moment of conversation. Rather
what is brought into focus through this segment is the critical importance of
organisational courses of action and their intersection with personal history
as a conjuncture through which professional practice emerges.

In the next segment I want to draw out the social worker's reliance on the
common-sense notion of family.

SW: uhm, so when you came into care you were separated from B (sister). Did
   you have contact with B or not?

T: I had somewhat contact but, uh, my mother didn't really want it, so me and my sister couldn't really have it ((clears throat)).

SW: Uhm, so visits with your mom how did they go?

T: Short and bitter at first.

SW: How long did it take for things to work out between you.

T: Oh well, three or four years. We just star, we are just, are getting there now, jist now we are starting to get back.

In this segment we see that the social worker relies upon the common-sense notion of family in contemporary society as including, parents – mother/father – and siblings – brother/sister, to effect an apparently smooth transition from a discussion of contact with a sister to contact with mother. Once again, the sense of this interaction depends on a shared background knowledge of family dynamics, history, and relations between the social worker and the child. Here the question arises as to whether or not the social worker was familiar with the child's and other family members' stories. Once again, the issue is that the sensibility of the conversation quite probably relies on a store of shared background knowledge available to the child and the social worker, albeit available in differential form. Thus, while the child may generate stories from her life through reference to lived day-to-day experiences, the social worker, may also share specific elements of such experience, but will also have as an available resource the documentary information on a file.

Each of these segments demonstrates a number of common features. First the social work interviewer has complied with the textual direction to explore the theme of relationships with parents, albeit expressed in the form of questions about visits, contact with, parents and/or more specifically mum. Second, the topic of relationships with parents is embedded inside the extended form of the interview, and is often approached in the context of other talk about contact with family members, whether a sister, brother, foster parent or so on.

Conclusion: The view from the other side

The discussion above has focused on the work of performing the interview through reference to the text from the standpoint of the social worker. Although I have outlined a number of different strategies social workers employ to apply the text to the situation at hand I have not addressed the ways that youth both appreciate and may even acknowledge and cooperate with, or resist the social worker's adoption of textual imperatives. In the following segment, taken from a Children's Aid Society Teen (CAST)[7] meeting, a young woman is addressing the agency's decision to pilot the "Looking After Children Project", which involved social workers working through a detailed workbook (which S referred to as "this whole package") with youth in care to thereby develop a "plan of care".

S: But we're all sitting around here and we're all taking about how our workers don't take enough time with us, our workers don't do this with us but,
maybe I got a more in depth thing of this whole package or whatever//

J: you did, you got a lot more than//

S: I got a lot more but, what I got out of it from what I heard that, is that the
workers are realising that they are not spending enough time getting at
the nitty gritty of what's goin on in our lives that..for them, like I mean
we can sit down with our workers and we can say, "alright," you know,
"how is your day?," an we all know as good as the next person, "fine" ↓,
or it'll be like a huge spiel, but with this in..instead of having te make you
talk there are questions there and stuff, and it jist seems like they're tryin
to find a way that they can narrow down what's goin on in our lives,
what's goin on, how they can help, and we're sitting here saying well
they're not gonna spend enough time with us. I mean this is once a year,
and I think, if I'm not mistake..mistaken, you said its not all gonna be
done in one chunk,

J: yah-

S: like its gonna be time and time, so its time that is spent with our worker that
these questions are maybe general and they may be going to other people
that are getting this thing done but the questions are..are..they're so direct
that its gonna help us to be able te talk, and it'll give us more time.

From S's observations we can see that she appreciates that "this whole package" despite reliance on standardised questions, "questions are maybe general", may nevertheless create a forum for social workers to get at the "at the
nitty gritty of what's goin on in our lives". S clearly appreciates that while the
worker may be performing a piece of generalised organisational work, it
nevertheless creates a possibility that her life might become a focus of
attention.

Although S entertained a positive understanding of the document and the
process of filling it out, I want to complete this chapter by examining the
understandings of other youth who did not share this view.

M: Uhm, just that, it's great and all and now they'll sit down with us an. and
put us inta a package, but then that's all like..like, mmmhm, okay's that's
all we are, is that like, kk, if you invested that time, like this is good
because its and advancement, but the truth is is that if the social workers
invested the time needed te sit down with J, and say te J, get a relationship going because that's what social workers do, they come there with
their paper, and they're like "Okay tell me...lalalalala," no wonder we
don't sit down with them and tell them what is goin on in our lives//

J: Not all workers=

M: not all workers[but its its the quota//[jist, jist a sec.

S: //[we hafta do that]

F: [yah [but that's a different sit.//

M: [Please, jist a second a I didn't interupt you=

SW: =yes=

M: =okay uhm, but then if with the package we're all generalisations, you plae..you take the problems and you go to the solution maker but we're each individuals, and I know you know this like, I..I'm not saying that you don't know this

Unlike S, M worries that all work that is referenced through such documents will simply result in superficial relationships aimed at getting the documentary work accomplished. These are relationships in which social workers "come there with their paper" and ask generalised questions that do not begin inside the lives of the youth, and to which the youth respond with equally stock and generalised answers.

In short, careful analysis of social worker's practices, as well as youth's practices when confronting texts, reveals a sophisticated repertoire of practical techniques for mediating the generalised and universal order of the text to the local and particular situation at hand. The range of understandings and background negotiations effected by both social workers and youth underscores the importance of acknowledging Garfinkel's insight against proceeding as if actors were "cultural dopes", "psychological dopes", or "judgmental dopes" (1967).

Perhaps what is most valuable in the tools of conversational analysis is the direction to examine members' talk carefully and in detail, as accomplishing the social scene in which they locate themselves and are located. What is most instructive in such an exercise is that we find that members do not proceed along one plane, and accordingly they are seldom simply unwitting agents of organisational or professional powers. Indeed, while they may find themselves working inside such forms of order they are hardly passive, hardly over determined, but always actively engaged, choosing, and determining subjects. Finally, while there may be tremendous inequality inside such spaces between social workers and youth, the youth themselves are hardly defenceless. As we have seen through excerpts from the youth, they understand what is happening to them when they meet with social workers. They chose whether or not to resist, when to resist, and how to produce compliance. Youth in interviews with social workers are clever and strategic, and have available to them the art of talk-in-interaction, which they deploy to create and to project images of self and stories of their lives.

Notes

1 In approaching texts I rely on Wittgenstein's (1967) notion of a 'language game' in which the good sense of words, such as 'text', emerge as expressed and used in context, day-to-day work, and practically situated exchanges. Although I begin by examining the ways that social workers used the text of the Interview Guide I created for a research project, their approaches to that text corresponded to techniques for managing organisational texts. As I listened to the audio-recordings, I heard and

recognised the very same methods I had used to work through organisational texts in my work with clients.

2 Hough notes, "All postmodern approaches will assert the centrality of discourse in structuring, at one and the same time, the world and the person's subjectivity" (1999:42). I do not dispute this claim. Indeed, it is my position that postmodernism is an anti-humanist idealism (Ryder, 2013), in contradistinction to humanist Marxist, materialist, realist, and even ethnomethodological and conversation analysis. Althusser, a structural Marxist, and Foucault, a post-modernist are united in a repudiation of humanism (Resch, 1992). Although Althusser favours a structuralist reading of the ideological interpellation of the subject (1970), Foucault pursues similar ends through a discursive interpellation of self into 'subject' positions and discursively rooted identities. For Althusser and for his protégé Foucault, people are träger, whether of structure or of discourses. Oppositely those doing EM and CA approach structures as the accomplished reflexive effect of actual people's interactive and engaged mundane congregational practices.

3 I was introduced by the director of personnel, who had arranged the meeting, to the social workers as a "professor at Carleton University" who was conducting research. Such an introduction invokes what Sacks has called a "membership inference rich representative" (Sacks, 1995:43), and accordingly provided those who were present with a series of devices for reading my performance, and their responses to my requests. As with the creators of child protection policy, I too was identifiable as an outsider, who although able to claim a certain expertise and authority, could not claim to know the actual youth and the actual organisation of day-to-day practice in the agency.

4 Derrida describes the trace as that which "cannot be thought without thinking the retention of difference within a structure of reference where difference appears as such and thus permits a certain liberty of variations among the full terms" (1997:46–47). While Derrida situates the problem of the trace inside western metaphysics, his analysis throws light on that which even in the absence of the text'remains as a residue of discursive "self-occultation" (47).

5 The social worker and the child recognise, as it were the truth behind Cicourel's analysis that "writing provides an abstract form of social control over different groups without the necessity of continuous face-to-face exchanges where oral and nonverbal conditions dominate interaction" (1985:161).

6 When I reviewed this passage with a student, who also happened to be an experienced clinical practitioner in the area of youth and addictions, he immediately recognised himself in the text. He outlined that when he has to fill out a form his approach is that, "It's not me who is saying this but somebody else. I want to maintain a personal relation. Our relation, not the structure's. I do it all the time. I say, 'I have these fucking forms that are totally useless.'"

7 CAST is a self-help and advocacy group directed by a social worker. I was an active member of CAST for about four years, meeting at the Children's Aid Society offices every Wednesday from 6:00 to 9:00. This allowed me to gain an intimate awareness of the day-to-day issues facing youth in care. The insights of the CAST youth were invaluable for sorting through the issues and dilemmas of social work with youth in care.

References

Abel, Charles M., & Johnson, H. Wayne. (1978). Clients' access to records: Policy and attitudes. *Social Work*, 23(1): 42–46.

Althusser, Louis. (1970). *Lenin and philosophy and other essays*. London, England: Verso.

Ames, Natalie. (1999). Social work recording: A new look at an old issue. *Journal of Social Work Education*, 35(2): 227–237.

Blake, Pamela. (2010). *Practice notes: The broken record. Perspective.* Toronto, ON: Ontario College of Social Workers and Social Service Workers.

Burman, Patrick. (1996). *Poverty's bonds: Power and agency in the social relations of welfare.* Toronto, ON: Thompson Educational.

Cicourel, Aaron V. (1985). Text and discourse. *Annual Review of Anthropology*, 14: 159–185.

Cumming, Sue, Fitzpatrick, Eileen, McAuliffe, Donna, McKain, Silvana, Martin, Catherine, & Tonge, Angela. (2007). Raising the Titanic: Rescuing social work documentation from the sea of ethical risk. *Australian Social Work*, 60(2): 239–257.

de Montigny, Gerald. (1995). *Social working: An ethnography of front-line practice.* Toronto, ON: University of Toronto Press.

Derrida, Jacques. (1997). *Of grammatology* (Corrected ed.) (Trans. Gayatri Chakravorty Spivak). Baltimore, MD: Johns Hopkins.

Edwards, R. L., & Reid, W. J. (1989). Structured case recording in child welfare: An assessment of social workers' reactions. *Social Work*, 34: 49–52.

Fook, Jan. (1993). *Radical casework: A theory of practice.* Crows Nest, NSW: Allen & Unwin.

Fook, Jan. (2001). *Social work: Critical theory and practice.* London, England: Sage.

Fook, Jan, & Gardner, Fiona. (2007). *Practising critical reflection: A resource handbook.* Berkshire, England: Open University Press.

Garfinkel, Harold. (1967). *Studies in ethnomethodology.* Englewood Cliffs, NJ: Prentice-Hall.

Hak, Tony. (1995). *Ethnomethodology and the institutional context. Human Studies*, 18, 109–137.

Holbrook, Terry. (1983). *Case records: Fact or fiction? Social Service Review*, 57: 645–658.

Hough, Gary. (1999). The organization of social work in customer culture. In Bob Pease & Jan Fook (Eds.), *Transforming social work practice: Postmodern critical perspectives* (pp. 40–54). London, England: Routledge.

Jones, Chris. (2001). *Voices from the front line: State social workers and new labour. British Journal of Social Work*, 31(4): 547–562.

Kadushin, Alfred, & Kadushin, Goldie. (2013). *The social work interview: The guide for human service professionals* (5th ed.). New York, NY: Columbia University Press.

Kagle, Jill Doner. (2008). *Social work records* (3rd ed.). Prospect Heights, IL: Waveland Press.

Kress, Gunther, & Hodge, Robert. (1979). *Language as ideology.* London, England: Routledge & Kegan Paul.

Leonard, Peter. (1997). *Postmodern welfare: Reconstructing an emancipatory project.* London, England: Sage.

Lipsky, Michael. (1980). *Street-level bureaucracy: Dilemmas of the individual in public services.* New York, NY: Russell Sage.

Little, Patsy. (1995). Records and record keeping. In Pam Carter, Tony Jeffs, and Mark K.Smith (Eds.), *Social working* (pp. 32–48). London, England: Macmillan.

Mullaly, Bob. (2018). *Challenging oppression and confronting privilege* (3rd ed.). Don Mills, ON: Oxford University Press.

Murray, Suellen, & Humphreys, Cathy. (2014). "My life's been a total disaster but I feel privileged": Care-leavers' access to personal records and their implications for social work practice. *Child & Family Social Work*, 19: 215–224.

Olson, Leslie A. (1993). Research on discourse communities. In Rachel Spilka (Ed.), *Writing in the workplace: New research perspectives* (pp. 181–195). Carbondale, IL: Southern Illinois University Press.

Ontario Provincial Service Employee Union (OPSEU). (2001). Peoplework not paperwork. Toronto, ON: Author. www.opseu.org/sites/default/files/media/policypap erpeoplework.pdf

Paré, Anthony. (1991). Ushering "Audience" out: From oration to conversation. *Textual Studies in Canada*, 1: 45–64.

Paré, Anthony. (1993). Discourse regulations and the production of knowledge. In Rachel Spilka (Ed.), *Writing in the workplace: New research perspectives* (pp. 111–123). Carbondale, IL: Southern Illinois University Press.

Prince, Katie. (1996). *Boring records? Communication, speech and writing in social work*. London, England: Jessica Kingsley.

Prochaska, J. (1977). Confidentiality and records. *Social Casework*, 58: 371–372.

Reamer, F. (2001). *The social work ethics audit: A risk management tool*. Washington, DC: NASW Press.

Resch, Robert Paul. (1992). *Althusser and the renewal of Marxist social theory*. Berkeley, CA: University of California Press.

Ryder, Andrew. (2013). Foucault and Althusser: Epistemological differences with political effects. *Foucault Studies*, 16: 134–153.

Sacks, Harvey. (1995). *Lectures on conversation (Volumes 1 & 2)* (Ed. Gail Jefferson). Oxford, England: Blackwell.

Smith, Dorothy E. (1990a). *Texts, facts, and femininity: Exploring the relations of ruling*. London, England: Routledge.

Smith, Dorothy E. (1990b). *The conceptual practices of power: A feminist sociology of knowledge*. Toronto, ON: University of Toronto Press.

Timms, Noel. (1972). *Recording in social work*. London, England: Routledge & Kegan Paul.

Wilson, S. (1978). *Confidentiality in social work: Issues and principles*. New York, NY: Free Press.

Wittgenstein, Ludwig. (1967). *Philosophical investigations* (The English text of the third edition) (Trans. G. E. M. Anscombe). Oxford, England: Basil Blackwell.

Zimmerman, Don H. (1976). Record-keeping and the intake process in a public welfare agency. In Stanton Wheeler (Ed.), *On record: Files and dossiers in American life*. New Brunswick, NJ: Transaction Books.

6 Getting started: Writing and erasing youths' stories

SW   Okay, u:uhm (22 second pause) {paper crackles at 5 sec} Uhm in terms of your relationships with other people, since coming into care, what has your relationship been like with the school, teachers, guidance counsellors, . . .

T   Thdat depends on if I'm havin a good day or bad day=

SW   =mmhuh=

T   =like fer- well- I get along with Donna and like the counsellor of the school, but even if I'm havin a bad day I can be like, "O:oh like you fuck off too."

SW   mmhuh=

T   =like, but I find I get along with school officials pretty well//[actually]

SW   [do you think]

T   (I'd a right fer)

SW   Yeah, do you think being in care has helped you//

T   yeah I think [that]=

SW   [get along]= in school?

T   Yeah I think it has because, if I hadn't all that, I think I would have probably depended on my mother to do a lot of my stuff, like I probably would have been like no you: go sign me up for highschool, no you: go switch my courses, and then youu go talk to the teacher and tell me that blah blah, instead of like becoming independent and having to do it myself

SW   Right

T   and, I found that living at Jim and Jenny's I became very independent because they wouldn't do NOThing for me, they wouldn't even take me to the docto::r=

SW   =um huh

T   Sooo

SW   So it was kinda of sometimes that's one of the down falls of being in CARE, right?

T   Yeah

SW   If you're not ready for independence, you're not, you're forced to be independent

T   Yeah, oh yeah, but=

SW   =On the other hand

T   it's better than, being in a predicament where you could be beaten up all the time . . .

SW   Uumm, if your mom, if it were up to your mom to do all this stuff for, how do you think that would have worked out?..

T   They'd shoot that out, I don't think, I don't even think I'd be in Y (city name) now, if 'd stayed with her, (if she would have taken me somewhere), I don't know, I really don't, know, like I've thought of it that way, I wonder how things would be if I lived with my mom, wonder if I'd loo::k the same if I lived with my mom, even you know=

SW   uhm huh

T   Like who's to say I wouldn't have become a fat pig like her, anorexic, or someum greasy or something, you know what I mean, . . . she barely makes by, for herself

Interviews, control, and power

The structure of the segment above, in which a social worker asks a question, and T, a young woman, responds, could have been taken from any interview in my collection. The interactive structure of questions, responses, acknowledgement tokens, and follow up questions is a cycle characteristic, if not the sine qua non, of interviews. To perform an occasion as accountably a social work interview is predicated on such asymmetry, expressed by different interactive positioning and participation. One person – a social worker – routinely poses questions while another person – a client – answers questions, providing details about her life, problems, thoughts, and so on.[1]

In this segment, the asymmetrical structure of questions and response allows T to talk about her experiences in her family and how living in care has created new possibilities, "Like who's to say I wouldn't have become a fat pig like her, anorexic, or someum greasy or something, you know what I mean, . . . she barely makes by, for herself". The interactive space of the interview, and T's relation with SW, allows T to address rather difficult and personal reflections about herself and her family. This ability to create and foster an interactive space where difficult, taboo, and potentially deeply stigmatising materials get talked about, emerges through both the professional capacity and the interactive skills of a social worker. This exchange, flows from an extended relationship between this social workers and T. Their relationship opens a space of trust, warmth, and care, such that the youth, T, feels able to identify such difficult content.

While it might seem that an interview expresses a power difference between the social worker and the client, I seek to caution against this simplistic view. An invocation of power as an organiser or explanator of an interview works to gloss and obscure the complex play of interactive practices and interaction involving both a social worker and a client. Against beginning by taking shelter in such a conceptual armamentarium, we can begin to discover both the art and complexity of social interaction by turning our attention to the details of talk-in-action. Our focus shifts from demonstrating the operation of concepts to an explication of social action. This provides a nuanced and complex view of an interview as an interactively accomplished occasion. We are concerned to track just how a social worker and a client worked together to co-produce the occasion as such with 'its' focus, meaning, and sensible accountability. Just how a social worker and a client perform and interact differently reveals deeply layered dimensions of social accomplishment that supersede a simple linear account of power.

Doing an interview relies on active and skilled participation of both the social worker and the youth. Consider the following from the above segment:

SW: ... since coming into care, what has your relationship been like with the school, teachers, guidance counsellors, ...
T: Thdat depends on if I'm havin a good day or bad day=
SW: =mmhuh=
T: =like fer- well- I get along with Donna and like the counsellor of the school, but even if I'm havin a bad day I can be like, "O:oh like you fuck off too."
SW: mmhuh=
T: =like, but I find I get along with school officials pretty well//[actually]
SW: [do you think]
T: (I'd a right fer)
SW: Yeah, do you think being in care has helped you//
T: yeah I think [that]=
SW: [get along]= in school?
T: Yeah I think it has because,

SW asks T to talk about how coming into care has affected her relationships in her school. Although SW reads the question from the interview guide, it becomes evident in her next turns that SW has formulated for herself what might count as an adequate response. T's first offerings are heard and responded to by the social worker with 'mmhuh' acknowledgment tokens. However, when T continued, "like, but I find I get along with school officials pretty well//[actually]", the social worker attempts, albeit unsuccessfully, to interrupt. It is important to ask, what might have prompted the shift from acknowledgement tokens as continuers, to an interruption?

What is going on? The social worker attempts to interrupt T's response, first by beginning "do you think", though T continues to talk (unfortunately I could not recover the words from the audio-recording), which leads the social worker to persist, "Yeah, do you think being in care has helped you//". Again, T interrupts, leading SW to make a further try to complete her question. She agrees, "Yeah, do you think being in care has helped you//". What informs the social worker's redirection? When we review the progression of T's response, we see that she begins by focusing on her relation with a particular person, Donna, but then shifts to getting along with officials generally. While SW responded to T's reflections about Donna with 'mmhuh', when T shifted from a particular relationship to the general, this prompted SW to try to interrupt. Was it the generality of the reflection? Was it that SW found T's first offering adequate or sufficient? Or, was it that what SW wanted from the question was greater reflection from T addressing the relation between being in care and actual interpersonal relations in school?

Minimally, we recognise that SW's interruption, and redirection, signalled a struggle to create a shared orientation or focus to the talk-in-interaction. Second, although it took a second try for SW to produce her full question, "do you think being in care has helped you", T responds, not by continuing to address relations with officials, but shifts to reflecting on the personal consequences in her life of living in care. This segment reveals a complex and subtle exchange in which both the social worker and the youth attend to, and work from each other's actions. The emergence of an interview as such articulates the capacities of both to engage the other to produce a shared sense of coherence and order, inside the interaction, and as this type of occasion as accountably an interview.

Our interest needs to be to explicate, or pull apart, in its details the artful performances of both the social worker and the youth in the coproduction of this occasion as an interview. While, it might be tempting to identify the worker's power to ask questions and to shape the topics for next turns, we need to guard against assuming that power runs in only one direction. Indeed, to pose the matter ethnomethodologically, we appreciate that power does not in fact run, but instead people run or interact in ways which they account for as instances of their power, competency, skill, knowledge, expertise, professionalism, abilities, and so on. Power is neither grammatical agent nor simple presence. By taking up tools from conversation analysis and ethnomethodology, what is brought into focus are the situated and specific interactions between a social worker and a youth for accomplishing this occasion as such.

The asymmetry of interaction, as a performed interview, while indicating a social worker's skills, capacities, experience, and powers to shape topics through use of questions, acknowledgment tokens, or formulations, is simultaneously dependent on the youth's disposition and willingness to engage the social worker. Further, in this occasion it is the youth, not the social worker, who tells her story, which indicates the client's positional power to hold the floor, and to be a focus or centre of attention.

As a social worker creates a space for a client, for the young person being interviewed it provides an opportunity to craft their story, to have another listen to that story, to have a sense that their story matters, and that they in turn matter. Conversely, if a social worker does not create a space for a client, the client can be expected to withdraw, or signal inattention, boredom, or even irritation and anger. Simply, the successful production of an interview is a cooperative achievement. In the preceding interview segment we see that T talks about her life, works through problems and issues at school and in her family, and uses the social worker as a resource. In this interactive moment the social worker limits her talk largely to acknowledgement tokens and to short questions designed to create space for T's story to emerge.

Through careful attention to transcribed interviews we recognise complexity, nuance, ambiguity, and paradoxical deployment of strategies in interaction. It is not simply a social worker who is an agent, but so too is a person in the position of being a client. Simply, the living and in vivo accomplishment of an interview relies on both participants' active work and play with structures, expectations, reactions, and possibilities. In the unfolding ambiguity and uncertainty of the moment, each participant listens and crafts responses from the other as well as the opportunities for their next turns. Simply, participants to a social work interview accomplish themselves and their positions interactively as accountably and warrantably instances of being a client and being a social worker.

For a social worker, the ability to elicit the client's story, to get a client to talk, to help the client remember that which was forgotten, and to aid in reframing, disturbing, and creating new insights, are all sources of professional satisfaction. As a good or successful interview unfolds it provides not only effective help to a client, but a provides a social worker with a space of interactive pleasure articulating and confirming the worker's experience, ability, insight, knowledge, and skills. Yet, a capacity to get the client to talk, and to disclose deeply personal materials, simultaneously demands a repression of the social worker's own experiences and stories. A warranted production of an interview should not become a place where as a social worker turns to the client for her own personal help. A worker's focus on the story of the client while providing the worker with a pleasure, simultaneously demands a professional control and self-regulation. Ultimately, the accomplishment of self-as-a-social-worker in the interview rests on suppression of an articulation of the worker's own needs and concerns, such that what is said is continually evaluated for strategic and tactical effect on the client. This focus on the youth's story speaks to the fulfilment of a practice art and professional skills. Being demonstrably professional demands suppression of a social worker's personal needs, such that what can emerge is a professional orientation. As participants to an interview interact with each other they struggle to achieve personal objectives in, through, against, and with other, albeit as masked, shaped, and formed by their respective fulfilment of positions as client and worker. The interactions with another while routinely a source of satisfaction and pleasure, are also occasioned by an inescapable frustration, tension, and struggle.

Schegloff's (1992) insistence that social categories (social worker and client) be demonstrably relevant to analysis of conversations is equally instructive as a caution against promiscuous reliance on social categories. Schegloff observed:

> The point is not that persons are somehow not male or female, -upper or lower class, with or without power, professors and/or students. They may

be, on some occasion, demonstrably members of one or another of those categories. Nor is the issue that those aspects of the society do not matter, or did not matter on that occasion. We may share a lively sense that indeed they do matter, and that they mattered on that occasion, and mattered for just that aspect of some interaction on which we are focusing. There is still the problem of showing from the details of the talk or other conduct in the materials that we are analyzing that those aspects of the scene are what the parties are oriented to. For that is to show how the parties are embodying for one another the relevancies of the interaction and are thereby producing the social structure.

(1992:109–110)

It is important to recognise the contrast between the approach to social categories and relations of power and authority proposed by Schegloff, and that of post-modernists. For example Foucault proposed that power "traverses and produces things, it induces pleasure, forms knowledge, produces discourse" (1980:119). Touraine noted that "power is thus everywhere and nowhere" (1995:164). Mullaly observed, "Both social structures and individuals are able to exercise power" (2002:22). Against these ways of thinking about power Schegloff directs us to focus on empirical, material, and at hand dimensions of in vivo social interaction. This way of working is decidedly outside postmodern foci on discourses, categories, and language in the abstract. In a move aligned with CA Smith advises, "What we call 'power' is always a mobilisation of people's concerted activities" (1990a:79–80). It is worth noting the suspension or bracketing of 'power' as such, through the phrasing, 'what we call power'. What is being proposed through conversation analysis, ethnomethodology, and institutional ethnography are alternative approaches, that bracket or suspend a too easy reliance on categories, discourses, and language, in favour of detailed analysis of in vivo interactions and practices. We shift our attention to the complex forms of interaction, differential forms of participation and positioning, for effectively producing an occasion not just as such, but as accountably and warrantably such, hence not just here and now but as potentially disputed, contested, and re-interpreted. Such that something like power seems to matter, must itself be accounted for as an effect of participants' actions, energies, and interactions.

It is in and through our bodies, conjoined with intention and will, that we expend energy talking, listening, working, and playing. That which we come to recognise and call power, as with all phenomena indicated through forms of language, escapes and overflows our naming and our words. Whatever it is that we intend, indicate, and point to as power, inescapably glosses, conceals, and over-writes, to thereby lose diverse phenomenal forms, diverse forms of being, and diverse concatenations of socially organised and located practice. Beyond power is a detailed examination of such practical conjunctures where one person's will comes to be expressed in and through material and social existence, in interaction with another's.

From out of detailed explication of the turn-by-turn nature of the talk-in-interaction as an interview, we can begin to explicate the artful accomplishment of various powers in, and as accomplished forms of interaction. That which might be pointed to as power is alive as that which is in hand, in speaking, in listening, in replying, in silence, in thinking, and in living. That which is pointed to as power is multi-form, myriad, and mystifying, as it articulates the visible and the invisible, the comprehensible and the ineffable dimensions of interaction. That which is pointed to as power is effected in members' achievements of this occasion as such. From out of situated action forms of order and the possibility of an accountability emerge, turn by turn, such that this work together, can be warranted not just for participants, but for transcribers, analysts, supervisors, and so on as a proper interview.

As people enter into the interactive work, of that which comes to be called an interview, they bring with them their experience, skills, aptitudes, abilities, talents, capacities, limits, deficits, and so on, which shapes the nature of the work that they can do in that setting. Though they can be counted on to try to effect some mastery and control over themselves, and perhaps over another, being able to do so articulates a personal history, life experience and education, and of course capacities. Each of us attempts to express our will in and against the materiality of the world. As the press of world rubs against our will we struggle, modify, and change both ourselves and a world.

That which we call power also speaks to the shaping of every-day relations, work and play between ourselves and others. Here the concept of power indicates or points to skilful navigation, accommodation, negotiation, compliance, resistance, or refusal in interaction with others. There power points to the difficulties of shaping one's imagination and will to that of another's imagination and will. The desires, intentions, and motivations which are articulated in and through action themselves originate in a synthesis between an individual in the every-day and every-night forms of interaction with others who co-inhabit a social landscape.

Through the plenitude of day-to-day activities of people at work and play emerges the replicative accomplishment of the orders of a society. Each of us recognise and struggle inside the seemingly dead weight of history, tradition, convention, custom, and culture. Yet, as we breath, act, and live, we remake these elements interactively with others to accomplish a present that shifts into a past. Every time we utter a word or struggle to articulate our thoughts and ideas with another, we bridge the phantoms of our past, our history, and our place to this here-and-now, to dialectically produce the sense of this moment as such. It is always, everywhere, in and through the mundane webs of actual, physical, here-and-now social interactions that that which we call history, tradition, culture, and society are realised, accomplished, and achieved.

Member's manifold powers, as incarnate expressions of their lives, are realised in the successful, warrantable, and accountable production of an occasion as an 'interview', that is as a moment that conforms to some ideality, or type of generalised form of exchange. The production of an 'interview' as such, that is its production as a warrantable artefact of this moment of work, relies on reference to social processes and social relations that extend beyond the moment of the interview itself. Studies in institutional ethnography (Campbell & Manicom, 1995; de Montigny, 1995; Smith 2005; 1999; 1990a; 1990b; 1987) provide helpful guidance to connect apparently local production of occasions to extra-local and institutionalised relations. This is an approach that bridges concern with the everyday worlds in which people live with attention to the more generalised accomplishment of forms of ruling those everyday worlds, hence with the practical operations of a 'ruling apparatus' (Smith, 1987).

Smith's institutional ethnography (2005) provides an important insight and extension to the ethnomethodological concept of indexicality. Smith's way of working does not forget, and continually seeks to articulate here-and-now local practices to extra-local or institutionalised or iterative forms of social relations. Hence, the here-and-now performance of a social work interview is enacted as potentially and actually articulated to future review and evaluation. Whatever is enacted here-and-now articulates participant's lives within matrices of social interactions, past, present, and future. Whatever unfolds as an interview is an artefact, or to use Smith's analogy, a "node or knot" "coordinating multiple strands or action into a functional complex" (1987:160). Central to a proper performance of an interview is the accountability of the occasion, hence how "members themselves and for themselves constituted the observability and reportability of what has happened" (161). Smith notes:

> When applied to the institutional context, the notion of accountability locates practices tying local settings to the nonlocal organization of the ruling apparatus. Indeed, the institutional process itself can be seen as a dialectic between what members do intending the categories and concepts of institutional ideology and the analytic and descriptive practices of those categories and concepts deployed in accomplishing the observability of what is done, has happened, is going on, and so forth. Thus, local practices in their historical particularity and irreversibility are made accountable in terms of categories and concepts expressing the function of the institution.
>
> (1987:161)

The focus of this chapter on interviews conducted between social workers and youth in care bridges both the practical and mundane practices of the participants as well as their self-referential accounting practices for connecting this moment to formal, organisational, and institutionalised social relations (Smith, 1987:160). The seemingly local practices of social workers and youth in care are always and everywhere rooted in, and accomplish articulations to forms of organisation that extend beyond the particular moment of the interview, the physical location of the interview space, and the face-to-face encounter between social worker and client.

While that which people do produces a social reality, they do so not just individually but collectively and in concert with each other. Accordingly, whether the object being produced is a commodity for sale, or an interview, the practices of its production articulate social relations that extend beyond the horizons of the participants. The practices of its production reproduce a form of work. The reality of the interview as such neither begins nor ends in the experienced sphere of the participants. Reciprocally, it follows that all knowledge producers, whether social workers, sociologists, or researchers, are themselves located or grounded in a horizon which provides only a partial view of the institutional organisation of their production and that explication of social order demands examining the web of social relations which although beyond immediate experience provides for its possibility. While what counts as knowledge expresses the social organisation of knowledge producers' actual experiences, and embodied locations, explication of that knowledge demands an articulation beyond the horizon of experience. I turn now to examine troubles with transcription as a means for explicating the social organisation in which interviews are produced and analysed.

Troubles with transcription

While an audio recording is ostensibly treated as a document of an interview there is an irremediable slippage between the actual occasion and the recording. Frank notes (1985):

> The relation of speech, tape and transcript exemplifies what Derrida calls 'differ-ance', which is perhaps most simply described (to the untutored) as a double pun (see Derrida, 1973: 129ff.; 1981: 27ff.). In one movement of this pun Derrida combines the verbs 'to differ' and 'to defer', the latter principally in the sense of 'to put off'. Thus, the tape and the transcript differ from each other, and the transcription represents a deferring, in time, of the tape which precedes it, just as the tape itself defers the presence of a conversation which took place at an (again) earlier time.
>
> (112)

Latour and Woolgar (1979) have addressed difference between event and recording, through analysis of "inscription devices." These include "machines, pieces of apparatus and technicians" (58) that are used to construct new objects that aim to indicate particular phenomena, in our case audio-recordings of living talk-in-interaction. Even as an audio-recorder produces the recording there is an electronic and mechanical delay between the moment of talk and the moment of inscription into a recording by the device. This first millisecond delay is compounded by further delays in the work of transcription. Between the spaces of the first delay and the second, the audio-recording is whisked away to be worked up in different contexts, by people who may not necessarily have been present when it was produced.

Because the document in hand at the point of transcription is an *audio-recording* and not a *video-recording*, the gestures, body expressions, physical arrangements of the room, ambiance, and so forth are lost to analysis. We cannot read the body signs in audio. The flush of a face, the dance of the eyes, the flourish of hand as gesture are all lost. The audio-recording is indeed a thin representation of talk-in-interaction, as it records or documents only the vocalisations of the participants. Although such mechanical inscriptions are routine, whether through telephone, radio, movies, or television, it must be recognised that not only does such technology provide for a separation of embodied, here-and-now talk-in-interaction from its technologically mediated forms, but that the sorts of analysis pursued in conversation analysis and this book rely on, and can only emerge from the availability of such technologies. Talk-in-interaction is always accomplished by living people in the concrete spaces of their lives, and audio-recording produced from those interactions are slim artefacts that point only partially to the plenitude and complexities of the occasion.

As we have seen, talk-in-interaction is not easily transcribed, as that which is uttered does not convert very smoothly into written language. People do not speak in full sentences marked by proper grammar or clear enunciation. They start, stop, mis-speak, mumble, mispronounce words, use hand gestures, and produce a variety of non-word vocalisations that are either poorly recorded, lost to the recording, and which do not lend themselves readily to transcription into words or even alphabetic orders. Additionally, the work of transcribing is an acquired art. When I first began producing transcripts of interviews with youth in care, I had to learn both how to format my transcripts so that they adhered to some standardised form, and second how to convert the talk I was listening to into text. In any given audio-recording there were many segments, including the one at the top of this chapter, where I was unable on first listening to recover readily sensible or coherent words, and meanings. When transcribing at home by myself I would stop, 'rewind' the audio to play it back, listen again, again, and again. If my spouse was home, I'd yell out, "Can you come here and listen to this? What do you think". When she was not able to make sense of a segment, I would review the conversation that both preceded and followed the ambiguous portion to look for possible matches with other turns of phrase. Sometimes I 'rewound' and replayed the audio further back to look for similar 'sounds' with the hope of identifying turns of phrase or a context for the utterance. Of course, as a native English language speaker, I relied on my own stock in trade of clichés, every-day expressions, and ejaculations to recover meaning from unclear passages. Additionally, I would play with the settings on the recorder, changing the pitch and tone, the speed of playback, and the volume. Sometimes, after multiple listenings, there would be a eureka moment, when I would be fortunate and 'get it', whereas other times, even after listening to a segment ten or more times, I would need to make a guess at what the participants were saying.[2] These guesses would be enclosed in brackets (). Obviously, when a reader reads a transcript they are encountering a complex work process, that is only hinted at in those passages enclosed in brackets. Furthermore, even those passages which are not contained in brackets, hence those which claim to represent talk-in-interaction accurately and without ambiguity, may have been produced as putatively unambiguous, only after repeated listening by different people.

When doing transcripts of interviews, I attempted to follow the conventions of conversational analysis outlined in some of the standard texts, notably those set out by Jefferson, and adopted by various primers in CA.[3] Sadly, when I looked at transcriptions presented in other's work, and compared them to my own, my constructions seemed remarkably unimaginative and prosaic. The cognoscenti in CA produce transcriptions that use a variety of unconventional spellings, creative alphabetic presentations of sounds, indication of pauses, gaps, and silences in micro-second intervals, complex overlaps of talk, and precise indications of rising or falling tone. Yet, in this recognition of differences in skills, exactitude, and competence in transcribing talk and sounds into text we recognise not only specialised skills, craftsmanship, conventions, and discourse, but different foci of attention.

Variations in the art and style of transcription is recognised among those who do CA. Hutchby and Wooffitt observe that, "A CA transcript embodies in its format and in the phenomena it marks out the analytic concerns which conversation analysts bring to the data", which they note are of two types, i.e. dynamics of turn-taking and characteristics of speech delivery (1998:76). Similarly, ten Have observes that there are "various conventions for transcribing" and notes that, "each system has its own theoretical and methodological 'bias'" (2007:32). Thus, for Jefferson, because the focus is on sequences of talk-in-interaction, considerable attention in transcription is given to capturing "the time line of the interactional stream" (ten Have, 2007:33). In this text the focus has been not on sequencing as such, but rather the co-construction of a particular type of sociability in and as an interview.

Analytic criteria for engaging the data

For those who do CA it is generally agreed that "transcripts are not the 'data' of CA" (ten Have, 2007:95). Hutchby and Wooffitt insist that "data consist of tape recording of naturally occurring interactions" (1998:73). Ten Have argues that in CA transcripts are "designed to reveal the sequential features of talk" (2007:96). It follows that for CA, properly speaking, what counts as the data is not the content of what people say, but rather the management and accomplishment of "sequential order of talk-in-interaction" (Hutchby and Wooffitt, 1998:75). Yet for social workers who take up tools from CA we cannot be indifferent to the content of that which is said in an interview. Must there be a bifurcation between analytic attention to the form or structure of the talk and to the content?

I believe that a solution can be found through the recognition that participants to talk-in-interaction are oriented to a variety of levels which practically serve to integrate structure and content. First, participants when engaged in talking intentionally talk about something, that is they are concerned to communicate specific content, not just any content. Matters of topic for social workers are relevant for the sensibility, organisation, duration, and forms of talk-in-interaction with clients, whether it is finding a job, being unemployed, dealing with mental illness, or child care. Second, the structure of the talk, that is its sequencing, repair, or recipient design, provides necessary mechanics for communication of content, and for production of the relationship. Third, talk, as content and structure, is designed to accomplish particular and specific forms of relationship, e.g. friendship, doctor/patient, social worker/client, parent/child, spousal, courtship, and so on. Fourth, this talk-in-interaction, hence this occasion, must itself be grounded in extended courses of actions of the participants, such that what transpires is accomplished with a view to its post-facto warrantability. For example, a talk that I might have at the kitchen table with my son, about matters he considers of import – e.g. his relationship with his friends and work – may very well be a remarkable matter, and may affect his subsequent courses of action, and precisely because I appreciate such ongoing consequential webs, that which I produce as my contribution to the talk is measured and weighed.

The complex facing participants to talk-in-interaction also greets anyone who would aim to transcribe talk. Given that transcripts of interviews usually span at least twenty pages, and that the topics addressed range widely crossing the life span of youth, obvious questions arise about the criteria that are used to sift through, select out, and develop a focus. Making sense of the data of audio-recordings, combined with the translations (ten Have, 2007:109) and transformations produced through transcription demand approaching data as itself embedded in extended courses of action and production. In this sense, the audio-record is an artefact of processes that are hardly transparent in the forms of the talk. This claim itself needs to be demonstrated, through the identification of lacunae, gaps, separations, and taken for granted practices that are employed to produce the audio-recordings as such. This book, just as with the participants in the interviews, sets out to tell a particular story. Of course, the story told in this text is markedly different from that told by the youths. Indeed, it is a story that is different than that imagined and solicited by the social workers who conducted the interviews. Further, it is a story that is delivered to a different audience than any that the participants may have intended. So then what structure do I adopt in this chapter to tell a story?

I begin by addressing the opening moves of participants to name, and thereby establish, the boundaries and forms of the occasion that follows. Of course, inside any generalised or ideal form there exists a space of ambiguity, and accordingly a terrain for contest, struggle, and indeed either transformation or repudiation of the form itself. The first focus of analytic attention will be the occasioned corpus of practice for producing the interview as such, that is as a prescribed form for interaction. Second, while the form of an interview is certainly distinctive with respect to "speech exchange systems" (Schegloff, 1992), what is of interest for the purposes of this chapter are the issues of participants' taken-for-granted competencies –knowledge, skills, and general-ised abilities – to enact this occasion as an interview. The success or failure of this occasion to stand as a proper interview emerges from out of the partici-pants' explicit orientation to a corpus of moves, strategies, and orientations for organising their interactive practices. To state the matter somewhat dif-ferently, borrowing from Baudrillard (1975), participants to an interview necessarily tie utilitarian exchanges marked by organisational relations to systems of symbolic exchanges marked by interpersonal relationships.[4]

Fortunately, for our analytic purposes the tension between the two dimen-sions of exchange are most visible in the utterances, requests, and orientations of the youth. The youths occupy a standpoint outside the work of the social workers and the researcher. While it may not be possible for the social work-ers or the researcher to enter this position, what can be noted are those moments of resistance by youth to the social worker's exercise of professional powers, and the responses of social workers, and to a lesser degree the response or attention of the researcher to such resistance. In the following I move to examine repertoires of inscriptive practices used by social workers to insert untoward instances into manageable, accountable, and warrantable frameworks, e.g. the child was acting out, being silly, getting off topic, not following directions, not listening, misbehaving, and so forth.

The socially organised context

Even though the socially organised background for the production of the audio-recordings are largely invisible and covert in the recording, it is both important and necessary to recognise from the first that the interviews emerge as a moment in, what Smith has called, a "mandated course of action" (1990b:157) wherein "the observed becomes ... a partial observation of an extended course of action to which we have no access" (1990b:157). At the most mundane level the production of the interview relied upon social work-ers engaging in a series of prior actions, that most likely included: contacting youth in care on their caseloads by telephone or during a visit; inviting these youths to participate in the research process; scheduling a meeting with the youths; arranging a meeting spot – usually at agency offices; picking up an audio recorder; arriving at the scheduled time; booking or finding a suitable interview room; and conducting the interview.

It this context the production of the audio-recordings while not a regular part of social workers' day-to-day work represented a variation of otherwise well-established organisational procedures and routines. Conducting inter-views was a part of what is for most social workers the stock-in-trade of their working day. Daily work at the front-line is replete with ongoing instances of contacting clients, arranging meetings, determining locations, and conducting interviews. Through such practices social workers initiate, orga- nise, and perform self-in-interaction in ways that accomplish their compe- tency and their professional powers (Friedson, 1986). This is a power to make occasions happen, and to direct or script those occasions in organisationally warrantable, sanctionable, and controllable forms.

Stepping back somewhat further, it is important to acknowledge that the participation of social workers in the project of interviewing youth in care about their experiences coming into care, and living in care itself emerged from out of considerable background research and organisational work. As the primary researcher either I contacted, or I had my research assistants contact key people in various child protection offices, whether across Ontario, in PEI, BC, Alberta, or the Yukon. Clearly, matters of recognised credentials, authority, legitimacy, and warrant were at work in fostering agreement between agency administrators and my research team. Interviewing and audio-recording of interviews is potentially a very dangerous enterprise. At stake are issues of confidentiality, access to privileged information, and the very safety of youths and the integrity of the agency itself. It would be inconceivable that a child protection agency would give permission to "just anybody" to interview youths and to produce recordings of those interviews.

Further, these interviews need to be understood to be artefacts of a com- plex institutionalised research process. In order to conduct this research funding was required to pay for equipment, supplies, travel and accommoda- tion, and stipends for graduate student research assistants. Before the project began, I had applied for the Social Sciences and Humanities Research Council (SSHRC) for funding. My application was not only reviewed by the SSHRC, but by my university's Research Ethics Board (REB). Once funding was granted, funds were transferred to the university research budget office. In order to receive payment I was required to submit expenses to a finance office, and payment was made once approval was received from the Director of the School of Social Work. Once university approvals were in place we needed to secure permissions and access, have social workers produce inter- views, and to have social workers refer children and youth in care on their caseloads for the research team to interview. In order to enlist social workers in the project, it had to be reviewed by administrators in Children's Aid Societies or in provincial and territorial government ministries responsible for child welfare. Once approved at senior levels, we needed to establish contact with child protection and youth services personnel and present the research project to them. In turn those who volunteered to participate con- tacted youth-in-care on their case-loads, arranged for interviews, and then conducted and audio-recorded the interviews. The audio-recordings had to be transmitted back to me and to my team of research assistants for transcription and review.

While such details may at first glance appear to be trivial matters the attention to precisely such matters is necessary for a proper explication of the data. Indeed, any adequate understanding of such in-hand objects as a computer stick containing an electronic audio-recording of an interview, demands explicating the social organisation which provides for the possibility of its production. At the most rudimentary level the audio-recordings are artefacts of a tremendously complex division of labour, organisational codes for regulating actions, and the insertion of a project into the discursive structures, evaluative protocols, and ethical language of professions.

Yet, beyond the formal recognition of the organisational contexts for the production of the audio-recordings, the question needs to be asked: Do these recordings reveal or articulate the social organisation of their genesis? If the recordings are artefacts of socially organised processes, will they reveal anything about those processes? Further, will the recordings as artefacts of actual practice be able to help us understand how these people who produced the recordings oriented themselves to socially organised forms of work at hand? Hence, can we recover from the recordings how the participants oriented themselves to a series of work processes in which they produced themselves interactively as the social worker, a child in care, a confident, a friend, a helper, a child protection worker, a bad girl, a bad boy, an abuser, a victim, and so forth.

Making and marking the occasion as an interview

The parties to these occasions – social workers and youths in care – repeatedly invoke conversational practices to mark off and thereby signify the production of this talk in interaction as producing a proper interview. In this sense the participants' talk reflexively transforms an occasion into a proper interview as such. Obviously as a minimum the production of the recording depends on mundane and seemingly inconsequential acts. These include turning on the audio-recorder, plugging in a good quality microphone, ensuring that there is a sufficient electrical charge for the period of the interview as well as sufficient memory or space in the device. Once the mechanical concerns with the recorder are settled, then the interviewer must determine where to place the microphone,[5] when to turn on the recorder, when to pause or shut off the recorder, and monitoring the device to ensure that it is actually recording the conversation and not merely sitting decoratively on the desk. Clearly some of these moments though not all will be recorded by the device.

Once the audio-recorder is turned on the talk-in-interaction becomes accountable as both participants recognise that what they say is being recorded. Consider the following two examples:

Y: Okay, this an interview with R conducted at the Children's Aid Society Office, (address), uh, the interviewer is Y.Y. okay, so ah you've read and signed consents, and you understand..

R: yah//

Y: all that, you understand the confidentiality//

R: yah

Segment two:

S: One, two, three, four, five-, (voice trails off) six, seven, eight, nine, ten. Hopefully this is now recording. Uhm, I'm S.S. I'm a social worker with the Children's Aid. Its the twenty-sixth of February, at at..at approx. approximately, a quarter after six p.m. Uhm, I am with a crown ward who I have been working with since she was thirteen. She will be eight-teen on the twenty-second of March. Uhm, this is her third time as a crown ward. Uhm, she came into care as a baby..

T: yah=

S: =and again at the age of six, and came into care the third time at thirteen.

T: °twelve° (softly),

S: Thirteen

T: mmh hu

In both examples the social worker is the first one to speak to the recorder. Although the social worker in the first segment begins by stating "this is an inter-view", the worker in the second avoids the device of naming the occasion, instead "counting off" and saying, "Hopefully this is now recording." She follows the explicit identification of recording by identifying both herself and the youth using organisational categories, i.e. "I'm a social worker with the Children's Aid", and, "I am with a crown ward". Both social workers' opening moves establish a trajectory for that which follows. The first social worker by naming this occasion an interview, and the second by referencing the recording, and their respective identities as a "social worker with the Children's Aid" and as a "crown ward", set out and pre-scribe the forms of that which will follow as observable and accountable.

Through the strategies of naming the occasion, and naming the institutionalised identities of actors, both workers reflexively shape the interaction that follows as a properly warranted and sanctioned interview. The very work of naming this occa-sion as an 'interview' is instructional and instructive. It not only shapes the forms of interactive work that will unfold, as both the social worker and crown ward can orient to their implicit expectations of their performance, but simultaneously sug-gests or offers up frameworks through which the substance or topics of talk will be shaped. That which transpires unfolds according to recognisable forms of war-ranted interaction such that what emerges turn-by-turn is accountably an interview between a social worker and a youth in care. Such openers indicate that however this occasion might eventually work itself out, it will be constituted inside the boundaries of professionally recognisable forms, that is as an interview, or as a moment of appropriately executed talk between a social worker and a client.

Further, in these segments both social workers communicate in their open-ings a sense that this is a performance, and indeed, this sense is recurrently expressed by both social workers and youths throughout interviews – more on this below. Both social workers identify significant elements to be addressed, whether that is respective roles, organisational location, signing of consents – thereby indexing professional concerns for confidentiality, safety of the youth, contractual interaction – prior histories of involvement thereby establishing both authority to speak on matters of fact and to lay claim to a past connection, and involvement between the social worker and the youth.

The abiding concerns of the social workers as expressed in their openers are sensible and recoverable only as read through the background structures of professional work. This is work that includes among its cardinal operative components matters of confidentiality, safety of youth, the best interests of the child, professional competence, and so forth. If we consider the following extract it becomes clear that the power of a social worker to execute a particular occasion as an interview that accords with a series of projected intentions is not always successful.

S: I am meeting with M. We are starting the interview now. (recording off-for an undetermined period of time)
M: I don't have to sit with you do I?
S: No you can sit over there. That's fine.
M: Ugh.
S: We are here to talk about you being in care, and all the things you can remember about being in care. So I'm gonna tap your brain and your memory. So ah, the first thing is do you remember why you came into care, and if you can't remember the first time, think about the second time or the third time . . . well think about, do you rememberv.. Okay, why don't we talk about the first time you came into care?.Okay, what do you remember about it? Do you remember me?
M: yah.
S: Yah, do you remember what happened?
M: No. Yah.
S: Yah. What?

In this example, the social worker S attempts to begin the interview, but something occurs off-record, so to speak, which leads her to turn off the device. After some undetermined period of time the recorder is turned back on, and the first voice recorded is the youth's, who asks, "I don't have to sit with you do I?" to voice a sense of displeasure. S responds by addressing the seating arrangement and ignoring the youth's audible expression of displeasure – "ugh." Rather than addressing potential problems in the relationship, the social worker presses on with her perception of the task, "We are here to talk about you being in care, and all the things you can remember about being in care. So I'm gonna tap your brain and your memory." The social worker asks the youth, "So ah, the first thing is do you remember why you came into care, and if you can't remember the first time, think about the second time or the third time . . .". Clearly, the troubles in the relationship have not been resolved, and M, having failed to have her complaint acknowledged and dealt with, continued to try to indicate that she is unhappy by withholding a response. Unfortunately, the social worker continues to ignore the troubles and presses on with extracting a response to her questions. Although M does respond she provides only minimal information, "Yah", and "No. Yah".

The recorded-interview as performance

Although interviews between social workers and youth in care are fairly routine productions, it is less common that those interviews are audio-recorded and submitted to a researcher for analysis. Further, the participation of the youth in the project appears to have been 'sold' to the youth by several social workers as an opportunity for the youth to tell their story:

S: So T's going to tell you her story.
T: Yo::, my story, lemme see ((clears throat)). I remember my first, my first trip to a group home. I was in H (group home name), it was just the worst thing I had ever seen in my whole life.

In this example the social worker is clearly oriented to at least two potential listeners, the youth and the researcher. She creates the opening for the youth to tell a listener, who although not physically present, is instructed to listen to the recording as a 'story'. The response of the youth is an apparently confident return based on the hip rejoinder, "yo::, my story", followed by the more uncertain "lemme see", a throat clearing, and then a direct launch into a tale about an episode in her history.

A review of this passage reveals a request by the social worker for a story, and the response by the youth that signifies compliance with the request, as well as an initial experience of anxiety, uncertainty about her capacity to produce and perform as expected. Her sense of uncertainty is clearly warranted, for from her standpoint the mundane question of "where to begin" is obviously a worry. How should she organise her story? Should she organise the story according to linear or calendar time? Should she organise it to address major traumatic events and episodes? Should she organise the story as a free association of themes, concerns, and interests? Should she let the social worker take leadership by asking more explicit questions? Additionally, she has to consider what will the social worker count as an adequate, coherent, and proper story or account of her life. Indeed, it is little wonder that she signals she is uncertain how to begin.

Just how the participants cue their activities to the production of the audio-recording is not always smoothly effected, and indeed, the recorder and the recording that results represent a meta commentary on the work at hand. In the following example, the social worker attempts to address both the youth and the recorder (or an anticipated listener). This results in a serious confusion, and a misinterpretation, that leads to the youth feeling insulted.

J: ... How did you get along with S, do you remember? S's your sister.

M: Hey, I know S's my sister, heh heh ((laughing)).

J: Okay, no, but I was doing that for the recorder, heh heh. Uhm.

M: My God, I'm not that dumb. Yah, my sister. How did I get along with S?

J: yah.

M: Okay. She was always in her own world. We were never in the house together. It was tough

In the first line the social worker introduces a question about S whom they both know to be M's sister, but adds, "S's your sister". Clearly, the nature of the relationship between M and S is not an accountable matter for either J or M in this moment of conversation – though we can easily imagine any number of possible scenarios in which it might be, e.g. if S did something to J that was not normally considered an appropriate action by a sister, if J indicated that either S's mother or father were not the same as M's, and so on. It is precisely because S's relation to M is known to the participants that J's explicit specification of the relationship, "S's your sister", is so untoward, surprising, and upsetting to M. To repair the misunderstanding the social worker indicates, "but I was doing that for the recorder", thereby making explicit her tacit reference to the background to her work. In this instance it would appear that M did not pick-up on or recognise that J was playing to an invisible audience that would access their talk through the audio-recording.

This incident illustrates the tensions that result rather routinely in interactions between social workers and clients. In this instance, a confusion was created because the social worker, but not the child, was oriented to the work at hand as producing a recording. From the standpoint of the child this interactive moment appears to have been situated in the work of answering the social worker's questions. Clearly, the social worker treated the interaction at hand as a piece of work, or as a moment in a more extended process that would ultimately absorb the particular interview as a piece of data.

Now it should come as no surprise that social workers are continually engaged in precisely such splits between the at hand work of the moment and the anticipated articulation of this work to organisational purposes. Social worker's motivations for proceeding as they do are hardly idiosyncratic, but rather express their organisational location. Each and every meeting with a client has warrant and significance to be actually or potentially reported on other later occasions for specific organisational purposes. For example, that a youth talks about drinking at a party, smoking marijuana, going AWOL may become remarkable matters to be discussed at a team meeting, in a running record, in a monthly report, in a referral for services, and so on.

Clients often experience the effects of such ruptures in the course of their meetings with social workers. Although clients may not have access to the background knowledge that informs social worker's questions and directions in interviews, they are able to tell when a question seems to "come out of left field", or "is about something else". When clients get together with friends to complain about a social worker's "stupid questions" what is most likely at issue is the disjunction between the client's understanding of the interview and the social worker's orientation to background concerns. Troubles in interviews develop precisely because clients are often unable to recover the theoretical and discursive forms that social workers rely on to conduct interviews.

It is precisely because social workers understand how particular occasions may be taken up and reworked within an extra-local organisational apparatus, while clients do not, that clients routinely feel confused, angry, and uncertain when interviewed by social workers, and other professional helpers. From the standpoint of clients the social organisation of institutional settings is largely invisible and hidden, with the result that while they may attempt to match their responses to what they imagine might be counted as a warranted response, they are not always successful in doing so. On the other hand the social worker may, due to his or her preoccupation with their own organisational location, lose sight of the standpoint, abiding concerns, and focus of attention of the client, with sometimes 'disastrous' results. The social worker's routine orientation to the task at hand, or the talk at hand, in addition to producing confusions such as addressed above, can also produce considerable resistance from the client, who may not want to invest themselves in the social worker's task.

In the following segment J (the social worker) and M had been discussing painting M's room in the foster home. M insisted that she wanted the room "black" and not "green with a border".

J: Actually a friend of mine painted her room black, and put stars and moons and stuff on it. It looked really cool. You'd like it. It's right up your alley, uh..
M: Are we almost done?
J: No. Why? Are you getting tired doing this?
M: Yah.
J: Okay, well what we can do is a couple more, and then we'll turn it off, and then we can begin at another time, okay. Is that all right?
J: Like is it taxing your brain or are you getting bored?
M: I'm getting bored.
J: Oh, well maybe we should make it more exciting?
M: No. I//
J: hee hee, hee, you should remember more.
M: I, eh(_).

The social worker seems to attempt to join the youth by matching of preferences or "judgmental propositions" (Boggs, 1990:108). The youth's petulant, "Are we almost done?", marks an obvious closure of an existing sequence, and a refusal to entertain a match of judgments, to thereby initiate a new sequence, that defiantly seeks to bring the social worker's project to an end. The youth closes the sequence on room decor without any obvious link, and invokes instead an opening to a potentially more confrontational series of exchanges.

The social worker when confronted with such obviously subversive demands for cessation of her project is placed into a bind. As a professional her response is conditioned by a series of imperatives to be respectful, courteous, and sensitive to the client's agenda. Further because this is an audio-recorded interview, the social worker is more vulnerable than usual as she is certainly aware that whatever response she crafts will be recorded, and accordingly will be listened to, reviewed, and evaluated. Yet, if the social worker consents to the youth's request she must abandon the project, turn off the recorder, and leave the job undone, which may also suggest failure or lack of skill.[6]

Indeed, for me as a social work practices instructor, the social worker in this segment does manage this exchange rather badly. Although what counts as the criteria for addressing either good or bad management of the client's response is not the focus of this paper, it is worth noting that the social worker relies on ordinary dis-preference for confrontation and conflict. Rather than exploring the youth's hostility to the interview directly the social worker suggests an insult "Like is it taxing your brain or are you getting bored?", and offers an explanation of the problem that places the responsibility for troubles solely on the youth. While in regular conversation we might expect that the adult would chastise the child for being rude or sullen, in an interview such a response would be recognisably and transparently inappropriate as it would blame the youth for troubles. Yet this social worker, rather than explicitly blaming the youth does so implicitly, thereby violating an axiom that healthy communication should be "clear and direct" (Will & Wrate, 1985). Furthermore, this social workers' passive aggressive response fails to maintain empathy or respect for individual difference (Biesteck, 1951).

The social worker faces the challenge throughout the interviews of ensuring her responses to the youth are warrantable as instances of professional conduct. Further her responses must be crafted to be demonstrably competent, appropriate, and skilful. The stock-in-trade of clinical social work courses use role-plays to explore how a social worker might use different techniques for managing resistant clients.[7] The social worker in this segment fails in her attempt to interest the child in the interview. To manage the child's resistance she tries "laughing it off" (Sacks, 1995:16). As Sacks points out "laughing it off" enables an actor to avoid treating an utterance as a "serious invitation", and thereby to avoid asking, "where would I be" (Sacks, 1995:16) if I took the utterance seriously. Indeed, if the social worker would have taken the client's utterance seriously she would have had to consider 'where she would be', hence would the interview continue? By laughing it off, the social worker slips away from addressing the issue of her ability to engage and interest the youth.

Constructive powers

Precisely because the domain of practice that brings social workers together with youths in care is intimate, personal, and private, the content of that discussed in interviews is potentially quite upsetting and unsettling. Although in the previous segment we encountered a social worker who dealt with potential conflict by laughing it off, more skilled workers are prepared to invite youth in care to be critical of child welfare services, and in so doing create a space for authentic expression of feeling, to thereby work through difficult life issues. Of course, such invitations are inherently dangerous as they may lead to not only criticism of child welfare services, but criticism of colleagues and even the social worker conducting the interview himself or herself. Yet by inviting youths to be critical, and allowing them to explore their feelings about child welfare, social workers also create an opportunity that allows them to provide re-interpretations of accounts that help youth to reframe and to make new sense of their lives.

Y: So these people who were around you when you came into care did they/ how did they affect you, did they help you, did they harm yu/ do you feel they harmed you, any//

S: At that time I was feeling they were harming me because I wasn't really used to that kinda invasion, just come in and kinda you know. Ah, I didn't understand why, cause I thought that was normal for me, I didn't know that wasn't normal=

Y: =the okay

S: but ah, I though ah, what the hell are they doing, you know? Like, just come in here kinda you know, like fine, my mom's consent that I should go, you know.

Y: Your mom was consenting?

S: yah, surely

Y: So did you, you were, you said earlier you were confused by the ah, the whole process and now your saying uhm that also you felt that people were, at that time you felt people were wanting to harm you, uhm, that's a pretty scary situation then.

S: yah

Y: did you ask? Do you remember if you ask any peo/ anybody what was happening?

S: uhm.

Y: be/btes/well you were pretty young eh?

S: yah, but I/I didn't really ask, I jj/jist was angry a lot, you know. I was jist ah, got really angry, and ah, fight back and jist not listen.

Y: Did anybody ever try to understand? yu/yu//[there were alota issues]

S: [I think alota] people did, they tried to understand but ah//

Y: did they try to make you understand though, did pee/people explain what was happening to you? . .

S: They, they did, they did I, in in certain ways, like..

Y: In a way that you could understand=

S: =not really=

Y: =not really, eh=

S: =it was too hard for me to understand=

Y: =uh huh

S: really, the way. I, I still wouldn't have understood anyway. Like its kinda hard to understand when somebody is taking you out of your house=

Y: =yah

S: like so what you know. But I don't know. I didn't really get to understand it perfect . . . . .

Y: hhhoo boy ((very soft sigh)) What/ what woul, could've been done different, what might have helped you at the time that you came into care?

S: okay, ah uhm, not really, nu/nu/nothing much different.

Y: nothing much different?

S: well, alla damage was done when I was at my house, so I donknow, I mean, there's nothing much you coulda done better

Y: okay

S: accept for maybe ah, if I needed like, a little treatments or a little counselling, that would've been the only thing.

In this segment Y (the social worker), asks a young man about his perceptions of "these people who were around you when you came into care", and "how did they affect you, did they help you, did they harm yu/ do you feel they harmed you". The social worker frames his question in the past-tense, thereby allowing S to craft an account that provides for slippage or change between what he might have felt then and what he feels or understands now. Y, by inviting S to address both negative and positive perceptions of the people he met after coming into care, creates an opening for S to speak critically about his experiences in care. Although, as noted, such openings are potentially dangerous, they also signal to the client that it is okay to be honest and to speak openly. Through such moves the social worker creates a space in which trust and a relationship can be developed, even if this might mean that the youth expresses anger, disappointment, or frustration with the social worker himself.

More importantly however, Y's invitation creates an opening for S to address his perception of the changes he might have undergone while in care. Y's invitation allows S to reflect, "At that time I was feeling they were harming me because I wasn't really used to that kinda invasion". S then develops a story that juxtaposes what he had come to accept as normal, "I thought that was normal for me, I didn't know that wasn't normal" when living with others and his new experience in care. Although S does not indicate specifically the ways that life in care was different, other than the fact that he was no longer living with his mother, he is able to articulate his sense of discomfort, albeit expressed as anger, "I jj/jist was angry a lot, you know. I was jist ah, got really angry, and ah, fight back and jist not listen." The social worker uses S's recognition of anger to ask an apparently neutral question, "What/ what woul, could've been done different, what might have helped you at the time that you came into care?" The neutrality of the question, that is it openness to either a positive or negative response, is used to good effect, as it presses S to respond with commensurate fairness or objectivity. He replies, "okay, ah uhm, not really, nu/nu/nothing much different." By modelling fair and reasoned examination of experiences Y leads S to an important recognition, namely that his sense of anger may not have been due to an actual but to a perceived injustice. His anger may have been as much about his own issues as about the type of treatment he received in care.

Through this moment of work we can see that Y uses his power as a social worker to model and to promote reasoned and fair evaluation of experiences. This is a power rooted in skilful use of questions that encourage S to answer honestly and fairly. This is a power rooted in a gentle use of professional knowledge and authority, rather than coercive forms of authority. By crafting a form of open and welcoming interaction with S, Y the social worker manages to not only perform an interview but to lead S to important insights about his life in care. Y's use of power is neither coercive or authoritative, but is rooted in practice knowledge and practice wisdom.

Summary and conclusion

The sub-title of this chapter is 'Writing and erasing youths' stories', and at times, as the author I have been guilty of both writing over and erasing the stories that youths were attempting to create in the interviews. I have crafted this chapter for an audience of social workers and other professionals which by extension does not include youth in care. In this sense, the youth's utterances are appropriated as objects to become part of an intellectual currency. Their stories are made to function for purposes other than those they intended. Their words and stories have been pressed into service for other tasks. Indeed, it is precisely in such moments of separation and appropriation that I along with my social work brethren rework the material from clients' lives into properly sanctioned professional assessments and reports. How then can we write youth's stories? Can we refuse to erase their stories? Is such refusal possible?

I have suggested that the process of writing and erasing youths' stories is achieved not just in the moments of an interview, but in the concrete forms for accomplishing an interview as such. I have argued that the interview is itself but a moment inside extended social relations. These are social relations marked by profound asymmetries of power based on age, education, and perhaps most importantly, formal organisational sanction. Just as social workers count what will count as relevant matters of fact so too do researchers. Though, youth are outside the loops of organisational and professional power they are not passive. Youth often actively resist the imposition of professional and organisational forms of power over their lives.

Neither social workers nor researchers can afford to ignore the ways in which the social organisation of their day-to-day working activities construct what counts as knowledge about people's lives. Social workers must not act as if their activities of arranging interviews, writing case notes, and identifying the points for analysis are incidental to the facts. Indeed, what count as the facts is thoroughly conditioned by the work of producing facts. Both social workers and researchers must acknowledge the profound reflexivity of that which they present as stories and accounts of the lives of others. Both social workers and researchers exercise professional powers to organise occasions, whether by producing interview guides, selecting the physical location for the interaction, structuring the dynamics of the interaction through routine adherence to established protocols, and so forth.

Yet, the conflicts at the heart of social work and social science methodology, of acting as if accounts were not reflexive, as if the knower and the known can be separated, are paralleled in the disjunctures between formal and informal practice. The attempt to construct relations of utilitarian exchange are challenged not only by social worker's clients but at times by social worker's themselves. An explication of the foundational conflicts at the root of professional practice suggests some directions for correctives, though correctives, as noted in Chapter 2, may be unfashionable for some ethnomethodologists, nevertheless they are a moral imperative for social workers.

As a first corrective social workers and researchers must acknowledge the fundamental disjuncture between the formal and the informal, the utilitarian and the symbolic, not as something to be solved once and for all but as a source of tension to be worked on and even played with. Second, both social workers and researchers must acknowledge their own position and forces pulling them one way or the other within this disjuncture. As professionals they find that the very forms of acceptable, warrantable, and proper practice are dictated by the exchange they have made between themselves and their employers, between themselves and their profession, and between themselves and their clients. Again, there is no simple solution. Their institutional location cannot be idealistically repudiated, and hence they cannot simply become friends with their clients. Social workers cannot "go native". Third, at the heart of social work and research are the powers to name, to analyse, and to order the experiences and lives of others. These are power that provide quite determinate pleasures, as the insights, resolutions, and solutions that a social worker might recognise in a client's talk can be communicated, in refracted and revised form back to a client (Buttny, 1996). These are powers which cannot be simply repudiated, neither through a romantic valorisation of client stories or narratives, nor through an uncritical elevation of experience over analysis. Finally, and perhaps most importantly, I have argued that youth are not "social dopes" (Garfinkel, 1967). Youth manage their encounters with formal, impersonal, and organisational workers by employing tremendously skilful devices. As social workers and researchers an acknowledgment of this skill is essential for competent and respectful practice.

Notes

1 Of course interaction is never quite this simple, as there may also be openings in which the client poses questions to a social worker, and a social worker is expected to answer. Though, however, what is likely is that such questions will be oriented to information gathering rather than to disclosure about personal life. Though even such general rules might be transgressed, as a mother involved with a child protection social worker might challenge the worker by asking, "Do you have any children?"

2 The challenge of developing adequate transcriptions of conversations was made more difficult by the fact that I am hearing impaired, and wear hearing aids. After the first few weeks I abandoned the hearing aids as I discovered that the compression devices in them limited the volume while increasing some distortion.

3 Fortunately there are a growing number of useful primers for doing CA. These include Psathas' introduction to conversation analysis (1995), ten Have's (2007) "practical guide", and Hutchy and Wooffitt's (1998) insightful overview of "principles, practices, and applications" of CA. Additionally, Schegloff's (2007) has produced an extremely detailed and comprehensive text entitled *Sequence Organization in Interaction*.

4 Baudrillard relies on Bataille and Kristeva to develop an analysis of utilitian exchange as differentiated by symbolic exchange. While the former is concerned with the production of use values for exchange within a political economy, the latter is centred in attention to "discharge, waste, sacrifice, prodigality, play, and symbolism" (1975:42). The challenge to humanity is that within a capitalist economy the latter is "overdetermined", with the result that the former is marginalised, devalued, and ideologically erased. Of course the erasure is never complete, for waste, prodigality, play, and symbolism although marginalised and displaced from the attention of serious research, continue to intrude as dynamic forces in our every-day lives, particularly in those of children and youth.

5 The production of a successful interview relies on absolutely mundane but essential practices such as the placement of the audio-recorder and microphone. Indeed, whether or not the voices of the participants are clear, audible, and can be transcribed from the vantage point of the researcher relies on precisely such skills, and of course the proper functioning of the equipment. In the process of transcribing recordings some were of much superior audio quality than others due to placement of the microphone relative to the location of the participants, and the proper operation of the microphone and recorder.

6 It may be worth noting that this social worker conducted only the one interview, and refused to conduct further interviews. Indeed, as a social worker myself, I found it very difficult listening to a recording without engaging in evaluative assessments of the interviewer's skill, empathy, engagement with the youth, and general practice competency.

7 In this case, a series of obvious correctives might be suggested that would include: Using open ended questions such as, "Okay, what is happening with you right now?", "What would you like to do now?", or "What would you like to talk about?" Addressing the youth's feelings, "You don't seem too happy about how this interview is going? Can we talk about it?", "You seem to have become frustrated and angry when we talked about your room at H. I guess it seems like others are always making decisions for you. Can you tell me how that feels?"

References

Baudrillard, Jean. (1975). *The mirror of production* (Trans. Mark Poster). St. Louis, MO: Telos.

Biestek, Felix. (1951). *The principle of client self-determination in social casework.* Washington, DC: Catholic University of America Press.

Boggs, Stephen T. (1990). The role of routines in the evolution of children's peer talk. In Bruce Dorval (Ed.), *Conversational organization and its development* (pp. 101–130). Norwood, NJ: Ablex.

Buttny, Richard. (1996). Clients' and therapist's joint construction of the clients' problems. *Research on language and social interaction*, 29(2): 125–153.

Campbell, Marie, & Manicom, Anne (Eds.). (1995). *Knowledge, experience, and ruling relations: Studies in the social organization of knowledge.* Toronto, ON: University of Toronto Press.

de Montigny, Gerald. (1995). *Social working: An ethnography of front-line practice.* Toronto, ON: University of Toronto Press.

Derrida, Jacques. (1973). *Speech and phenomena* (Trans. David B. Allison). Evanston, IL: Northwestern University Press.

Derrida, Jacques. (1981). *Positions* (Trans. Alan Bass). Chicago, IL: University of Chicago Press.

Foucault, Michel. (1980). *Power/knowledge: Selected interview and other writings 1972–1977* (Ed. Colin Gordon). New York, NY: Pantheon.

Frank, Arthur. 1985. Out of ethnomethodology. In H. J. Helle and S. N. Eisenstadt (Eds.), *Micro-sociological theory: Perspectives on sociological theory (Volume 2)* (pp. 106–116). Beverley Hills, CA: Sage.

Friedson, Eliot. (1986). *Professional powers: A study of institutionalization of formal knowledge.* Chicago, IL: University of Chicago Press.

Garfinkel, Harold. (1967). *Studies in ethnomethodology.* Englewood Cliffs, NJ: Prentice-Hall.

Hutchby, Ian, & Wooffitt, Robin. (1998). *Conversation analysis.* Cambridge, England: Polity.

Latour, Bruno, & Woolgar, Steve. (1979). *Laboratory life: The social construction of scientific facts.* Beverly Hills, CA: Sage.

Mullaly, Bob. (2002). *Challenging oppression: A critical social work approach.* Don Mills, ON: Oxford University Press.

Psathas, George. (1995). *Conversation analysis: The study of talk in interaction.* Thousand Oaks, CA: Sage.

Sacks, Harvey. (1995). *Lectures on conversation (Volumes 1 & 2)* (Ed. Gail Jefferson). Oxford, England: Blackwell.

Schegloff, Emanuel A. (1992). On talk and its institutional occasions. In Paul Drew & John Heritage (Eds.), *Talk at work: Interaction in institutional settings* (pp. 101–134). Cambridge, England: Cambridge University Press.

Schegloff, Emanuel A. (2007). *Sequence organization in interaction: A primer in conversation analysis (Volume 1).* New York, NY: Cambridge University Press.

Smith, Dorothy E. (1987). *The everyday world as problematic: A feminist sociology.* Toronto, ON: University of Toronto Press.

Smith, Dorothy E. (1990a). *The conceptual practices of power: A feminist sociology of knowledge.* Toronto, ON: University of Toronto Press.

Smith, Dorothy E. (1990b). *Texts, facts, and femininity: Exploring the relations of ruling.* London, England: Routledge.

Smith, Dorothy E. (1999). *Writing the social: Critique theory and investigations.* Toronto, ON: University of Toronto Press.

Smith, Dorothy E. (2005). *Institutional ethnography: A sociology for people.* Lanham, MD: AltaMira.

ten Have, Paul. (2007). *Doing conversation analysis: A practical guide*. London, England: Sage.

Touraine, Alain. (1995). *Critique of modernity* (Trans. David Macey). Oxford, England: Blackwell.

Will, David, & Wrate, Robert M. (1985). *Integrated family therapy: A problem-centred psychodynamic approach*. London, England: Tavistock.

7 Relationship in an Interviews

E: I was dead fer two minutes.

G: What↑

E: Yep, I hawa, I was eight years old, went down a foot ravine, on a bike, BMX

G: yah

E: there was a sharp turn, I made that turn, and there was a big bouwlder there

G: oh lord=

E: =I was going fast enough that I hit that bouwlder dead on=

G: yah

E: it made me go inta the air about ten feet across, I was bein skidded on my back, I was still being skid fe about five feet, hit anothew big bouwlder with my head, and tuwn my body vewtical-cal, then I was on my stomach. And I was dead fer two minutes wight then, and getting back, and I woke up in a house, it was my fwiends house.

G: jeeze=

E: =and I said wow,

G: that's pretty scary.

E: and yecan, outta body expewience.

G: didja, youreally did

E: yah

G: an outta body experience. Yah, well that's pretty awesome

E: but it's jist,

G: yah yah

E: strange

G: huh

E: because I was, my body was dead but not me

G: Didja see yerself

E: I was walkin around

G: no

E: but when I came too I was ina house

G: heh, that's amazing

E: I din thought I got myself hurt, but when I=

G: =yah=

E: =stood up, I walked, an forgot about the bike

G: didja hafta go to the hospital

E: Yah, I spent about two months, them picking at my back gettin all the rwocks out.

G: Was there any concussion.

E: mm uh.

G: no eh.

E: my head wasss like a rwock

G: yah

E: like all I got when I hit those rwocks with my head, all I got was a big like, big goose egg

G: yah

E: what covered right there. My head wasn't split open or anything, even though I hit that rock.

Introduction

The preceding segment is from an interview I (G) conducted with Ed[1](E). During the interview Ed related a story about a bicycle accident that was both extraordinary and fantastic. He claimed that he had been dead for two minutes, that he hit a boulder with his head, that he had an out of body experience, and that despite such obvious trauma he claims that he did not suffer a concussion because as he explained "my head wasss like a rwock". Just as fascinating as his story might be, so too is my response. I do not directly dispute or contradict Ed's fantastic claims. The closest I come to challenging Ed was when I responded to his claim of having had an out of body experience by asking, "didja, youreally did". What is going on here? What sort of work are Ed and I doing together? What sort of work is Ed doing by telling and developing this story? What sort of work am I doing in my responses as a listener to his story? How do I receive the story, and what work do I do with Ed's story?

Indeed, the ways that I respond to Ed's story provides for the possibility of building a relationship of trust. Conversation analysis (CA) allows us to unpack the issues of trust-building as effected turn-by-turn, thereby bringing our attention to strategies for avoiding trouble, bypassing tensions, and managing potential disagreements. Through a turn-by-turn analysis CA allows us to see issues of timing and strategy as practically effected between participants. Unlike previous chapters where I employed segments from different interviews, in this chapter I focus on a single interview which I conducted with a seventeen year old Indigenous youth in northern Canada. Through detailed focus on this single interview I seek to draw out the utility of CA for social work practice at the front-line. It is precisely because CA draws attention to the accomplishment of social scenes as in vivo practice, through talk-in-interaction that social workers can better come to understand as a detailed matter the ways that they accomplish interviews and other interactions with clients.

By focussing on talk-in-interaction, conversation analysis gives us tools for addressing the complex work achieved interactively through telling stories, and the activities of listening to stories. In this segment, we can see that what is at work in a turn-by-turn fashion appears to build a particular type of relationship, which minimally can be described as involving an interviewer and an interviewee. Of course, beyond this basic or simple description of the relationship, are other dimensions, for constructing relationships, hence, dimensions of difference and similarity between participants. For example, can we see signs of a relationship across professional and personal dimensions, across ages and life experiences, across gender, across urban and rural experiences, across racial identifications, across class and life opportunities, and so on? Indeed, if we ask what sort of relationship is being accomplished in and through the talk recorded in this segment, we can begin to explicate the strategies deployed by the participants turn by turn for not only communicating a story, but for defining and building a particular form or type of relationship.

Fortunately, as the interviewer, I can reflect on this segment, and on the interview as a whole. I can approach this piece of data with a knowledge of why my participation contributed to its structure as it emerged. While any reader of the segment can see, that I refrain from overtly stating my opinions or voicing my viewpoint, or expressing overt scepticism concerning Ed's tale, as the interviewer I recognise these as strategies for keeping Ed on side, for building an alliance with him and for communicating an acceptance of his understanding of reality. As this is our first and only meeting, my objectives are to win Ed's trust to the extent that he will provide me with a voluntarily produced and useful – for my research purposes – narrative of his life.

Our work performed in this segment, although bound by the fact that it was a single interview rather than a sustained case-work relationship, nevertheless reflects or mimics interactive forms necessary for building and sustaining helping relationships generally. In many ways this interview parallels the first meeting in any helping relationship. Social workers begin as strangers to clients, and as such they need to work through the sorts of issues Shulman (2016) identifies, i.e. can I trust this person, what does he or she want of me, can we work together? While fantastic stories and claims might be noted, as material to be explored in subsequent meetings, in first meetings they may be allowed to let pass, with minimal interrogation or challenge. That fantastic stories are not initially challenged does not mean that they are unremarkable, but only that for the interviewer or social worker the time is not deemed right to raise critical challenges, either in the form of questions, or elaboration. Simply, what is said, turn by turn, is shaped strategically. Social work turns, when shaped as 'interventions', are informed by background relevances, references, and professional consideration. As interventions turns are shaped to perform certain types of work, quite apart from explicit or overt content.

The work I perform as a listener, the ways that I communicate that I am listening to Ed, and my approach to Ed's claims – i.e. accepting them, exploring them, and not explicitly challenging, ridiculing, or dismissing them – reveal a great deal about social work strategies for relationship building. If Ed's claims are patently untenable, how should I, or any other social worker respond to Ed? Should we challenge him? If we should challenge such claims, when and how should challenges be formulated? How might Ed or any other client respond to our challenges? In this nexus of challenge, response to challenge, and social worker's responses to client responses we can better unfold the practical accomplishment of that which is called respect, understanding and empathy.

I experienced this as a particularly difficult interview. In that which follows I will take up this difficulty as a providing a point of entry for an explication of the art of interviewing. As the interview began I repeatedly miscued, misunderstood, and felt that I was not joining with Ed. I struggled to establish rapport, and though I think that by the end of the interview I managed to do so, it was an achievement not easily won. Yet, by noticing and attending to that which is difficult, and that which did not go well, we can also make explicit not only that which makes an interview go well, but the dynamic tension between ideal and reality that structures interview situations. Indeed, what is it to go well? What is the nexus of desire, imagination, intention, expectations, self-reflective and self-critical analysis, in contradistinction to that which actually happens, which informs arriving at an assessment that the interview went well?

An interview that does not proceed as desired or expected illuminates both participants' expectations and differential practices for producing the occasion as such. The discomfort produced in an interview that goes badly works to bring into focus the often-tacit expectations and preferred forms for organising interviews. Through such seemingly trivial matters as silence or pauses and gaps, interruptions, evidence of repairs, length of turns, and sequence structure social workers can better come to understand the in vivo mechanics of such problems as disagreement, sullen withdrawal, anger, stubborn defiance, and so on.

In focussing on troubles in this interview I confess to feeling somewhat vulnerable. Could the troubles be a sign of my deficiencies, lack of skills, ineptitude, and incompetence? Certainly, such evaluative matters are a repeated source of anxiety for social work students, and even for experienced practitioners. Such anxieties are a primary reason why so much resistance occurs when students and practitioners are asked to audio-record their interviews with clients and to submit those recordings for analysis by others. Though it may be hubris I must confess that I am not really bothered by such concerns. Rather, it is my strong sense that the sorts of troubles I identify in this chapter are similar to those that arise in any interview situation, and in most encounters with clients. Troubles are not solely the effects of personality, but rather are in large part the structured effects of the challenge of performing a relationship through talk-in-interaction. Troubles are at the very core of talk, and as such are rooted in our human condition.

The forms of an interview are not just a matter of personality, and not only emerge from out of complex interactional dynamic, but through reference to institutional context and relevances in which co-participants shape each other's responses (Malone, 1995). Further, the interview must in turn be recognised as one moment, or fragment in the life stream of the participants, who have come together often from out of profound life differences (Kohler Riessman, 1993). From out of their differences they may rely on different methods to organise narratives and the hard work of coming to understand different lexicons, different ways of ordering a life-world, and different ways of producing self. These can be seen in the very forms of interaction. An analysis of the interview is needed which brings into focus the complex practices for constituting self as an interviewer, and reciprocally for constituting self as the interviewee. Of course, these interactive practices articulate other shadings and nuances of self-construction and self-representation in interaction with others that include moral and ethical ontologies as male, Indigenous, white, educated, tough, honest, brave, kind, loyal, and so forth.

As the interview unfolded our talk-in-interaction articulated complex socially organised background practices for indicating and performing both similarities and differences, tracking across socially recognised signposts of age, race, class, and so on. Indeed, in what follows I will examine our interaction as doing masculinity. Of course, following Schegloff's (1992) dictum of relevance, this description of interaction as "doing masculinity" is a gloss, particularly given that neither Ed, nor I, explicitly name it as such in our talk. Yet, what informs my deployment of the gloss of masculinity? What am I pointing to as somehow a performance of being and acting male? By naming that which is at work a performance of masculinity, am I transgressing the strictures of CA by presupposing that which, if it is to be asserted, must be discovered in the conduct of the materials (Schegloff, 1992:110)? However, by examining detailed analysis of talk in interaction I aim to produce a compelling case that though not named, such practices for doing gender and marking off difference are an essential component for explicating the nature of interaction between Ed and I on this occasion. Simply, the sensibility of the interaction relies on unnamed although drawn on capacities, orientations, and forms of being in the world, we call gender.

Research or social work

It may be asked whether the fact that the interview was conducted as part of a research project rather than as a moment of social work vitiates its applicability and relevance for social work practice. Although this is certainly a fair question, I argue that the objectives of the research project, it's staffing, and the organisational settings in which interviews were conducted created a similarity with front-line social work practice. The interview I conducted with Ed, by virtue of being conducted in a child protection office, and as organised with the assistance and cooperation of social workers in that office, of necessity reflected general social work principles and practices. Further, although my objectives in the interview were organised by the objectives of the research project, these were to help social workers understand the experiences of youth in care by inviting youth into a dialogue about their lives. The putative claim that the project would advance a collective understanding of the experiences of youth in care was anticipated to advance front-line practice in child protection generally.

Precisely because my objective was to give youth in care a voice, that is to create a forum in which they were invited to speak about their experiences, it was necessary that I as an adult be committed to listening to, reflecting on, and digesting what they had to say. I also recognised that as a former social worker and as an adult that I might have some life wisdom that might be a resource to youth in their struggle to make sense of their own life experiences. In all interviews I was bound by legal and ethical requirements to identify and to protect children and youth at risk. Though the interviews were conducted for research purposes, in any cases that arose where I or my researchers came to believe that youth might be at risk, we were bound to report, and indeed we did routinely report this information to the child protection authorities under whose auspices, and in whose offices we conducted interviews. The fact that the interviews were conducted under the auspices of child protection agencies and organisations of necessity meant a continual orientation, and monitoring of risk to youth in care. Finally, it must be noted that when doing interviews with youth in care I drew on my knowledge and experience as a former child protection worker.

A central objective in the design of the research project that generated the interviews with youth in care was to combine data collection about youths' experiences with helping processes rooted in social work. The focus on providing help, counselling, support, and referral would not normally be part of conversation analysis. CA researchers in their focus on talk-in-interaction in ordinary conversations, or their analysis of talk-in-institutions, approach participants sociologically, that is, the objective is to understand what is being done, not necessarily to help people to do it better. For social workers a focus on talk-in-interaction must always be informed by an orientation to providing assistance, easing emotional trauma, problem solving, and so forth. To approach interviews as a social worker is to always ask: What can I learn from this occasion that will allow me to improve my practice? What can make me a more effective helper? What do I need to know to allow me to understand better the problems, difficulties, and issues raised by this client? What can I say or do that will help this person to cope with or resolve their problems?

The interviews conducted for this project also differed from those of conventional qualitative sociological research. While a research interview may be oriented to eliciting the "depth of detail from respondents" (Hermanowicz, 2002:481), in social work an interview must also be oriented to building a positive professionally congruent relationship that accords with ethical principles of social work practice. Pawson, speaking as a sociologist, summarises that the purpose of an interview is to "advance data in order to inspire/validate/falsify/modify sociological explanation" (1996:295). Against this way of understanding interviews in social work we must always aspire to build trust, respect, honest engagement, and accordingly some form of helping process.

From within my standpoint as a social worker I am obligated, and must perform my relationship with Ed as accountably ethical, that is as subject to review by colleagues and other social workers, as ethical in the details of its performance. As a social worker, there is an abiding sense that an interview with a youth in care, cannot be conducted solely for research purposes, nor simply to gather data. Against such instrumentalities a social work interview must foster communication, understanding and respectful sharing of our places and being in the world. As a social work interviewer, I cannot exploit a youth's experience simply to produce a story for research. Rather the process, and the relationships we create, albeit only for this hour or so, are as important as the data derived from the encounter. Further, as an adult who believes that he possesses some life experience and wisdom, I felt obliged to counter those elements of youths' stories that were hateful, self- or other destructive, or patently false and harmful to themselves and others. Yet, as an adult, and as a father of three adult children, I recognise that timing, tone, and presentation are essential when challenging youth about their beliefs, no matter how problematic. To challenge a youth in an interview requires both understanding and skill. Challenge must be joined to not only understanding but empathic recognition and openness to hear, and to join a young person in an examination of the profoundly emotional nature of the transitions in life, experience, and existence brought about by coming into care and living in care. These are experiences of profound loss and often grief, both visible and invisible, tangible and intangible (Crenshaw & Hardy, 2006; Hardy & Laszloffy, 2005).

In addition to the concerns for trust and respect, as a social worker I am also aware of the need to recognise a youth's privacy, to step back from intrusive questions about painful and traumatic events, to safeguard the youth's emotional safety, and at the same time to be alert to issues that might put the youth at risk. In my past work as a forensic social worker, responsible for producing extensive bio-psycho-social assessments, I learned how to lead clients to confess details of their activities (e.g. criminal offences) that were often against their immediate interests, resulting in additional charges, or withdrawal of their privileges, and which accordingly they preferred to keep secret. While Hermanowicz may express a preference for "getting to the core of people", getting past their "protective shell", and making them "crack" to "show their inner workings" (2002:481), such objectives are, except for quite specific types of social work, not acceptable.

Mazeland and ten Have point out that what is said in an interview situation has a "triple orientation", that is first as a description of the "life world of the speaker", second as having a "local relevance" – oriented to the interview situation itself – and, third, as data or materials for analysis to be used by the researcher (1996:1). While this threefold taxonomy is helpful in part, the notion of "local relevance" is a gloss as it conflates issues of work with issues of play, an instrumental orientation with an expressive orientation, utilitarian exchange with symbolic exchange, and exploitation with caring. To understand what is transpiring in and as an interview we must look beyond the content of the talk-in-interaction, to explore the ways that the talk performs both locally relevant and extra-local institutionally sanctioned forms of social relationships. In this case our concern is to examine how people use talk to effect and navigate and to produce as local and institutional matters dynamics of power and control as negotiated, whereby one person positions self as an interviewer and another as an interviewee or client.

Entering the interview

For an interviewer each interview is fraught with potential difficulties. First, an interview creates a situation in which two strangers come together, ostensibly to talk about issues identified by the interviewer, and about that which the interviewee is supposed or presumed to have some experience or knowledge. Pawson observes that "subjects ponder (mostly in silence) – 'who is this person?', 'what is she after?', 'why am I being asked?', 'what have others said?', 'what should I be saying?'" (1996:306). The meeting of strangers creates a series of anxieties along with practical difficulties. Just as I enter the office with my agenda so too does the interviewee.

Indeed, in this interview, even before the audio-recorder was turned on, Ed began by pushing his chair, which was near the corner of the desk in the middle of the room, back to the wall, announcing "I need my space". Although I did not immediately follow up on what I observed to be a remarkable claim the theme of space proved to be tied to not only trauma, but to an assertion of autonomy. As will be addressed in more detail below, a key theme organising both the content and the talk itself was Ed's forceful assertion of his need for space. Ed used the content or subject of space to account for a series of violent and confrontational events in his life, as well as to indicate those relationship forms he preferred, namely those that respected his space. Ed uses the form of space, that is the physical management of his body, and its relation to others, to mark off the boundaries of his participation, to set the terms for his engagement in the interview, and to assert his autonomy as an actor. As will be outlined below, analysis reveals that Ed employs space to assert forms of power and control that work for him not only in the interview process but across various forms of interaction.

The specification of a focus or topic serves not only to lend an organisation to the interview as it unfolds, but retroactively, when being reflected on, transcribed, and analysed, the form and content of that which is recorded can be evaluated in light of conformity or divergence to the topics identified in the Interview Guide (Appendix A). For instance, because the interview was designed to address the issue of living in care, a major concern was to determine the number of placements that the youth had lived in since coming into care. The work of tracking through a youth in care's placements usually required some attention to a chronology of events. Attention to chronology in turn served as a tool for redirection, such that the interviewer could identify confusion about chronology as an invocation or reference to topic, i.e. now where were we? The routine matter of getting off topic, talking about seemingly irrelevant events in one's life – e.g. a lengthy story about a bike accident.

Naturally, the accomplished construction of a simple linear narrative organised by chronology was rarely possible and indeed would have been disadvantageous, as discussion would often range over a host of other relevant issues that were thematic rather than chronological. An interviewee might begin by addressing one issue, only to be reminded of another, and then another, and so forth, until what had been one topic became transformed into a wholly new topic. As a result a critical task of the interviewer is to redirect the talk back on topic, but of course, performing such an exercise demands having some sense of what might count as on topic, hence what is relevant for the task at hand. Furthermore, given that the focus of the interaction and the interview is research and as such presupposes the possibility of discovery, it follows that the notion of topic must express a considerable degree of elasticity, such that what is deemed to be on topic cannot be easily defined, cannot be easily regulated and is open for discoveries to be made.

Troubles from the start

Let us turn now to look at the following segment taken from the very beginning of the interview.

G: Wh what's cha been up to today.
E: Out walkin around being tirwed.
G: Yah, late night↑
E: Naw, went to bed early, woke up too early.
G: mmhuh

This would normally stand as a rather ordinary opener. It has a familiar, though formulaic colloquial quality, such as might characterise a greeting between family or friends. When asked, "Wh what's cha been up to today", Ed responds that he has been "out walkin around being tirwed." Note that my next turn could have taken any number of possible directions or choices.[2] I could have asked where he had been walking around; whether it was the walking around that made Ed tired; or I could have focused on being tired, to explore what it was that contributed to this state. However, I chose to not pose a series of questions, fearing that would make me seem inquisitorial and invasive.[3] Rather than pose a second question, I responded by formulating a possible explanation, "Yah, late night", expressed as a question, with a rising tone at the end of the word "night". The form of response gave Ed an opportunity to disagree, correcting me (providing a repair), by responding, "Naw, went to bed early, woke up too early". Clearly, my interpretation was rejected, and Ed's proffered his own account to explain his tiredness.

An understanding of why I proffered "late night" as an explanation for Ed's fatigue, is not simply a matter of motive, but points to an ordinary adult repertoires of at-hand or common-sense, or what Sacks called "inference rich devices" (Sacks, 1995:41), for assembling not only identity categories, but the characteristics of those people assigned to such categories. My response to Ed was informed by generalised assumptions about teenagers, staying up at late night parties, drinking, drugs, talking with friends, and not getting enough sleep, especially during the summer when school regimens are disrupted by summer vacations and changing routines. However, Ed disputed my assumptions and frameworks. My reliance on such a 'inference rich' categories and categorisation devices proved to be a candidate incorrect inference, or at least not a preferred version. Of course, for Ed it might not have been the preferred version, not because it was it was not an accurate conjecture about his previous night's activities, but because it was the proffered version. Hence, it might have been rejected simply because it was the version produced by me as the interviewer.

In the next segment we see what appears to be a simple enough confusion.

E: because when I woke I jist, I have a window right in front/ of me.
G: A what? A window, ooh, what win/
E: I noticed when I woke up it was six o'clock, but it was bwight, bwight, like this.
G: What do ya look onto.
E: What do I look onto?
G: Yah what does yer window look on to.
E: Oh, ah, it not my window, it was my fwends, I was up at his place last night.
G: Oh yah, do, ah sleep over.
E: Mmmhuh, yah

Ed explains that he awoke at "six o'clock" because "it was bwight, bwright". The good sense of his statement depends on our shared context of life in northern Canada. The interview was conducted on June 17, in northern Canada, just before the summer solstice, which is the longest day of the year, when there is no darkness at night. By "six o'clock" it would indeed be bright outside. As the interviewer, I knew this, as I had spent the last week camping in a nearby park, and had faced the challenge of sleeping in a tent under perpetual daylight.

Rather than address the patent reality of bright light at six, I formulated my next turn, relying on an assumption that he was speaking about awaking in his own room. My question "What do ya look onto" without an understanding of shared context might appear to be off topic, however, in context, it signals that a more interesting issue is to develop an understanding of Ed's living arrangements. Unfortunately, my assumption that Ed awoke in his own room proved false, which in turn left me wondering why he had stayed with a friend, and what his own bedroom was like?

Only slightly later, as I returned to explore Ed's living arrangements in more detail and connection with his family, the following exchange occurred.

G: Where're ya livin these days.
E: Forest Glen (pseudonym)
G: Forest Glen, with who?
E: mmhum, my dad, and my bwother, and thwee of my cousins, and my aunty.
G: What's yer dad's name.
E: I'm named after my dad.
G: Oh yer dad's Ed too.
E: But his Smith, is his last name.
G: Smith
E: yah
G: So who's name is Jones
E: It's my mom
G: uh huh, and who's yer mo, and you live with yer dad and your brother.
E: Yes, but I ain't gonna say all their names.
G: Well just so I can, just when you, cause later you'll mention their names. How, okay, older brother, younger..younger brother?
E: Older

The preceding segment begins with a simple question to determine where Ed is living. He responds by stating with "my dad, and my bwother, and thwee of my cousins, and my aunty". In my next turn, I ask for his dad's name, and this is where trouble once again begins. Ed outlines that though he shares his dad's first name, he does not share his dad's last name, Smith. My response, Smith, signals my recognition that Ed had been identified in the referral to me as Ed Jones, and an expectation that children usually assume their father's surname. This disjunction results in my next question, "So who's name is Jones". Ed tells me that Jones is his mother's surname. Clearly, this apparently simple fact that Ed uses his mother's surname, and not his father's, but claims to live with his father, warrants exploration. Yet, at this moment in the interview, having worked through my confusion, I begin by asking "who's yer mo", but effect a repair, interrupting myself, to state "and you live with yer dad and your brother". Ed counters, "Yes, but I ain't gonna say all their names."

Ed's refusal to respond to my question marks both real and potential trouble. It is what Schegloff calls a dispreferred response (2007). He writes,

> The summons–answer sequence is a sequence designed to mobilize, secure, or establish the availability, attention, and aligned recipiency of its addressed target. The two main types of response are the go-ahead and blocking responses. The former embodies what the sequence is designed to do – it displays (or at least claims) the attentiveness of its speaker; the latter embodies a problem in its realization.
>
> (2009)

As the interviewer, I feared that my attention to Ed's living arrangements, and with how these reveal his family relations, might elicit irritation and anger. I worried that Ed was feeling frustrated, angry, possibly hostile toward me. Such feelings would of course signal my failure as an interviewer and jeopardise the success of this interview, especially if Ed refused to continue or cut off further discussion. As Peräkylä, a psychoanalyst who also uses CA to make sense of his work, observed: "It is possibly conflict of some sort that makes us aware of choices that we make in interaction" (2011:229). Indeed, when faced with Ed's refusal, I needed to determine how to proceed in my next turn.

The dilemma I faced was whether or not to give voice to his refusal, or to name my fears? I feared that by confronting Ed, exploring the issue of his refusal, and demanding an explanation that this might only reduce the likelihood that Ed would continue to participate in the interview and to tell me his story. Although, I knew that Ed had signalled something that pointed to trouble, the question was how to respond. In retrospect, when doing the analysis I realised that I might have said, "When you say you don't want to provide the names of your brothers and sisters I wonder whether you find doing this interview brings back bad memories? Or, do you think that I'm prying into personal and private stuff?"[4] Such a question would have created an opening for Ed to respond, "you're right", however, such an opening might also have led him to add, "let's end it now."

So why didn't I name my fears, name his frustration, and work through our interactive difficulties? Was it a tactical decision to not name troubles, or was it fear of worsening the situation, or inviting an attack on me? As the interviewer I had to choose whether or not to ignore or disattend troubles or to react to them. Clearly that which is ignored does not cease to exist, but rather is allowed to 'pass' without comment (Garfinkel, 1967). It is purposefully made unremarkable. To act as though trouble is ignored, or not made remarkable, is a requirement of all social interaction, otherwise parties to talk-in-interaction would never move off ambiguities. Indeed, sense is never delivered all at once or fully intact, but emerges turn-by-turn in a process of interaction.

That which is ignored while still existing does allow attention to be focused elsewhere, perhaps on more positive or fruitful avenues. Troubles that are treated as remarkable can at the same time create an escalating spiral of confrontation. Indeed, I anticipate that by sidestepping confrontation at this point, I will still attain my objectives of identifying siblings, as I expect that later in the interview Ed will of necessity come to use the names of his brothers and others. While his refusal heightens the potential for ambiguity and confusion in what has already proven to be a difficult interview, it also poses a taunt or challenge to overcome and work through resistance to arrive at a relationship of trust and cooperation. The ideal of the end or objective of the interview shapes the artful use of time and responses.

Although I chose to not press Ed to explain or address his refusal, I had already identified that his motivations and purposes for contradiction and refusal likely pointed to his need to assert his autonomy and control in the interview process. At the very least, Ed demonstrated resistance either to his identity as a youth in care, or to participating in the interview itself.[5] Whether the resistance was a manifestation of personality, a reaction to previous interviews with social workers, or a personal reaction to me as an interviewer remained an open question. Such needs had to be respected. Minimally, we can see that Ed felt that it was necessary to indicate a refusal to provide the names of the people with whom he lived. This is a need that expresses his assertion of the boundaries and limits of his participation in the interview. This is a need that carves out the space of his cooperation.

As we can see through the next segment Ed uses correction and disagreement to assert his independence and to effect control over the interaction. Ed's assertion of independence is revealed in his response to my continued attempt to determine his living arrangements.

G: ... So right now are you, are you in care, are you.
E: Yah, I'm in care of this place.
G: but you're livin with yer dad
E: Yah
G: Okay, what's that about.
E: It's what my court order said.
G: that you hafta live with your dad.
E: no. I don't hafta live with my dad if I don't want to. I'm capable of living where ever I want. I can live on my land.
G: yah
E: If I wanted to
G: yah do you do that?
E: If I wan to, but which I don't have it staked out yet.
G: You don't eh?
E: u uh

My question about whether or not Ed is "in care" designates a legal status, in which control over his life, that is custody, is assumed by the government office where the interview is being conducted, "I'm in care of this place." Yet, picking up on the previous point, I observe, "but you're livin with yer dad", which is an unusual situation for a youth in care, as normally it is safe to assume that a youth in care is not living with their parent(s). I express this confusion by asking "Okay, what's that about", to which Ed replies, "It's what my court order said", to which I pick up on the concept of an 'order', hence a court commanding a course of action to observe, "that you hafta live with your dad".

In what was by then becoming a familiar pattern, Ed responded by disagreeing with my conjecture. He states, "no. I don't hafta live with my dad if I don't want to. I'm capable of living where ever I want. I can live on my land." Ed makes it very clear that regardless of any court order he is master of his own life. Ed asserts that he can determine with whom and where he lives. Even though he does not own land, he imagines that he could stake out land and live there independently. Ed's claims for mastery operate not only at the level of content but define an interactional dynamic affecting the structure of power in the interview. As the interviewer Ed's responses to my questions made me feel very confused. Had my question been misunderstood? Did Ed not understand the operation of a court order? Was Ed asserting his ability and his right to determine where he lived regardless of institutional orders? Ed's response put me off balance and undermined my authority as the interviewer. Ed's continual contradiction of my formulations allowed him to create his own agenda for the interview, and to oppose mine. Was Ed using puzzles, contradictions and paradoxes to assert his control over the process?

Constructing gender?

Throughout the interview Ed produced a series of stories that by addressing difficult events in his life communicated a preferred version of himself as a moral actor. I want to explore two instances of such self-representation. The first followed from my attempts to determine family composition, to which Ed begins by addressing his parent's relationship:

E: then they brwoke up, and went their own ways, and she:: kinda went and
   got, her actually was goin out with my ah, foster dad,
G: yah yah
E: I jist call him call him foster dad=
G: yah yah
E: because he was there more years than my real dad was=
G: yah
E: so, and he had ah, three other kids, and two of them died,
G: oh
E: two of my baby bwothers.
G: how did that happen
E: wahhaw, they was jist babies, this one had a breathing pwoblem, and one
   had a heart pwoblem. Mmm so, I don't worry about that, I jist jist
   natural te me.

G: yes

E: I don't worry about you know one dies, lives,

G: yah

E: to me it's jist the way the wowld works.

G: yah

Though the chronology of Ed's account is sketchy, it does seem as though his step-dad fathered three other children (assumed to be with his mother), of whom two died in infancy. Along with reference to the specific deaths of two siblings, Ed makes a claim about how he deals with or manages death and loss generally, "I don't worry about that, I jist jist natural te me", and in an elaborating move he repeats, "I don't worry about you know one dies, lives". While the details of the hardship are unsettling, it is important to look beyond the content to the way that presentation of issues is tied to presentation of self, or to what Goffman called impression management (1959). Goffman's explanation that understanding impression management provides insight into "social establishment", that is, "any place surrounded by fixed barriers to perception" (1959:238), provides a series of useful metaphors or insights into this moment of interaction. Indeed, the metaphor of barriers brings into focus the ways that Ed erects and then relies on conventional and taken-for-granted practices of being a man, that is being strong, brave, coura- geous, to allow for certain types of presentations of self, and to preclude other less preferred versions, e.g. that he might become distraught, crying, depressed, anguished, etc. Further, Ed is able to deploy a barrier to weakness erected . through a proper masculinity, by in turn successfully relying on my acceptance of the good sense of this framework. E's strategy works, for I quite clearly collude with and support the good sense of his account of dealing with hardship.

Ed claims that he is able to deal with and manage extremely difficult if not traumatic life events. He claims that he does not "worry about that", hence that he is able to push concerns about life and death out of his mind. This is suggestive of fearlessness. Ed portrays himself as oriented to a pragmatic fatalism, a fatalism rooted in ready to hand understandings of 'being a man'. A man just gets on with his life and accepts with courage the travails of mis- fortune. The recovery of sense from this presentation of self is something that both Ed and I as a male interviewer know how to do. Ed does not need to explicitly claim that he is brave, that he has courage, or that he is a survivor, for through this segment Ed's approach to life is clearly communicated and is demonstrative of all of these attributes. It is not that Ed is uncaring or unfeeling. Rather, Ed recognises "it's jist the way the wowld works." It needs to be noted that Ed's claim to understand, pragmatically and without delu- sion, how the world works is simultaneously designed to convey that he is not a child, he is not bound to illusion or to a fantasy that the world might be otherwise. Clearly, Ed's strategy for self-representation is resonant, and therefore successful as I do not challenge his version of reality, or even his understanding of self.

The next segment began with my question about why Ed no longer lived with his mother.

G: So what was goin on with her that you're not livin with her, and you kept comin inta care.

E: NAhh, I didn' wanna live with them. Jist didn' wan to. Got too tiwred.

G: How?

E: Nothin, te do, the same thin' over and over=

G: =yah=

E: =arguments=

G: =yah=

E: =te me, my bwother, my kid sister-[ster]

G: [yah]

E: -ster, P would fweek out, and end up tryin te frow at knife at us or somethin.

G: Who's P?

E: my kid sister. The one who got the singing job.

G: Is that right. Tryin te throw a knife at you?

E: Yah.

G: So a lotta fightin goin on in the home.

E: Yah, and afta she did that mom jist said, "you wanna do that P, listen I won't care, if you got beat up by them". An I jist said, "heh, I ain' goin te beat her up."

G: yah=

E: =maybe I might defend myself but I ain' goin' te beat her up.

Ed follows up his claim that he left his home because he "Got too tiwred", and explains why with a single word; "arguments". Ed then claims that his sister P threw a knife at him, the details of which Ed chooses to not provide, nor which I as the interviewer press for, instead allowing it to pass. However, what is remarkable is the next segment in which his mother is presented as giving Ed and his brother permission to beat up their sister, and to which Ed reports, "An I jist said, 'heh, I ain' goin te beat her up.' ... maybe I might defend myself but I ain' goin' beat her up." In this passage Ed is plainly communicating a picture of the sort of man he is. He is a man who would not beat his sister, a girl/woman, even when provoked. He is a man who will not use violence against his sister, and we might by extension presume, a man who will not use violence against those weaker than him. He is not a bully. He is a man able to exercise restraint even in the face of provocation. Again, as a male interviewer I do not challenge, but rather collude and agree with E's version of proper action, through the acknowledgment token "yah".

In this passage Ed presents himself to me as a young man who inhabits a moral universe marked by some sense of respect for those weaker than himself, even when they are angry with him and threaten his safety. We also see that Ed sets the limits to his behaviour. He demonstrates that he is an autonomous actor, who despite seeming to have been given permission by his mother to beat P, that he will set his own moral compass, and the course of his own actions. In this sense Ed creates a parallel structure similar to that governing whether or not he lives with his father. He is the master of his own life.

Space and safety

When I attempted to explore why Ed had been placed in a facility for young offenders, he provided the following explanation.

E: cause I was, it was in fronta J's office, but she was in J's office, cause, I was standin at the door, and she kept on invading my space, and tellin me te get out an everything, but I said no, "I wanna say my piece", you deserve fwhat you get

G: mmhuh

E: and the next thing she push, and I said, whoa, what didja do that for, and she did that two oth, two other times before that, one in frwont of a long flight of stairws, which was leavin downstairs, and I got lucky there, and then there's another time, this was another flight of stairws

Ed explains that troubles arose because a staff person was "invading my space", and refusing to allow him to "say my piece". The importance of the observation "I wanna say my piece" should not be overlooked as it articulates E's demand for respect, that is a demand to be heard and listened to. J's refusal to let Ed say his piece is an affront to his integrity, which then couples with the claim that she violated his space.

The theme of space arises not only in relationships of confrontation, but as a key to respect, hence to respect Ed is to respect his person, his right to speak, the integrity of his words, and his space.

E: -n't, but my real dad, I don't know, don't care. He does what he wants, I do what I want.

G: yah.

E: nn, an I don' interfere with his business, and he doesn' interfere with mine.

G: He doesn't?

E: He rwespects my space and everything, an so.

G: yah. You need te ha, you need te have yer space.

E: mmhuh, my dad respects that=

As we have seen before Ed is intent to assert his independence. For Ed to be properly human is to be autonomous, and to have his space respected. Ed demands the right to control his own life, the recognition of this right by others, and accordingly the right to manage who enters and who is barred from his own space.

As the interview progressed I was curious about the function of 'space' and its importance for Ed. I suspected that it was a significant issue, most likely representing some form of trauma, or violation of his space, whether in the form of past physical or sexual abuse. It was clear that Ed was a young man who would allow himself to be approached, and touched only on his terms, and not on the terms of others in positions of authority. The following extended sequence began as Ed revisited the theme of space, and the ways that troubles arose when others violated his space.

E: it takes three, three cops te pin me down. An took them a good bout twenty minutes=

G: iz that °right°

E: for I went went down.

G: iz that right

E: and the only reason that is 'cuz one got on my back and I smashed him against the wall

G: mmuh

E: and everything-thing, friggin, and I was'nt doin nothin-thin, and I jist said "shoot me-me-me" an I don't achtully mean shoot, me-me, what I'm tryin te mean, is like knock me out man, like shit, like, but when he grwabbed me wrist te handcuff me, I said okay man, don't mess around, you're in my space, and if you do that again, I'm gonna, and he didn' get out, so I did what I hadta do, an

G: mmhuh

E: mm I don't care if it's the cops or anything, like, they're invading my space=

G: =yah=

E: =I will get them outta my space=

G: =yah=

E: =neither way I can=

G: =yah=

E: =like, n'aw was even a hundrwed percent, and I was alwready thrwashing thrwee cops-s, and that was only as fifty percent.

G: yah

E: If I was at a hundrwed it would take bout five co:awps then.

G: So what's this space. How much space..ce

E: I have an arms length space.

G: Yah

E: S, so if anyone's in my space of an arm's length, I'm not gonna be too nice.

G: Wh what makes yer space important for ya? When did that become important for ya.

E: That came important te me when I was a little baby=

G: =yah=

E: =when I's a baby about five years

G: yah, tell me bout that.

E: I don't want to.

G: No

E: mm uh. It's done an over with he's go' his punishment, it's over.

G: oh somebody hurt you.

E: no. Not me, my little sister-ter,

G: yah=

E: =but, I didn' wan te see it, but I woke up at that time.

G: I see, an, so she was being sexually abused=

E: =yes=

G: =and you saw that. Did that happen to you?

E: Noo:if ee, after I woke up, I' kinda faked slep, and when he came try doin thin'k te me, like, put the diaper over me-m', b' that's all he did with me, an=

G: =yah=

Quite apart from a theme of male braggadocio connected to physical prowess this sequence is important as Ed returns to the theme of space, and the violent consequences meted out to those who violate his space. Ed's approach to the interview, and indeed to life, is one of carefully delimiting the entry of others into his space, both as expressed physically and through disclosure of personal details. Ed carves out his space both through the management of his body, and even through the form of his talk with others. My dilemma as an interviewer was to build trust, by demonstrating my respect for the boundaries of Ed's space while at the same time, pressing into spaces of discomfort to produce a story which would explain his valorisation of space itself. The puzzle I faced was how to open up the issue of space without seeming to invade his space.

Clearly, the issue of space was an important element in Ed's story, particularly as it was connected in his confession of having witnessed the sexual abuse of his sister, and perhaps having also been a victim. Once Ed disclosed the incidences of sexual abuse, I was faced with a problem. Such disclosure, quite apart from being a 'taboo' subject (Shulman, 2016) almost invariably awakens painful and traumatic experiences rooted in an experience structure of memory and being. Indeed, it is at the level of experience structures in memory, that is remembrance of what actually happened, as detailed violations of one's body, articulated through language, that the event as revisited evokes pain and discomfort. For the purposes of my interview, I did not need to explore the details of the violation. I only needed to know that sexual abuse had occurred in Ed's past, and that it had had definite effects on his presentation of self and on the practical techniques he used to manage social situations with others. Just as I needed to respect Ed's space, I needed to win his respect. He demanded that I respect his privacy and his need to determine which elements of his story he would share and which elements he would keep to himself. As a researcher I was acutely aware of the limitations of my position.

As a social worker I was also aware that opening up trauma without ensuring some means for follow up, and ongoing care, was irresponsible. Yet at the same time I could not let the connection between sexual abuse and space go unremarked. I also felt that it was essential that Ed struggle to disentangle the connection between his sexual abuse and his insistence that others respect his space. Understanding the ways that these elements were connected was particularly important, as Ed's perception that others had violated his space seemed to have resulted in criminal charges and violent confrontations with people in authority and power. As a social worker I could not resist trying to 'help' Ed by supporting his assertion of space as integral for his integrity, and at the same time, helping him to use other less confrontational and violent strategies for protecting himself.

This next segment begins by Ed outlining that the man who sexually abused him has been "locked up". Ed noted:

E: but's that's what's done an over with//
G: But, no, but you see, it's not done and over with, because you see you need yer space.
E: See, I need my space, you wanna know why?
G: =Yah
E: Because I respect=
G: =yah=
E: =other people's space=
G: =yah=
E: =so, also=
G: =yah, cause//=
E: =an I, I like te be at arm's length, either way=
G: =ah yes, I yes, I [underst]and that.
E: [iz' not], iz not always b'cause that but=
G: =yah=
E: I don't think of that like, as like why'm I respect my own space-s, and respect other's people's space
G: [absolutely right] (space)
E: I'ts just like, I count fer that wa=
G: =Good fer y'=
E: =like if anyone came up an wreally touched me, like, go like that, an I did'n wan it,
G: yah=
E: =and tell im, w'd please don touch me.
G: don't do that
E: mm
G: good fer you=
E: =like, I don' wan te be touched, when I want te be touched I'll=
G: =you'll let im know.
E: yah=

G: =right on Ed=

E: =like=

G: =right on. Now is that a problem a school that peop, people'll..

E: No it's not a problem at school, like not much kid'zll go up an go// "hey"

G: "Hey man how's it goin"

E: Like when I'm at school, like I really won't care like if anyone touched me, cause they're all my frwends=

G: =yah I see

E: at school. Like . . .

G: Okay, so one of the ways that you kinda deal with that kinda threat is say look, this is my space, you don't invade it.

E: Yah, like I only do that to people-ple-ple that I don' like that much=

G: =Yah

E: like frwends and all that=

G: =mmuuhh

E: its totally diffewent.

G: good. No that's cool. It's cool.

Although Ed insists that the matter is done and over with, I do not accept this version. I openly disagree. I note, "But, no, but you see, it's not done and over with, because you see you need yer space." Ed recognises the challenge, and responds, "See, I need my space, you wanna know why? (G Yah) Because I respect= (G yah=) =other people's space= (G=yah)=so, also=(G=yah, cuz//)=an I , I like te be at arm's length, either way." E's response is fascinating, and seemingly characteristic. He insists that it was not what others have done to him which makes him value space, but rather, that it is the choices he has made, what he values, what he respects, which makes him demand his own space, and "other people's space". Tacitly, Ed is declaring that unlike those who have violated his space he respects the space of others. He is not like his abusers and tormentors who do not respect the space and integrity of others.

Conclusion

This chapter examines in detail a troublesome interview. Though the interview began badly, as I felt a certain awkwardness, and unsettled feeling about how to approach Ed, as it progressed my sense was that Ed became more comfortable sharing details of his life, although always on his own terms and within his own limits. The puzzle I faced as the interviewer was figuring out how far and how hard to push Ed for details, to ensure the coherence of the narrative, while ensuring Ed's continued cooperation in the interview. Clearly as the interviewer, attempting to help Ed produce a coherent and cogent story of his experience in care, I needed to ensure not only Ed's cooperation but commitment to sharing often intimate and personal details.

In this sense the interview may be thought of as a dance between strangers, in which we entered with different abilities and different agenda's. My agenda was to guide Ed through an exploration of his life in his family of origin and his life in care that made sense, had coherence, and was topically relevant. Ed's agenda, although less accessible as a subject of the research, can be determined in part through the interview transcription. Throughout the interview Ed did manage to communicate a strong and clear picture about the type of young man that he was. He was not an abusive man. He was not a bully. He was not a physically or morally weak man. He was an independent man. He was a man who made choices over his own life, and did not impose his choices over others. The glorious element of the interview is that it provided Ed with an opportunity to tell someone else, albeit a stranger, who he was. I provided an opportunity for him to say, this is what I believe, this is who I am. Clearly Ed felt that his story was worth telling and worth being heard.

The challenge I faced as an interviewer was figuring out how to coordinate the dance of talk-in-interaction such that Ed felt that he had a stake in continuing our work together. Through turn-by-turn moves we worked together to produce a story which resonated with the important issues of his life. The nightmare at the margins of our interview was the possibility that I might offend, communicate a lack of respect, or show disinterest in Ed's story and thereby loose his commitment to the process.

Though this interview began with troubles, and though by the end I certainly felt that it had gone well in general, it was only in the process of analysis that I came to appreciate that *space* operated not only at the level of content and meaning, but at the level of interactive processes. Space was deployed by contradiction, correction, disagreement, and refusal to share information. These were the ways that Ed managed to protect his space within the interaction. Ed's trauma reverberated throughout his life, in not only moments of high drama, such as physical battles with police, but in the everyday workings of his talk in interaction such as our interview together. The difficulty I faced is that I was not just a researcher, but was always also a social worker. As a social worker I was a moral agent, committed to 'helping' people to work through and to resolve conflicts and pain in their lives. Accordingly the interview was centred not merely around the collection of information, but also a practice of guidance and direction.

Curiously, although this book is dedicated to leading social workers to examine the utility of EM and CA for practice, I must confess to being pleasantly surprised by the sorts of discoveries that emerged when working with this case example. Through each working and reworking of analysis new insights piled on others. For example, where I began by simply identifying 'trouble' in Ed's refusal to name his siblings, in later analysis I came to recognise the problems with my response to his refusal. The attention CA gives to exploring turn by turn talk-in-interaction brings into focus the micro-movements whereby participants bring about, as living practice, a relationship of a particular sort. The attention CA gives to turns allows us to ask: What is it that these people are doing with each other in their utterances, in their listening, and in their responses? It is my firm belief that CA has tremendous utility for close case analysis.

I feel that I have only skimmed the surface of possibilities in this chapter, but it is my hope that it has pointed to the potentialities of CA for social work on a case by case basis. CA through an analysis of turn-by-turn talk unfolds the complex weave by which people connect their mundane, taken-for-granted, and largely unremarkable practices to the foundational philosophical and moral issues of our society.

Throughout this chapter we have seen how both Ed and I struggled to craft a particular representation of self for another. We did this work turn-by-turn in the most mundane micro-moments of our practices. In this interview Ed's responses must be read not only as communicating the events of his life, but as displaying and affirming a moral orientation to the world. His is a moral orientation that infuses the most mundane and ordinary decisions and actions of his life. His is a moral orientation that shapes his view of self and his evaluation of others. It is essential that social workers recognise that it is not only themselves, as professionals bound to codes of ethics, and professional values, but their clients who interact and work from out of such complex moral universes.

Notes

1 Ed is a pseudonym, as are all proper names associated with this case example used in this chapter.
2 The recognition of choices, as Garfinkel points out, provides an entry for ethnomethodological study. When formulating policies for EM Garfinkel observed: "any occasion whatsoever be examined for the feature that "choice" among alternatives of sense, of facticity, of objectivity, of cause, of explanation, of communality of practical actions is a project of members' actions" (1967: 32). Similarly, Schegloff, indicates that an omnirelevant issue for the participants for any bit of talk-in-interaction is "why that now" (2007:2).
3 Buttny found that "some therapists ask few direct questions, but instead attempt to elicit information from the clients by 'telling them something about themselves'" (1996:128).
4 My avoidance of trouble, hence my decision to avoid naming Ed's refusal, is quite similar to the refusal of the social worker in Chapter 10, to address the relationship dynamics in the youth's demand, "Adopt me". Avoidance of moves to make relationship dynamics explicit points to the ego needs of workers. Yet, addressing such dynamics can in fact provide important inroads for developing honest and open dialogue and trust as power issues are dealt with. Clearly in this segment I succumbed to fear rather than pursuing effective social work.
5 Ed's resistance is similar in form to that identified by Benwell & Stokoe, in their analysis of student's resistance in educational settings. They note: "The category 'resistance' provides a useful gloss for indicating, in broad terms, how students might be constructing and assessing their disposition, performance and activities" (2005:126).

References

Benwell, Bethan, & Stokoe, Elizabeth. (2005). University students resisting academic identity. In Keith Richards & Paul Seedhouse (Eds.), *Applying conversation analysis* (pp. 124–139). Houndmills, England: Palgrave Macmillan.

Buttny, Richard. (1996). Clients' and therapist's joint construction of the clients' problems. *Research on Language and Social Interaction*, 29(2): 125–153.

Crenshaw, David A., & Hardy, Kenneth V. (2006). Understanding and treating the aggression of traumatized children in out-of-home care. In Nancy Boyd Webb (Ed.), *Working with traumatized youth in child welfare* (pp. 171–195). New York, NY: Guilford.

Garfinkel, Harold. (1967). *Studies in ethnomethodology.* Englewood Cliffs, NJ: Prentice-Hall.

Goffman, Erving. (1959). *Presentation of self in everyday life.* Garden City, NY: Doubleday Anchor.

Hardy, Kenneth V., & Laszloffy, Tracey A. (2005). *Teens who hurt: Clinical interventions to break the cycle of adolescent violence.* New York: Guilford.

Hermanowicz, Joseph C. (2002). The great interview: 25 strategies for studying people in bed. *Qualitative Sociology*, 24(4): 479–499.

Kohler Riessman, Catherine. (1993). *Narrative analysis.* Newbury Park, CA: Sage.

Malone, Martin J. (1995). How to do things with friends: Altercasting and recipient design. *Research on Language and Social Interaction*, 28(2): 147–170.

Mazeland, Harrie, & ten Have, Paul. (1996). Essential tension in (semi-) open research interviews. In Ilja Maso & Fred Wester (Eds.), *The deliberate dialogue: Qualitative perspectives on the interview* (pp. 87–113). Brussels, Belgium: VUB University Press.

Pawson, Ray. (1996). Theorizing the interview. *The British Journal of Sociology*, 47(2): 295–314.

Peräkylä, Anssi. (2011). A psychoanalyst's reflection on conversation analysis's contribution to his own therapeutic talk. In Charles Antaki (Ed.), *Applied conversation analysis: Intervention and change in institutional talk* (pp. 222–242). Houndmills, England: Palgrave Macmillan.

Sacks, Harvey (1995). *Lectures on conversation (Volumes 1 & 2).* Oxford, England: Blackwell.

Schegloff, Emanuel A. (1992). On talk and its institutional occasions. In Paul Drew & John Heritage (Eds.), *Talk at work: Interaction in institutional settings* (pp. 101–134). Cambridge, England: Cambridge University Press.

Schegloff, Emanuel A. (2007). *Sequence organization in interaction: A primer in conversation analysis (Volume 1).* Cambridge, England: Cambridge University Press.

Shulman, Lawrence. (2016). *The skills of helping individuals, families, groups, and communities* (8th ed.). Toronto, ON: Thompson Brooks Cole.

8 Child protection and entries into care

A: yah, an, my mom left him and stayed in Moose Town, an she jist drank. That's all she did. She'd buy a bottle and sit by Moose lake all by herself, jist sit on the bottle an get drunk by herself. Cry and think about what she's done an what's she'd doin, an how bad it is. An she'd jist pray she said.

J: So how is that for you, if mom was drunk who was takin care of you when you were with her.

A: When I was with her we'd be takin care of ourselves, we'd usually be sittin at her house. She'd leave us fer days, but there'd always be food in our room.

J: So you became pretty self sufficient pretty quick.

A: yep

J: waz that, ho' how did that feel as a little kid.

A: It was normal

J: it was normal

A: it's what we grew up. It's just like now, we don't see how people could live the way they have lived in their perfect families, and not knowing what is going on an happening to some people=

J: =yah=

A: =thinking their problems are jist the biggest in the world, an to other people they jist seem like petty little things=

J: =yah=

A: that we wouldn't even think twice about

Sadly, stories like A's, a First Nations woman living in northern Canada, are not uncommon among children and youth in care. These are stories of broken relationships, parental addiction, violence, abuse, poverty, racism, and social marginality. Kelly notes, "Children who come into foster care constitute one of the most vulnerable groups in society and typically experience maltreatment, parental substance abuse or mental health issues, poverty, and separation from their families" (2017:7). Granofsky states, "Children-in-care are vulnerable and disadvantaged. They have by definition been deprived of consistent attachment figures and have suffered abuse or neglect of some kind"

(2010:9). Beyond the realities of abandonment and of repeated and egregious parental failures are the imaginings, yearnings, and desires of these children. Against the realities of abandonment, children and youth struggle for reclamation by holding onto shards of care. A explains, "She'd leave us fer days, but there'd always be food in our room." A reaches for, recovers, and holds onto the claim that despite her mother's drinking she ensured that her children had food and that they would not starve. Yet A knows that lurking behind the food was her own pain, fear, loneliness, and abandonment. The pain of such abandonment is profound and reverberates throughout A's life. As A grew older, and as her social purview expanded she realised that what she had come to accept as normal was not how people in other families lived. This realisation lead her to recognise another form of abandonment. She identified the indifference and lack of attention that other people, other parents, and other families pay to families in crisis. She explained, "we don't see how people could live the way they have lived in their perfect families, and not knowing what is going on an happening to some people=". A's call, along with that of many other children and youth in care, is that others pay attention to the plight not only of children but their parents.

A's story is made sensible and is existentially rooted in her mother's own despair and trauma. A noted, "She'd buy a bottle and sit by Moose lake all by herself, jist sit on the bottle an get drunk by herself. Cry and think about what she's done an what's she'd doin, an how bad it is." Not only do children in need of protection suffer, but so too do their parents. The stigma and shame of failed parenting, failure to provide, and failure to meet social expectations is passed on through the generations. A's decision to participate in the research was rooted in a need to declare that the voices of children and youth in care and their families be heard.

In this chapter and the next I attempt to develop some core themes for social work practice following from analysis of interviews with youth in care. Precisely because this text draws on tools from conversation analysis, we turn now to pay particular attention to the voices of youth, as they tell and narrate the stories of their lives in interaction with social workers and research interviewers. A turn to conversation analysis, and careful attention to the stories of youth, is vital not only for research and understanding of child protection, but to ensure good practice. Munro, observed:

> All too often, children are not fully recognised as active participants either as a source of knowledge about what is happening in the family or as a source of opinions about what should be done.
>
> (2007:23)

It is vital that we listen to children and youth as they talk about their lives in their families of origin, coming into care, and living in care. By listening to children and youth social workers can not only come to understand what young people need and want while in care, they will also come to appreciate the imperative of ensuring that social supports are provided to children and their families before child protection interventions become necessary. Over the course of the research project, we interviewed almost 100 youth across three provinces and one territory. In addition, I attended CAST meetings for four years. Although decades had passed between this research and my former work as a child protection worker, I was struck by the continuing resonance of familiar themes in the lives of children and youth in care, and for their families of origin. Such themes are nicely summarised by Bazalgette, who examined the experiences of youth in care in the UK: 1) positive experiences of care; 2) disrupted relationships – frequent foster home, group home changes, and change of social workers; 3) going missing from care – running away, being on the street, returning to family; 4) stigma and discrimination against children in care; 5) poor quality and harmful care – emotional neglect and rejection in care; and, as a summary, 6) ensuring young people's voices are heard (2014:27).

Not surprisingly many youth come into care from horrific home environments marked by parental alcohol and drug abuse, mental illness, poverty, and neglect and abandonment, physical, sexual, and psychological abuse. While entry into care was often not idyllic, and created frustration, anger, and disappointment with foster parents, social workers, and group home staff, many youth whom we encountered, despite multiple placements and moves, were eventually able to live in a place of safety and support. Again, Bazalgette's findings correspond with those presented in this book. Bazalgette noted, "Nearly all of the young people who took part in detailed 'life story' interviews felt that their contact with the care system had enhanced their life changes in some way" (2014:29). Later she added that young people "explained that entering care had enabled them to be removed from very harmful or dangerous situations" (2014:29).

This chapter focuses on the movement from family of origin into living in care. It deals with the transition period, and focuses on narratives of youths' lives at home with their families, and their reflections on their new life in care. The challenge the youth faced was being able to produce a coherent and sensible account of life in their family of origin which could explain the remarkable and extraordinary need for apprehension and placement in care. As we have seen in previous chapters, the stories that get produced in interviews, and as we see below in CAST meetings, are shaped in an interactive co-production of relevance and meaning that recovers a working and identifiable sense through narrative. That which is talked about as relevant emerges from out of intimate familiarity with life inside a child protection system. Most youth recall being apprehended, being placed in an emergency home, moving into a group home or foster care, being assigned a social worker, changing schools, making new friends, and so on. Youth in care find themselves absorbed into a world of talk and accounts of social work professionals, foster parents, group home parents, psychologists, and counsellors.

That which emerges as youth's stories articulates their recognition of the systems into which their lives have been taken-up. Their talk is not just a here and now turn-by-turn processes of relationship building, but articulates their location and awareness of being children or youth who have become subject to the orders and governance of child protection law, agencies, and organisations. Their narratives are informed by tacit or implicit political understandings and positions concerning preferred versions for accounting for troubles in families of origin, personal responsibility, and the authority of child welfare agencies.

Despite the social organisation and the politics informing children's stories or narratives, this recognition does not vitiate either their value nor our ability to learn from that which they have to say. Barron notes, "Allowing youths a voice in matters that directly affect them is a starting point for change" (2000:122). The voices of youth not only deserve but need to be heard as they provide clear direction, and lesson for change in child welfare practice.

Youth in CAST

I was extremely fortunate to have been able to participate in a Children's Aid Society Teen (CAST) group. We would assemble at the local CAS offices, and meet every Wednesday evening from about 6:00pm to 9:00pm. The CAST group, and program of support to teens in care was led by a youth worker with several decades of experience, who had dedicated his life to creating spaces for dialogue with youth. An average of twelve to fifteen youths attended every meeting. The organisation of meetings was rather informal, as youths would check in, there would be a discussion about what type of pizza to order, and talk would proceed. Usually topics turned to problems with social workers, problems with foster parents, or group homes, or troubles at school with teachers or fellow students, and so on. I was given permission by the CAS and the group to audio-record meetings. These recordings posed quite specific challenges for transcription. Sometimes youth might talk at the same time. There were interruptions. Some youth, especially when talking about sensitive material, talked softly. Sometimes it was difficult to make out from the recording what was being said due to simultaneous conversations, noise from moving chairs, rustling paper, or laughter and other vocalisations. Despite whatever technical challenges the recordings posed for transcription these hardly mattered. Involvement in CAST allowed me to come to know a strong and energetic group of young people who despite trauma, abuse, and neglect proved not only personally resilient, but committed to improving the lives of others in care. The opportunity to be involved in CAST was a highlight of my week, and gave depth and life to my research, as I came to know many of the youths over extended periods of time, in the intimate spaces of safety in the group.

The voices of the youths point through the moments of the interviews to their desire to tell the interviewer about the realities of their lives in care, to

agree to be interviewed, and to arrive at child welfare offices for the interviews. Although I had considered using only those accounts created in interviews, I decided to include stories of youths created at CAST meetings in this
and the next two chapters. While it is the case that the stories generated in
CAST meetings are shaped by members' struggles to make themselves heard
in competition against sometimes up to twenty youths, and to hold the floor,
and while such an interactive crucible may have contributed to their pithy
clarity, additionally they serve to bring into focus the publicly available ways
that youth talk about living in care to each other. Indeed, the stories produced
in CAST meetings, perhaps due to such interactive dynamics generally present
articulate and efficient statements of experiences in care.

In using segments from CAST meetings it must be acknowledged that a
sub-text of much of the talk performed in the group was designed to develop
and promote a positive image of youth in care. This is the politics of the
group. CAST is a support group that seeks to educate others about youth in
care. It seeks to establish that children and youth in care are not to blame for
their situation, that they are as 'normal' as other youth. CAST aims to help
youth in care see themselves as sane, reasonable, intelligent, honest, and
worthwhile. The youths' talk in the CAST group was routinely directed to
countering what they perceived to be negative stereotypes about youth in
care, and as a result talk often turned to affirming the worthiness of youth in
care. In CAST youth often focused on planning and executing activities that
promoted positive images of youth in care, whether through setting up tables
in malls for youth services events, attending youth symposia, or providing
education to other youth in schools, children's services professionals, and so
on. For example, CAST members provided education to CAS employees and
potential foster-parents through regular scheduled and special presentations
and seminars. CAST youths provided liaison with other youth and community organisations. They invited influential guests – among whom included the
government Minister of Community and Social Services – to their meetings
to lobby for policies that improved the lot of children in care. They organised
special events for youth in care, that included various fund-raiser, sports, and
activity days, "Youth Achievement Award Celebrations", and Christmas
dances. Additionally, youths used weekly meetings to provide mutual aid, to
help each other talk about and work through difficult issues of daily living,
and to build solidarity and support.

The segments of talk from CAST meetings must be interpreted as operating
in and against such extended group purposes and organisational debates.
Group members' turns at talk were heard and reviewed by other members
inside and against such background frameworks for promoting a sense of the
worth, achievement, and entitlement of children and youth in care. Stories
about life in care blended accounts of life experiences with political statements designed to counter negative and damaging public stereotypes about
problem kids, problem families, and dysfunctional child welfare systems. Yet,
while such factors need to be recognised as structuring accounts, for youths

participating in CAST their talk was not just about 'performance'. Their talk in the group was part of a collective effort to make sense of and work through difficult and challenging life issues surrounding living in abusive and neglectful families, coming into care, and living in care. The group provided an opportunity for youths to speak about their experiences, to be listened to, to find commonalities, and to share their struggles to work through and make sense of often painful life experiences. It is precisely this focused nature of CAST meetings that makes the youths' talk so valuable for social workers who wish to improve services to children and youth in care.

Listening to youth

The analysis pursued in the chapter of youths' talk about living in care is oriented to a simple foundational proposition, that good social work is built on face-to-face relations and personal commitments to clients. To provide effective child protection, family service, and to be genuinely helpful demands commitment that social workers spend time with children and youth, and their caregivers.[1] It is through the development of close working relationships that social workers build the trust necessary to allow young people in care to talk about their experiences and to confide in an adult when there are problems in their placements. The essential foundation of a trusting relationship with children and youth in care is the same as that of any other relationship, namely that people demonstrate their commitment to each other by spending time together in activities that are mutually enjoyable. A helping relationship is not comprised only of talk. Social workers need to have the time available at work to be able to get to know children and youth on their caseloads. They need to have the freedom to build relationships marked by loyalty and commitment, both to children and youth, and to parents. Building such commitments demands meeting children and youth in normal activities, whether going to movies, going bowling, working on cars, or going to lunch. Social workers in child protection need to make demands that allow their workdays to be reorganised. They must have the resolve and confidence to push paperwork aside and to make getting to work with and to know children and youth their first professional priority.

Social workers must listen to the voices of children and youths on their caseloads. By inviting them to talk, and by listening to what they have to say, social workers can move beyond a dysfunctional politics of child protection. By being with and by listening to children and youth they can develop case plans and interventions that begin with the needs of clients. Kadi comments, "all systems of oppression – from child abuse to racism to ableism – function most effectively when victims don't talk" (1996:11). The task of social workers is to help children and youth to talk about and work through their experiences so that they can become active agents, along with their parents, professionals, foster parents, and others, in the determination of viable and humane intervention plans. Talk and listening to clients are correctives to the ideological positions and reductionism in which propo-nents of family preservation square off against those who argue for the "best interests of the child".

Talking with youth reveals that what matters are not abstract debates about family preservation[2] (Berry, 1997; Goldstein, Freud, & Solnit, 1979) or the "best interests of the child" (Bala, 1991), but having a safe place to live and having adults in their life who listen to them, are interested in them, and are committed to them. Talking with youth in care reveals the intimate relation-ship between child abuse and neglect and poverty (Hughes, 2000; BCMSS, 1992; Garrett, 1999; Parton, 1985). Talking with youth in care reveals the conflicting dynamics of sympathy for their parent(s) and the difficult recogni-tion of the reality that despite desires sometimes youth cannot live at home.

As child protection services across the country have moved to embrace standardised risk assessment tools, e.g. Ontario Risk Assessment Model (ORAM), and measures of parenting, e.g. Looking After Children (LAC), social workers find increasing portions of their days absorbed by paperwork. Garrett writing about the problems with LAC worried:

> Clearly the task of child-care social work is, in part, underpinned by a willingness to form judgements about standards of parenting and these must be informed by reflective professional assessments; social work cannot and should not be held fast, or paralysed, by an arid and reduc-tionist cultural relativism ... Yet social work needs also to be alert to how a seemingly omniscient 'objective' discourse on parenting standards can be used to regulate and discipline the socially and economically margin-alised children and families who make up most of the service user population.
>
> (1999:33)

Against the ideological impulse towards a professional objectivism and the machine enhancement of organisational powers and authority, social workers need to reach out to those who become clients to forge solidarities and loyalties. It is in the crucible of talk and dialogue that social workers mediate their values, knowledge, and organisational mandates with the realities of clients' lives. It must be recognised that such shifts towards dialogue with cli-ents are dangerous, unsettling, as they threaten to strain loyalties, commit-ments, powers, and authority in such fashion that they will inevitably create crises both for social workers and for their agencies.

The hard choice for apprehension

As social workers talk to children and youth, and conduct investigations, they recognise that some live in family situations of horrific and unacceptable abuse and neglect. Apprehension of children and youth has been and will continue to be necessary for many. Child protection services provide an escape from homes marked by extreme parental incapacity, and serious risk of physical, sexual, and emotional abuse. Removal from their families, and placement in care becomes necessary to prevent serious injury and death. While it is necessary that some children and youth come into care, simultaneously parents who become involved with child protection services need to be offered supports to manage their problems, receive mental health and addictions treatment, resolve issues of violence and abuse, and become better parents.

The advocates of family preservation argue eloquently for the need for enhanced resources to support families. Working from an ecological position (Berry, 1997; Cimmarusti, 1992) they argue that becoming a better parent is nearly impossible so long as a people feel vulnerable, overwhelmed, and stressed (Berry, 1997). A single mother cannot be an effective parent while struggling on her own to cope with alcohol or drug addictions in a community without viable treatment options (Haydon, 2004). A parent can hardly provide a safe home for children if affordable and adequate housing is not available in her community. It is difficult becoming a better parent if there is little hope for improvement in one's life due to a lack of education and training opportunities. It is difficult raising a family if there are few opportunities for secure, rewarding, and good paying employment. It is difficult being a good parent if one feels beaten down, inadequate, stupid, uneducated, and a failure (Burman, 1996; 1988; Kadi, 1996; Baxter, 1988). Becoming a better parent is difficult indeed if one is filled with self-loathing and self-hatred arising from the grinding effects of poverty (Corby, 2000:209). Hughes, writing in the Toronto CAS newspaper argued

> It takes more income to participate in our society than to subsist. And we will never effectively address the pressing issues of participation in the work force, successful child development, education, and improved health unless we address fundamentals like poverty.

(2000:1)

While the problems in youths' families of origin are variable they are usually rooted in the grinding effects of poverty and social marginality. Parental incapacity, whether due to mental illness or developmental delay, physical disability, drug or alcohol abuse, or unresolved anger and rage, predictably results in poverty (National Council of Welfare, 1999; 1997, 1979[3]; Swift, 1995). By definition poverty creates limited access to housing, emergency income support, necessities of life – food, clothing, and recreation, substance abuse treatment and care, and so on.[4] As programs have been eliminated which helped people to provide individual and family counselling, to gain education and skills, and to find decent employment, the vulnerabilities and risks to children increases. In home environments marred by poverty, addictions, mental illness, and despair the only viable option left to child protection social workers is removal of the child.

J: so you were born here in X (city), but then your family moved.

C: Yah, we useta move a lot.

J: mmhuh, ah, do you know why you moved a lot, °why was that°

C: uhm, my mom told me that we moved alot because my dad was in a gang

J: do you have any memory of that

C: uhm, kinda yah

J: yah

C: when I was a liddle kid I useta see a lotta drugs. Like there'd be a table right in fronta me and there'd be coke all over the table

J: mm . . . okay, so do you have any memory of being three

C: yah

J: so do you remember where you were taken when you were three

C: yah, I was taken to:oah a group home me and my liddle brother lived in.

C, as with other children in care recalls that "we useta move a lot." The theme of frequent moves is recurrent among children in care, most likely arising from the problems of finding and keeping decent housing, particularly for those with troubles with the law, and who have drug and alcohol problems. If C's claim is factual that, "I useta see a lotta drugs. Like there'd be a table right in fronta me and there'd be coke all over all over the table", this would on its own comprise grounds for determining that she was in need of protection. The Institute of Medicine and the National Research Council, *New Directions in Child Abuse and Neglect Research*, reports that, "Parental substance abuse, history of child abuse or neglect, and depression appear to have the strongest support in the literature as risk factors for child abuse and neglect" (2013:S-2).

The effects of a lack of social service supports for parents and their children can be glimpsed through the details of the following segment.

J: How was it growing up with mom.

M: Pretty good, she'd tell me what's right and wrong, and help with me my math homework.

J: So what was not so good about it?

M: When I was twelve we started having arguments and stuff, about making my bed and stuff.

J: And going out.

M: Yah.

J: were rules strict at home.

M: Yah a little bit. I was only allowed out an hour a day.

J: Were you allowed to go out with friends.

M: yah

J: How did school go.

M: I did very well in school. Last year I got better grades. I'm going into grade nine.

J: Great. What changed last year that you did better.

M: At first of grade eight didn't get along with teachers. I would leave school, go out, hang around all day.

J: What changed.

M: since moving into the group home I was scared to do that because I'd get into trouble for it.

J: So that made a difference to your studies, yah great

J: So:o humm, did something happen sort- a:around October that ah:eh that ahh instigated you leaving the home? . . . . . . (6 sec)

M: uhm: me . . . . (13 sec) uhm, me and my mo::m we:e fought physical at one time, and that's what uhm, me moved into a group home.

J: okay, so you, you and your mom got into a physical altercation, do you remember what it was over?

M: No

J: was that the first

M: yah

J: Who called the children's services.

M: Think, my counsellor at school.

J: did you go to school and tell your counsellor?

M: I think the counsellor I was seeing with my mom, told family services. We both went and told her, and she called children's services.

J: do you remember who came to talk to you from children's services?

M: No

J: A social worker?

M: Yah. I went to the seventy-two hour room here.

J: How did you get here? Who brought you here.

M: The police

J: I'm missing part of the story. How did the police get involved? Who called the police.

M: I think my mom called the police during the fight, and the police came and brought me here. Then after I was here for seventy-two hours, I went to a group home, and

J: Do you remember how you felt coming in here?

M: I felt nervous.

Although it is not addressed in this segment, later in the interview M revealed that the arguments with her mother revolved around M's problems with drugs, alcohol, suicide attempts, boyfriends, and even prostitution. Clearly, her acting out behaviours were beyond the control of her mother. M begins the interview by only very elliptically suggesting, "When I was twelve we started having arguments and stuff, about making my bed and stuff", to which J adds, "And going out", leading M to respond "yah". J then asks, "were rules strict at home" to which M responds by elaborating, "Yah a little bit. I was only allowed out an hour a day." If M's account can be relied on, it would seem that her mother did try to reign in her daughter's acting out and dangerous behaviours, albeit without success, and it would seem without apparent external support. The tragedy is that the situation escalated to the point, as M explains, "me and my mo:om we:e fought physical at one time, and that's what uhm, me moved into a group home."

Any parent who raises teenagers knows how difficult and challenging this phase of life can be, both for the youth and for the parent. Limits, rules, and boundaries are all tested and redefined. Stern prosaically notes, "Family conflict increases during adolescence as teens seek to assert their independence and parents react to the disruptions in family life developmental change create" (1999:181). For parents and their teens to survive healthy social supports and emotional and physical resources are essential. Parents and their teens need to have other adults and, when necessary, skilled professionally staffed services to turn to for guidance and support. Parents and their teens require a broad range of resources to weather the developmental changes and tensions of teenage years.

Although we cannot recover any substantive understanding regarding the quality of parenting in M's home, we can recover sufficient detail from her story to begin to sketch the lineaments of trouble. She was one of five children in a home with a single mother who attempted to deal with her acting out behaviours on her own. She was able to live in her mother's home, without prior involvement from child protection services for twelve years. This points to potentially adequate if not strong and resourceful parenting. The tragedy is that the vulnerabilities of her mother, combined with M's serious acting out behaviours, obviously led to crisis situations that resulted in M entering care.[5] If M's mother could have been provided with sufficient resources, with counselling services, and with family respite, might M have been maintained in the family home? Such a question can only be answered in the presence not the absence of social services and community resources.

Silva Wayne, writing the "Afterword" to Elizabeth Cameron's story of her troubled relationship with her son Keith, who became a permanent ward, notes, "What chance is there for a child of a parent who has been rejected as a child and who is presently financially stressed, emotionally drained, isolated, un-tutored, unsupported and unsure?" (1984:161). When working with clients whose lives are shaped by realities of systematic deprivation, loss, abuse, and hopelessness, the vulnerability of parents shapes the vulnerabilities of their children. It is imperative that social workers struggle alongside parents to build face-to-face solidarities, supports, respect, and care.

While some youth are brought into care in order to protect them from horrific abuse and neglect, for many youth entry into care becomes necessary simply due to effects of poverty and lack of substantial resources to support their family of origin. The relationship between child protection services and poverty is persistent and clearly documented (Stokes & Schmidt, 2011; Jonson-Reid, et al., 2009; Drake & Zuravin, 1998). It is obvious to social workers that when parents face the stresses of unemployment, underemployment, precarious employment, resulting in inadequate housing, dangerous neighbourhoods, and not having enough money for food, clothing, and entertainment, that parents and children suffer together. Parents living under stress, marginalisation, and racism will predictably suffer mental health problems or engage in substance abuse. Yet, addictions treatment, respite, home support, public housing, and other social services are often not available to parents and children.[6] Battams, who conducted research for the Vanier Institute of the Family, reported:

> Household income can have a significant impact on child and family wellbeing, as it has been identified as one of the most significant social determinants of health. Family income levels can affect many aspects of life, such as overall living conditions and psychological functioning, and it can influence health related behaviours, such as diet quality, physical activity levels, tobacco and alcohol use. Research has also identified income as the "strongest predictor" of food insecurity.
>
> (2018:7)

Today, as in past, social workers are obligated to articulate the personal to the political. This requires engaging in a politicising dialogue with children and youth, and their parents, to explicate the relationship between personal troubles and the organisation of social and economic inequalities. Poverty, racism, gender inequality, ableism, and so on, emerge as the effects of a capitalist political economy, which leaves social workers and social service agencies to pick up, patch, and try to repair the personal breakdowns that follow from exploitation, alienation, and marginalisation. Indeed, social workers need to take sides, and to build working solidarities, loyalties, and commitments with those who become clients, to promote social advocacy and struggle. Only in a context of honest dialogue, which bridges social injustice to personal suffering, can social workers develop the necessary relationships that will enable them to talk realistically with parents about life problems, responsibilities, and choices as articulated to complex social and economic backgrounds.

Of course, not all of the problems families face can be resolved through dialogue. Further, although social workers can easily imagine services that might aid parents and children to stay together, the reality is that such services are simply not available or accessible. No matter how much social workers may feel frustrated by the disjunction between their imaginings and the realities of social service provision, they must ultimately adhere to an uncomfortable pragmatism, in which there must be a firm commitment to protecting children from harm. A social worker's or a parent's desires for drug treatment cannot protect a child from harm when a parent fails to care for themself also fails to care for their child. A social worker's or parent's desire for decent housing cannot protect a child from living in firetrap or in a high crime neighbourhood. A social worker's or parent's desire for employment cannot feed a child when there is no food in home. Beyond desire, beyond imagination, and beyond the painful insights into what might be, social workers face the hard decisions bred from the realities of people's daily lives.

It is against the world as it is organised, and as it can be modified realistically that social work action must be forged. It is in and against hard and difficult realities that social workers find themselves constricted in their choices and their actions, and compelled to continue to bring children into care.

When children and youth are brought into care social workers need to enter into dialogue, to listen, and draw on the child or youths' strengths and resources to develop an appropriate plan of care.[7] The National Youth in Care Network, 'Backgrounder', 'Voice', notes,

> Youth in care feel that their voices are not being heard. The notion of having a voice and being heard is crucial to the development and empowerment of young people. There are different ways for youth in care to have a voice. The most critical and important way is to be allowed to provide input in the formation of their plan of care.
>
> (NYCN, 2005)

Children and youth who are involved, by social workers, in their own care planning and processes can be helped to invest in, and to be committed to, working cooperatively with foster parents and group home parents to achieve healthy and viable life goals. Similarly, Cocker and Allain observe: "Communicating with looked after children and ascertaining their wishes and feelings is not a one-off event but should represent an ongoing dialogue linked to the care planning processes of assessment, planning, intervention and review" (2008:63). It is vital that children in care know that their voices matter, that they are taken seriously, and that they have a sense of input and control over their life in care. While children will continue to need to be brought into care, the disruption, loss, and alienation of the process demands that as social workers develop plans of care, that they take the time and exercise the patience necessary to enter into sustained dialogue with those children and youth. Social workers can play an instrumental role in helping to make children feel listened to, respected, safe, and cared for. Apprehension, and care outside their family home can offer safety, respite, and planning for next steps. These can include developing interventions and plans to restore family functioning, or if needed placement with relatives, friends, and others in the youth's community of contacts.

Social workers' commitments to children and youth must combine with the confidence that not just child protection, but child and family welfare are noble enterprises. Social workers must be advocates for both children and their parents. For too long child protection services have been provided on the cheap, and even youth in care recognise that child protection is a welfare service.

J: How long didjew stay there?
S: I don' know,
J: abo:out, [a year:er]

S: [it wasn't that long], it wasn't that long. Uhm, maybe almost a year cause I was there fer my birthday, and my birthday came and I got all these retarded clothes an hhh, jist cheap things, and I was like, "this is a waste of money, like come on people", ya know, you gotta be thankful, because when you're livin here you don't get what ya want=

J: =hheh, okay=

S: believe me you don't get [anyth]ing good like, you don't like, oh, I'm not saying that like te be a little snot, but you gotta be grateful for what ya get, because you're not gunna get a whole lot, because yer parents if they don't buy it, you don't get it, that's the way it is, that's the way I see it, but some people are lucky, and they get a lot.

Once in care children and youth learn that the services they receive are poorly funded, stigmatising, and inadequate.[8] In a CAST meeting one young woman observed.

H: I think of the Children's Aid as a single parent, low income family with twenty-two kids, ((laugher)) and/

I: that's so funnheheh.

H: an and that's why, like that's why I'm satisfied, eh I'm eighteen, you guys got me to being eighteen you know, in in two days, its your birthday fer me, you know, and so that's why why I don't hate you guys or anything, but I just, seeing so much that can be done.

Commitment to children and youth in care demands placing their interests over those of agencies and governments. Social workers need to lobby vigorously both for the rights of children in care and for the rights of poor parents who become involved in child protection systems.

Life in limbo

During the 1980s a consensus emerged that "being in care adds psychological disturbance to social deprivation" (Elliot, 1991:572), and that, "being in care" should be treated as a "last resort" (567). The result was a shift in legislative provision, that incorporated the principles of "least disruptive intervention" (Barnhorst & Walter, 1990:18) family support, and prevention (Rosenbluth, 1995:233). Correspondingly, during the 1980s social workers increasingly turned to the philosophy and treatment approaches of family preservation.[9]

> Intensive FPS (Family Preservation Services) were developed in the 1970s and fostered by the Adoption Assistance and Child Welfare Act of 1980, which requires states to make "reasonable efforts" to prevent the out-of-home placement of children. In the late 1980s and early 1990s, most states instituted family preservation programs.
>
> (Littell & Tajima, 2000:406)

Despite the rhetoric of family preservation (Bala, 1991; Rosenbluth, 1995) during the 1980s and 1990s increasing numbers of children continued to be brought into care across Canada. Farris-Manning and Zandstra writing on behalf of the Child Welfare League Canada (CWLC) noted, "Over the last decade, studies have shown that in Canada, the vulnerable population of children in need of protection is increasing significantly", and reported that their data indicated that in 1998/1999 there were a total of 46,397 children in care across Canada, excluding Quebec (2003:2). More recent Statistics Canada data from 2011 indicates that there were 47,885 children in foster care, about 0.5% of all children in Canada under age 14 (Cuddington in *The National Post*, Sept 19, 2012), and that particularly in the western provinces First Nations children continue to be disproportionately represented among those in care.

Behind the statistics are the realities of the lives of children and youth in care, and the every-day fabric of lived experiences. Unfortunately, too often the every-day lives of many children and youth in Canada continues to be an experience of disruption, movement, and dislocation from one home to another. We see this articulated clearly in the next segment taken from a CAST meeting dedicated to exploring the issues of coming into and being in care. All the youth present at the meeting spoke of continuous disruptions in their lives both before and after coming into care.

R: ... I.I was away from home, you know. I lived with my father. I lived with my aunt. I was always..I never lived at home that much so, and moving away from home was always relaxing.

A: Well I went from my mom's, to my grandma's, back to my mom's, to my grandma's, back to my mom's, to my dad's...

SW: uh huh.

A: so I was used to always being shuffled around packing my stuff so, one more move wasn't anything.

D: Me? I don.I don't remember but I came into care when whenever I was two, and I was in and out of care until I was ten, so that.that part I don't remember a thing. That from ten and up I do.

A: I felt that all the love that was given to me was just taken right back, but the only person I could count on was my grandma, my aunt and my uncle, uhm, felt that I was (was just maybe) a bouncing ball, went from home place to another, that's what happened to me exactly. One foster home to another. Eventually () I.I was never going to get friends. I was going all over the place. Going to a different school...

SW: Didja hafta change schools or anything?

G: Yep, oh I got used to that, cause I was flown, cause first I was from Africa, then I moved to the States, then I moved to Montreal, then I moved. So I.I got used to movin. It..it doesn't bother me the part about moving.

The theme of constant movement from one home to another, one relative to another, and one home to another, points both to the attempts of the parents to keep their children in their own families, and tragically to the incapacity of both parents and family members to provide the necessary stability for their children. It is in the wake of such incapacities and parental and family failure, that children are brought into care.

The tragedy is that sometimes for years before child protection workers become alerted to problems, and even after they become involved with a family, children and youth are left in a state of limbo. The authors of the Sparrow Lake Alliance report *Children in Limbo* (1996) outline,

> Limbo is a prolonged period of time in which a child is subjected to lack of continuity of relationship with major caregivers, manifested by ongoing confusion, conflict or uncertainty about parent figures, parenting authority, parenting techniques, family relationships, past history and especially future plans.

(1)

For children and youth in care, their lives are often marked by repeated moves within their families of origin, repeated attempts by child protection authorities to help parents to care for their children, repeated attempts to reunite children with their parents, repeated failures of such attempts, and repeated entries into care, repeated moves through different placements in care, and repeated changes of core staff.

The obvious trauma of living in limbo, of suffering through a childhood without durable and reliable adult attachments, led to a "permanency planning" approach to child protection practice. Although the objectives of providing children and youth in care with stability are admirable, the complexity of the family problems, the lack of viable treatment and family support options, and the operational inertia of legal and court systems all conspire to make permanency planning more an ideal than a reality. Pike et al. (1977) promote permanent planning for children in foster care and envision that social workers can follow an ordered and orderly decision tree to determine whether or not a child's parents can provide an adequate home, whether or not treatment is viable, and whether or not a child will need an alternative permanent placement.

Yet against the imagination of social workers clients face the realities of lives wracked by uncertainties. A loss of an apartment, a new abusive boyfriend, a loss of a job, or a growing addiction, may wreak whatever plans, contracts, and commitments parents might have made with social workers. A commitment to undergo treatment may fail due to lack of facilities, eligibility requirements, distance, cost, and so on. The fervent and committed desire of a parent to have a child return home may be vitiated by the circumstances of life on the edge of poverty. The professional desire for order, while seemingly viable from inside the orders of organisational work, becomes chimerical for clients whose lives are marked by poverty, poor health, mental illness, addictions, and vulnerability. While social workers cannot abandon the need to develop contracts and plans with clients they must at the same time recognise that the order they imagine might come to exist in client lives is vitiated by the social forces that produce disorder and chaos in the lives of the most marginalised.

In the next segment B, a young woman addresses the problems with attempts to preserve families in which children are abused or neglected.

B: Well I can't personally remember my first entrance, but from my records and from what I've been told, and from a little bit that I can remember, sometimes you can get in, and they say, "Oh you can go home now." Yet they know what you are coming from is hell, be it physical, sexual, mental, emotional abuse, they know that nothing has changed, you know, in a month a person can't reverse themselves like that, but they still put you in that situation, again and again and again and again and again, and I think they finally realise it won't work. Maybe they should give the parent one more chance, but I remember I was put back in my home maybe six times before they finally got it through their thick head, you know. Nothing's going to change, so it was my reintroduction into my birth home that was upsetting, not necessarily going back into CAS. I always thought CAS was a haven.

B, a young woman, makes a passionate plea that her interests and welfare need to be placed before the wants of the parents. Her words provide an important corrective to an ideologically driven practice that places the priority on the principle of family preservation, rather than honest assessment of the child's best interests. B protests, "they know what you are coming from is hell, be it physical, sexual, mental, emotional abuse, they know that nothing has changed, you know, in a month a person can't reverse themselves like that, but they still put you in that situation, again and again and again and again and again". The repetition of "again and again …" discloses the frustration and pain of being subjected to ideologically driven and dysfunctional cycles. Social workers must be able to listen to the voices of youth in care, as correctives to the worker's own beliefs, desires, and thoughts about best practices. The voice of youth creates a disjunction that unsettle professional presumptions, approaches, while simultaneously disturbing the rhetoric and ideology of child protection, helping, and service.

Social workers need to be able to combine careful assessment of parental capacity and motivation through close dialogue with a pragmatic assessment of available services to weigh the actual possibility of constructive family change. Unfortunately, there are some families marked by physical and sexual violence, predatory behaviour, hatreds, and mental and emotional dysfunction that should not be preserved. Despite almost sixty years of second wave feminist critiques of the family, identification of problems of male violence, sexual abuse, and exploitation, the romanticisation of family and family preservation persists. Corby reflects on the turn from a primary focus on protecting children from their parents, to a family supportive approach, and observes that "events in the preceding 20 years created an awareness of the fact that families could be dangerous and distressing places for many children" (2000:49). Social workers require a courage of conviction born of clear adherence to social work values to arrive at and carry out difficult decisions on behalf of children and youth. In the crucible of child protection there can be no room for moral or epistemological relativism. The palpable danger to children and youth in dysfunctional families routinely demands recourse to apprehension and placement in care.

This young woman's story is a caution against the arrogance of a professional belief that skilled intervention can bring about necessary change in a relatively short span of time. Although many parents with debilitating alcohol and drug problems can and do seek help, and get their additions under control, the period of time in which their lives are in crisis places their children at serious risk (Hayden, 2004; Reid et al., 1995). Sometimes it takes years and even decades before parents are able to regain control over their lives. Some of those who survive their alcohol and drug habits recognise, as does Morrisseau, "I came to a point where I was running out of choices. I could continue to drink and die as a result of suicide, or I could go through a kind of mental collapse" (1998:16). The problem child protection workers and children in care face is that in the five, ten, or twenty years it takes for the parent to kick a habit and otherwise get in control of their lives, childhood is lost, or as Owen so aptly observed, "Every childhood lasts a lifetime" (1996). The problem is that children cannot afford to wait for their parents to become parents.

Against the forms of idealism and collusion that would see social workers hold out hope for change without sufficient cause, this young woman's story stands as a corrective. Her voice cautions social workers against colluding with parent(s) in a folie a deux based on optimistic, politically correct, and naive idealisations. Though social workers are increasingly urged to recognise that parents of children in care are oppressed due to their race, gender, ability, or class (Mullaly, 2002); are encouraged to critique the organisation of child protection that blames mothers generally (Swift, 1995); and, are chastised for failing to protect their children from sexual abuse (Carter, 1999), they must nevertheless be able to develop realistic assessments and interventions into difficult and unpalatable realities of peoples' every-day lives. Social workers at the front-line are required to commit to protect children from abuse and neglect. They must hold a child's wellbeing and life paramount despite the politics of oppression, and even despite a desire for solidarity with parents. Children have a right to be protected from harm. Children need to live in homes with adults who take responsibility for their safety, security, and care. Harm or death of a child rightly brings into question the parents' capacities and judgments, regardless of whatever oppression a parent might suffer due to gender, race, ability, sexuality, or class. Social workers must beware of a collusion of hope that creates a mutual pretence that work and change has been achieved. Social workers must beware a dysfunctional collusion rooted in an 'illusion of work' (Shulman, 2016).

The fundamental issue is not an either/or approach to family preservation versus apprehension and placement in care. Nor is the issue choosing to speak to children and youth and not with parents. Rather social workers need to establish dialogue with both children and with their parent(s), as well as other existing or potential care givers. It is in such moments of honest dialogue and forthright discussion that a social worker speaks to their assessments and tests these against parental reactions. Honest dialogue is not necessarily comfortable, safe, or non-threatening. Honest dialogue demands that social workers engage with parents and with children to communicate their professional and organisational obligations to make difficult choices. Honest dialogue demands that social workers allow parents to understand their obligations, their powers, and their assessments and the implications of these for their work. Honest dialogue means helping parents to understand that their children may need to be apprehended and taken into care.

Social workers must demand that every custodial parent must be committed and able to provide minimum standards for their children. When parents are unable to provide minimum standards social workers must make the hard choice to bring and keep children in care. Pike et al. propose that social workers ask themselves, "If the child were returned home tomorrow would I have concern for the child's welfare" (1977:14). Although this is an enigmatic formulation, it forces social workers to recognise their moral responsibility for children on their caseload. Certainly, while there are genuine risks in separating children from their families, there remains nevertheless, as children in care will argue, a compelling necessity to continue do so.

Notes

1 Although this book has focussed on the voices of children and youth, social workers need to recognise that most of these young people continue to have emotional and practical ties to their families of origin. Many teenagers and young adults in care, even permanent or crown wards, continued to have some contact with one or both of their parents. Youth established contact with their mother or father once they became old enough to venture out on their own without adult supervision.
2 Kelly and Blythe provide a succinct overview of the genesis of family preservation in the United States, which they indicate grew out of the "crisis being observed in out-of-home care" (2000:30), the recognition that children entered care often due to family poverty, and that many children were "in unnecessary out-of-home placements" (31).
3 The Canadian National Council of Welfare was created in 1962, fully reconstituted in 1970, to become the national centre for research on poverty and the issues affecting families and children. Sadly, in 2012 the Conservative government of Stephen Harper ceased all funding, thereby shutting down the Council.
4 Conway while arguing that "poverty, unemployment and economic stress have been frequently associated with child abuse" acknowledges two primary sources of opposition to this argument, the first coming from "feminist writers who dislike any argument that deflects central attention away from the patriarchal family, and male

supremacy" and from others who oppose linking child abuse to lower economic status (1993:82).

5 An older study by Reid, Kagan, and Schlosberg of a prevention program counselling service in New York reported that children and youth who required placements tended to be from families with "fewer resources, used services less, made less progress, and were less satisfied with agency's efforts". They added that "adolescents in the placed group were more likely to be at risk of placement because their behavior problems were more numerous and more threatening to the community" (1988:33).

6 The political decisions made by right-wing governments can have serious deleterious effects on vulnerable families. For example, the Conservative provincial government in Ontario, led by Mike Harris from 1995 to 2002, resulted in a 39% increase of children in care. This increase coincided with the decision to reduce welfare rates by 21.6% (Moscovitch, 1997:85) and to "tighten eligibility" (86). There were 10, 919 children in care in 1997, 14,100 in 2000, and 18,126 in 2003 (OACAS, 2004).

7 The National Youth in Care Network, has demanded a greater voice for youth in care for many years. The 2002 Report, *Who Will Teach Me to Learn: Creating Positive School Experiences for Youth in Care* (2001), similarly to more recent documents outlines, "Youth who are actively involved in determining the course of their own lives are not only more satisfied with their lives, they are also more successful in their transitions to independence" (7).

8 This view is shared by foster parents who complain that they are a cheap "dumping ground for society's problem children" (Kendrick, 1990:4) (also cited in Miedema, 1999:32).

9 Krane took a feminist position to argue, "protection efforts which conform to least intrusion and support for children in their homes come about through the obligatory, yet invisible, labour of women in families" (1997:59). She outlined that mothers' protection of children is a form of work that should be recognised and supported with "tangible aid" (72), and that "addressing the material conditions of mother protecting is necessary" (72).

References

Bala, Nicholas. (1991). An introduction to child protection problems. In Nicholas Bala, Joseph P. Hornick, & Robin Vogl (Eds.), *Canadian child welfare law: Children, families and the state* (pp. 1–16). Toronto, ON: Thompson Educational.

Barnhorst, Dick, & Walter, Bernd. (1990). Child protection legislation in Canada. In Nicholas Bala, Joseph P. Hornick, & Robin Vogl (Eds.), *Canadian child welfare law: Children, families and the state* (pp. 1–16). Toronto, ON: Thompson Educational.

Barron, Christie. (2000). *Giving youth a voice: A basis for rethinking adolescent violence.* Halifax, NS: Fernwood.

Battams, Nathan. (2018). *Modern family finances: Income in Canada.* Ottawa, ON: Vanier Institute.

Baxter, Sheila. (1988). *No way to live: Poor women speak out.* Vancouver, BC: New Star.

Bazalgette, Louise. (2014). The views of looked after children and young people on the care system. In Tom Rahilly & Enid Hendry (Eds.), *Promoting the wellbeing of children in care: Messages from research* (pp. 25–51). London, England: NSPCC.

Berry, Marianne. (1997). *The family at risk: Issues and trends in family preservation services.* Columbia, SC: University of South Carolina Press.

British Columbia Ministry of Social Services (BCMSS). (1992). *Protecting our children, supporting our families: A review of child protection issues in British Columbia.* Victoria, BC: BCMSS.

Burman, Patrick. (1996). *Poverty's bonds: Power and agency in the social relations of welfare.* Toronto, ON: Thompson Educational.

Burman, Patrick. (1988). *Killing time, losing ground: Experiences of unemployment.* Toronto, ON: Thompson Educational.

Carter, Betty Joyce. (1999). *Who's to blame? Child sexual abuse and non-offending mothers.* Toronto, ON: University of Toronto Press.

Cimmarusti, Rocco A. (1992). Family preservation practice based upon a multisystems approach. *Child Welfare,* 71(3): 241–256.

Cocker, Christine, & Allain, Lucille. (2008). *Social work with looked after children.* Exeter, England: Learning Matters.

Conway, John F. (1993). *The Canadian family in crisis (revised).* Toronto, ON: James Lorimer.

Corby, Brian. (2000). *Child abuse: Towards a knowledge base* (2nd ed.). Buckingham, England: Open University Press.

Cuddington, Wayne. (September 19, 2012). Census 2011: Canada's foster children counted for first time. *The National Post.*

Drake, Brett, & Zuravin, Susan. (1998). Revisiting the myth of classlessness. *American Journal of Orthopsychiatry,* 68(2): 295–304.

Elliot, Doreen. (1991). Substitute family care for children in Britain. *Social Service Review,* 65: 564–581.

Farris-Manning, Cheryl, & Zandstra, Marietta. (2003). *Children in care in Canada: A summary of current issues and trends with recommendations for future research.* Ottawa, ON: Child Welfare League of Canada.

Garrett, Paul Michael. (1999). Mapping child-care social work in the final years of the twentieth century: A critical response to the "Looking after Children" system. *British Journal of Social Work,* 29: 27–47.

Goldstein, Joseph, Freud, Anna, & Solnit, Albert J. (1979). *Before the best interests of the child.* New York, NY: The Free Press.

Granofsky, Brigitte. (2010). Life narrative and voice are children's rights. In Birgitte Granofsky (Ed.), *There are not wizards: The child welfare conundrum* (pp. 7–12). Toronto, ON: Sparrow Lake Alliance.

Hayden, Carol. (2004). Parental substance misuse and child care social work: Research in a city social work department in England. *Child Abuse Review,* 13: 18–30.

Hughs, Colin. (Spring 2000). Child poverty and child welfare. *Communicate (CAS Toronto),* 12(1): 1.

Institute of Medicine and National Research Council. (2013). *New directions in child abuse and neglect research.* Washington, DC: National Academies.

Jonson-Reid, Melissa, Drake, Brett, & Kohl, Patricia. (2009). Is the overrepresentation of the poor in child welfare caseloads due to bias or need? *Children and Youth Services Review,* 31(3): 422–427.

Kadi, Joanna. (1996). *Thinking class: Sketches from a cultural worker.* Boston, MA: South End Press.

Kelly, Susan, & Blythe, Betty J. (2000). Family preservation: A potential not yet realized. *Child Welfare,* 79(1): 29–41.

Kelly, Wendy. (2017). *Understanding children in foster care: Identifying and addressing what children learn from maltreatment.* eBook: Palgrave Macmillan.

Kendrick, Martin. (1990). *Nobody's children*. Toronto, ON: MacMillan.

Krane, Julia Elissa. (1997). Least disruptive and intrusive course of action … for whom? Insights from feminist analysis of practice in cases of child sexual abuse. In Jane Pulkingham & Gordon Ternowetsky (Eds.), *Child and family policies*. Halifax, NS: Fernwood.

Littell, Julia H., & Tajima, Emiko. (2000). A multilevel model of client participation in intensive family preservation services. *Social Service Review*, 74: 405–435.

Miedema, Baukje. (1999). *Mothering for the state: The paradox of fostering*. Halifax, NS: Fernwood.

Morrisseau, Calvin. (1998). *Into the daylight: A wholistic approach to healing*. Toronto, ON: University of Toronto Press.

Moscovitch, Allan. (1997). Social assistance in the new Ontario. In Diana Ralph, Andre Regimbald, & Neree St-Amand (Eds.), *Open for business, closed to people: Mike Harris's Ontario* (pp. 80–91). Halifax, NS: Fernwood.

Mullaly, Bob. (2002). *Challenging oppression: A critical social work approach*. Don Mills, ON: Oxford University Press.

Munro, Eileen. (2007). *Child protection*. London: Sage.

National Council of Welfare. (December 1979). *In the best interests of the child*. Ottawa, ON: National Council of Welfare.

National Council of Welfare. (Summer 1997). *Healthy parents, healthy babies*. Ottawa, ON: National Council of Welfare.

National Council of Welfare. (Spring 1999). *Preschool children: Promises to keep*. Ottawa, ON: National Council of Welfare.

National Youth in Care Network. (2001). *Who will teach me to learn: Creating positive school experiences for youth in care*. Ottawa, ON: National Youth in Care Network.

National Youth in Care Network. (2005). *Current themes facing youth in state care: Backgrounder series #4: Voice*. Ottawa, ON: National Youth in Care Network.

Ontario Association of Children's Aid Societies. (2004). *CAS Facts: April 1, 2003 – March 31, 2004*. Toronto, ON: Ontario Association of Children's Aid Societies.

Owen, Jan. (1996). *Every childhood lasts a lifetime: Personal stories from the frontline of family breakdown*. Brisbane, Australia: Australian Association of Young People in Care.

Parton, Nigel. (1985). *The politics of child abuse*. London: Macmillan.

Pike, Victor, Downs, Susan, Emlen, Arthur, Downs, Glen, & Case, Denise. (1977). *Permanent planning for children in foster care: A handbook for social workers*. Portland, OR: US Department of Health, Education, and Welfare.

Reid, Grant, Sigurdson, Eric, Christianson-Wood, Jan, & Wright, Alexandra. (1995). *Basic issues concerning the assessment of risk in child welfare work*. Ottawa, ON: Family Violence Prevention Division Health Canada.

Reid, William J., Kagan, Richard M., & Schlosberg, Shirley B. (1988). Prevention of placement: Critical factors in program success. *Child Welfare*, 67(1): 25–36.

Rosenbluth, David. (1995). Moving in and out of foster care. In Joe Hudson & Burt Galaway (Eds.), *Child welfare in Canada: Research and policy implications* (pp. 233–244). Toronto, ON: Thompson Educational.

Shulman, Lawrence. (2016). *The skills of helping individuals, families, groups, and communities* (8th ed.). Toronto, ON: Thompson Brooks Cole.

Silva-Wayne, Susan. (1984). Afterword. In Elizabeth Camden, *If he comes back he's mine: A mother's story of child abuse,* (pp. 155–165). Toronto, ON: Women's Press.

Sparrow Lake Alliance. (April 1996). *Children in limbo.* Ottawa, ON: Canadian Resource Centre on Children and Youth (CRCCY).

Stern, Susan B. (1999). Anger management in parent-adolescent conflict. *American Journal of Family Therapy*, 27(2): 181–193.

Stokes, Jacqueline, & Schmidt, Glen. (2011). Race, poverty and child protection decision making. *British Journal of Social Work*, 41: 1105–1121.

Swift, Karen. (1995). Manufacturing "bad mothers": A critical perspective on child neglect. Toronto, ON: University of Toronto Press.

9 Stories of coming into care

Social workers engaged in child protection recognise that children and youth suffer physical, psychological, and social harms from abuse and neglect. This recognition is self-evident. Additionally, the process of separation from family and multiple placements while in care, either in group homes or foster care, can contribute to traumatic experiences of separation and loss. Clearly, apprehension of children from situations of risk of abuse and neglect articulates our recognition, of relative harms, in which we weigh the risk of serious injury and death against the risk of emotional harm occasioned by separation of the child from family, friends, and familiar environments.

We know that neglectful and abusive family situations create elevated risks for conduct or behaviour problems (Docherty, et al., 2018; Jaffee, et al., 2005; Oswald, et al., 2009), psychological problems (Springer, et al., 2007; MacMillan, et al., 2001), additional health care and special educational needs, attachment disorders, substance abuse, eating disorders, and so on. Oswald, Heil, and Goldbeck, state the obvious, "Children living in foster care often experience threatening situations such as neglect, domestic violence, physical, or sexual abuse in their family of origin" (2009:462). However, while the process of coming into care can be traumatic, when examined against the background of a child's family of origin, it is not surprising that for many children and youth coming into care can be experienced as protective and nurturing. For youth, coming into care despite troubles in group and foster homes, movement through multiple homes, and adjustment difficulties is often occasioned by a sense of relief and escape from untenable home environments. Indeed, Wiener in his forward to *Understanding Looked After Children*, opened by observing:

> It is increasingly recognised that a period of safe, secure and stable family life can be deeply healing for a child who has been deprived of these things in their birth family.

> (2007:5)

It is certainly the case that children and youths are harmed in multiple ways, physically, developmentally, neurologically, cognitively, etc., by abuse and neglect. Yet, attention to resilience, following Garbarino, leads us to be attentive to ecology, complexity, culture, and to the framework of moral expectations and judgements social workers bring to evaluate success or failure (Garbarino, 2005) of the protection processes. It is important, as Unger advises, that we study "the multiple pathways that children, their caregivers, and communities travel toward health" (2005:xvii). The provision of foster care and group homes, extended family placements, and placement with friends needs to be evaluated as foundational elements in the complex work of helping neglected and abused children.

The old chestnut, 'if you go looking for trouble you will find it', is a worthwhile caution for social workers. Unfortunately, professional expectations that neglect and abuse of a child will inevitably lead to trauma may result in the formulation of questions by the interviewer, which in turn elicit responses that match or anticipate a framework for finding and discovering trauma as present. Schwartz noted, "Trauma survivors' belief systems inevitably get reinforced in treatment ..." (2000:6). An advantage of a turn to conversation analysis is that it discloses the reflexivity of the practical activities of social workers and youth and the co-construction and shaping of interviewer questions and youth responses. What emerges from interviews, the questions posed by interviewers, and the responses and voices of youths, articulates a reflexive complexity, which is both essential and incorrigible. That is, the co-construction and enactment of accounts and stories is woven into the substantive material itself. The forms of representation are shaped by talk-in-interaction.

With this in mind, I turn to the following segment, in which the social worker, interviewing P, a youth in care, provides a framework suggesting trouble.

SW: How did you feel? What were your feelings? Were you frightened, confused, apprehensive?
P: Ah...anxious, I was scared, angry and very confused yeah.
SW: Ah, didn't anything in the way you do things, did you have any reactions after coming into care? Any change in the way you act?
P: I was a bit calmer, um..That's about it. I mean ah, no real changes in my actions, my reactions.

Although the social worker asks if P might have felt "frightened, confused, apprehensive", and while P is prepared to work through this framework, P responds by providing modifications to the adjectives, i.e. "anxious ... scared, angry, and very confused." The social worker, who most likely was alert to the potentiality that P was parroting back his words, followed with a question designed to elicit an elaboration of personal details. The social worker asks, "Any change in the way you act?" P responds, "I was a bit calmer". About a minute later P explained:

P: When I first came into care she (the social worker) explained, ah some things that, ah were available at Child/ and with ah the Children's Aid, the fact that I was going into a foster home. At that time I had thoughts about the foster home...I heard stuff about the foster homes. There were group homes and things like that and just stuff I heard in the washrooms about the foster homes at school. But ah, when I moved in it was quite the opposite actually. Ahh, I was surrounded by families, caring families

Indeed, when P was provided with an opportunity to develop his own understandings and story about coming into care, he generated a reflective account that addressed the complex interplay between feelings, expectations and attitudes of others as sifted through his own experiences in care. P indicates that despite expectations and understandings about foster homes held by other youths that he "was surrounded by families, caring families" For many children who come into care, the new opportunities provided by foster care, that is to live with adults and in families where there is interactive attention and routine care – meals, bedtimes, provision of clean bedding and clean clothing, and conversations – can be quite unlike life in their family of origin.

The next segment is from a youth who, on hearing about the project, wanted to meet to discuss his experiences in care. Although he was nineteen years old, the woman who had raised him from childhood was about to adopt him. For him, escape from his mother, who had a serious problem with alcohol abuse, was a relief from horrific neglect and suffering. At one point he explained.

G: but now yer gunna be adopted so
C: yep
G: okay, well . . .
C: its like ah awesome since I got here. Like I didn't like being left alone, and down d's hungry
G: you remember that
C: yah
G: were you hungry a lot
C: yah
G: how long would you be left without food for
C: I I don' know, like long time, jis . . I don' know I'd like go te some, some-ones place I guess, runn over
G: mmhuh. Do you remember being sad during those times er
C: Ah:h I didn' really think, cause jis hungry, jis like survin, tryin te survive, i's likes ah, like a word survive.

For C the palpable memory of hunger and its effects are profound. Hunger and the physical sensations of discomfort and pain, while palpable, are also occasioned by a child's biological and instinctual turn to a parent to reduce discomfort (Glaser, 2000). The failure to provide comfort leads to anxiety, stress reactions, and cognitive disorganisation, and as child grows older to loneliness, a sense of abandonment and betrayal. When C, reflecting on coming into care, observes, "its like ah awesome since I got here. Like I didn't like being left alone, and down d's hungry". For C being in care means no longer being "left alone" and "hungry". It should be noted that C's positive feelings toward his foster parent, and positive response to this care, attention, and affection reveals both the depth of young peoples' resilience, and the interdependence of youths' sense of self and health upon the care by others.

In the following L, a youth in care describes her horrific home situation.

B: I'm going to be interviewing you around your experiences of coming into care and also how it's been for you to be in care um in in the CAS care

L: mm mmm

B: maybe you can just start by telling me um how it was that you . . umm came into care, what were the circumstances surrounding that?

L: ah the first place, when I went to the first, went to the Children's Aid, I had been had sexually abused, and mentally abused and beatened by my mom, and a friend of my mom's had sexually molested me and a fr- my step-sister had called the police and uh . . . she went, the police went got a social worker and came to see me and took me away Christmas Eve.

B: And how old were you then?

L: I was around fifteen, sixteen when I went to a foster home.

B: ok, you said something around when you were eleven something happened

L: ah, I was around eleven years old, I'd been ahhh fff til eleven, four til eleven I'd been raped, and umm all my life I'd been . . badly abused, and my family couldn't take it anymore soooo they called.

B: They called when you were eleven?

L: Ya

B: They called the Children's Aid?

L: mm mmm

B: And what happened when they called?

L: Well the police had told them ok keep her there, make sure she don't go nowhere ah the social worker came, we talked and I told her what everything what happened happened, that this man had raped me and things like that. We went to court, and my mom beat me and I described what she used, she hit me with a board, umm she smacked me all over different places . . and . . . . hhhnnnaaa ((nervous laughter))

B: [you're doing fine] no that's what we want to hear is is is how it was for youso when you were eleven did you go into care at that time

L: ya

B: so, were you in care from eleven on?

L's description of life in her family of origin provides a readily recognisable case of a "child in need of protection" (Ontario CYFSA, 2017:Sect. 74(2)). L speaks of sexual abuse, mental abuse, physical abuse – i.e. "beatened by my mom" – and other forms of abuse, albeit not specified in detail. L claims that not only did her mother fail to protect her from rape and sexual abuse from her male partners, when she disclosed the rape, her mother responded by punishing her.

Of course, as B elicits and listens to L's story, the coherence of the narrative is as interactively achieved through talk. Obviously, L's mother is not in the room either to counter nor oppose L's story. While this research project and these interviews only involved youth in care, arriving at a workable understanding of L's story requires speculating or hypothesising about the motivations that could have led L's mother to attack rather than to support her when she disclosed sexual abuse. For example, Carter, in her research with mothers of sexually abused children, noted that a dominant feature was the mothers' financial and emotional dependency on the child's abuser (1999). An understanding of women's dependency allows us to recognise just how threatening a disclosure might be to whatever family stability, security, and place a mother might have not only for herself, but any other children, and for the victim. Additionally, again, as Carter indicates, many women suspect that abuse has occurred, though they know that they 'failed to see' and 'failed to act'. Such recognitions combine with the shame of sexual abuse, and the perception of the sordid, secret, and taboo nature of sexual assault against a child. Furthermore, the intergenerational nature of sexual abuse, where women whose children are sexually abused often were abused themselves, expectedly triggers strong emotional reactions and traumatic memories. Such volatile emotional content can easily generate traumatic rage which in turn becomes projected and displaced in attacks on a child who discloses. Once again, it needs to be recognised that such interpretive frameworks and considerations cannot be readily derived from the talk-in-interaction itself. They can only be recovered by locating this achieved moment of talk inside of broader understandings about social realities and psychological dynamics. In this segment of talk, there is both the said and the unsaid. There are indeed choices[1] made by participants that shape next turns and responses.

In a recognition of missing elements, describing social context, history, and the dispositions of others in her life, we press up against the horizons of conversation analysis and ethnomethodology. As we have seen in previous chapters, while Schegloff, and others who do conversation analysis, might insist that explanatory categories and the consequentiality of context need to be derived from the conduct of the materials (1992), in fact, the achieved sense of interviews relies on social workers' "vulgar competence" (Garfinkel, 2002) as members of the profession. Thus, occasions are entered into and interpreted in a complex process of articulating the unfolding here-and-now to complex background understandings. Hearing, accepting, and determining next turns – acknowledgement tokens, questions, emotional supports, and so on – demands drawing on extensive background knowledge, about therapeutic technique, trauma, psychological processes, child abuse, and specifically the sexual abuse of children and its effects, not only on the child, but on all other family members. Understandings from practice and research are vital for unpacking the dynamics which might have allowed L to suffer abuse in her family of origin. The work of listening to, and interpreting her story as a social worker relies on complex professionally frameworks, or scaffolding. L's story is taken-up and as interpreted using various theories about psychological trauma and risk, functional and dysfunctional family dynamics, child attachments, parental capacities, and the effects and harms that result from child abuse and neglect.

Just what might have led L's mother to ignore, deny, collude with, or punish her, when she disclosed having suffered sexual abuse? Carter (1999) in ethnographic research where she interviewed twenty-four mothers of children who had been sexually abused, identified a pattern of inter-generational trauma and abuse. For instance, she found that "only two of the twenty-four women ... were not victims sometime in their lives of some form of violence from males" (1999:67), and added that seventeen had been "victims of child sexual abuse themselves". She added that seventeen mothers did not know that their child was being sexually abused. Social workers recognise the imperative to hear and to interpret such stories in the context of sexual violence (Carter, 1999), and male power and violence (Walker, 2009; Lundberg-Love & Wilkerson, 2006; Walker, 1990; Pizzey, 1974), women's economic and social inequality, the vulnerability of single parent mothers, the etiology and symptomology of alcohol and drug abuse, and the issues of intergenerational trauma and abuse (Guishard-Pine, et. al., 2007).

Indeed, over the course of the interview, L claimed that her mother had problems with alcohol and drug addictions, mental illness and hospitalisation, and economic and emotional dependency on abusive men. Lundberg-Love & Wilkerson, outline,

> Some battered women with histories of childhood physical or sexual abuse may have used drugs and/or alcohol since a young age to numb the effects of victimization. Unfortunately, the use of drugs or alcohol as a coping mechanism may also numb the battered woman to the risks of violence and reduce her ability to protect herself and her children.
>
> (2006:42)

While L suffered sexual violence from the men in her mother's life, she also suffered physical violence and abuse from her mother, as she hit her with a board, a belt, and her hand. What were the sources of her mother's anger? Was the mother a victim of physical and sexual violence herself (Carter, 1999)? What were her mother's frustrations, vulnerabilities, and fears? As might be expected, L revealed that when she first went into care that she attacked other children, and was eventually placed into detention. Pezzot-Pearce and Pearce observe, "Some foster and adopted children may, for example sexually abuse other children in the home, torture animals, or steal from parents or the community" (2004:12).

In the details of her story L produces a narrative that any child protection worker would readily recognise as warranting apprehension and placement in care. Further, the early onset of persistent sexual abuse, beginning at age four and continuing to age eleven, invites the social worker into a disclosure of extremely disturbing and troubling material. B, the interviewer, in hearing L's laughter (that which I have identified as 'nervous laughter') recognises that L has been talking about difficult, hurtful, and often shameful personal information. The social worker responds, "[you're doing fine] no that's what we want to hear ..." L's story makes patently obvious "candidate correct" (Pollner, 1974:40) instances of reasonable grounds for apprehension, removal from family, and placement into care.

In the next segment, another young person, a male, N, describes his entry into care. He claims that entering care provided an escape from a physically abusive and torturing older brother and a neglectful and indifferent father.

G: What's happening at home.

N: Me and brother just had incidents. Me and my brother didn't get along. We got along for a while, and then, what's it like getting beaten up by my big brother. We really hated each other.

G: Yah, how come?

N: I don't know. I didn't hate him, but he hated me at first. It was jealousy at first, new sibling in the home. He used to just kick the fuck right outta me. Beat me up man.

G: Hurt you?

N: Oh yah, slit open my leg once with a knife. Used to beat me up.

G: Did you need stitches.

N: No, no I didn't tell no one. Let it heal by itself. It wasn't really fights. He would just torture me.

G: Yah

N: I tried to fight back, but it didn't really work, I got my butt kicked, yah.

G: Was he a big guy.

N: It wasn't that. Uh, fast, fast, he was fast eh. Studies a lotta martial arts, he's a fast guy. Talented you could say, eh, and uh, just he was smart you know. He didn't just beat me up, he'd mess with my head and stuff. Play head games with me and stuff, get me all weirded up, and beat me up and stuff. Tie me up and stuff. Tie me up, stuff dirty socks in my mouth, tied me up with no water for about a day eh.

G: Are you serious?

N: Yah, (laugh). Ended up phoning. Used to problems, like trying to kill myself a few times. Tried to hang myself, branch broke, tried hanging myself upside down, blood rushed to my head, didn't work, you know. After a while couldn't take it anymore getting my butt kicked, you know. Couldn't, couldn't tell my dad about it, my dad has never known I'd have my butt kicked by C (big brother). Never told him eh. Not a rat. Learned not to rat at an early age eh. I used to use a lotta excuses to get outta the house. Told my the social worker. The social worker came to pick me up.

> My dad said, "you wanna leave pack your stuff, you know". Okay, I packed my stuff, and
> G: How old were you then?
> N: Twelve.

This young man reported being unable to tell his father because he didn't want to be a 'rat'. It is important that we tease out the multiple dimensions of 'being a rat' and not 'ratting'. First, it needs to be recognised that 'ratting' or telling can be extremely dangerous for the victim. Wiehe observed, "Victims appeared to live in constant fear of further abuse. Attempts to scream or cry out for help often resulted in further abuse" (1998:173). It should also be noted that N reported that he 'learned not to rat at an early age'. How did he learn this? What happened when he reported abuse? Was it followed by more serious and painful abuse? Second, for many teenagers, especially those who are marginalised by racism, poverty, ethnicity, or language the code of silence, the shame of informing on friends, and the social expectation to not 'be a rat' continues to be a powerful. Further for marginalised youth, those authorities who might offer protection, whether teachers, counsellors, social workers, or police, are not to be trusted. Youth who are told by family and friends that authorities will break up the family, take them away, and destroy their lives learn to adopt a 'code of silence' which proscribes disclosure of abuse and exploitation.[2]

For N not being 'a rat' compelled him to maintain silence in the face of serious sibling abuse. Unfortunately, this interview did not explore N's understanding about what made 'being a rat' problematic. Was he simply fearful that if he told, that he would face the secret retribution and punishment of his brother? Did N adopt the framework that 'being a rat' was something to be reviled as shameful? But what would make 'ratting' as a practice shameful? Was it because being a rat meant dependency and turning to others for protection, rather than living by a machismo code of self-protection, self-preservation, and aggressive response to bullying?

N observed that when at age twelve he told his father about the abuse he had suffered, his father reportedly responded "you wanna leave pack your stuff ..." Though, for social workers, and most others, this seems hard and uncaring, it is consistent with research. Garcia et al. reported the link between sibling conflict and "rejecting parenting". Their research examined "whether rejecting parenting accounts for the relation between destructive sibling conflict and conduct problems" (2000:45).[3] Further, they add, problems between a parent and a child can 'spill over' into destructive sibling relations. Bank, Burraston, and Snyder (2004) also examined the links between "ineffective parenting",[4] "sibling conflict", and developmental outcomes. Similarly, Wiehe, reported that,

> Another common parental response (to reports of sibling abuse) was to become very angry and discipline both the perpetrator and the victim

with corporal punishment. In some instances, the perpetrator would be so severely corporally punished (Whipped, beaten with a belt) by a parent that the victim felt badly for having reported the abuse to the parent.

(1998: 174)

Although we have focussed on N's story, it is important that we also ask, what were the dynamics that might have led his brother to treat N so viciously? What anger, rage, frustration, and jealousy lead to systematically victimise his younger sibling? Was he acting out his own experience of neglect and rage? Was he modelling parental behaviour (Wiehe, 1998)? Was he re-enacting pathological patriarchal and abusive relationships with his younger sibling? If N's narrative is accurate, we need to also consider the communication dynamics within this family (Will & Wrate, 1985) that would have allowed such secrets and silence to be sustained? Caffaro observed that, "sibling relationships and their contribution to developmental outcomes can be understood only in light of processes involved in other family relationships" (2014:5).

So then, just what might cause a parent to overlook such systematic abuse and torture? N suggests an answer when he notes that his father had serious problems with alcohol abuse and addiction. A parent whose mind and functioning is continually affected by alcohol and drug abuse and who can barely attend to his or her own needs predictably fails to attend to the needs of dependent children. In the absence of parental attention, care, and guidance, both N and his brother were forced to rely on primitive and pernicious rules to survive. Sadly, both in N's home, and again in the young offenders detention facility where this interview was conducted, not ratting and thereby enduring suffering were important tools for survival.

The lives of youth in care are usually marked by parental problems that often render them incapable of caring either for themselves or their children. There is little surprise in this. But what is surprising is the degree of honesty and insight that many youths in care demonstrate when talking about the family situations that resulted in entering care. In the following segment T introduced herself to a new member:

T: My name's T, nineteen years old, I've been in care for approximately seven years. I've been involved with CAST for two and a half years, uhm, one of the youth involvement workers there, she's nice. Uhm, I've lived in four different group homes, two foster homes, and currently I'm in a change right now. I've been living with my grandma for about a year and a few months, ah, room and board, an tomorrow morning I'm moving out on my own completely. So, I'm kinda, right now, I'm more nervous about moving then (seeing me pack everything else though)((laughter))

T: Uhm, I came into care because my mother physically abused me and was an alcoholic. I tried to live with my F..ather, didn't work out, cause of his wife, I didn't get along with her, and uhm, I moved to my grandmother's, itws, oh well, three years ago, an uhm, pretty much my whole life in care has been pretty good, its been a better experience than some people would have thought. People think that coming into care, that the agency will screw you around and everything, but as my family says it's the best thing that they've ever been done, so...Keep it short and sweet, huaa

For many youth, it seemed to them that coming into care was in large part the result of parental choices. Many recognise that their parent(s) chose a partner or spouse, drugs and alcohol, or something else over caring for them. Children interpret their sense of parental abandonment and failure to protect them as rejection. For T's mother alcohol is more important than caring for her. For T's father his new wife is more important than caring for her. For T's father's wife something else, perhaps competition with T for her father's affection, is more important than caring for her. For T, and other youth, the response to such systematic rejections by family members is to become angry and enraged, and to express this in ways that are identified as behaviour problems. Of course, as youth become more difficult to control and act out in destructive ways, these actions compound to legitimise their parents' decisions to "kick them out of the house" and "put them in care".

In the preceding segment T acknowledges the stereotype that the CAS "will screw you around and everything", but plays her own experience against expectations. She claims that her experience of coming into care was beneficial and perhaps surprisingly, that her family shares this understanding. It is worth considering, if T's account is correct, just what T's family members have seen that led them to see coming into care and living in care as beneficial. Just how have they come to see that care by others is better for T than the care that they could have provided? Did they need to overcome a sense of their own failure? Was there a sense of jealousy or envy that strangers were able to care for T in ways that they could not?

In the next segment another youth, with Foetal Alcohol Syndrome (FAS), addresses the positive aspects of coming into care, in comparison to life in her family of origin.

J: I was put in care because I have a disability my father didn't know much about it, an he couldn't take care of me because he was sick, as he was abusing. I was in three places, three group homes and a foster home. I preferred the foster home cause it had more of the family setting. I felt like it..I never had a family setting, cause my family was all over the place, you know, an I felt very comfortable in it. There was no ch.checklist for chores, no li..it, a family setting, and I felt really good about that.

The presence of Foetal Alcohol Syndrome expresses chronic problems with alcohol beginning even before a child is born. The presence of FAS points to the mother's incapacity to make healthy decisions either for herself or for her foetus. Jones points out that "some affected children have witnessed or been subjected to abuse and neglect early in their lives" and that "affected children and their families may have needs which are so severe that early institutionalization or multiple home placements have been a reality" (1999:81).

In the next segment another youth tried to reconcile some negative experiences she had in care by referring to some of the long-term positive outcomes of her life in care.

D: I came into care whenever I was two, an, well, I was sorta in and out of care until I was ten, and and I don't rea//and I don't really like room, uhm, I'm sorta, I'm sorta, heheh, excuse me. Uhm, like I don't sorta like remember anything about those years, but, anyway, uhm, and then at ten years old I went to a foster home, and I was there for seven years, and uhm, the first five years were really good, until like the last two were then, and for some reason it fell apart, uhm, and then I moved, to to uhm, ah ah, Meadow Vale, ahm, and uhm, uhm, and I'll pass about that one. Uhm, and, heha, I mean it was a good home. I mean, I don't really like you know, like think anything bad of it, but then it closed down, uhm, just a few months ago due to budget cuts so, uhm, so like I never really stayed there long enough, like I was only there for three months, and then I was on my own, so and, and like now I'm on my own, and ah, it's great.

It is tragic that a foster home where D had lived for seven years, and where "the first five years were really good", that something changed during the last two years, and that "for some reason (it) fell apart". Although the life circumstances of foster parents, whether disease, divorce, relocation, unemployment, and so on, can result in the breakdown of a foster home, it is imperative that children and youth are informed and consulted before being moved to another home. Social workers and foster parents need to discuss the move openly and honestly with children and youth in care. A failure to engage children and youth in discussions about the issues in a foster home, and the need for relocation, means that they will fabricate stories on their own about why they were moved. In the absence of open dialogue, children and youth, who have already suffered abuse and neglect, can be expected to speculate, and to develop stories. Unfortunately, these are often stories in which they are to 'blame' or where they feel themselves responsible for the placement breakdown. Alternatively, absent a coherent account, they can hold to variously competing and conflicting stories which leave them feeling confused and disoriented.

D reports that for at least two years before being moved to another home something had changed in the home. However, whatever it was that was different remains vague and is not specified, i.e. "some reason". The question is whether this indicates that D is withholding sharing her understanding of the causes of the placement breakdown, or whether she does not in fact know what these were. In any event D needs to have a narrative or story for understanding and processing her move from a home where she has lived for seven years. Further, the fact that this placement broke down and that she needed to be relocated likely reinforces D's sense that others are not committed to her, nor are they prepared to support her. The danger of course, though it is not articulated, is just how such a perceived lack of commitment by others affects her sense of self. Has D internalised this rejection as somehow articulating her own lack of value or worth? Is it the unreliability of others, unprocessed feelings of rejection, and lack of commitment that leads D to assert, "like now I'm on my own, and ah, it's great". So what is great about living on her own? Is it that she is free of having adults in her life who failed to act in ways that demonstrated concretely and materially their commitment to her?

Traumatic entries into care

The next segment returns to analysis of an account produced in an interview with a young woman who had multiple experiences of coming into care. In the following she talked about one particularly traumatic and disturbing entry.

G: So, for you coming into care what did that feel?
M: U:hh, I don't know, coz care has been something I've known all my life [so:o]
G: [Oh you have
M: [it's not..]I do remember the last time=
G: =OK=
M: =I went into care. We had gone to uh . I went to daycare at the time and I think I might have talked to the therapist there, in fact I think what I'm remembering is the PHX daycare=
G: =Mm:hm=
M: =because daycares don't usually have=
G: =a therapist=
M: =exactly, u:h:mm and I remember talking..I don't remember talking to her but I must have about what went on at home=
G: =Yeah=
M: =becoz one day the therapist asked her to come in and they talked alone for a while, while I was playing with my friends and then u:h:h mom came out really upset and said "We have to go home, we have to go home" and we walked home and I was behind her and she kept on saying, "The police are going to come, The police are going to come; We have to go, We have to go." And eu:hh I went home and sure enough the police did come and I'll never forget but I saw mother arrested an:d I can't remember the charge
[but it waz

G: [that's right], we spoke-we spoke about that=

M: =I'll never..I'll never forget that. U:h:mm very...that hurt me, that disturbed me. She gave me ten dollars an-an said (background noise and sigh from G) Get yourself a treat or something coz I can't get you one an (-)=

G: =Yeah=

M: =An:d, eu:hh, sh-I can't remember the charge but the charge was something to the effect of neglect of a
[child or assault]

G: [yeah, yeah (something)]

M: [or something like that. Uh-my father was involved with me but u:h:mm I can't remember (-) like I remember him but I can't remember if he was good to me or if he was bad to me=

G: =Yeah=

M: =Things are really fuzzy with me=

G's question, "what did that feel", creates an opening for M to address her feelings about coming into care. M's response, "U:hh, I don't know, coz care has been something I've known all my life", as with so many other children and youth in care, articulates a life-long process. While many youth in care do not have a memory of the first time they entered care they often experience inchoate emotions and feelings. When M states, "I remember talking .. I don't remember talking to her but I must have about what went on at home", and though the interviewer did not explicitly pick up on the theme, it is quite likely that M is expressing a sense of responsibility and perhaps even guilt for talking and for disclosing events that led to her coming into care. M continued, "=becoz one day the therapist asked her to come in and they talked alone for a while, while I played with my friends and then u:h:h mom came out really upset". M indicates that she was responsible for setting in motion the chain of events that led to the police coming and arresting her mother. It is this matrix of responsibility and the drama that makes this chain of events memorable. Indeed the events that matter are those that create the deepest emotional impacts, "And eu:hh I went home and sure enough the police did come and I'll never forget but I saw mother arrested". The effect on M of her mother saying, "Get yourself a treat or something coz I can't get you one" and then seeing her mother taken away must be acknowledged.

By engaging youths in dialogue social workers provide an opportunity to work through their life stories. By talking with social workers youth are able to share their understandings, and to elicit another's reflections and analyses. Youth, such as M, who struggle to make sense of the chain of events that led to her coming into care need access to adults who know how to care, to listen, and to make sense of the existential complexities of life in families and life in care. Indeed, as M tells her story we need to try to imagine her world. We need to try to imagine how these events would have looked for her as a child. By engaging in dialogue and listening we can empathise with her pain and confusion, and we can help her examine the boundaries of her responsibility and to explore her own sense of guilt. By being in dialogue we can work with her to help her to craft an account which makes such difficult and potentially destructive feelings explicit, while suggesting new ways of making sense of these events. It is very likely that M holds herself responsible for the fact that her mother was arrested and faced charges for child neglect. Only by listening to M's story can we identify, and work through the perceptions and under-standings M has concerning her entry into care. Precisely because such understandings have been built up impressionistically from reflections on her childhood, it is critically important that they be examined and reworked through dialogue. M's primitive story when shared with a social worker, cre-ates an opening for a mutual examination of responsibility. M needs to be helped to recognise and to appreciate that even if she said something that led to child protection intervention, that she was not to blame. It was her mother who had a primary responsibility and obligation to care for her and to protect her. Simply, children and youths need the help of responsible and skilled adults, social workers, foster-parents, and group home workers, in order to recognise that it is the adults in their lives, not they themselves, who are responsible for their care and the fate of their families.

In the following segment N, a nineteen-year-old woman, reflects on the trauma of abuse and her decision to take action to get out of a bad home situation.

SW: Hi N. Thanks for participating in this research project. Information you give us may help improve services for children in care. N can you tell me about, how did you come into care?

N: How did I come inta care? Well my mom physically assaulted me. Beat the snot out of me, and I left there. I decided I wanted to get away from home. I didn:t want to be there. I didn:t care where I was, who I was with. I just didn:t want to be with her, and then I signed a form with Children:s Aid, an...

SW: so it was by..so you:wre apprehended then? After you phoned the Chil-dren:s Aid?

N: uhm,k I kinda met them at the hospital?

SW: mmhuh=

N: =like cause certain therapists, because of what happened, I had to go=

SW: =mmhuh=

N: =the hospital=

SW: =mmhuh=

N: and then that's the first time I'd ever ever even met Children's Aid=

SW: =mmhuh=

N claimed that her mother "beat the snot out of me", and as a result of the beating she needed to be taken to the hospital – though how she got to the hospital and who took her is not specified. Clearly, for N the beating was a mark of significant emotional and physical pain.

A remarkable feature of N's account is her insistence that she was the agent of the action, "I left", "I decided", "I didn't want", "I signed a form", and so on. While this may indeed have been the case, it is important to recognise, that N's account affirms her agency in the process. What must be acknowledged is N's need to be in control of her life, which is not an unusual feature of adolescence. The social worker who was familiar with N's case history knew that N had entered care at age ten, however, the follow up expresses some level of discomfort with N's version of events. When the social worker asks, "so it was by..so you:wre apprehended then?", she expresses her confusion. This is a confusion rooted in an understanding that N's sense of her own control over the process might not be correct. Simply, apprehension is not something that the child does, but rather it is something that an adult social worker does to a child. The social worker's question elides N's account of agency, to suggest an alternative set of events that corresponds with how the social worker understands that child protection services actually works.

N addresses a traumatic event in her life through the use of a colloquial and brutal expression, "Beat the snot out of me". Albeit graphic she avoids communicating in detail the physical injuries and bodily consequences were of the beating. How viciously was she beaten? Where was she hit? Was she hit in the face, on her head, on her torso, or on her limbs? Was she hit with open hands – slaps – or with closed fists punches? Were there bruises? Did she suffer a concussion? Were bones broken? Were there lacerations? Were the police called? Why was she hospitalised afterwards? What action was taken as a result of the beating, other than N's decision to leave the home? The social worker did not explore the chain of events nor the nature of the beating. This decision may speak to the function of the interview, which was designed to provide an overview of coming into care and living in care, rather than to provide therapy, counselling, or to prepare evidence for court. Different functions would have led to very different forms of enquiry between the social worker and the youth.

Independent of the issues of interview function, it must be acknowledged that social workers will back off pursuing such details as they may be considered to be too painful and re-traumatising for the client. Some preferred strategies are to encourage youth to volunteer details on their own, to wait until later in the interview when other difficult issues have been addressed, to suggest links and segues back to traumatic materials, to interject more difficult topics after trust has been built and the youth is more comfortable, or simply to wait anticipating that the youth will get around to talking about the traumatic materials in more detail. The dynamics of whether or not to pursue painful material are complex. Decisions about whether or when to press a young person to address difficult events in their past reflects the social worker's own desire to avoid pain, the balancing of curiosity against respect for personal privacy and emotional space, and the relative merits of drawing out painful material and its overall relevance to the intervention and treatment plan. Ultimately, the core question is whether eliciting painful memories and stories from a youth's past will contribute to helping them at this moment, or harming them.

Throughout this interview, and indeed throughout most interviews, despite a mythological expectation that social workers will help clients deal with painful material from their pasts, the more common pattern is for social workers to collude with clients in glossing over the particular remembrances which informed stories of trauma. Thus, N's claim that her mother "beat the snot out of me" combined with some later details, in particular hospital admission, is allowed to stand as a warranted account of 'what actually happened'.

Entry into care before memory

As we have already seen above, many youths find the task of providing a coherent story about their first entry into care difficult and challenging. This is especially true for those youths who entered care in infancy or early childhood. Young people's stories about entering care when less than five or six years of age can be expected to be impressionistic fragments of emotional memory. They produce stories that rely on synthesising impressions with the stories and accounts provided by older siblings, adults, and even agency records. For many youth their first entry into care does not even comprise an 'experience':

SW: Uhm, so okay he was two, a::nd you were born in XX (province).

A: yah, uhm, I guess after probably moved te YY (province) somewhere's an between there I don't remember it at all

SW: right

A: I've seen pictures, but it doesn't ring a bell. That's what I've noticed that most of my life is a blurr, because I've seen so many different things.

SW: right

A: s s

SW: Well jist do yer best, if you don't remember something, tha that's no problem.

A: hhyah

SW: I don't expect you to remember back te when you were five months ol: lhh:d heh. Uhm, e, as far as going inta care at five months old what do you know about that.

A: I:: really don' know, know anymore.

In the above A's recollection of coming into care is rooted in the time before memory, when she was five months old. In such a situation, A's only resource for telling the story is reliance on what others have told her and pictures. Indeed, A warns that much of her "life is a blur". The metaphor of a blur indicates that which is not clear, uncertain, and confusing, but which the youth seeks to penetrate and to understand to thereby discover some form of coherence. What possible resources might social workers provide to help youths to craft stories about their lives? Social workers who may have worked with the child at the point of entry into care, or who come onto the case in later years, nevertheless have access to agency records through which they can assist the child or youth to construct some sense of their past.

For youth who have no memory of coming into care the events leading to entry into care call out for interpretation and understanding. Carol Shipley, in *Love, Loss, & Longing: Stories of Adoption*, provides a quintessential expression of this compulsion. Writing about her own adoption, she observed:

> Dorothy and Frank brought me home from the hospital to a small house in the village. 'The baby' was unusually quiet and still. I cannot seem to use the first person 'I' to describe myself at this point of entry into my new family. It's as though I am viewing the baby as if she were not me. The abrupt separation from my birth mother created a primal wound, a rift that was deep and wrenching.
>
> (2013:25).

Similarly, March, who was herself adopted, and who studied those adoptees who had established contact with their birth mothers, notes, "individuals construct or build their own reality from the tools that their social world provides" (1995:16). For adoptees "their biographical discontinuities intruded on the process of social interaction" (45) with the effect that "they could not manage their self presentations effectively" (45). Similarly youth in care, in order to function socially among peers, in group homes, and at school, are impelled to search to find patterns and to make sense of events that seem chaotic and confusing.

SW: do you have any knowledge about what was happening when you first became involved with social services?

B: no I can't remember right back then, but I know that as a kid I dealt with it, it was fine, but as I grew older it kindaf, it didn't, I started rebelling against people

SW: okay, has anyone ever told you why you were taken into care at two?

B's response is fascinating because she insists that "I know that as a kid I dealt with it, it was fine, but as I grew older it kindaf, it didn't, I started rebelling against people". If B is unable to remember coming into care, how is it that she can claim to have a memory of dealing with being in care? What might B be referencing when she says, "as a kid I dealt with it"? What does dealing with it mean for B? How was living in care 'fine'? How does she know that she began "rebelling against people"? In what ways are the actions she points to as 'rebelling' tied to the dynamics identified by March, that is B's loss of continuity and the struggle to create an identity interactively with others while living in care?

B's account expresses a desire to find some sense in her experience, and to display her sense and understanding to the interviewer. Although the social worker lets B's account stand as adequate, it is only by exploring such functional glosses that social workers reach out to youth to help them to develop more sophisticated and reflective understandings about their lives. It is very likely that B's account relies on synthesis of other's versions of her behaviours over the years, and as such says as much about B's memory as it does about the interpretations of adults around her.

Given the dynamics of identity construction and the attendant confusion and stigma surrounding coming into care it is critically important that social workers be prepared to work with youth in care to help them to construct a viable, congruent, positive, and healthy story about themselves and their relationship to their family of origin. The child or youth must be helped to understand the boundaries between their own personal responsibility and parental and family responsibilities. Young people need to be engaged in a dialogue around self-image and worth that works through the conflicting emotions and degradations of self that many youth in care have experienced in their families of origin.

For most children and youth in care separation from parents means that they are either not available as a resource for reconstructing narratives about their childhood, or that they are negative, hostile, destructive, and unsuitable resources. It is precisely because memories of our early childhood are blurry or fuzzy that we must rely on adults to help us work through the inchoate impressions of childhood memory. Unfortunately, for many youth in care there has been little continuity in their lives. Their parents may be absent. They may be separated from extended family members. They may have been moved through a dozen or more foster homes (Kaplan, et al., 2009; Holland & Gorey, 2004). The result is that they must cling to whatever fragments, imaginary bits, and contributions from others that they have been able to synthesise into an account.

In the absence of stories provided by committed adults, children employ whatever resources are available to piece together a coherent story of their life:

SW: Uhm, and do you have any connection with yer original family at this point.
C: I don't rememb- I don't know if I do or not. I just know that I . . mm . .
    know what my mom looks like, cause I have bir, my birth pictures, a:[nd]
SW: [okay]
C: pictures of her::, pictures of me:: and pictures of everybody else, hehe
SW: So what have you been told about your birth mom?
C: That she: brang me to the foster home because she couldn't take care of
    herself so obviously she couldn't take care of me.

The loss of parents, siblings, and other family members, combined with frequent disruption and movement through multiple placements strips away collective memory and narrative resources from which children and youth in care can construct viable and healthy stories of their lives.

SW: Are these your biological parents.
K: My mom for sure but not my dad.
SW: Do you know your biological father?
K: No.
SW: Is your biological father the same as your brother & sister.
K: I don't think so, nobody knows.

This confusion about identity of fathers was common. It usually signified the absence of a consistent father in the lives of many young people. For those children who grew up in a single parent family, usually mother led, the absence of a father meant that there was one less adult resource available to the child for constructing a viable personal identity. Similarly, the uncertainty about the parentage of siblings articulated problems of transitory relationships and communication between parents and children.

G: yah, and what a'bout yer dad. Were yer mom and dad together er::
C: No my dad is in XY, I think like, a hundred miles ou' north o' M (city)
G: Oh yah
C: I didn' never see my dad before
G: never
C: no.
G: didju ever want to
C: a:ahh, yah, yah, I'd like te see im
G: huh, never met him
C: mm uh

The fact that C has never seen or met her dad while perhaps remarkable for most children and youth is common for many youth in care. It is difficult seeing what it is that C imagines a dad to be, and how talk about a dad is relevant for her life. Although today with an increase of divorce, separation, and common-law relationships a great many children do not have ready access to their fathers,[5] and though being a child raised in single parent mother led families is normal – statistically – the issue of a broken relationship or the absence of any relationship with a father continues to be a remarkable and an often lamented matter[6] which many children and youth in care identify.

Respecting autonomy

The following segment underscores the importance of intervening with young people in ways that emphasise their autonomy as well as their ability and right to make choices.

A: My situation, from the beginning my whole experience was that I absolutely needed some help trying to figure out some stuff for myself, and
dealing with some of the problems I was having at the time, and as soon
as that was alerted to the Children's Aid they helped right away. I moved
into an emergency home, I moved into a treatment home, and then next I
moved to a transition home right now. The whole thing has been very
much positive. I've always been able to express what it is that I want and
need, and most of the time, well yah, I've come to some agreement with
the workers or the people I was dealing with, or the people that were
trying to help me. So for example, I got a job through the CAS, I got
involved with youth organization, I got all the treatment that I needed. I
live in a house now that's basically one of the best homes that I've ever
lived in. Everything's provided for me, and that's what I like, and I think
that's one of the best things that could've ever happened in my life, the
help of the Children's Aid, right there!

Although A is a bright and articulate young man who was able to make
viable plans for his life, equally important in his success was that he was
able to find social workers who made the effort to listen, to respond, and
to work collaboratively with him, in the project of helping him to meet his
own needs.

In contrast to the above the next segment demonstrates the obvious
negative consequences that follow from failing to consult or to respect the
opinions of young people.

G: yah, did people give ya many choices about where ya were gonna live
when you were younger?
E: No. They'd gave me no choice.
G: None eh?
E: mm uh,
G: do you think they should've
E: yah, but still I'd wather stay'ed with my foster parwents.

Unlike the previous segment, this young man makes it clear that the lack of
choice and self-determination he encountered fed his anger, resentment and
hostility towards the agency. Further it is quite likely that while this young
man may have been much better off in care than with his family of origin, his
perception that he did not have any choice shaping his care had the dysfunctional effect of enabling him to deflect both his own responsibility and that of
his family for his life in care. The failure to give children and youth realistic
choices by involving them in extensive explorations and discussion of their life
situations sets into place a series of dysfunctional patterns for coping with life
in care. In the above we see that in the absence of consultation and choice this
young man directs his anger and resentment towards the very agency that is
mandated to keep him safe.

A recurrent theme that was expressed in interviews with youth in care is that too often the adult professionals in their lives failed to provide youth with sufficient information, and to help them to obtain a sense of mastery over the direction of their lives. It is imperative that social workers join with youth, spend time with youth, listen to them, and help them to explore and to make choices about where they will live, when they will move, or what supports they will receive.

I will end this chapter with two lengthier segments, taken in order from a single weekly CAST meeting. The first segment has been selected because it so ably demonstrates the ways that talk-in-interaction in a group setting operates along several dimensions simultaneously. In the following segments the lead social worker (SW) and I (G), begin by talking to S about his experiences of coming into.

G: How old were you?

S: I think twelve. I went into care by agreement.

G: I see . . So one day you're living at your mother's then next.

S: Yah, I went for five days, they thought that we were just at each other's throats. So I went for five days, at ah treatment home, and then ah, and then I went home, and it didn't stop, its continued, it kept on doing it, and it stay.stayed the same, and ah so they put me into the same group as my brother, and one day that was it. And, one day they came and got me.

SW: Can you remember when you were a little kid, and you went into foster care system. {loud coughing}

S: I can't remember why I went in or what happened. I think at that point I truly was an innocent and that I didn't, or at least they did..or naive to what..what was going on. They just said, you are moving to this place, and I..I remember being ah, I guess really confused as to why, like I just didn't know why I was moving. I wasn't a bad kid or anything like that, I just didn't know the reason why, and then they put me into the P, the PHX[7] for hyperactivity or something, and I didn't understand why (that either), especially with the kids around me, you know, its like there were kids that were stabbing each other, peeing on the walls, and doing just crazy things, and I was, then..I felt like I was, you know, Jack Nicholson, in One Flew Over the Cuckoo's nest, heheh [((loud coughing))]

G: [You felt this?]

S: But no I felt like I didn't belong there. It was pretty scary, or then I thought, maybe I did belong in the home I was put in.

G: So the scary part for you wasn't being away from.from your home, it was being in this place with people that you didn't necessarily want to be in the place with.

S: Yah, the scariest thing was that.that, you know what I.I was away from home, you know, I lived with my father. I lived with my aunt. I was always, I never lived at home that much so, and moving away from home was always relaxing. I was more scared that people thought I was an idiot, or crazy, or stupid, than. that was what I was most afraid of.

G: okay

First, S[8] seems to claim that the process of coming into care, and leaving his family of origin was not in itself traumatic, although his placement in the psychiatric hospital was certainly disturbing. G links the facts of placement to emotional experience, "So the scary part for you wasn't being away from.from your home, it was being in this place ..." S responds, repeats the reference to feelings, "Yah, the scariest thing was", to then return to addressing events and their emotional effects, "I lived with my aunt. I was always, I never lived at home that much so, and moving away from home was always relaxing." Rather, what mattered to S was that people not think that he "was an idiot, or crazy, or stupid".

S makes it very clear that what was most frightening was the belief that perhaps he did "belong" in this reportedly rather dysfunctional hospital ward, and therefore that there was indeed something seriously wrong with him. S provides an overall framework, in which coming into care was a positive event in his life. O takes up this framework to claim the next turn and to display a sense of thematic relevance and topical cohesion.

O: I was going to say, when I first came into care, I knew I was gonna go away. Like I was living with my father at the time. When I, like when I was living with my mom, she goes threatening me, you're gonna go into.. I'm gonna send you to children's aid. I had a few friends in care, and I knew what it was like in the children's aid, an uh, and uh, I phoned, I phoned the group home, I phoned the children's aid, when ah, when I was living with father, and I said, I don't wanna live with my father. I couldn't stand it with my family at all, and so what they did is they phoned a social worker also, and I came into care, I think about three weeks later, and like leaving was fine, itwasju.. I felt fine at the time.

G: How old were you, again, O?

O: I was twelve, thirteen at the time/ [no thirteen]

G: [twelve] thirteen=

O: =and ah I went from my dad's house to the children's aid group home, and like moving was fine, I don't know what it wasn't so much scared, I was nervous because I was moving to a new place. I was so used to moving that it became a routine, so moving into a group home was fine, but ah, I felt, Idonknow, I think I felt more nervous than scared, but..

G: So you'd been moving around from your dad's to mom's too..

O: Well I went from my mom's, to my grandma's, back to my mom's, to my grandma's, back to my mom's, to my dad's=

G: =uh huh

O: So I was used to always being shuffled around packing my stuff so, one more move wasn't anything.

G: I see=

O: =So wh.when I went to the group home I.I planned it, and my dad plan-ned it, so it was okay, and then like it was just another move, and then there was the children's aid. I've..I've (guess gotte) know the agency pretty well, I was always at the agency on B. street so..

G: Before?

O: Well like va..visiting my worker all the time, and so I was pretty much..and before that, before I came into care I was in counselling with my mom, like trying ta, like family counselling, so I knew the agency pretty well, before I even came into care, [so]

G: [hhm], hhhm It sound's pretty much parallel to S {{previous speaker as above}}

This segment begins as O explains that "I knew I was gonna go away" and adding, "I had a few friends in care, and I knew what it was like in the Children's Aid." As with N who appeared in a previous segment, central to O's account is communicating a sense of self-determination and control over the process. She explains, "I phoned, I phoned the group home, I phoned the children's aid, when ah, when I was living with father, and I said, I don't wanna live with my father." It is precisely because of her sense of having determined and controlled her entry into care that O is able to claim, "I think about three weeks later, and like leaving was fine, itwasju. I felt fine at the time", a theme which she repeats later. As noted O's turn followed S's at the CAST meeting, and in response to S, she works through, and modifies the themes of constant moving and family disruption to craft her own story.[9] In this sense O's story is topically coherent with S's story. O makes it very clear that in her family of origin that moving was routine, so that when she finally moved into care that it too was not unusual but routine. Further, it seems from O's account that she knew the social worker, that going into care was supported by her parents, and that she knew about and supported her plan of care. The importance of her involvement in the care process should not be underestimated. Those youths who felt involved in the process of planning their move into care generally communicated a sense of control, agreement, and accordingly less disagreement with the decision-making that led to entering care.

Conclusion

This chapter has made a strong claim that social workers must listen to youth. They need to spend the time that is necessary to move beyond surface ren-derings of stories about coming into and being in care to an exploration of the issues raised through these stories. Clearly the interviews from which the segments addressed in this chapter were derived did not afford an opportunity to dig into the depths of the issues youth raised. Indeed to have done so would have been inappropriate and would have made the interviews, which were largely conducted with strangers, quite uncomfortable. Yet, the ongoing social work relationship, built across multiple contacts, and conducted over the spaces of lived time, afford social workers with opportunities, and indeed the necessity of helping youth in care to work through and find functional meaning in the stories about their lives.

What does entry into care mean for children and youth? Children and youth who enter care often struggle to make sense of experiences which have a profound impact on core issues of personal identity and belonging. Kools, who interviewed 17 adolescents in foster care, observed, "Living in long-term foster care was found to have a primarily negative impact on the central process of adolescent identity development" (1997:266). She identified problems with institutional structures of care of children, the diminished status of the foster child, stereotypes about foster children, and various impacts on the self, interpersonal relations, and independence (1997). In my research, we spoke to many children and youth who identified their personal struggles with memories of physical, emotional, and sexual abuse. They had to work through traumatic memories of having been blamed by their parents for family troubles, and having been removed from their own homes. While it is in and from our families that we usually come to discover who we are, for children and youth in care their families often proved to be dangerous and damaging places. The effects on self and their personal assimilation of shame, stigma, anger, rage, and hatred all need to be explored. Social workers at the frontline of child protection must be allowed to devote the time and resources that are necessary to build trusting and healthy relationships with children and youth in care, and only then can a positive and healthy reclamation of youths' experiences and viable plans for their futures become possible.

Although I have suggested that the stories youth tell in interviews cannot be taken up as unproblematic or as naively representing what actually happened, they open up for immediate review the contours of youth's lives. Their stories articulate what matters to them as worthy of telling and accounting for. Their stories speak to the struggles in their lives to make sense and to find coherence and meaning in often disturbing events. While in previous chapters I have focused on the reflexive nature of stories, in this chapter I have focused more on their reflective nature, that is their nature as reflecting the contours of a socially organised world in which their experiences and memories emerge, both as rich and rewarding, and as impoverished and miserable. While the shape and texture of what gets told as a story arises from within the practical interactions between the youth and the interviewer, both struggle through their talk to reference and point to the contours of a socially organised world in which their interaction and talk is located.

Notes

1 Garfinkel, suggests that when examining any occasion ethnomethdologically, that we start by focusing on "choice among alternatives of sense, of facticity, of

objectivity, of course, of explanation, of communality of practical actions" (1967:32), and to see these choices as members' actions. To understand the choices a social worker must make requires member's knowledge, or what Garfinkel calls "unique adequacy" (2002), that is those methods that member's use to do the work of occasions.

2 Tafler, a reporter with the Globe and Mail, in a piece entitled "The code of silence: Replacing the 'rat' mentality", wrote about the difficulties the police encountered obtaining information from eight teenagers who were present during the beating death of Rena Virk in November 1997 (2000). The article documents the fact that "dozens of young people" knew about the beating and murder but remained silent.

3 It should be noted that their research focused primarily on maternal parenting, whereas the transcript presented above involves two boys and their single parent father.

4 Ineffective parenting was defined as "poor problem-solving skills, poor supervision skills, and parent conflict bouts" (Bank, et al., 2004:107).

5 Eichler observes, "one of the greatest complaints both women and children make is that most non-custodial fathers do not interact enough with the children" (1997:76). For a comprehensive examination of the issues facing non-custodial fathers see Mandell's *Deadbeat Dads* (2002).

6 Eichler notes, "Family disruption is by no means a new phenomenon. When life expectancy was lower, it used to be relatively common for children to lose a parent and for partners to lose a spouse to death" (1997:31). Similarly Conway outlines, "In the 1960s the overwhelming majority of female single parent families resulted from the death of a spouse (63 per cent), the next largest group resulted from separation or divorce (35 per cent), and only two per cent were headed by single (never married) mothers. By 1996, 54 per cent of such families resulted from separation or divorce, 20 per cent from death of spouse, while 25 per cent were headed by single mothers" (2003:24).

7 PHX is an acronym for the name of psychiatric hospital S was sent to, i.e. Psychiatric Hospital of X.

8 Although this chapter focuses on the substance or content of youths' stories about coming into care, the form of S's turn is remarkable. He provides an 'entertaining' account replete with dramatic language – i.e. "one day you're living at your mother's then next", "I truly was an innocent" –; and colourful similes – i.e. "I felt like I was, you know, Jack Nicholson, in One Flew Over the Cuckoo's nest". S's obvious story telling ability worked to good effect as he was able to hold the floor for a sufficient period of time to develop an account of his experiences coming into care.

9 In the group meeting youth used the repertoire of previous accounts to respond to each other, and accordingly to shape their own accounts, both as similar and as different. The youth's reports of actual remembrance, about coming into care need to be understood as being both about memory and about performing their place in the group. Their stories emerged through a sophisticated melding of at-hand, thematic, and topical structures, presentations of self, and didacticism (i.e. having others accept their opinions, understandings, beliefs and points of view).

References

Bank, Lew, Burraston, Bert, & Snyder, Jim. (2004). Sibling conflict and ineffective parenting as predictors of adolescent boys' antisocial behavior and peer difficulties: Additive and interactional effects. *Journal of Research on Adolescence*, 14(1): 99–125.

Caffaro, John V. (2014). *Sibling abuse trauma: Assessment and intervention strategies for children, families and adults* (2nd ed.). New York, NY: Routledge.

Carter, Betty Joyce. (1999). *Who's to blame? Child sexual abuse and non-offending mothers*. Toronto, ON: University of Toronto Press.

Conway, John F. (2003). *The Canadian family in crisis* (5th ed.). Toronto, ON: James Lorimer.

Docherty, Meagan, Kubick, Joanna, Herrera, Carolina M., & Boxer, Paul. (2018). Early maltreatment is associated with greater risk of conduct problems and lack of guilt in adolescence. *Child Abuse & Neglect*, 79: 173–182.

Eichler, Margrit. (1997). *Family shifts: Families, policies, and gender equality*. Toronto, ON: Oxford University Press.

Garbarino, James. (2005). Foreword. In Michael Unger (Ed.), *Handbook for working with children and youth: Pathways to resilience across cultures and contexts* (pp. xi–xiii). Thousand Oaks, CA: Sage.

Garcia, Monica M., Shaw, Daniel S., Winslow, Emily B., & Yaggi, Kirsten E. (2000). Destructive sibling conflict and the development of conduct problems in young boys. *Developmental Psychology*, 36(1): 44–53.

Garfinkel, Harold. (1967). *Studies in ethnomethodology*. Englewood Cliffs, NJ: Prentice-Hall.

Garfinkel, Harold. (2002). *Ethnomethodology's program: Working out Durkheim's aphorism*. Lantham, MD: Rowman & Littlefield.

Glaser, Danya. (2000). Child abuse and neglect and the brain—A review. *Journal of Child Psychology & Psychiatry*, 41(1): 97–116.

Guishard-Pine, Jeune, McCall, Suzanne, & Hamilton, Lloyd. (2017). *Understanding looked after children: An introduction to psychology for foster care*. London, England: Jessica Kingsley.

Holland, Patrick, & Gorey, Kevin H. (2004). Historical, developmental, and behavioral factors associated with foster care challenges. *Child and Adolescent Social Work Journal*, 21(2): 117–135.

Jaffee, Sara R., Caspi, Avshalom, Moffitt, Terrie E., Dodge, Kenneth A., Rutter, Michael, Taylor, Alan, & Tully, Lucy A. (2005). Nature x nurture: Genetic vulnerabilities interact with physical maltreatment to promote conduct problems. *Developmental Psychopathology*, 17(1): 67–84.

Jones, Kathy. (1999). The ecology of FAS/E: Developing an interdisciplinary approach to intervention with alcohol-affected children and their families. In Jeanette Turpin & Glen Schmidt (Eds.), *Fetal alcohol syndrome/Effect: Developing a community response* (pp. 80–87). Halifax, NS: Fernwood.

Kaplan, Sandra J., Skolnick, Lourise, & Turnbull, Ayme. (2009). Enhancing the empowerment of youth in foster care: Supportive services. *Child Welfare*, 88(1): 133–161.

Kools, Susan M. (1997). Adolescent identity development in foster care. *Family Relations*, 46(3): 263–271.

Lundberg-Love, Paula K., & Wilkerson, D. Karen. (2006). Battered women. In Paula K. Lundberg-Love & Shelly L. Marmion (Eds.), *" Intimate" violence against women: When spouses, partners, or lovers attack* (pp. 31–46). Westport, CT: Praeger.

MacMillan, Harriet L., Fleming, Jan E., Streiner, David L., Lin, Elizabeth, Boyle, Michael H., Jamieson, Ellen, Duku, Eric K., Walsh, Christine A., Wong, Maria Y., & Beardslee, William R. (2001). Childhood abuse and lifetime psychopathology in a community sample. *American Journal of Psychiatry*, 158(11): 1878–1883.

Mandell, Deena. (2002). *"Deadbeat dads": Subjectivity and social construction*. Toronto, ON: University of Toronto Press.

March, Karen. (1995). *The stranger who bore me: Adoptee–birth mother relationships.* Toronto, ON: University of Toronto Press.

Ontario. (2017). *Child Youth and Family Services Act.* Toronto, ON: Author.

Oswald, Sylvia, Heil, Katharina, & Goldbeck, Lutz. (2009). History of maltreatment and mental health problems in foster children: A review of the literature. *Journal of Pediatric Psychology,* 35(5): 462–472.

Pezzot-Pearce, Terry D., & Pearce, John. (2004). *Parenting assessments in child welfare cases: A practical guide.* Toronto, ON: University of Toronto.

Pizzey, Erin. (1974). *Scream quietly or the neighbours will hear.* Harmondsworth, England: Penguin.

Pollner, Melvin. (1974). Mundane reasoning. *Philosophy of the Social Sciences,* 4(1): 35–54.

Schegloff, Emanuel A. (1992). On talk and its institutional occasions. In Paul Drew & John Heritage (Eds.), *Talk at work: Interaction in institutional settings* (pp. 101–134). Cambridge, England: Cambridge University Press.

Schwartz, Harvey L. (2000). *Dialogues with forgotten voices: Relational perspectives on child abuse trauma and treatment of dissociative disorder.* New York, NY: Basic Books.

Shipley, Carol Bowyer. (2013). *Love, loss, and longing: Stories of adoption.* Winnipeg, MB: McNally Robinson.

Springer, Kristen W., Sheridan, Jennifer, Kuo, Daphne, & Carnes, Molly. (2007). Long-term physical and mental health consequences of childhood physical abuse: Results from a large population-based sample of men and women. *Child Abuse & Neglect,* 31: 517–530.

Tafler, Sid. (March 31, 2000). The code of silence: Replacing the "rat" mentality. *The Globe and Mail.* Toronto, ON. www.theglobeandmail.com/opinion/the-code-of-silence-replacing-the-rat-mentality/article766901/

Unger, Michael. (2005). Introduction: Resilience across cultures and contexts. In Michael Unger (Ed.), *Handbook for working with children and youth: Pathways to resilience across cultures and contexts* (pp. xv–xxxix). Thousand Oaks, CA: Sage.

Walker, Gillian. (1990). *Family violence and the women's movement: The conceptual politics of struggle.* Toronto, ON: University of Toronto Press.

Walker, Lenore. (2009). *The battered woman syndrome.* New York, NY: Springer.

Wiehe, Vernon R. (1998). *Understanding family violence: Treating and preventing partner, child, sibling, and elder abuse.* Thousand Oaks, CA: Sage.

Wiener, Andrew. (2007). Foreword. In Jeune Guishard-Pine, Suzanne McCall, & Lloyd Hamilton (Eds.), *Understanding looked after children: An introduction to psychology for foster care* (pp. 5–6). London, England: Jessica Kingsley.

Will, David, & Wrate, Robert M. (1985). *Integrated family therapy: A problem-centred psychodynamic approach.* London, England: Tavistock.

10 Social workers and children and youth in care

J: And didjew get a chance te check out T's place before you moved in the-there?

S: No:oo. Tee- Yah, actually I did yes, cuzz the day of my birthday they they like took me up there, and they had this friggin (bee) and then stuff happened, and there's these idiots comin up sayin yer blah blah blah and stuff, and they were jist cummin in and telling me from M (town) these stupid social workers, telling me, "Ya:ah well yo- it was your decision te move up here". No it wasn't I tell you that much. I had this idiotic s:social worker, and if I ever see I will punch her right in the mouth [because]=

J: [id]=

S: =I hate her that much. Like I wouldn't, like I don' know, I could jist. Like I can't stand her, because she was so mean te me. She said it was my choice if I wanted te move with this place. The first day I went up there and I went and I looked, and no:o actually I don' wanna live there, "Well you already said you would so!" I never said that at a:all. I didn'. . I cannot trust any social worker. Their guy that works here, J::ehh, I I, don' wanna even talk te him no more. I'm not talkin te anyone, I toll them, "They're gunna get me outta here". They don' listen te me. I have this little thing, that I. If they don' get me outta here, I'm jist gunna do it myself, because I'm sick of this crap, they're not even listening te me anymore. It's at the point where anything goes. You know. It's lih:hke heh. Whatever.

J: oh yah (softly)

Care and worker authority

S clearly expressed her dissatisfaction, anger, and rage at the social workers whom she believed were responsible for placing her in a home she disliked. She exclaimed, "these stupid social workers, telling me, "Ya:ah well yo- it was your decision te move up here". No it wasn't I tell you that much". Quite clearly a major source of S's frustration is her sense that not only was she not listened to, but that the social worker(s), in her opinion mistakenly, claimed that the decision to place her in T's foster home was based on her own expressed wishes. S counters that she did not make this choice and that the social worker is wrong. S speaks to a deep conflict, or reality disjuncture, between her version and that of her social worker. She insists that she was not consulted and that she did not agree to the placement with T. While the source of S's anger and frustration cannot be pinpointed, what emerges clearly from this segment of talk is the imperative for social workers to talk to youth in care, to consult with them, to listen, to ensure that youth know that they are listened to, and to take the preferences, wishes, and understandings of youth seriously. Indeed Bush and Gordon, who interviewed 370 children in care, found that "the practice of promoting informed choice among children in foster care could reduce the number of placements that break down" (1982:310). Of course, this makes sense, as cooperation and coordination between social workers, care-providers, and youth, can work to mitigate resistance, anger, and rebellion.

In this chapter I focus on the issues youth raised concerning their relationships with social workers. Not surprisingly the primary issues youth identified speak to the dynamic tensions between their needs and wants and the institutional organisation of child protection work. Youth face a tension that arises between their informal and locally organised lived realities and their encounter with the formal organisation of child protection practice. The tension they identify is analogous to that expressed across a variety of different disciplines in a variety of ways. These are the tensions between play and work (Baudrillard, 1975),[1] symbolic and economic capital (Bourdieu, 1990),[2] symbolic and utilitarian exchange, and expressive and instrumental reason (Taylor, 1989).[3] Prosaically expressed, these are the tensions between the personal and political.

Interactions between children and youth in care and child protection social workers are accomplished in an interface that joins local to extra local organisations and informal to formal relations, and which as a result generates tension and irremediable contradictions. Social work is a paid practice. It is a professional practice. It is an organisational practice. As such, social work and child protection bind organisational mandates and forms of action to local sites. Social workers are called on to resuscitate, reconstitute, and accomplish in the forms of their every-day practices otherwise dead letters of legislation, policy, and procedures. In the here and now interactive moments of engagement with children and youth in care social workers struggle to knit face-to-face activities to extra-local orders. From the one side, child protection social workers are pulled to enter into the every-day realities and lives of youth in care. These are realities that in their contours are largely situated in private, personal, and family domains of life. From the other side, child protection social workers are pulled into the universalised, temporally transcendent, and extra-local realities of textually organised institutional orders. Social workers in and through their day-to-day activities construct the perpetually unstable bridges of a practice that oscillate between the shores of personal and organisational relations.

Social workers performing child protection work enter into a utilitarian relation of exchange with their agencies and organisations through which a day's working activity must be accountable and warrantable as comprising a series of proper instances of professional child protection practice. Individual social workers enter into encounters with clients as employees of an organisation. An integral component of their work is to transform face-to-face encounters, living talk, and relations into the textually mediated order of organisational rules and policies. However, those who are skilled in their work also recognise the slippage, leaks, and concealment between that which is produced as formal accounts of work, and the actual shape, contours, and relations of practice.

Social workers need to be able to develop strategies to ensure that youth in care do in fact receive 'care'. Either the social worker provides a source of 'care' or they must ensure that someone else, whether a foster parent, a youth worker, a relative, or even a parent provide that care. Children and youth in care often hunger for attachment, commitment, and caring from adults in their lives. Laursen and Birmingham argue that the provision of care is closely associated with the ability of youth in care to overcome predictable hardships in their lives. They describe seven characteristics of caring relationships which they identify as trust, attention, empathy, availability, affirmation, respect, and virtue (2003:244). This seems to be a simple enough list, and indeed in the pages to follow most of these themes will be repeated as we encounter youths' voices as they describe their relationships with social workers. The needs of young people in care demand that social workers understand and are prepared to grapple with the complex collisions and contradictions between the loyalties of face-to-face relations and the obligations to effect impersonal organisational mandates, policies, and professional orders.

As noted in the previous chapter, work with children and youth in care is fraught with hurt feelings, anger, acting out, and destructive interpersonal relations. Social workers who work with youth in care must be vigilant in their pursuit of consistent, clear, and honest practice, informed by a strong sense of humility. Humility is a corrective against a worker's sense of outrage following predictable personal attacks and criticism from children, youth, and their parents. Humility is a guard against failed expectations, rejected plans, and client resistance. It is not that humility demands lowering expectations, but that it demands realistic and compassionate expectations. Humility demands accepting successes and failures as rooted in the realities of a world which in its complexity and range is beyond the control and authority of child protection practice.

Relations at the front-line are imbued with a professional responsibility to 'help' that demands the exercise of judgment and leadership (Turner, 2002). As helping relations social workers struggle to effect interpersonal dynamics of face-to-face care, emotional commitment, and compassion, inside of organisational imperatives for measurement, standardisation, and containment as expressed in organisational and professional records and accounts. Yet the very organisation of child protection work demands the production of judgements or 'diagnoses' (Turner, 2002) whether expressed in files and reports, referrals, or court documents. Through their day-to-day contacts with youth in care social workers gain access to the most personal, intimate, and private dimensions of youths' lives. All the while however social workers are expected to apply analytic tools that take up organisational policies and procedures manuals to order and make sense of youths' accounts. Social workers need to transform in vivo and lived talk into warrantably professional accounts. To do so social workers deploy what Garfinkel has called a "documentary method". This is a way of working that extracts discrete details from the ground of people's lives, such that they become "the document of as pointing to, as standing on behalf of a presupposed underlying pattern" (1967:78).[4] It follows then, that child protection social work demands taking up the problems and issues of people in their families, not just as they are presented, but always and irremediably as interpreted through organisational and professional orders. On the one hand child protection work demands exploring, uncovering, and addressing the most intimate contours of people's lives in their families, while on the other hand it demands expressing these in organisationally warrantable documents and forms.

These work processes of translation and transformation, while problematic, nevertheless remain necessary within an organisational location. In front-line practice social workers join with clients, both youth in care and their parents, to help them to work through, struggle over, and if possible resolve tensions, conflict, abuse, and neglect.[5] Work devoted to taking up people's lives in their families and people's work and play, of necessity creates a tension, if not a contradiction between the "personal and political" (Hamos, 1978). In social work, attempts to work through this tension can take a variety of forms across a continuum. At the one extreme social workers can retreat into a rigid professionalism. This approach can be seen in a strict orientation to the 'job', adherence to the letter of 'policy', and a hyper-attentiveness to marking off professional boundaries. At the other extreme are those social workers who invest their lives in their work, who bring children and youth in need into their homes, and who in so doing collapse the boundaries between work and their personal lives.

Although child protection is paid and organisationally regulated work it generates encounters with children and youth who crave and demand relationships of friendship, loyalty, love, and affection. The interface between children's needs and fantasies and the realities of the work confronts social workers with enormous and at times unbridgeable challenges. Child protection is replete with contradiction, and yet is a field that demands firm assessments (or diagnoses), judgements, and action. It is a field where inaction can result in the death of a child, while action may break up a family. It is a field with a potential for disastrous failures and tremendous success. While children may die or be subject to abuse creating permanent injury at one extreme, at the other through intervention children may come to have a mother or father who may learn to become effective parents. At the front-line social workers must struggle to develop strategies that transform a job and work into a commitment and a calling. Yet, though work becomes more than a job, they must manage to create a space and boundaries in which they can maintain their position as 'officers' of organisational and agency mandates and their own personal health and happiness.

In the realities of our actual life courses, and in the actions of any at-hand moment of practice, there is never purity, never complete authenticity, never transcendence of socially organised grounds. Good social workers must understand and explicate, both for themselves and for clients, the contradictions, tensions, pulls, and struggles that arise from the grounds of their practice. Social workers need to be able to name and to identify these grounds and these realities for clients, so that clients can understand the implications of their actions and the requirements of social work response to those actions. Social workers in their face-to-face encounters with clients must struggle to mediate the so called 'cold hand of the state' with the warmth of their own personality, while clearly communicating their adherence to professional and organisational boundaries and values.

That which social workers can accomplish here and now, as human, authentic, genuine, and congruent, is always mediated, always cobbled together, and always achieved in balance across the sharp edges of an inescapable institutional reality. The option of hiding behind a rigid wall of professional defences fails to meet the needs of children and youth in care, yet the option of going native, by becoming a 'parent' or a 'friend' to those children and youth, may be a violation of organisational policies, professional ethics, and client needs. The challenge child protection social workers face, and indeed I suspect all workers face, is to develop a thoroughly reflexive understanding of their practice, in which they recognise the necessity of the forces structuring that which they do, and the possibilities for innovation and change in that which they can do. Through a reflexive understanding social workers can struggle to reach through the dead letters of the organisation, to move across legislation and policy, to thereby pull employment, position, categories, rules, and regulations into an 'authentic'[6] encounter with people in the face-to-face and daily activities of a working day.

Precisely because social workers enter into the daily lives of children and youth in care, and as this entry is organised in part by the demands and needs of these children and youth, it will of necessity require a form of practice which as caring, committed, and engaged is attuned to symbolism and play. Work with children and youth is inherently dangerous as their desires for connection, commitment, and caring – their transference[7] – calls forth the desires of social workers to respond as caring adults and parents to their needs – counter-transference – which threaten personal boundaries, organisational and professional boundaries, and ultimately the ability of the worker to maintain a 'helping' social work relationship. Child protection work, precisely because it is focused on children and youth, whose daily worlds are centred in the concerns of play and caring, gives rise to the apparent paradoxes of playing at work and working at play.[8]

Struggles against objectification

The following segment taken from an interview between a social worker and a young woman on her caseload provides a glimpse of the ambivalence both the social worker and the youth experience as they negotiate through the troubles arising from the tensions between work and care. A focal topic up to the point of this segment was M's "eating disorder" which then led the social worker (L) to ask:

L: Are there any meals you like?

M: No

L: heh heh heh heh heh heh except pizza, once in awhile right? heh, uhm, and the odd ice cream as long as it's healthy

M: Yah

L: Yah, okay uhm...

M: Well if you ever see me maybe we can have an ice cream together. You never come to see me unless it's something like this.

L: Ah, hah ho ho ho. Actually you know it's funny cause I was doing the base...I..and I think you're right.

M: uhhuh (softly)

L: uhm, I ah..I mean I see you probably more than I see a lotof of other kids.

M: Yah about once every two months.

L: No, actually I saw you four times since you left.

M: Yah all in one month, heh heh

L: Heh, heh, heh, no no, actually I saw in . you in November. I saw you in December, and I saw you in January, and twice actually in February . So you'd like it to be a bit more than that.

M: Yah

L: How often would you like to see me?

M: every day

L: That's not really realistic though is it?

M: Adopt me

L: Adopt you! And you'd live at my house

M: Yah

L: and not eat my food and complain about it

M: Yah

L: Yah he heh

The segment begins as the social worker, following up on the discussion of M's eating disorder, asks a sarcastic or ingenuous question, "Are there any meals you like?"[9] While the worker's turn was shaped as a question, the youth correctly recognises the sarcasm, and implicit criticism, to respond, "No".

The social worker believing that she had scored some sort of moral victory responds with laughter, and moves to answer her own question by suggesting, "except pizza ... and the odd ice cream as long as it's healthy". Her suggestions rely on a stereotypic attribution of youth tastes, that mockingly offers an oxymoron of healthy pizza and ice cream, to implicitly suggest that M dislikes everything. M refrains from countering the worker, allowing the victory to stand, by demurring, "Yah". By signalling indifference M manages to leave the social worker without a comeback, as she responds, "yah, okay uhm..."

M recognises that she has managed to catch the social worker off guard, and moves to develop a counter attack. M takes up the opener provided by "ice cream" and reshapes it into a challenge. M responds, "Well if you ever see me maybe we can have an ice cream together". M's counter is fascinating. First, although M and L are clearly together doing this interview, and are accordingly seeing each other, M observes, "if you ever see me". While M might have simply misspoken, could it be that M is claiming that the social worker never really sees her as she actually is? Although I am hesitant to state the matter as such, it does seem that M has raised a problem that might be rooted in an erasure of her individuality and subjection to an organisational category. Rather than being seen for who she is, she is seen as just another child in care, and just another 'case'. M's complaint is that this way of working with her fails to recognise her needs for personal attention and care. The challenge for this social worker, and social workers in general, is to figure out how to look beyond the child as a case or a member of category to see the complex realities of a person, whose life extends beyond this moment of work.

By asking the social worker to take her for ice cream M expresses her desire for a relationship that is beyond work and beyond interviews. M expresses a desire to have someone in her life who will engage her in activities that are enjoyable, pleasurable, and playful and not "something like this." M's suggestion "maybe we can have an ice cream together" issues a challenge to the worker to shift the ground of the relationship. M imagines that their relationship need not look like this. M challenges the social worker to relate to her as a friend, as a parent, and as a caring adult, not as an interviewer. M challenges the social worker to recognise that she is more than just another youth in care to be probed in an interview.

M and the social worker are situated in two very different realities (Schutz, 1973)[10] despite interacting together at this moment. M wants the social worker to engage her in something other than work, while for the social worker, work is the only legitimate (and perhaps the only safe) base for engagement. The social worker is not prepared to leave her location inside the work. M indicates that she is unwilling to cooperate and collude with the social worker's project. These sequences signal that there are serious troubles in the relationship and the work. Rather than address the trouble explicitly the social worker's first response is to try to laugh it off, "Ah, hah ho ho ho", and then conceding "Actually you know it's funny cause I was doing the base...I..and I think you're right". Yet, rather than pursue the line of thought that might follow from "I think you're right", the social worker assumes a defensive move, as she counters, "I see you probably more than I see a lotof of other kids."

The 2.5 second pause, when the social worker hesitated after saying, "cause I was doing the base" is a self-initiated self-repair, as the social worker stopped herself from completing the utterance, precisely because the next most likely word would have been 'count' or 'tally' or some such other indication of number. I suspect that the social worker stopped herself because any such utterance would have confirmed M's implicit claim that she was just another case, another number, and another thing to be counted. Indeed, M's next turn suggests that she recognises the cover-up, as she responds to the social worker's defence by countering, "yah about once every two months." Thus, M raises the issue of number, albeit in the context of contacts rather than as signifying that she is just one among many cases.

Unfortunately, the social worker fails to understand that M's challenge is not about frequency of visits, but the form and orientation of the time they have spent together. M has said that she wants a different type of relationship while the social work wants a connection founded on a clearly defined work relationship.[11] These the two people though sharing this moment together are oriented to quite different projects. M wants care and commitment and the social worker wants a working relationship. When the social worker asks, "How often would you like to see me?", M responds clearly and unambiguously, "every day". M's has trapped the worker in the contradictions of her position. Sadly, the social worker's response fails to explicate these contradictions, relying instead on a formulaic invocation of 'reality'. The social worker's reply, "that's not really realistic though is it?", implicitly relies on, but does not explicitly address, the issues of professional boundaries, the organisation of a worker/client relationship, rules and regulations at work, and perhaps most importantly, the social worker's own disposition toward this young woman. M, again proving that she is wise to the social worker's game counters, "Adopt me".

While M's demand "Adopt me" could be heard as a literal request that the worker adopt her, it also needs to be heard as a demand for a more personal relationship with the social worker. It is a troubling of the form of interaction and the instrumental relationship unfolding in this interview. M's demand is a clear repudiation of the social worker's project. M demands that she be treated as a person, as an individual, as someone worth spending time with on her own merits, and not as an object to be studied. M's demand is reflected by Bazalgette's research with youth in care, which identified "the need to increase opportunities for social workers to spend time with children and young people in care" (2014:18). Further, M's demand "Adopt me" declares her resistance to objectification by pushing the social worker to step outside the boundaries of a professional relationship, and consider what it might mean to engage M as a person. The demand to be adopted is a request that the social worker embrace M in her plenitude. M seeks a foundational interpersonal commitment that transcends professional boundaries.

In summary, while the social worker's 'intervention' might not be counted as an example of 'good' social work, M's articulation of demands and challenges is absolutely brilliant. M recognises and then exploits the disjunction between L's attempts to appear to be caring and sensitive and the realities of L's interaction with her as work. Further M uses this disjunction to put L on the defensive and to advance her resistance to L's project of doing the interview. Indeed, this social worker's responses are so thoroughly unsatisfactory precisely because she fails to acknowledge and to explore the relationship dynamics identified by the youth. Even though the youth has exposed the contradictions at the core of the social worker's practice, the social worker attempts to laugh off, and deflect the youth's complaints.

The youth challenges the social worker by implicitly stating that the social worker does not care for her, and that she is just another piece of work. Unfortunately, the social worker refuses to address M's concerns openly and directly. Had the social worker responded to M's concerns 'honestly' the work and the relationship might have moved in a more positive direction. An honest and open acknowledgment of M's concerns could have taken any number of forms. The social worker might have said, "I am guessing that you feel that I don't care for you?" "When you say we only get together for something like this you are telling me that I only treat you as a case, or a number, or just another kid in care?" "Are you saying that you want someone to really care for you, and that though I say I care, I really don't?" "I think you are right, I have been unable to get closer to you because I am always so wrapped up in my work." "What do you think we can do about it?" The trajectory of such responses is to open up as a topic of discussion the troubling issues of commitment and care that circulate and define the form of M and L's relation. These are issues which resonate deeply with youth in care, and most probably with M herself, as they likely articulate and reflect lifelong dynamics of abandonment, abuse, and rejection.

While M in the previous segment sought to signal her repudiation of objectification,[12] challenging the social worker to adopt her, the young woman (A) in the next segment sought to avoid a relationship with her social worker.

J: right. Who was yer worker at that time.

A: uhm, when I was at C's it was still SW, I believe

J: SW's been here for ever hasn't she.

A: yah, yah

J: that's kinda nice te have a consistent person.

A: yah

J: how's that relationship?

A: Between SW and I? I don't like it. I don't like the fact of havin a social
    worker hanging over my shoulder tellin me what te do, when te do it, or

asking me te do things. I coulda. I jist don't like meetings with her. She'll ask me things an what'll m'm, what am I gunna do, an it's like I haven't planned that far ahead, an she seems te keep pushing for it=

J: =mmhuh

A: jist feels like I'm possessed by someone, I'm someone's d/ doll or toy, they can call, anytime

J: ha how would it be better. Is it because you don't want any social worker?

A: Yah basically.

J: basically

A: I wanna lead a normal life like other people, then again what's normal

J: °right° . .

A: It's the saying on the washing mach:heh:ine it's not a person

J: hh, °yah°

When J asked, "how's that relationship?", A replied, "I don't like it. I don't like the fact of having a social worker". For A to accept her social worker's attention might very well have signalled a betrayal of family loyalties. For A to accept the social worker's attention would have been to recognise her need for others outside her family. As with M above the theme of objectification emerges, albeit more explicitly as A explained, "jist feels like I'm possessed by someone, I'm someone's d/ doll or toy, they can call, anytime". J, the interviewer, happened to be an extremely skilful youth worker. As a result she recognised that the dynamics behind A's repudiation of her social worker were not necessarily interpersonal as much as they were an expression of internalised conflicts and divided loyalties. J gave voice to this possibility when she asked, "Is it because you don't want any social worker?" A's response, "Yah basically", indicates that the problem is not with this particular social worker but with social workers in general. The fact that A is a youth in care forces her dependence on a social workers and other strangers rather than her own mother, father, or family.

Demonstrating commitment

In the next short segment from a CAST meeting, B, a young man compares his social worker to other workers.

B: I think my social worker is a good social worker, because when you told her the situation, she listens and then she does something about it. I never had another social worker, but most people from what I heard, is that they (the social workers) listen but they never actually try.

From this young man's understanding of the essential elements for good social work practice we can begin to understand the foundations of good practice with children and youth generally. First, social workers must be prepared to listen and to struggle to come to understand and synthesise into workable projects that which youth express as their wants and needs.

Second, the social worker must demonstrate a willingness to not only make commitments but to follow through with those on behalf of children and youth. Given that many children and youths' lives are marred by broken relationships, broken promises, and violated trust, social workers must be scrupulous in carrying out their commitments.

J: What are the qualities of a good social workers.

K: I don't know. Somebody really good with kids, that understand them well enough, somebody to keep their wits about them, and be as organised as possible.

J: Why do they need to be organised?

K: Because most social workers take on a lotta kids.

J: Do you find that a problem?

K: Really I haven't met a social worker that wasn't organised.

J: Have you had problems with social workers not calling you back?

K: No. I don't call SW, I tell FP (foster parent) and she tells SW.

What might K mean by invoking as a criterion for a good social worker, "Somebody really good with kids"? Although this is a rather stock phrase, K must envision some characteristics of being 'good with kids'. While these are not addressed directly in this turn or K's next turns, we can catch a glimmering of what matters to her, namely "somebody to keep their wits about them, and be as organised as possible". At first glance K's assessment seems to be more what we might expect from a supervisor than from a youth in care, however her concerns begin to emerge in her next turn, as she explains, "Because most social workers take on a lotta kids". Clearly, K recognises that she is just one "kid" among many others "kids" on her social worker's caseload.

J, the interviewer, interprets the implications of K's remarks, by responding, "Have you had problems with social workers not calling you back?" Indeed, this is a very familiar theme among youth in care, who complain quite vociferously when their calls are not returned in short order. Why does returning phone calls matter for youth in care? When a social worker returns a youth's call it signals that the worker cares. It says that the worker takes the youth seriously. By returning the youth's call the social worker suggests that the youth matters. By returning the youth's call the social worker suggests that this youth, albeit one among many on his or her caseload, is not just a 'bit of work'. Yet by failing to return a youth's call, the social worker gives an indirect message that the youth's concerns, the youth's sense of urgency, and the youth himself or herself does not matter. Indeed, even though youth recognise that a social worker's failure to return a telephone call may occur due to caseload demands – as we will see below – the problem is that youth also then come to feel rejected and unimportant. Unfortunately, these feelings often resonate and reverberate with real abandonment and trauma. For youth who starve for affection such indirect signals can readily become fuel for anger and resentment.

In the following segment B talks in a very open way about the ways that R her social worker has demonstrated commitment to her over the years.

J: very fun heheheh, uhm. Do you ah, do you talk te R about how you feel
B: no, no she asked, like we're pretty close, she's been my social worker since I was eight, so she's been there, seen me through everything, mostly. And she was at my graduation too,
B: ...[cause her]
J: [wuz she]=
B: =son graduated as well=
J: and how do you get along with her
B: very good
J: yah, so what qualities does she have that make a good social worker
B: a very, ki::nd ve:ry she can listen. She can also make me feel more con-fident. . She's not too pushy but she has helped me make it

Just as functional parents and family members demonstrate commitment to chil-dren through ongoing, regular, and routine participation in events and activities in their children's lives so too must social workers. Although R may have attended the graduation ceremony for her son, she communicated that she was there to celebrate B's graduation as well. While B does not provide specific details of just how R built a relationship of trust and closeness, the sense of her account implies that R must have interacted with B in such ways that B recognised her presence at the gradua-tion as well as R's recognition of her. B provides a wonderful summary of what makes R a good social worker when she observes, "she's been there, seen me through everything, mostly", and "She can also make me feel more confident." B does not suggest that in being there and seeing her through everything R ceased to be a social worker. Instead, what she makes visible is the way that by expressing an ongoing commitment, and engaging in shared celebratory practices, R was able to form a lasting connection to B.[13]

The damage of broken commitments should not be underestimated. It is vitally important that social workers not make promises that they are unable to keep. The following segment offers a contrast as F discusses problems with her social worker LM.

F: I'ss:s L, kay' that was my, my old social worker, LM=
G: =uh huh=
F: =when I first went to the receiving home, she said, "Oh, I won't even be there for like a month", an I ended up stayin there fer eight months. I hated it. I hated her for it. She onl', she said I'd only be there for like two three weeks=
G: =yah=
F: =I ended up there for eight months. She said, "Oh we'll getcha a foster home right away" she didn'//
G: how old were you then

F: I was fourteen. She didn't get me a foster home right away. I I was mad at, so I didn' care, like I tried, in September . . in ninety, ninety-seven, September, uhm, I tried, I quit drinkin for like cuz I useta drink all the time, she told me if I smarten up, if quit AWOL'ing,[14] if I listen by the household rules, she'll get a foster home. So I quit drinkin for a month. I quit AWOL'ing, so that was like a month and a half=

G: =mmhuh=

F: =that I was being good for a whole month and a half, an she never did nothing. She didn' find me a foster home, an I jist fuck it, an went out an got drunk.

G: so when social workers don't do:o [what they]

F: [I' they they]=

G: =say they're gunna do

F: yah, they tal', they lie too much, they, they don't tell you, they don't know how to tell you things, like I don' know

The central dynamic of F's complaint is to talk about a series of broken commitments. First, LM indicated that he would be in the receiving home "for like a month" but "I ended up stayin there fer eight months". The result of this broken promise was that "I hated her for it." F claims to have sunk into a despair of drinking and AWOL'ing. F claims, "she told me if I smarten up, if quit AWOL'ing, if I listen by the household rules, she'll get a foster home." F explains that despite, "being good for a whole month and a half, an she never did nothing." The perception of broken promises provides F with a device to legitimise his behaviour, as he states, "I jist fuck it, an went out an got drunk."

In the following we can see the difficulties both youth in care and social workers face making relationships work. The youth, J, is talking to G about his female social worker, BC, and frames his complaint at two levels, the first addressing her failure to intervene effectively on his behalf, and the second addressing his perception that to be heard or listened to requires "kissing ass".

G: now do you have a social worker at the office, at the office

J: yah

G: who's that

J: BC

G: B, do you ever go in and talk to her

J: no pointless, it's li talking to the wall

G: how so

J: jist like, ah don know, she's like tal- I don know man, she's (-)

G: yah, oh you mean in terms of the receiving home

J: no I don't talk to her about that, I don know, it's jist like, I don't expect anything from her

G: no

J: sorta ah, she wouldn't do nothing anyways

G: yah

J: I was gunna move out, "oh you hafta be good an all that stuff", it's like, well it's hard te be good in a place like that, jist not gunna happen

G: I'm never sure what being good is

J: oh like phone, the rules, going to bed

G: yah

J: kissing ass, and doing all this stuff

G: yah at sixteen it's bit hard te kiss peoples' ass that you don't like

J: I don' kiss anybody's ass

G: what does mean

J: brown nosing

G: yah

J: yah sucking up shit like that, don't do that

Certainly social workers can expect that young people in care can be confrontational, angry, and difficult to reach, however, it must be recognised that these behaviours are signs of necessary pride, strength, and independence. Indeed, this young man's refusal to 'kiss ass', 'brown nose', or 'suck up', points to his desire to maintain personal integrity in his situation of extreme dependence on others. While J's responses to his social worker will likely be perceived as confrontational, they demand skilful negotiation, and re-framing such that their positive and constructive dimensions can emerge.

It is by making substantive commitments and promises which can be fulfilled, and which are fulfilled, that social workers communicate in direct and actionable ways their dedication to youth. The paradox social workers face is that as services are cut and as the demands for organisational accountability increase, the range of services which they can deliver to youth in care diminishes. As social workers' ability to adhere to their commitments is vitiated by cutbacks and a politics of surveillance, they must seek out and determine that which they can continue to provide, and that which they might be able to attain through pressure, struggle, and political action.

It is vitally important that social workers struggle to uphold the commitments they make to children and youth, even when these commitments place them in conflict with their agencies. Indeed, it should be expected that loyalty and commitment to children and youth in care will most likely create conflicts with agency and organisational policies. Commitment to youth demands opposing cutbacks and the dismantling of services and even making vigorous demands for the creation of new and expanded services.

Interpreting the organisation to youth in care

Social workers have the advantage over youth of being inside the organisation. As professionals they are familiar with the ways of professional sense making, professional categorisation procedures, and agency policies and mandates. As insiders it is critically important that social workers act to help children and youth in care understand the organisational systems which have power and authority over the course of their lives. Social workers need to take the time to share their knowledge of organisational and professional forms of action with children and youth.

Yet, precisely because social workers have such authority and power, whether derived from their organisational and professional locations, or from the composite features of their personal life history – e.g., their education, class position, physical characteristics, etc. – they must continually self-evaluate their use of that authority, as it affects the mundane form of their interactions with children and youth. Shulman has addressed the issues of professional and organisational power under the rubric of what he calls the "authority theme" (2016). He characterises conversations about authority as a taboo, that is as indicating the seen but unsaid dimensions of interaction and as violating taken-for-granted codes. As a result, problems that arise between people, that are rooted in their differential authority are often very difficult to address, particularly for the person in a subordinate position. To counter this taboo Shulman advises that social workers make explicit links between troubles in the relationship or in the work and issues of authority and power. He outlines that by laying out such connections for clients a new culture is created in which clients learn that this person with authority is open to negative feedback, that the social worker will not punish, is nondefensive, and is open to change (2016).

The imperative to share this knowledge can be seen quite clearly in the following extract from a CAST meeting. The sequence begins with the CAST social worker's question to the group. J, a young woman, responds first, followed by S, a young man, who indicates that his court hearing for crown wardship had occurred that very day.

SW: Did anybody ha, get an opportunity to speak at their wardship hearing.
J: I did.
S: My wardship hearing was this mornin=
T: =W:ow=
S: =I didn' go.
T: You didn' go, heheh
SW: It's on consent.
S: Crown, I don' know, crown ward whatever.
SW: But it's a, so you didn't go, you signed a paper that said that you were in agreement with it=
S: =my mot[her signed]
SW: [your moth]er signed an agreement sayin you were in agreement with it.
S: yah. yah. I signed something. I don' remember what it was//
T: hehehe=
SW: =yep=
T: =he's aware of his legal rights, hehehe.

Given the extremely momentous organisational implications of a hearing for crown wardship, and given the legislative requirement that the court take "into account the child's wishes" (Ontario CFSA, 1990:sect 61.1(e))[15] it is remarkable that the hearing occurred without S being present. The social worker's continued questioning is designed to determine whether or not his colleagues had acted properly to protect S's rights. Although T, a young woman who is also in care, responds with laughter, the social worker attempts to determine whether or not policy was followed. He begins first by suggesting, "It's on consent", eliciting an obviously incorrect or mistaken response, "Crown, I don' know, crown ward whatever." The social worker continues to determine if policy was followed by suggesting, "you signed a paper", to which S replies, "my mot[her signed]", leading to overlapping speech as the social worker looks for some other way to get at the issue of consent. Finally, the social worker's search is rewarded as S admits, "yah. I signed something. I don' remember what it was".

This exchange underscores the need for social workers to ensure that they work assiduously to help youth to understand policies, procedures, and their rights within the web of legislation and policy that interlocks child protection with foster care, with courts, with police, and so on. It is essential that social workers take the time to help young people understand the complex legal and institutional systems, in which others operate with authority over their lives.

Choosing priorities: Documents or children and youth

Children and youth in care recognise that the increased amount of time social workers are required to do paperwork will have a negative or deleterious effect on their relationships. In what follows, I focus on a discussion at a CAST meeting among youth in care who had attended an orientation and training session on the adaptation of the British "Looking After Children" (LAC)[16]Assessment and Action Records (AAR). From this discussion we can better appreciate the sorts of choices that social workers must make when confronting the conflicting demands for organisational accountability and for relationship building with children and youth in care.

The LAC Assessment and Action Records are yet another series of standardised instruments introduced into child protection, that have been ostensibly designed to provide monitoring of progress, and improvement of services to children and youth in care. While the youth in the following segments address their comments to LAC they also give voice to the pervasive problems and tensions in relations between youth in care and their social workers. Their comments address the troubles that arise as social workers attempt to balance meeting the needs of youth and the needs of the organisation for accountability and compliance.

The segment that follows begins with a discussion on LAC, however it very quickly becomes redirected to address the caseload demands faced by social workers. The youths' reflections raise a series of doubts and worries, not so much about the utility of LAC, but the effect of LAC on their relationships with their social workers. In the following segment CSW is the CAST Social

Worker, A, B, P, T, and M are youths; and LSW is the social worker responsible for promoting LAC in the agency. LSW also led the workshop on LAC with the youths.

CSW: and so I say, how is this going to interface with a plan of care, and is it gunna replace a plan of care?

P: Yah that's what I wanted to ask actually.

LSW: Yah, this, this will be the plan of care, but you can appreciate with all the questions that you may wanna just say, okay, fer the next three months, six months, we're just gonna talk about three things. And we're gonna work on those three things, so your plan of care comes out of here.

T: When we were//

CSW: And as you do that document nobody will ever complain about seeing their worker, because their worker, is gonna hafta..[be there very frequently]

LSW: [the worker sits] down [and goes through this] it

M: [but that's just dumb]

LSW: won't be done in just one sitting, it'll be [done over two]

B: [what are the quest/]

M: [that's just dumb], because the social workers already have huge cases,

B: yah

T: but

M: and like,

A: there's no theme

M: I don't believe in this at all.

LSW: well=

M: sorry.

This segment demonstrates a fascinating struggle by youth to gain the floor. It begins with the CAST social worker asking, "how is this going to interface with a plan of care, and is it gunna replace a plan of care?" P follows by affirming that, "Yah that's what I wanted to ask actually." This leads LSW to respond in a detailed turn, that addresses the ways that LAC will work as a plan of care. Following her description T attempts to interject, "When we were//", but is interrupted by CSW, who argues for the positive effects of LAC, "And as you do that document nobody will ever complain about seeing their worker, because their worker, is gonna hafta. [be there very frequently]". LSW's overlapping observation "[the worker sits] down" supports and reinforces CSW's claim that the LAC will create more opportunities for social workers to spend time with youth. M clearly disagrees, and attempts first unsuccessfully to interject her views over and against the social workers' mutual praise of LAC, "[but that's just dumb]". LSW attempts to ignore M's remarks and continues to talk. B also attempts to interject, albeit, not with a criticism but by using the tactic of posing a question, "[what are the quest/]". She too is ignored. This leads M to repeat her criticism, in another effort to gain the floor, "[that's just dumb], because the social workers already have huge cases". At this point the youths take over the floor. A argues, "there's no theme", and M adds, "I don't believe in this at all".

Despite the CAST social worker and the LAC social worker's arguments the youths hold to their position, as they are not buying into the virtues of LAC. M argues against the CAST social worker's claims that social workers will be spending more time with youth in care by relying on her knowledge that social workers already have "huge cases". M claims that the extra time demanded by LAC will conflict with the existing demands on social workers' time. The obvious question is where will they make up time.

Later during the meeting M returned to the theme of overwork:

D: The average number of social workers that a youth in care has by the time they leave care, is like, a lot, and if this is the same social wr/ are you saying that this social worker that is asking all these questions is their regular social worker, seeing them many more times than they already do?

J: Well, in order to do this they are gonna need to see people//

D: a number of times

M: How, there's there's only twenty four hours in a day fer a person, and we're already, cannot get the social workers out there enough to see the people that they're supposed te be seeing//

For M and for other youth getting time with their social workers is a struggle. They need to work very hard to ensure that their social workers will listen to their concerns and act on their demands. M understands that the time demands created by the need to complete the LAC will be one more source of competition – along with that of other youth on the worker's caseload – against getting her own needs satisfied.

Yet not all youth were as pessimistic as M. In the following segment we can see that T, who had attended the training, was prepared to envision a series of positive effects following from LAC.

T: I got a lot more but, what I got out of it from what I heard that the workers are realising that they are not spending enough time getting te the nitty gritty of what's goin on in our lives, that fer them, like I mean we can sit down with our workers, and we can say, alright, you know, how is your day, and we all know, as good as the next person, "fine", or it'll be like a huge spiel, but with this it . instead of having te make you talk, there are questions there and stuff, and it just seems like, they're trying to find a way that they can narrow down what's goin on in our lives, what's going on, how they can help. And we're sitting here saying well they're not gonna spend enough time with us. I mean this is once a year, and a, I think if I'm not mistake, mistaken, you said something like, "It's not all gonna be done in one chunk, like it's gonna be time and time", so it's time that is spent with our worker that, these questions are maybe general, and they may be goin to other people that are getting this thing done but, the questions are.are so direct that it's gonna help us te be able to talk, and it'll give us more time.

Clearly T is optimistic. She believes that social workers "are realising that they are not spending enough time getting te the nitty gritty of what's goin on in our lives". T believes that social workers do want to know what is happening in the lives of youth, and in her life. While she has accepted the message that LAC with its "questions there and stuff" will provide an opportunity for youth to address their issues, she envisions a strategic alliance with the document with the hope that it will require workers to spend more time with youth in care, and further, that through the use of LAC, "it's gonna help us te be able to talk". In short T is prepared to embrace LAC as a means to be able to have a social worker pay attention to her, to listen to her, and to spend time with her.

In the next segment T's positive view is challenged by M, and by F who joins the discussion.

T: … and another thing is, like I mean, if we're saying right now, that our social workers don't spend enough time with us, then maybe this is a way that they can have the time// [te sit down].

M: [But the rea]son they don't spend the time with us is because they have bi/big caseloads. It's not because they're coming back here and having three hour coffee breaks. That's not the reason.

T: Yah, but that's not our problem. [If they]

F: [but it is] our problem=

T: if they, have the//

M: but it is our problem

T: No, I'm saying about this, if they're gonna take the time and do something like this, then.

M: It's not time. It comes down to money. There's not enough social workers to go around to put this out//

Clearly, T, M, and F, although disagreeing about the relative value of LAC for social work practice, are in agreement that social workers need to have time to spend with youth. While T is hopeful that "maybe this is a way that they can have the time// [te sit down]", M is so anxious to counter this view that she interrupts T, to argue, "[But the rea]son they don't spend the time with us is because they have bi/big caseloads". Although T attempts to hold to her line of argument, by countering "that's not our problem", her turn is first overlapped by F who disagrees, "[but it is] our problem", and who is then interrupted by M, who repeats F's words insisting, "but it is our problem".

These youth in care recognise that the demands of the work exceed the time available to staff. Clearly, youth in care recognise that their social workers have multiple demands at work that go beyond simply meeting their personal needs, however they also recognise that the organisation of social workers' work makes it difficult for them to meet their needs. Youth in care want and expect social workers who will express their care for them in face-to-face and genuinely communicative relations. In the next segment M continued to voice her concerns about Looking After Children documents by arguing that what mattered to her was not that the forms get filled in but that there be genuine communication between herself and her worker.

M: Okay, uhm, but then, if with the package, we're all generalisations, you ta, you take the problems and you go to the solution maker, but we're each individuals, and I know you know this, like I.I'm saying that you don't know this

SW: mmhuh

M: but i.it, that's why it frustrates me is because it's really just putting us into a box, and saying well hey, this box has one problem, and they're's always one solution, but that's not the[case]

SW: [well] but the solution does not come from here, and the plan doesn't come, you know the action doesn't come from here, but the solution comes from the people that can make the difference, yourselves, the social worker, and the person you're living with.

M: I think of//

SW: You're the one's that develop what's gonna happen, and have control over that.

This young woman's insight that "we're all generalisations, you ta, you take the problems and you go the solution maker" is a brilliant attack on the managerialism that envisions that records, documents, and standardised forms can improve practice. She recognises that the solutions to her problems and those of her fellow children in care will not emerge from artful completion of forms but rather through the work and the care that get performed between people.

It must be recognised that for many children and youth in care, their lives are marked by disruptions not only in their family of origin, but after coming into care. Many youth in care experience multiple moves in receiving, group, and foster homes. Over time their social workers also change. As they move they change schools and lose contact with teachers and friends. In the face of such disruptions and losses agency records can provide a source of continuity, a record of their lives and movements, and a substitute for shared memory provided by family and friends. Given such uncertainties in the lives of children and youth in care, access to agency records is imperative, as these documents may represent the only form of autobiography readily available to a child or youth in future.

In the next segment M, L, and A, all young women in care, talk about the need for agencies to try to retain committed and caring social workers.

M: Social workers have kids of their own too, you know, they can't always, you know.

L: Yah, I know, my old social worker had to quit her job[to uh],

A: [yah, mmhuh]

L: had to quit, quit

A: she ah, because more than a year ago, she asked me if she could have part-time instead so she, she could spend time with her children, and ah, C (name), I think it was, finally told her a year after asking, "either you keep your job full time, or you retire". She jist decided te retire.

L: and I think that's good fer her=

A: =yah=

L: =because, she made the right choice. I thought of becoming a social worker, and I'm not gonna go back on my word, but uh, like there's nothing we can do, well there's things we can do, but we're the receiving end of everything, uhm. But i/ I hate. I guess because of all the cuts, and I guess it kinda discourages the social workers to see what the kids are going through, and to see how much they hafta deal with and yadda yadda yadda, but they're forgetting like, their, their quality of work is going down, ah, they don't seem like they care. Like my social worker wrote me, huh, she wrote me a letter she wanted me to fill out a form and put it into, put it into X(city), and she hasn't seen me for a long time. In fact I've only seen her maybe once. She didn't ask anything like, "how are you? I'll be seeing you.", anything, anything like that. When we did the . ah, plan of care, like, "I'm so glad this is over now, I won't hafta worry about it for another three months", and ah, sure it seems logical, but, ah//

A: thanks a lot.

L: Yah, exactly, oh you won't hafta deal with me for another three months, I'm I'm almost thinking I should throw a fit or something jist to get their attention. Uhm, because like, I don't know about you, but I feel, I feel so, if/ I could go to a Macdonald's and get more personal service.

It is critically important that social workers recognise that children are not ignorant or stupid. They are often very quick to recognise false and deceptive relations. They are also sensitive to various ploys social workers use to get through the work. In the above, it is very clear that the youth wishes to be given priority, and to be recognised as more important than the organisational demand for proper record keeping.

Clearly, there is a pressing need for good records, that is effective, comprehensive, thorough, and which provide detailed information. Such records are necessary in child protection especially given the potential for serious injury, harm, and death. Further, for many youth in care, their case records comprise a primary, if not sole, source of information about their past, albeit expressive of institutional priorities and forms of knowledge. The primary purpose of records in child welfare must be to meet the needs of youth in care. Too often in recent years recording keeping has shifted away from client needs towards enhancing supervision, monitoring front-line worker compliance, and organisational risk reduction. The move towards standardised record keeping produces a semblance of 'best practices' while diverting workers from face-to-face, spontaneous, and individually directed interaction. For agency records to provide a source of memory for children and youth they must be written with a voice of passion, and informed with a knowledge that can only be developed in close and caring relationships with those children and youth.

Conclusion

The core of effective social work practice is nothing fancier, newer, or more innovative than genuine care, attention, respect, and time in relationships. Felix Biestek, in his classic *The Casework Relationship*, stated, "The relationship is the soul of social casework. It is the principle of life which vivifies the processes of study, diagnosis and treatment and makes casework a living, warmly human experience" (1957:v). Biestek's message is more than mere homily. He provides vivid redirection for child protection and child welfare practice in the new millennium. While the desperation occasioned by a generation of neo-liberal cuts to state provision threatens to send social workers scrambling for security in the form of standardised documents and rigid adherence to policy and protocols, I have argued that a radical and more effective response is found by forging face-to-face relations, loyalties, and solidarities with children and youth in care. The most effective response is to remain focussed on building relations, caring and effective solidarities day-by-day. Although relationships are inherently dangerous, they are indeed the stuff of personal and social change.

Curiously youth in care recognise that which skilled social workers know, and this is "relationships matter most" (Snow & Finlay, 1998). Snow and Finlay, a researcher and Chief Advocate in the Office of Child and Family Service respectively, talked to youth in care in Ontario and found:

> Youth identified relationships with staff as the single most critical factor for healing. Respectful interactions, feeling cared for and not being judged, give youth a sense of belonging and safety which increased their ability to trust. These factors are the essential building blocks for self esteem and the ability to develop interpersonal relationships.
>
> (1998:5)

Youth in care hunger for care. Youth in care hunger for support that transcends the boundaries of existing child protection agencies. They require more contact with social workers than can be provided by a single appointment once a month. The type of contacts and commitments that youth in care need are not any different from those that people who have the good fortune to grow up in healthy families need. Youth in care need ongoing, continuous, and compassionate support that is provided not only during moments of crisis, but through the day-to-day routines and ordinary episodes of their lives.

Although I have not been able to address the vast range of issues raised by youth in care, it is important to recognise that the orientation to child protection must be supplemented by an orientation to child welfare, as broadly defined. The focus on protection, while essential, is but a first step towards providing children in need with good parenting. Many families of origin could be salvaged if adequate resources and supports were available, but the reality is that child protection and family welfare is provided on the cheap, so the result is that children are brought into care. Social workers who are clear about their loyalty to children and youth in care can translate their commitments and convictions into a force for social change, not as drama, but as day-to-day pressure, lobbying, and transformation of their agencies and organisations. A clear focus on children and youth in care demands being an advocate for services and supports to help them to develop optimum abilities and capacities.

As children and youth move across the life span the forms of service and support that they need is transformed. Yet it is clear that while a drive for autonomy, self-control, and independence increasingly comes to be exercised by adolescents and young adults in care, and by those who have left care, as with all of us, the need for social and economic support continues. A study by Andrew West (1995) in Britain, sponsored by Save the Children, answered the question, "Who should provide support?" with the following:

> Well over half of those surveyed specified social services in various guises – as social workers, residential social workers or leaving care workers. A few said support should come from family and friends, while others thought social services should fund the facilitation of post-care groups or that support should come from older care leavers.
>
> (19)

The paradox faced by children and youth in care is that the care they need from family is often unavailable, and that even when they come into care, the forms of institutional practice through which child protection is accomplished produce social relationships where care, compassion, and commitment are difficult to secure. From the standpoint of social workers, the demands of children and youth in care often seem insatiable and unrealistic. From the standpoint of social workers these are demands that seem to require them to abandon their professional standpoint, the boundaries of working relationships, and often the rules of the work itself. The difficulty of work with children and youth is that often they are indifferent to such boundaries and restrictions. What youth in care need, and what they demand, are relationships founded in love and commitment. The puzzle social workers face is figuring who is best suited to provide sustenance for such needs.

I am sure that there is no perpetually happy resolution to the tension in child welfare. Child welfare work challenges the boundaries for professional and organisational action in ways rarely faced by social workers in other fields. Certainly, while I worked in forensic psychiatry with the criminally insane I never felt the slightest inclination to befriend or bring any of my clients home to live. This was not the case when I worked in child welfare. In child protection I met children who, though they needed love and commitment, were living on the street, or as temporary residents in receiving and group homes. These children needed someone to reach out, make a commitment, and to make the extra effort to provide them with a safe, secure, and loving home. As a social worker I saw their needs, yet often I could not see any available resources to meet those needs. The desire to rescue these children butted against the realities of my work, my life, and my family. At times I felt as though I was betraying the youths with whom I worked, by using a rhetoric of care but seeking safety behind professional boundaries and the routines of work. I knew that these young people needed a home, needed responsible adults to be committed to them, and needed parents, yet I also recognised that the foundation of my relationships with these youths was as a child protection social worker. I believed that that which I could give these youths, although not parenting, not a life-long commitment, and not a home, was nevertheless of value. Much as the early functional social workers argued, I believed in my agency function.

While such were the choices I made, I have worked with and met many social workers over the years, for whom I have deep respect, who have invested themselves in the lives of children and youth in care by becoming foster or adoptive parents themselves. I have also met many social workers who have left the field of child protection and child welfare precisely because it was such difficult work. I too am an emigré from the tumult of the field. Through this book, however, it is my hope that in some small way I can help a new generation of social workers to recognise the value of child protection work, and to enter the field with a sense of profound humility in the face of complex human needs.

Notes

1 Baudrillard (1975) develops a critique of Marx and Marxists generally. He argues against what he describes as a modernist ontology that focusses on productivity, utility, objectification, and as such foundational for human existence (34). This over-valorisation of labour, and dismissal of play, reproduces "the esthetic and humanistic virus of bourgeois thought" (39) rooted in an "absolute idealism of labour" (37). Against an ontology of labour he draws attention to free play, discharge, waste as "a realm beyond economic value" (47). Such a 'realm beyond' points to the revolutionary implications of an ontology and ethics that moves beyond social relations of labour, utility, exploitation, and commodification to consider relations of play, pleasure, caring, compassion, commitment, and love.

2 Bourdieu (1990) addresses symbolic capital in contradistinction to economism which he portrays as a form of ethnocentrism that applies "categories, methods ... or concepts which are the historical product of capitalism" (112–113). This is "a universe of relations between man and man based, as Marx says, on 'callous cash payment'" (113) or "naked self interest" (113). Just as anthropologists must beware

of transporting the categories of a capitalist social formation to other societies, so too should we as social workers beware of reducing the complexity of family relations to forms of economic calculation.

3 Taylor (1989) attempts a mediation between the distinctly modernist forms of instrumentalism and subjective expressivism as he argues that it is necessary to acknowledge or recognise the 'goods' that follow from both forms. Taylor calls for a method that gives "full recognition to the multiplicity of goods and hence to the conflicts and dilemmas they give rise to" (514). Ultimately, Taylor recognises that a purely secular outlook fails to recognise transcendent goods in the form of a spiritual orientation rooted in a fundamental orientation of 'agape' (516), that is the capacity to see the good in human beings. Such 'seeing good' is the necessary foundation for social work.

4 See Smith (1990; 1974) for her analysis of the 'documentary method' identified by Garfinkel.

5 Foucault's analysis of surveillance, regulation, and panopticism (1995; 1980) has been extended to address the policing or regulation of families (Margolin, 1997; Donzelot, 1979), in such fashion as to displace from view both the necessity of intervention for preserving life, and the salutary effects of that intervention for children, youth, and their families. Although I agree that a foundational dynamic of child protection was, and continues to be, the regulation of working class and poor families, the development and organisation of child protection expresses complex human relations and situations. Beyond an impulse for regulation are the impulses of care, compassion, and concern that drove the earliest 'friendly visitors'. Such impulses continue to be at the heart of good front-line practice. To fail to recognise the motivations of social workers to help is to insult and denigrate the efforts of a vast cadre of workers who struggle to help people to live lives of dignity, respect, and hope. Social workers struggle for authentic, genuine, and congruent practice, which as the early advocates of 'functional social work' recognised, must combine agency services with client needs as mediated by the personality and skill of the social worker (Smalley, 1970).

6 Authenticity is a term often misused by social workers to designate a nativist, pure, and unspoiled form of practice. Practice, precisely because it is always situated, grounded, and co-produced interactively is correspondingly always impure, spoiled, and contaminated. What I seek to point to through the notion of authenticity is a reflexive practice marked by self-awareness, awareness of socially organised ground, awareness of limitations, awareness of client capacities, and awareness of the elasticity of possibility for change. An authentic practice is of necessity a practice informed by a reflexive analysis of the dialectic in which one's own individual personality is mediated by the dynamics of institutional relations.

7 The importance of such issues as transference and counter-transference was readily recognised by those social workers who used a so-called diagnostic approach influenced by the insights of psychoanalysis and psychotherapy. Hamilton writing in 1937 observed, "clients tend to bring into this case work relationship feelings and attitudes and behavior which they have experienced with others" (1937:151).

8 Notice that "playing at work" is readily understood – from a managerial standpoint – to be problematic, as it could interfere with productivity and output (Braverman, 1998; 1975). Yet, as Roy outlined, playing at work or making a game at work is often the only way to survive monotonous, boring, routinised, and Taylorised routines (1959). On the other hand, "working at play", something we can easily imagine teachers, art therapists, play therapists, child care providers, and social workers doing, is not only not problematic, it is to be extolled as an effective form of practice.

9 The question, "Are there any meals that you like?", is heard as 'sarcasm' both by virtue of the tone of its delivery and by the use of the modifier "any". More

genuine or innocent questions might be, "Are there meals that you like?", "What meals do you like?" – though with this formula an emphasis on the word 'do' could easily be interpreted as sarcasm – or "What do you like to eat?".

10 Schutz (1973) wrote of "multiple realities" by which he indicated a world of everyday life, a world of phantasms, a world of dreams, and a world of scientific theory. Similarly the struggle that emerges in this segment articulates the tensions between the realities of M's desire – her phantasies, ideals, and needs – as conjoined to L's orientation to a reality of work, professional relationships, and idealisations of 'interviews'.

11 Hegar's insight that children in foster care need to "build emotional ties to those adults who act as parents to them" (1983:44) applies equally to the relationship between children in care and their social workers.

12 The problems of objectification between adults and children, as within social work relationships with children and youth, are profound. Polakow makes the following observation about the treatment of young children, "The world in which children live – the institutional world that babies, toddlers, and the very young have increasingly come to inhabit and confront – is a world in which they have become the objects, not the subjects of history, a world in which history is being made of them." (1982:188)

13 Though it may see trite, it must be acknowledged that from time to time there are exceptional adults who through their work as teachers, counsellors, foster parents, social workers, and so on come to provide children with life shaping guidance and mentoring. Many of us as adults can look back with affection on perhaps one or two adults who through their care and attention were able to effect a profound transformation in our lives as we came to recognise through their eyes our own worth.

14 AWOL is an oft used acronym for "absent without official leave".

15 The Ontario Child and Family Services Act was repealed on April 30, 2018.

16 The *Looking After Children Project* was developed in the UK by the National Department of Health following passage of the 1989 Children's Act. Soon after it was piloted in several Canadian provinces, including Ontario and British Columbia. It has been adopted in Ontario. The University of Ottawa Centre for Research on Educational and Community Services (CRECS) has played a central role in promoting the Ontario Looking After Children (OnLAC) project (Lemay & Ghazal, 2007). Their most recent report indicates, "At present, 43 of the 48 CASs in Ontario use the main OnLAC tool to assess young people's service needs and monitor their outcomes, namely, the most recent (2016) version of the second Canadian edition of the Assessment and Action Record (AAR-C2–2016)" (CRECS, 2017).

References

Baudrillard, Jean. (1975). *The mirror of production* (Trans. Mark Poster). St. Louis, MO: Telos.

Bazalgette, Louise. (2014). The views of looked after children and young people on the care system. In Tom Rahilly & Enid Hendry (Eds.), *Promoting the wellbeing of children in care: Messages from research* (pp. 25–51). London, England: NSPCC.

Biestek, Felix. (1957). *The casework relationship.* Chicago, IL: Loyola University.

Bourdieu, Pierre. (1990). *The logic of practice.* Stanford, CA: Stanford University Press.

Braverman, Harry. (1975, 1998). *Labour and monopoly capital: The degradation of work in the twentieth century.* New York, NY: Monthly Review Press.

Bush, Malcolm, & Gordon, Andrew C. (1982). The case for involving children in child welfare decisions. *Social Work*, 27: 309–314.

Centre for Research on Education and Community Services (CRECS). (2017). *Ontario Looking after children (OnLAC)*. Ottawa, ON: Author.

Donzelot, Jacques. (1979). *The policing of families*. New York, NY: Pantheon.

Foucault, Michel. (1980). *Power/knowledge: Selected interview and other writings 1972–1977* (Ed. Colin Gordon). New York, NY: Pantheon.

Foucault, Michel. (1995). *Discipline & punish: The birth of the prison* (Trans. Alan Sheridan). New York, NY: Vintage.

Garfinkel, Harold. (1967). *Studies in ethnomethodology*. Englewood Cliffs, NJ: Prentice-Hall.

Hamilton, Gordon. (1937). Basic concepts in social case work. *The Family*, 18(5): 147–156.

Hamos, Paul. (1978). *The personal and the political: Social work and political action*. London, England: Hutchinson.

Hegar, Rebecca L. (September, 1983). Foster children's and parents' right to a family. *Social Service Review*, 57(3): 429–447.

Laursen, Erik K., & Birmingham, Scott M. (2003). Caring relationships as a protective factor for at-risk youth: An ethnographic study. *Families in Society: A Journal of Contemporary Human Services*, 84(2): 240–246.

Lemay, Raymond, & Ghazal, Hayat. (2007). *Looking after children: A practitioner's guide*. Ottawa, ON: University of Ottawa Press.

Margolin, Leslie. (1997). *Under the cover of kindness: The invention of social work*. Charlottesville, VA: University of Virginia Press.

Polakow, Valerie. (1982). *The erosion of childhood*. Chicago, IL: University of Chicago Press.

Roy, Donald F. (1959). "Banana Time": Job satisfaction and informal interaction. *Human Organization*, 18: 158–168.

Schutz, Alfred. (1973). *Collected Papers I: The problem of social reality*. The Hague, Netherlands: Martinus Nijhoff.

Shulman, Lawrence. (2016). *The skills of helping individuals, families, groups, and communities* (8th ed.). Toronto, ON: Thompson Brooks Cole.

Smalley, Ruth. (1970). The functional approach to casework practice. In Robert W. Roberts & Robert H. Nee (Eds.), *Theories of social casework* (pp. 77–128). Chicago, IL: University of Chicago Press.

Smith, Dorothy E. (1974). The social construction of documentary reality. *Sociological Inquiry*, 44: 257–267.

Smith, Dorothy E. (1990). *Texts, facts, and femininity: Exploring the relations of ruling*. London, England: Routledge.

Snow, Kim, & Finlay, Judy. (1998). *Voices from within: Youth speak out*. Toronto, ON: Office of the Child and Family Service Advocate.

Taylor, Charles. (1989). *Sources of the self: The making of modern identity*. Cambridge, MA: Harvard University Press.

Turner, Francis J. (2002). *Diagnosis in social work: New imperatives*. New York, NY: Haworth Social Work Practices Press.

West, Andrew. (1995). *You're on your own: Young people's research on leaving care*. London, England: Save the Children.

11 Conclusion: Seeing 'the social' in social work

For many progressive social workers this must appear to be a peculiar and perhaps an unappealing book, as little attention has been given to dominant themes in contemporary social work, that is oppression and anti-oppressive practice, identity and intersectionality, post-modernism and post structural 'disruptions' of social work. However, it must be 'confessed' – thank you Foucault – that such omissions have not been accidental. This work has aimed to articulate an abiding and persistent focus on actual people's activities and interactions, against a turn to study of structures, language, discourses, and ideologies. The focus on talk-in-interaction as practice, hence as constitutive of social occasions and social orders, represents a deliberate turn toward a Marxist epistemology, wherein, "the ideal is nothing else than the material world reflected by the human mind" (Marx, 2010:19). The material world in turn is worked on by people, not in some abstract isolation, but communally, in society, in webs of social relations, and through socially organised in vivo, embodied, and lived activities and practices. Through these matrices people come to develop, together communal understandings of their world.

In this work, I take seriously Smith's understanding that, "The concept of social structure hypostatizes what is external to the individual subject active in it" (2005:67). Against writing about, or treating structures – whether child protection offices, law, or the state as subjects or as agentic – I propose a return to an examination of people's every-day activities, for producing the operations, warrants, accounts, and cogency of that we call structure. Whether this is a child protection office, a government ministry, a hospital, a police detachment, that such institutional forms and orders come into being is possible only as produced day-in-day-out by a cadre of people at work who act and interact. Order emerges as social workers talk to clients and write reports, as directors review caseloads and manage workplaces, and as support staff file, create spreadsheets, compile data, and so on. By turning to ethnomethodology (EM) and conversation analysis (CA) we can find both direction for enquiry and lineaments for developing a new grammar and a new way of speaking about action. Through EM and CA we can begin to track peoples' local and situated activities as interacting, unfolding, phenomenologically constituting, accounting and warranting social orders. People bring structures and institutional orders into being through talk, work, and play. That which we point to as structures becomes subject to explication as effects of people's congregational practices for articulating multiple here-and-now situations to extra-local relevances and orders.

Talk-in-interaction, as iterative, predictable, developed in time, is a practice. Of course, activities understood as practice simultaneously articulate a here and now, an immediate engagement and action in the world, as well as a life course. Practice accomplishes this specific moment of activity as such, that is as an interview, a report to the court, a team meeting, and so forth, while simultaneously referencing and articulating local sites to extra-local orders. The turn to social interaction is both a recognition and a celebration of actual peoples' lives and actions as producing moment by moment accountable and warranted institutional orders (Boden, 1994). Against a turn to structures, and against the hypostatisation of 'things' as agents, actors, and subjects, the turn to the incarnate activities, or practices of people in situ, provides a pathway for explicating the mundane accomplishment of the every-day orders of our lived world.

The every-day accomplishment of an inhabited, and experienced lived work, is admittedly equivocal, ambiguous, and paradoxical. As people interact, they dance in the light and the dark, that which is present in thought and lurks in the recesses of a conscious and preconscious ocean of memories and submerged phantoms. As people talk and engage with each other, they do so as incorrigibly embodied, and in and through their bodies, they talk, move their hands, respond with alterations of pitch, speed of talk, volume, and so on. As they talk, they interact with others to modulate and shape their next turns, as the other acts and reacts with them, each engaged simultaneously in external acts that articulate internal dialogues and readings of each other. In the immediacy of interaction they shape both what is said, and what is left unsaid, in an anticipation and an intention to produce this occasion as this sort of social interaction, and as this sort of social moment. A focus on interactive practices moves social workers to suspend inscription of every-day events into a categorical professional armamentarium, to examine just how people actually go about producing the every-day orders of their lives, including a social worker's own practices at work and at home. Further, social workers' practice and understandings of clients can be enhanced by a quite simple focus on interactive practices as constitutive of social realties. Social workers sense-making needs to begin with practices, as socially organised, as situated, as embedded in lived time, as arising through the concerted energy of people's bodies, as expressing diverse intentions, fleeting thoughts, conscious articulations, and unconscious murmurs. It is in the every-day activities of people in the world that social worlds come to be shaped and formed.

As noted, the focus of this book is not on discourse, language, or even communication as abstracted generalities apart from actual people's situated interactive activities. This work takes seriously Vološinov's insight that:

> Signs can arise only on interindividual territory ... It is essential that the two individuals be organized socially, that they comprise a group (a social unit); only then can the medium of signs take shape between them. The individual consciousness not only cannot be used to explain anything, but, on the contrary, is itself in need of explanation from the vantage point of the social, ideological medium.
>
> (1973:12)

A recognition of 'interindividual territory' or space, opens up for consideration the importance and value of beginning with peoples' practical, lived, and every-day activities, as it is in their social interaction that they produce their lives, social orders, forms of consciousness, and knowledge. A simple focus on what social workers and youth did in the moments of interaction allows us to explicate just how they quite practically went about making or constituting occasions as warrantably and accountably 'interviews'. It was through in vivo and face-to-face activities that interviewers and youth joined to create talk-in-interaction which they could treat as an interview, and as a space where youth could tell their stories about coming into care and living in care. The focus is simply on people's activities as constitutive and as bringing into being a lived and experienced world. How do some people work or shape themselves and their interactions with others into moments of social work practice, and how do others work or shape themselves and their interactions into recognizable forms as youths or as clients who tell their 'stories'?

The attraction of both ethnomethodology and conversation analysis is a resolute focus on people's concerted in vivo and situated doings. Against a fetishisation which treats social relations as structures, whether the economy, ideology, or the state, as overdetermining forms of life (Althusser, 1977; Althusser & Balibar, 1977), or a post-modernist turn, which erases 'the subject' and which in an avowed anti-humanism attributes agency to discourses and to 'power' (Foucault, 1995; 1980)[1], through EM we refuse to discard the unpredictable, confusing, welter, buzzing, enigmatic, and contradictory field of people in social interaction. Further, through EM and correspondingly through an abiding attention to just how, just when, and just where people in interaction, in concert, and congregationally, produce day-after-day, with no time out, their lived social orders, we develop an empirical, rather than ideological account of just how social orders and societies come to produced.

EM and CA, while not at all rooted in Marxist theory, provide a grammar and vocabulary of practical interaction. Oddly, the focus on social interaction, or practice provides a link to Marxist attentions. If indeed a central problem of capitalist societies is the alienation inherent in forms of social relations between labour and capital, and the resulting fetishisation of commodities – simply, that which we produce – it behoves those of us who are privileged as 'intellectuals' in capitalist society, to return our attention to our own practical activities, in congregation with others, for producing as cogent and as realised the contours of social work. By turning to just how we actually go about doing our work with each other, and with those who are positioned and who position themselves as clients offers a profound and foundational view of social work practice.

So it is that we struggle against transformational grammars that treat the things we produce as subjects with agency (Billig, 2008; Fowler, et al., 1979; Kress & Hodge, 1979).[2] So it is that we need to bracket those forms of talking, writing, and thinking which treat our things as the actual subjects. We 'bracket' Foucault and his approach.

> What makes power hold good, what makes it accepted, is simply the fact that it doesn't only weigh on us as a force that says no, but that it traverses and produces things, it induces pleasure, forms knowledge, produces discourse. It needs to be considered as a productive network which runs through the whole social body, much more than as a negative instance whose function is repression.
>
> (1980:119)

Whether it is power or any other artefact of social interaction, our objective as social workers is to return to a muddling through of people in their lives, working and playing with each other, and congregationally achieving for quite practical purposes their own living sense and sensibilities in the world. As social workers we need to stop talking about social work, power, discourses, ideologies, or even the state as the agent or actor doing this or that, or producing this or that effect. Instead we need to develop and cultivate a grammar which allows us to think, speak, and write about action and agency as an expression of actual peoples' socially organised relations and forms of work and play. In EM and CA what is – that is the ontology of things, both material and social – is as realised and brought into being with an essential, or inescapable reflexivity. By attending to human activities, or actual doings in situ, we can begin to trace the practical, though complex accomplishment of experiential contours of a lived world. EM and CA provide a lexicon, a way of writing and thinking, which restores a focus on mundane activity here-and-now. These ways of writing provide an important redirection and revivification of a humanist Marxism in contradistinction to a structural Marxist anti-humanism and to post-modernist anti-humanism. EM and CA begin to provide us with a lexicon for expressing practical activities as constitutive. EM and CA offer to restore individuals as social subjects in interaction, coming to be themselves, while bringing into being the orders of an every-day world.

It needs to be seen that the epistemological focus of EM and CA on practical activities as that which produces social orders provides a connection to a Marxism that insists that there is an intractable and real material world, which is brought into being, and into thought, through quite mundane, everyday, and practical activities or forms of life (Marx & Engels, 1976). Marx and Engels set out their materialist method in the German ideology, and asserted:

> Men are the producers of their conceptions, ideas, etc., that is, real, active men, as they are conditioned by a definite development of their productive forces and the intercourse corresponding to these, up to its furthest forms. Consciousness ... can never be anything else than conscious being ..., and the being of men is their actual life-process. If in all ideology men and their relations appear upside-down as in a camera obscura, this phenomenon arises just as much from their historical life-process as the inversion of objects on the retina does from their physical life process.
>
> (1976:36)

To work from Marx, we begin with 'real, active people' in interaction, as engaged with each other, in the processes of making their lives. The life process is not simply production in a factory or an office, but must include making meals at home, intimate sexual relations, having children, raising children, and so on. Life processes must include not just the work of the body, but the work of talk, interaction, and social cohesion and organisation. The life process is both work and play (Baudrillard, 1975). The world that is for us is the world that we bring into existence through the congregational forms of activity, as science, as philosophy, as linguistics, and as social work.

The world of child protection work is oriented to simple instrumental and ethical[3] questions, which while perhaps beneath the attentions of male philosophers (O'Brien, 1981)[4], are rooted in the congregational practices on which each of our lives depend: Are there adults who will feed a child? Is a child hungry or malnourished? Is a child being abused, physically or sexually? What harms to the body, development, and mind will a child suffer as a result? Is a child being cleaned, clothed, and cared for, or is a child at risk of infection, hurt, and harm? Is this child at risk of death? Such questions provide sufficient impetus to recognise and hold onto the empirical organisation and accomplishment of a lived and all too real world. This is not just any 'real' world, or a 'real world' as abstract, but a world we are born into, are nurtured in, developed in, and grow older in. This is a 'real world' with readily identified every-day forms of order, whether cooking, eating, talking, cleaning, clothing, and so on. We not only inhabit but collectively bring into being recognisable lived contours of an accomplished real world from which, as Garfinkel so usefully observed, there is no time out (2002).

What does it mean to insist that we live, move, are part of, and come to understand a 'real world'? It means that social workers must struggle to study that which is, not just as it appears, but just how it is brought into being reflexively, day-by-day, moment by moment through the concerting of socially organised and lived activities. It means that that which 'is' must be recognised as reflexively constituted, and that an ontology of the world emerges, day-after-day in the coordination of everyday practically effected congregational activities. How we think about a world is rooted in and expresses the forms or shapes of how we live with each other in the world. The apparently abiding structures of our work express just how we go about producing our lives with each other in its minute and ceaseless interactional details. The recognition of the essential reflexivity of every-day activities is reflected in the heart of social workers' attention to 'practice', even though 'practice' has rarely been recognised as the foundation for thought and knowledge. The recognition of the essential reflexivity of socially coordinated activities is necessary for coherent and effective social work practice.

If our accounts are embedded and interactive, and as such bound to an essential reflexivity doesn't this vitiate or undermine the claims that there is a 'real world'? It only does if we posit a rigidly representational epistemology, that is a machine knowledge, whereby each word is imagined to operate in an exclusive binary, off or on, this or that, without equivocation or contextual variation. Nor does a recognition of essential reflexivity demand a slide into the postmodernist relativism, such as we see in Parry and Doan's *Story Re-visions*:

> A story told by a person in his/her own words of his/her own experience does not have to plead its legitimacy in any higher court of appeal, because no narrative has any greater legitimacy than the person's own. Therefore, attempts by others to question the validity of such a story are themselves illegitimate. They are coercive, and to the extent that such methods are used to silence or discredit a person's stories, they represent a form of terrorism.
>
> (1994:26–27)

Essential reflexivity points to the interactive and social accomplishment of order and accounts. Every account or story as produced does in fact answer to the 'higher court of appeal' and this court is nothing less than the actual, embodied, and empirical forms of life of the story teller and listeners. Clearly, social workers can only adopt such aversion to judging stories at their grave peril. In the press of social work practice the comfort of relativism is chimeric, as it only 'defers' the necessity to make judgements.

The problem with Parry and Doan's account, and that of other postmodernists is that it assumes that all that exists are stories or narratives. Stories as fetishised become something that we carry around inside of us rather than that which we produce interactively, with others who participate with us, in socially organised contexts of daily life and interactive experience. Stories are told from out of our lives. When my grandmother told me how to capture wild yeast, in order to make sourdough bread, her story referenced a being in the world along with yeasts, wheat, sugars, salt, ovens, and 'bread'. Every story is told for another, and a story told by a client with a social worker emerges, is shaped, developed, and analysed turn-by-turn. A client's story as told in an interview, while produced in interaction with a social worker, is also told for a potential audience of others, especially in child protection, where it might be retold to the police, to a judge in court, or to other professionals. So just as a story emerges here and now, so too might it potentially be retold elsewhere later. In a telling of a story, the storyteller is continually weighing, measuring, and calculating the effects of his or her story on another and the ways that that story will shape another's views of the storyteller. When a story is told face-to-face, that which emerges is woven into the fabric of each other's facial and bodily gestures, and responses. A story emerges in rising and falling tones of voice, with greater or lesser rapidity, with few or many stops, starts, hesitations, self-corrections, and so on.

Every story is produced for a listener. The implications of such a seemingly simple insight is that whatever coherence, sense, correctness, and legitimacy any story has is always and everywhere subject to a 'higher court of appeal', and this court is accomplished in the responses of another. Through examination of such matters as self-initiated self-repair (Schegloff, 2007; Hutchby & Wooffitt, 1998; Schegloff, Jefferson, & Sacks, 1977) we see that speakers, as they talk to another, themselves are constantly evaluating the production of their own talk, and the responses of another, to effect as a routine matter 'repairs' of utterances. Through examination of such mundane matters as turns and sequences, combined with attention to question/answer structures again, we can see that the matter of a 'story' is not a single person's, but an interactive construction articulating the joint work of speakers and listeners (Manusov, 1996). Through analysis of response tokens we see that talk as it unfolds is continually subject to evaluation by listeners.

In short, producers of talk-in-interaction are continually engaged in making their talk accountable as an interview, and performing their own accountability in the unfolding of talk as interviewer and interviewee. Unfortunately, despite the good intentions, and positive directions of narrative therapy and corresponding attention to stories and accounts, especially White and Epston (1990) and more recently Payne (2006), the post-modernist foundations of the approach too often result in an idealist descent into relativism. We can recognise the over-valorisation and fetishisation of 'stories' when White explains, "we live by the stories that we have about our lives, that these stories actually shape our lives, constitute our lives, and that they 'embrace' our lives" (1995:14). Similarly, Freedman and Coombs insist, "since we can't objectively know reality, all we can do is interpret experience. There are many possibilities for how any given experience may be interpreted, but no interpretation is 'really' true" (1996:33).

Yet, beyond talk, even beyond talk-in-interaction, and beyond the in-vivo interpretation of that talk, is the foundational bedrock of material embodied life in a world with others. In order to be able to 'talk' one must learn a language and the rituals of interaction as a child. One grows up within a community of others, not just through talk but through the interactive practices of care and attention. Children are born as members of our evolved and evolving human species. As Gopnik points out:

> Childhood literally couldn't exist without caregivers. Why do we go through a period of childhood at all? Human beings have a much more

extended period of immaturity and dependence, a much longer child-hood, than other species, and this period of immaturity has become longer as human history has gone on.

(2009:10)

The evolutionary and species dependent foundations are never more present than in child protection work. If we cease to provide an infant with food and water she will die. If we cease to provide affection and love she will not thrive. If we cease doing the work of changing diapers, picking up, holding, com-forting, nursing, feeding, burping, and so on, a child will be at risk of sores and disease. We know from the neuroscience, that:

Infant primates, both human and non-human, are highly susceptible to social perturbations in maternal care. While the mother's brain has been 'maternalized' by the hormones of pregnancy generated by the foetal extra-embryonic placenta, the infant's developing brain requires social stimulation from a mother committed to providing the emotional rewards of suckling, huddling and grooming. It is clear that the process of infant socialization benefits from this close relationship and, because this occurs during early brain development, mother–infant separations are likely to have long-term consequences.

(Broad, Curley, & Keverne, 2006:2208)

Being in the world as human, and correspondingly human interaction, depends on our conception, prenatal development, birth, and post-natal development. We not only think, and talk, we rely on each other to produce the contours of our every-day and experienced world.

If by objective and "really true" Freedman and Coombs mean that we cannot produce knowledge divorced from our 'real' place in history and society then I concur. But, they do not mean this. We do not simply interpret, we act. Every act is in its embodied, interactive, and socially organised character embedded in a commitment and a realised interactive co-production of a world that can be known, can be manipulated, can be used, and can be consumed. Clearly experience, if by that we mean life and our capacity to survive each day, is always far more than interpretation. Experience and life itself is action.

As social workers we do need to recognise that some versions are preferred over others. We do need to insist that there are truths, not just meaning. While post-modernists may celebrate the breakdown of 'truth' and 'grand narratives', a social worker in child protection needs to establish how this child's arm got broken, how that child's lip came to be lacerated, whether or not the bruises on this child's buttocks are from a fall or from a spanking. In child protection work we recognise that physical, emotional, and sexual abuse of children is harmful beyond the bruises, broken bones, and tears to the flesh. Such acts destroy the fabric of social relations and the integrity of human existence.

In the ambiguities and complexities of every-day practice good social workers come face-to-face with their judgments, their values, and their theoretical frameworks. They use these to make sense of the cases they encounter. This ground in one's own life, one's own understandings, and one's own preferences – which are not just one's own but are developed in interaction, in day-to-day work, and in an articulation of textual realities to every-day life – are the foundations of practice. The glorious aspect of child welfare is that its emergence is a clear testimony to the celebration of the value of humanistic care. Child welfare is a celebration of the values that say that all life, even that of the smallest, weakest, and most vulnerable child, is sacred. Child welfare is rooted in values that declare that indifference, brutality, and abuse against children are not to be countenanced. Child welfare is a quintessential expression of social work values that side with a post-enlightenment humanism that affirms the right of people to live with dignity, in comfort, and with the support of a community, that recognises their individuality. Child protection at its core is a declaration against relativism, against the laziness that would pretend that all versions of reality are equally valid, and against justifications for violence and abuse.

As social workers engage and work with clients they rely on general rubrics, frameworks, evaluative criteria, and categories to sort through emerging and unfolding stories. What counts as relevant or becomes remarkable and worth further examination is shaped by complex background factors. These include the personal characteristics and identities of the social worker, the nature of the social worker's professional education and training, the context of the interaction, the organisational purposes for the interaction, and so on. Of course, as a professional, subject to professional regulation, organisational mandates, job descriptions, and responsibilities, a social worker must abide by institutional considerations when interviewing a youth in care. For example, a social worker is required to take action should they believe that a child is in need of protection or is in danger of harming themselves or another.

When doing child protection a social worker's exercise of professional judgement can routinely become a matter of life and death. Relativism and deconstruction bump against the imperative to make real-world judgements about risk, causes of injury, and potential for harm. In such calculations an empirical world matters: a parent's relationship with a child matters; parental capacity to care for a child matters; whether or not a child is fed matters; whether a child is dirty and covered in urine and faeces matters. Children who are abused or neglected need to be separated from their parents; and, if there are no other family resources, these children need to be 'placed' in homes or group homes. Indeed, the recognition that there are forms of practice that can count as and be accounted for as social work practice, against other forms of practice which are not social work, which are unprofessional, which are abusive, which are manipulative, and not acceptable, arises from out of a real ground, real social relations, and real socially organised interactions.

As readers have moved through this book, it has been my hope that you would have recognised in the close analysis of talk-in-interaction the ways that interviews with clients are not neutral, innocent, nor unbiased disclosures of people's actual lives. Further, it is important to recognise not only that interactively produced accounts are both indexical and reflexive, but that they cannot be otherwise. Indeed, I hope that readers will have recognised that not only are they not neutral or objective, they should not be. As social workers our task is always partially educational or pedagogic. As workers we need to be prepared to join with a child to say: "No, it is not right that you were sexually abused." "No, you are not responsible for the abuse you suffered." "Yes, you have a right to live in a home with loving parents." By using tools from conversation analysis we have examined the active co-production of the 'interview'. An interview is a specific type of occasion in which institutionally organised, warranted, and sanctionable forms of talk are produced to organise this occasion. The accomplishment of an occasion as an interview emerges out of professional education and training, as well as through a reflexive articulation of here-and-now interactive practices to legal and state institutional 'structures'.

It must be recognised that the focus in this book has been on children and youth in care. We did not talk with either parents or substitute care providers, i.e. foster parents or group home workers. My focus has been to present the voices of youth in interaction with social workers and interviews. Although many children and youth spoke about their parents in a harsh and condemnatory manner, in fact many youths who entered care as infants or as toddlers, once they are old enough ventured out on their own seek out their birth parents. Even youths who suffered abuse and neglect as children or entered care as teens often search for reconciliation and rapprochement with their parents. While child protection is a necessary 'service' it is equally clear, as I indicated in previous chapters, protection must always be supplemented with other forms of family support service. It is far too easy in child protection to lose hope and to fall into mother or parent blaming (Swift, 1995), or to side with children against their families. Child protection cannot be divorced from the political project of defending working class, poor, and marginalised families. Parton addressed the inherently political nature of child protection when he observed,

> So while we are encouraged to take a broad definition of child abuse, and there is considerable evidence in the research studies that the vast majority of children and households subject to child protection interventions are living in poverty and come from the most marginalised and deprived sections of society, nowhere is it suggested that policies that reinforce and deepen these social ills are themselves either abusive or contribute to the numbers of children in need. Issues of patriarchy, social class, racism and the impact on children and families of increasing social divisions and isolation ...

> (1997:11)

Blaming occurs when the situation of children and their families is analysed without attention to the social organisation of their lives or when due attention is not given to the details of people's lived social experience. Blaming occurs once sustained and focused dialogue and communication have broken down. Blaming is fuelled by the loss of resources, increased worker frustration, and misdirected anger. Blaming is sustained so long as people lose hope that they can reclaim control over their lives.

Loyalty and commitment

Today, social workers face the perplexing problem of figuring out how to keep the social in social work. The rise of the political right has shifted the focus to individualisation, pathologisation, and blame rather than on viable social policies and social change. Keeping clients at the forefront of practice and forging positive and respectful working relations with clients moves social workers beyond blaming, towards genuine empathy and support. Social workers must ally themselves with clients to demand social services that support people in the realities of their lives. Social workers and their clients have seen the erosion of government support for public and co-op housing, supported care for the chronically ill, health care, 'employment insurance', social assistance, and public recreation (Armitage, 2003; Raphael, 2001; Armstrong & Armstrong, 1996). These losses couple with the loss of high paying and unionised employment in manufacturing and industrial sectors and their replacement by non-unionised, part-time, and minimum wage employment in the service sector (Jackson, 2004; Beck, 2000).

Taking sides and honouring loyalties is not easy. At times it is even dangerous. Social workers who take the sides of clients against their agencies risk their own status in the organisation. They risk sacrificing future promotions and advancements through a career structure. They even risk dismissal itself.[5] Indeed the challenge of honouring loyalties and taking sides is so intense that social workers can easily abandon the side of clients, abandon the side of poor peoples, and in child welfare, abandon listening to the voices of children and youth. It is simple enough to retreat into compliant adherence to rules, regulations, and policies. We are only too familiar with those moments when we too have lapsed into hostile cynicism concerning clients, into moves of separation and differentiation between ourselves and 'those people', and into depression and despair. At the other extreme social workers can lose their sense that there is a 'reality', that this reality can be known, and that there is 'truth'.

Social workers, especially those seduced by a post-modernist promise of critical and deconstructive disruption of dominant discourses, can only too easily lose a sense of their own moral centre. For example, Rossiter et al. (2000) observe, "we have come to understand professional ethics as an effect of power which also produces power" (2000:86). If, indeed, being a social worker is merely an effect of power and discourse, then the possibilities of subjects in interaction resisting and shaping new ways of being is chimerical. If self as a subject, agent, and actor is repudiated, all that remains is a play of difference, discourse, and language. If I am reduced to only that which is interpellated, and become only a 'träger' or bearer of structures, then I am compelled to retreat into confusion and despair. While Rossiter desires innocence, following Foucault, she moves away from innocent knowledge "to develop a space that allows us assess the governmentality ... that creates the potential for trespass" (2000). Yet, problems of innocence, the postulation of trespass, and so on, emerge only at the juncture where people are separated from the complex material webs of social relations and life itself. Of course, in the recognition of fundamental sociability, there can be no 'innocence', but only negotiation, compromise, ambiguity, and unfolding of understanding and life-in-interaction with others from which there is no time out (Garfinkel, 2002). So, while social work is performed on behalf of state agencies, our work, like our lives, can never be pure. Our work, while putatively designed to help clients, is always and incorrigibly controlling and political. Our talk-in-interaction articulates this gesture, that rise in volume, that shift in tone to extra-local and institutional forms of order, theories, professional knowledges, accounts, frameworks and stories. In the face of these relations and these complexities there can be no retreat.

Rossiter fears that she is teaching students "to do social work by not being a social worker" (Rossiter, 2001),[6] though just what this refusal might look like as a practical matter, other than standing in line at a welfare office, is difficult to discern. The paradox Rossiter identifies emerges for her precisely because she has placed herself, and social work inside of a conceptual apparatus or an 'idea' of social work. Indeed, if social work is written about, and thereby treated not only as a grammatical subject but as an agent, and if she is to be a social worker, then by definition she must be subordinate to the profession as subject. That which is disattended are the choices, responsibilities, in vivo activities and relationships, in which Rossiter and others bring themselves into being as subjects who bring social work itself into being. Despite an intellectual and methodological orientation which demands erasure of herself as a subject, her actual and embodied being in the world seems to inform her desire for trespass. Perhaps in a recognition of 'bad faith' (Sartre, 1978), and to her credit Rossiter searches for pathways out of innocence. She proposes that social workers find comfort in "being in uncertainties". She calls on social workers to recognise the power of their own professional stories to dominate clients. She asks that social workers examine what makes "some stories visible and others invisible" and adds that social work accounts need to "be enriched by the knowledge of their clients" through experiential knowledge. While these are laudatory redirections it is important that we add that for students to gain such 'knowledge of clients' they must be in interaction with those people. For social workers the problem is not merely a position in "capitalist, imperialist countries", not just that they "occupy a place of pain and doubt" but that they act, perform, and come to be congregationally with others, in these particular, identifiable, and sensible ways as social workers.

The articulation of social work as thing, as subject, as corpus, and as agent is indeed an epistemological problem. I share Rossiter's desire to reform social work, her recognition of the politics of our work, and her appreciation of our location as practitioners within institutionalised forms of action. However, against a nihilistic deconstruction of discourse and ideas, I turn toward social practice and empirical or material relations, as the wellspring and source of fissures, ruptures, and solidarities which counter professionalism and relations of power inequality. Of course, Rossiter is correct when she observes, "our professional stories of helping are partial and fallible" (2001), but so are all stories, including those we produce in dialogue with clients. A way forward is through a commitment to engagement, to dialogue, to listening, and to reflection. Social workers need to engage in a hermeneutic and reflexive exploration of self, in which our own lives, character, habits, and actions are rooted in a lived world shared with those with whom we work (McBeath & Webb, 2002). They must struggle to realise in and through their practices a reflexive epistemology in which choices are made about the relative merits of different and conflicting accounts and stories. They must struggle to make sense of and evaluate client stories. Simply, social workers must exercise, to borrow from the language of Canadian Catholic bishops, a "preferential option for the poor" (CCCB, 1996:6; Lind, 1983). While social workers need to interrogate, question, and resist the forms of domination within their agencies, they must also recognise that operation in and through the mandates and powers of child protection are essential for the protection and preservation of children's lives.

Social workers need to find an ever-changing balance between a sense of certainty and moral correctness on the one hand, and an opposing sense of uncertainty and moral relativism on the other. As an educator of social workers, I have despaired in class when I hear social work students make authoritative pronouncements about clients from 'dysfunctional families', about children with 'attention deficit disorder', or teens with 'anger management problems'. Although I agree that such descriptions are necessary and appropriate, I worry that too often they signal a retreat into pathologising discourses rather than a detailed assessment made on the basis of dialogue and discovery. On the other hand, I have also despaired when I hear students abrogate their authority, and their responsibility to exercise this authority. I cringe when I listen to them claim that "I don't want to be 'judgmental'" or that, "I don't have right to impose their values on clients", or that "A client's narrative must be respected". Against such formulations I have tried to steer a course through the dangerous shoals threatening to seduce social workers in the direction of an authoritarianism founded in the putative objectivity of facts, and a moral relativism founded in a retreat from the real world.

Despite the desire to experience the satisfaction of face-to-face work with people, social workers doing child protection today often find themselves prevented from forming functional, caring, and helpful working relationships with clients due to the very organisation of their workplaces. In child protection social workers have faced an unmanageable escalation of caseloads, administrative demands, and time spent completing on-line forms and records. As face-to-face time with clients is sacrificed to data entry social workers are in danger of losing touch with people's every-day realities. The separations between social workers and clients breeds working environments marked by lack of trust, hostility, cynicism, withdrawal, and despair. In the space of separation between themselves and clients social workers are in danger of adopting agency priorities against those of their clients. They are in danger of putting their loyalty to the agency before loyalty to clients. They are in danger of losing sight of the politics of the social in social work.

Just as problems in a dysfunctional family often escape the attention of family members, the shift to machine technology in social work seems to have escaped professional consciousness. It is unfortunate that social workers have often colluded with the technological imperative to produce standardised, measured, systematic, regulated, and uniform products, with the mistaken belief that adopting such 'tools' will improve their practice, or make their work more accountable, and more scientific. Yet, the insights of early social workers, that ours is work which can never be scientific, controlled, and regulated (Taft, 1933), seems to have been lost precisely because anxiety rooted in uncertainty impels an obsessive embrasure of machines with their promise of control. Writing in 1933 Taft noted the shift in her own thinking about therapy:

> It has developed from the notion of a reform of the 'other' through superior knowledge of life and psychology, a concept closely allied to that of scientific control in the field of emotions and behaviour, to my present acceptance of … a therapy which is purely individual, non-moral, non-scientific, non-intellectual, which can take place only when divorced from all hint of control, unless it be the therapist's control of himself in the therapeutic situation.
>
> (1933:v)

Today, we see that social workers are obsessed by developing and demanding adherence to professional codes, orders, and epistemes for determining correct or right practice. A focus on clinical skills development is substituted and used to erase a fundamental being with clients in moments of uncertainty, ambiguity, and mutual discovery.

The imperative for control, regulation, and formal accountability in turn results in a turn away from clients and a focus on record-keeping. The turn to risk assessment and systematic record keeping, such as those developed for the Looking After Children project, have prompted progressive social workers to complain about the time consumed by record-keeping. Novell,[7] writing in the Guardian in 2014 observed,

Child protection social work in particular has become so bureaucratic and paper-laden that 80% of a practitioner's time is spent form-filling rather than supporting service users. The less time you spend with the person that you are supposed to be supporting, the less you understand their needs and wishes and the less likely you are to advocate for them effectively. And because you are unable to build up a strong professional relationship, a breeding ground for resentment is created when service users feel big decisions are being made for them, rather than with them.

(2014)

For front-line social workers the obligation to complete a crushing pile of record-keeping conflicts with a desire to do face-to-face work with clients. The demand for data entry into electronic records is an expression of Taylorisation (Braverman, 1998)[8] of social work, a machine demand, to produce a product which is measurable, which conforms to standards, which meets quality control expectations. These demands are patently antithetical to social work practice with others, for unlike pieces of paper or on-line records our clients cannot, and should not, be measured, made to conform to standards, or be expected to meet 'quality control' expectations, though such demands had a brief legitimacy during the period of mental hygiene, eugenics, and social purity.

Today each social worker is forced to weigh and to make fundamental choices in the workplace. Do they commit themselves to clients or to paperwork? Is their primary loyalty to those people who are clients, and to muddling alongside these people, or to the organisation and to their employment? Do they join with clients to explore, examine, and understand ways to survive daily life and to find some comfort and happiness? Or, must social workers commit themselves to the structures of professional alienation, organisations, and institutionalised ways of being? Do they seek their own safety inside and behind the wall of institutional structures, professional theory, and knowledge? Do they, stand with clients against the organisations which employ them, and which through the organisation of services contributes to the generation of angst in client's lives?[9] Thus social workers must choose to give voice to uncertainty, ambiguity, and complexity of people's lives or to adopt the cool rationality of manufactured certainty, measure, and determinacy. Social workers must choose between a loyalty to people in the in vivo struggles of their lives and the array of technocratic diagnosis and assessment offered through various measurements, standardised assessment tools, and records. The factors influencing the weighing of the balance are complex.

So, at its root this book is about loyalties. It is also about obligations. What are the obligations of front-line social workers? How can we, who are social workers, find our way through the conflicting obligations to self, career, and our own families, to risk our positions, and to take the often uncomfortable, disturbing, and stigmatised side of our clients? How can we accomplish a personal integrity, build alliances with colleagues, express loyalty and dedication to children and youth in care, and to their families? There are no simple answers to such questions, though part of the solution lies in a two-fold commitment to truth and courage, informed by a foundation of love and faith in the capacity of people to live authentically and humanely. Such concepts need to be resuscitated as central to a proper social work orientation. Yet in calling for a return to truth, courage, love, and a humanistic faith, I can anticipate indulgent 'tut tuts' and envision gentle smirks breaking out on the faces of post-modernists. Surely allegiance to humanism is a sign of backwardness. For post-modernists the imperative is to deconstruct and to drive out of consideration all forms of 'pernicious' humanism, and to demonstrate that each of us, in our consciousness, our resistance, and our lives, comes to be as effects of discourses and power. The subject, along with a desire for 'truth', becomes a curious artefact of antiquated modernist and rationalist projects. How could anyone demand that truth and courage be placed front-and-centre in good social work practice.

Despite the post-modernist turn away from humanism, truth, and courage, fortunately those doing child protection are inoculated against such idealist retreats by the pressing urgency of matters at hand. Child protection demands determining if the child was 'injured', how the child was 'injured', who 'injured' the child and so on. Further, in arriving at such assessments a social worker needs to rely on the courage of his or her convictions and his or her sense of the rights of a child. Post-modernist approaches that would equivocate about 'truth', that would treat all narratives as equal, cannot survive in child protection work. Indeed, it is a commitment to truth as not just my truth, or his truth, but our truth as examined, explored, and worked over which is at the core of helping relationships. It is a commitment to truth as a shared project, as something that we muddle towards together, that preserves the 'social' in social work (Smith, 1999). It is precisely because there is a 'we' that works together, that affirms certain values, certain codes for preferred ways of being together, that we turn away from moral relativism, and work to protect children. It is a commitment to these socially held moral truths to which we seek to enlist parents, as we struggle with them to build relationships that are marked by respect, by caring, by reciprocity, by accommodation, and so on. It is our commitment to the truth that hatred, anger, violence, and manipulation of others are not preferred, not acceptable, that motivates us in our practice.

The issue of courage must also be addressed. Every day as social workers enter the doors to their offices they must make tough choices. They face people who are usually the most marginalised and vulnerable. From their own life space of having employment, having a steady income, having a university education, and having a professional position, they enter into face-to-face work with clients. Whether they meet their clients in run-down apartment buildings, fast-food restaurants, or agency offices, social workers take from these encounters the fragments of lived interaction. These fragments, memories of sounds, smells, and feelings, must in turn be worked up into some form of professional account. This professional retelling of a client's stories also requires courage. The temptation facing social workers is to lapse into the easy and comfortable spaces of professional narrative, by inserting details of this person's life into general categories and frameworks of the professional and organisational discourses.

Social workers require courage to question the forms of what counts as service in their organisations. They need courage to make the links between this client's problems and that client's problems and to name the social relations and dynamics that create hardship in people's lives. They need courage to speak to the social contexts which organise people's lives, and which shape the decisions that people make. Social workers need courage to not only question, but to challenge the organisations in which they work, and to which they owe their own living. Social workers need courage if they are to be clear about where their primary loyalties lie, and if they are to pursue the 'truth' of their moral obligations. It does indeed require courage to affirm the social, and to move beyond pathologising individuals. It requires courage to move beyond 'blaming' parents, for abuse and neglect, toward speaking of 'responsibility' and choices inside and against the contours of lives systematically gone wrong.

Truth and courage are at the core of good social work practice. Social workers doing child protection need a firm sense of the truth of the social ties that bind our lives together. They must be artful practitioners to recognise the truths behind the cultivated ignorance and self-deceptions in some client accounts. They must be able to recognise the truths behind the minimisations, the denials, the distortions, and the lies they face in every-day practice. In recognising these 'truths' they must be able to reach through lies to the possibility of humanity and caring in all people's lives, and unfortunately they must also be able to recognise those occasions when these possibilities are cut-off or adumbrated at this time.

I have argued for an affirmation of loyalty to people in the every-day and every-night spaces of their lives. In writing each chapter I struggled to navigate between the shoals of scientism, objectivity, and a practice that worships regularities and those of post-modernist relativism in which there can be no truth. To find a path through these treacherous waters I have followed maps written in the day-to-day activities of living people. These are maps that are etched not just by the words people have spoken but track the shorelines and forests of their material lives. They contain more than the stories people tell, as they address their work and their play and their relationships with others. They are not just documents but are the forms of life enacted day-by-day outside the office. These are maps sketched in the places and spaces in which multiple, myriad, personal, and institutional social relations are effected. These are maps inscribed by living activities, transforming practices, and rooted in the plenitude of people's every-day worlds. Ultimately social workers must keep the social in social work. To keep the social in social work demands a primary attention to the actual activities, actual practices, actual performances, not just of clients but of ourselves as social workers.

It is essential that we recognise that our own lives are interwoven with the lives of those who become our clients. We find ourselves confronting horrific situations where the interests of parents conflict with their children, and where spouses and partners become threats to each other's lives. In such conditions social workers need tools rooted in the substance of reality. They need tools to explicate or pull apart for analysis the complex articulations between peoples' every-day lived activities, and lived realities, and the articulation of these practices to a matrix of social relations that combine to knit together the world as we come to know it. EM and CA provide tools for examining in a simple way, the artful, wondrous, mundane, and largely taken for granted every-day practices people employ in concert with each other to produce here, there, and the every-where contours of a lived and experienced world.

The voices of youth in care

To end this book, it is fitting to take a segment from a CAST meeting where youths in care talked to other youths in care about coming into care. In reading this last segment it is important that we recognise and remember that, despite enormous hardship, loss, and abandonment, in joining with others we find a simple joy and bonds that enable us to survive this vale of tears.

JULIE: Amber

AMBER: I don't remember much but uh, well I actually have three different stories of why I'm in care. Uhm, one my mom was young, didn't know howte control me, was on drugs, yada yada yada.

JULIE: heh, that good on the tape, yada, yada, yada, so the youth say, sorry, go on, heheh

AMBER: Uhmmhehe, num/ like the second story I::s I was out of control, and I asked te be in children's aid, and I really don't think if I wil:red ask te be in children's aid, and the third one, well, thhhe (snort) I was told I was picked up from school and children's aid just took me away cause they had complaints that my mom was like doing drugs and stuff like that, so I don't know, I'm just trying te find out the truth.

JOHN: Have you had the same social worker the whole time.

AMBER: Hell no

JULIE: Hell no, heheh,

AMBER: I've had like twelve different social workers so itw's kinda confusing, and I like, I know when I came in all's I remember is like, I was crying. I didn't know what te do I was scared, uhm, I felt like alone, cause my first foster home they put me in, well the little/ the, I lived with three little girls uhm, and a foster mom and dad, and the foster dad like pulled my hair, and so did the little girls. They washed my hair with peroxide, and like, I don know, I remember so much of that an, sh, yah, it was a bad experience.

RACHAEL: Did yer hair grow in blond.

AMBER: Yah, heheheh, and it started fallin out, and it's like, I didn' understand why because here I am, like if I were a little girl and my hair's fallin
out, and like, I didn't know what was happenin, and then I called my
mom. I don't remember how I did, I just remembered, like I was told I was
gonna be able te visit my mom. Never saw my mom for like a whole two
months, that I lived there, and then I moved into a foster home and I lived
there for five years, and like that foster home, made me like welcome. They
did things, they comfort me, you know, they like changed my life.

JULIE: so that's from ssi, what age didja come inta care again?

AMBER: Five.

JULIE: So from five te ten you were in that foster home.

AMBER: Yep

Notes

1 Despite differences in attention and focus, Althusser and Foucault join in a methodological anti-humanism. This is an anti-humanism which postulates people as
träger or carriers as structures or as governed through discourses. The link between
Althusser and Foucault is sympathetically addressed by Montag, "Althusser's central thesis (ideology interpellates individuals as subjects) only takes on its full
meaning in relation to what we might call Foucault's reading of the materiality of
ideology, a notion re-written as the 'physical order' of the disciplines" (1995:75).

2 Fowler and the East Anglian School developed a critical analysis of routine and
simply effected transformations, or nominalisation, the use of 'noun phrases over
verb phrases', and the 'use of passive voice' (Billig, 2008:785). Indeed, as Billig
notes, when first encountering this work it was exciting and changed forever how we
read texts, not only headlines but scholarly works. Indeed, attention to nominalisation, as a practice, leads us to ask, just how is it that we write in ways which
eliminate subjects, that is people from sentences, to thereby treat categories (social
work, interviews, values) as active agents. Perhaps my favourite example is from
Dominelli, who wrote, "Social work is suffering a crisis of confidence as it faces
constant attacks from policy makers, practitioners, clients, academics and the lay
public" (2004:3). In this splendid example, we step back and ask, who are these social
workers who are suffering? Are all social workers suffering? Or, are just some suffering? What can we do to help these poor souls? Simply, we recognise that the object in
question, social work is a reification or a fetishisation, which is derived from actual
people's practices. This formulation lifts whatever people feel and do out of the feeling and doing, to treat it as an 'object' for scholarship and intellectual elaboration.

3 Adams, in a paper that examined Aristotelian virtue ethics, as developed by Aquinas,
reflects that there were three types of good that defined the human telos: "(1) to maintain
ourselves in existence and (2) to reproduce ourselves and care for our offspring. In contrast to other creatures, it is also a good for humans (3) to develop and use the powers of
rational thought and, in consequence, to know and love God" (2009:94).

4 O'Brien, perhaps as a result of her former career as a midwife in working class dis-
tricts, had an astounding ability to develop pithy and insightful aphorisms which disturbed conventional forms of patriarchal thought. When writing about her feminism
she noted, "We are laboring to give birth to a new philosophy of birth" (1981:13). She
notes that, "there is no philosophy of birth yet it is of birth we must theorise" (24).
O'Brien's recognition that patriarchal philosophers either forget or denigrate women's

'labour' in giving birth, was cleverly summed up in the chapter title, "Sorry we forgot your birthday". O'Brien's insight that something as seemingly 'animal' as birth is fully social, and paramount for an adequate understanding of our forms of life.

5 The case of Jane Scharf, a care worker in an Ontario group home who was fired following speaking out in opposition to use of physical restraints in the group home where she worked provided a poignant reminder of the dangers of siding with clients (CMAJ/JAMC, 2002), though as a result of her hunger strike the Province of Ontario reversed course and banned the use restraints on young children (Coalition to End Child Restraints, 2002).

6 McBeath and Webb, although identifying with postmodernism, are particularly harsh when addressing Rossiter et al. (2000), who they describe as "vulgar postmodernists" (2002:1031). They criticise the claim by Rossiter et al. that "social workers are therefore a homogenized result of determining discourses". McBeath and Webb refer to this characterisation of social workers as a preposterous reading "akin to the functionalist structural Marxism of Althusser" (2002:1031).

7 Novell's opposition to bureaucratic demands for production of records, echo's Hilton Dawson's 2009 clash with Ed Balls, the Children's Secretary (Williams, 2009). Similarly, in Canada, the Ontario Public Service Employees Union (OPSEU) published *Peoplework not Paperwork*, and launched a campaign to protest increasing workloads and "flawed funding formula" (2001). The report noted that "frontline protection workers spend 70% of their time attending to 'administrative' expectations" (2001:3).

8 In 1980, I completed a MA thesis, *The social organization of social workers' practice: A Marxist Analysis*, which extended Braverman's (1975) analysis of scientific management, as it was then being applied to child protection work, e.g. time audits, managerial control over task assignment, productivity measures, and so on.

9 Beck (2000; 1999; 1992) has outlined the reflexive relationship between social risks and the "systematic way of dealing with hazards and insecurity induced and introduced by modernization itself" (1999:21). The social forms which generate child abuse and neglect as problems generate the attention to these 'problems' in the form of state controlled government ministries and Children's Aid Societies.

References

Adams, Paul. (2009). *Ethics with character: Virtues and the ethical social worker. Journal of Sociology and Social Welfare*, 36(3): 83–105.

Althusser, Louis. (1977). *For Marx* (Trans. Ben Brewster). London, England: NLB.

Althusser, Louis, & Balibar, Etienne. (1977). *Reading Capital* (Trans. Ben Brewster). London, England: NLB.

Armitage, Andrew. (2003). *Social welfare in Canada* (4th ed.). Don Mills, ON: Oxford University Press.

Armstrong, Pat, & Armstrong, Hugh. (1996). *Wasting away: The undermining of Canadian health care*. Toronto, ON: Oxford University Press.

Baudrillard, Jean. (1975). *The mirror of production* (Trans. Mark Poster). St. Louis, MO: Telos.

Beck, Ulrich. (2000). *The brave new world of work* (Trans. Patrick Camiller). Cambridge, England: Polity.

Beck, Ulrich. (1999) *World risk society*. Cambridge, England: Polity.

Beck, Ulrich. (1992). *Risk society: Towards a new modernity*. London, England: Sage.

Billig, Michael. (2008). The language of critical discourse analysis: The case of nominalization. *Discourse & Society*, 19(6): 783–800.

Boden, Deirdre. (1994). *The business of talk: Organizations in action.* Cambridge, England: Polity.

Braverman, Harry. (1975, 1998). *Labour and monopoly capital: The degradation of work in the twentieth century* (25th anniversary ed.). New York, NY: Monthly Review.

Broad, K. D., Curley, J. P., & Keverne, E. B. (2006). Mother–infant bonding and the evolution of mammalian social relationships. *Philosophical Transactions of the Royal Society B,* 361: 2199–2214.

Canadian Conference of Catholic Bishops (CCCB). (October, 1996). *The struggle against poverty: A sign of hope in our world.* Ottawa, ON: Author.

Canadian Medical Association. (August 20, 2002). *Canadian Medical Association Journal (CMAJ),* 167(4): 386.

Coalition to End Child Restraints. (November 18, 2002). Home Page. http://end childrestraints.tripod.com/

Dominelli, Lena. (2004). *Social work: Theory and practice for a changing profession.* Cambridge, England: Polity.

Foucault, Michel. (1995). *Discipline & punish: The birth of the prison* (Trans. Alan Sheridan). New York, NY: Vintage.

Foucault, Michel. (1980). *Power/knowledge: Selected interview and other writings 1972–1977* (Ed. Colin Gordon & Trans. Colin Gordon, Leo Marshall, John Mepham, & Kate Soper). New York, NY: Pantheon.

Fowler, Roger, Hodge, Bob, Kress, Gunther, & Trew, Tony. (1979). *Language and social control.* London, England: Routledge.

Freedman, Jill, & Coombs, Gene. (1996). *Narrative therapy: The social construction of preferred realities.* New York, NY: W. W. Norton.

Garfinkel, Harold. (2002). *Ethnomethodology's program: Working out Durkheim's aphorism.* Lanham, MD: Rowman & Littlefield.

Gopnik, Alison. (2009). *The philosophical baby: What children's minds tell us about truth, love and the meaning of life.* New York, NY: Farrar, Straus and Giroux.

Hutchby, Ian, & Wooffitt, Robin. (1998). *Conversation analysis: Principles, practices, and applications.* Cambridge, England: Polity.

Jackson, Andrew. (2004). Reorganizing unions solidarity forever? Trends in Canadian union density. *Studies in Political Economy,* 74: 125–146.

Kress, Gunther, & Hodge, Robert. (1979). *Language as ideology.* London, England: Routledge & Kegan Paul.

Lind, Christopher. (1983). Ethics, economics and Canada's catholic bishops. *Canadian Journal of Political and Social Theory/Revue Canadienne d théorie politique et sociale,* 7(3): 150–166.

McBeath, Graham, & Webb, Stephen A. (2002). Virtue ethics and social work: Being lucky, realistic, and not doing one's duty. *British Journal of Social Work,* 32: 1015–1036.

Marx, Karl. (2010). Capital, Volume 1. In *Karl Marx & Frederick Engels, Collected Works (Volume 35).* London, England: Lawrence & Wishart.

Marx, Karl, & Engels, Frederick. (1976). The German Ideology. In *Karl Marx & Frederick Engels, Collected Works, 1845–47 (Volume 5).* New York, NY: International Publishers.

Manusov, Valerie. (1996). Changing explanations: The process of account-making over time. *Research on Language and Social Interaction,* 29(2): 155–179.

Montag, Warren. (1995). "The soul is the prison of the body": Althusser and Foucault, 1970–1975. *Yale French Studies,* 88, 53–77.

Novell, Rebecca Joy. (December 10, 2014). I want to fight for social work but I will not fight for bureaucracy. *The Guardian: International Edition.*

O'Brien, Mary. (1981). *The politics of reproduction.* London, England: Routledge & Kegan Paul.

Ontario Public Service Employees Union (OPSEU). (2001). Peoplework not Paperwork. Toronto, ON: Author. www.opseu.org/sites/default/files/media/policypaperp eoplework.pdf

Payne, Martin. (2006). *Narrative therapy: An introduction for counsellors* (2nd ed.). London, England: Sage.

Parry, Alan, & Doan, Robert E. (1994). *Story re-visions: Narrative therapy in the postmodern world.* New York, NY: Guilford.

Parton, Nigel. (1997). Child protection and family support: Current debates and future prospects. In Nigel Parton (Ed.), *Child protection and family support: Tensions, contradictions, and possibilities* (pp. 1–24). London, England: Routledge.

Raphael, Dennis. (2001). From increasing poverty to societal disintegration: How economic inequality affects the health of individuals and communities. In Pat Armstrong, Hugh Armstrong, & David Coburn (Eds.), *Unhealthy times: Political economy perspectives on health and care in Canada* (pp. 223–241). Don Mills, ON: Oxford University Press.

Rossiter, Amy. (2001). "Innocence Lost and Suspicion Found: Do We Educate For or Against Social Work"? *Critical Social Work*, 2(1): (electronic publication no pagination).

Rossiter, Amy, Prilleltensky, Isaac, & Walsh-Bowers, Richard (2000). A postmodern perspective on professional ethics. In Barbara Fawcett, Brid Featherstone, Jan Fook, & Amy Rossiter (Eds.), *Practice research in social work: Postmodern feminist perspective* (pp. 83–103). London, England: Routledge.

Sartre, Jean-Paul. (1978). *Being and nothingness.* New York, NY: Pocket Books.

Schegloff, Emanuel A. (2007). *Sequence organization in interaction: A primer in conversation analysis I.* Cambridge, England: Cambridge University Press.

Schegloff, Emanuel, Jefferson, Gail, & Sacks, Harvey. (1977). The preference for self-correction in the organization of repair in conversation. *Language*, 53(2): 361–382.

Smith, Dorothy E. (1999). *Writing the social: Critique theory and investigations.* Toronto, ON: University of Toronto.

Smith, Dorothy E. (2005). *Institutional ethnography: A sociology for people.* Lanham, MD: AltaMira.

Swift, Karen. (1995). *Manufacturing "bad mothers": A critical perspective on child neglect.* Toronto, ON: University of Toronto Press.

Taft, Jessie. (1933). *The dynamics of therapy in a controlled relationship.* New York, NY: Macmillan.

Vološinov, Valentin N. (1973). *Marxism and the philosophy of language* (Trans. Ladislav Matejka & I. R. Titunik), New York, NY: Seminar Press.

White, Michael. (1990). *Narrative means to therapeutic ends.* New York, NY: W.W. Norton.

White, Michael (1995). *Re-authoring lives: Interviews and essays.* Adelaide, Australia: Dulwich Centre Publications.

White, Michael, & Epston, David. (1990). *Narrative means to therapeutic ends.* New York, NY: W.W. Norton.

Williams, Rachel. (October 23, 2009). Balls clashes with social work leaders. *The Guardian: International Edition.*

Appendix A

Issues to be addressed in the interview

- **The processes of coming into care**

  - How did you come into care?
  - If you were apprehended, what was process which occurred when you were apprehended? What are your memories of being apprehended:

    - Can you tell me what you felt when you were first apprehended? Were you frightened, relieved, anxious, confused?
    - What were the circumstances surrounding your apprehension?
    - When you were apprehended did the social worker or police officer explain what was happening?
    - What might have helped you at the time of apprehension?
    - Where were you placed when first apprehended? With strangers, friends, family? In town? Out of town? In the same neighbourhood? Outside the neighbourhood?

  - What changes occurred between you and your family?

    - Were other siblings apprehended? Were they placed with you or were you separated from your siblings?
    - Did your parents have access? Did your parents visit?
    - If they didn't visit what do you think prevented them from visiting?

- **The experience of being in care**

  - How long have you been in care?
  - Where have you lived since coming into care?
  - Have you changed placements?
  - If you were moved from one placement to another what was the process?

- Did you get to visit with the foster parents or group home workers at the new placement before being placed? How many times? How long before?
- Who wanted you to change placements? You, the foster parents or group home workers, the social worker, your parents, others?
- When you changed placements was the need for the change explained to you? By whom?
- Describe each placement to the best of your ability. Focus on what you liked or disliked about the placement. What made this placement enjoyable or difficult (e.g., other children, the condition of the house, the food, entertainment, the neighbourhood, etc.) ... ?

- What adjustments have you made

  - How have you changed? since being in care?
  - How have your relationships changed with nuclear family – parents and siblings – and extended family – cousins, uncles, aunts, grandparents, neighbours, and friends.
  - Has your relationship with others changed as a result of coming into care? How has it changed:

    - with school teachers, principals, counsellors, students;
    - with friends;
    - with others – e.g., school yard taunts and stereotyping?

- What issues arise for you being in care? What has arisen in terms of:

  - issues of self, stigma, image, confidence, sense of belonging;
  - emotional and mental health issues, depression, safety issues;
  - issues of relationships with foster parents or group home workers;
  - issues of relationships with other children in the home;
  - financial issues, allowances, jobs, spending money, toys, gifts, etc;
  - issues of daily life, different routines, bed-times?

- What do you think would make being a child/youth in care better for you? For other children/youth in care?

Appendix B

Transcription Symbols

Sequences in Talk:

=	latched, where one speaker closely follows the other without a gap or pause
-	represents distinct stop or cut off of the prior word
/	self interruption and self-repair, speaker continues to talk
//	abrupt or hard interruption and stop –self or other initiated
S: ... [tick] T: ... [tock]	simultaneous or overlapping utterances

Morphology of Sounds in Talk:

do::g	colons indicate preceding sound has been stretched, two colons indicate a longer stretch, approximately a second.
DROP IT	loud or increased volume
<u>Drop it</u>	firm, confident, bold and precisely stated
°sorry°	softly spoken and low volume
↓	falling intonation
↑	rising intonation
, .	volume and sound decreases into the pause.
fer-	slight continuation to end –not quite a sound stretch.

Addenda to Talk in Transcription

(this that this)	ambiguous utterances
(–)	verbal sound recorded but indecipherable
(name)	deleted identifying information, (name), (town), (organization)
((cough))	descriptions of complex verbal sounds –moans, laughs, cries, etc.
{}	non-verbal background noises, and may include talk from other speakers who are not part of the interview
{{explanation}}	explanations of material inside transcribed segment
(door bangs)	stage directions, and information not recorded, e.g., tape-recorder is turned off

Pauses/Gaps/Silence in Talk

.	periods and spaces accompanying periods (..) (. .)represent pauses or gaps in talk. These are approximate indications of duration. A period without spaces represents a short pause of less than a second, whereas, a period with a space before and after represents a full second.
Heh.he	< 1 second
Heh . he	1 second
Heh..he	>1 second and <2 seconds
Heh . . he	2 second
Heh ... he >	>2 second and < seconds
Heh ... he	3 seconds, etc.

A time indicator, e.g. (6 sec), (13 sec) will be provided for lengthy gaps in talk

Index

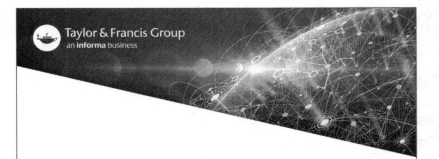